Management Accounting

Management Accounting

Principles and Applications

Hugh Coombs

David Hobbs

Ellis Jenkins

⑤SAGE Publications

London ● Thousand Oaks ● New Delhi

First published 2005

SAGE Publications Ltd
1 Oliver's Yard
55 City Road
London EC1Y 1SP

SAGE Publications Inc.
2455 Teller Road
Thousand Oaks, California 91320

SAGE Publications India Pvt Ltd
B-42, Panchsheel Enclave
Post Box 4109
New Delhi 110 017

Library of Congress Control Number: 2005901200

A catalogue record for this book is available from the British Library

ISBN 1-4129-0843-4
ISBN 1-85396-383-6 (pbk)

Typeset by C&M Digitals (P) Ltd., Chennai, India
Printed on paper from sustainable resources
Printed in Great Britain by Alden Press, Oxford

CONTENTS

LIST OF ILLUSTRATIONS

Figures

Tables

Case Studies

Exhibits

PREFACE

Management accounting may be seen as a practical tool aimed at solving the day-to-day financial management problems facing decision makers in the private and public sectors. We feel, however, that this is too narrow a view of the potential of the subject. Accordingly, we have gone beyond this view. In this book, while we have looked at the practical techniques that can help managers and students solve management accounting problems, we have tried to approach the subject in a way which ensures coverage of technical financial topics in an accessible style while making appropriate reference to research. In addition, the book goes beyond techniques to recognise qualitative issues by attempting to identify analytical and critical issues of relevance to decision makers at all levels in a variety of organisations in both the private and public sectors.

While chapters contain exhibits and examples, we have introduced case studies from the end of Chapter 2. These can be approached on many levels such that students from a wide range of backgrounds and experience can benefit from working through them either in whole or in part. The case studies are intended to be underpinned by reference to the research literature to gain maximum benefit. We introduce some of this research literature in the practical context of each chapter in order to encourage further reading. Readers can thus contextualise the issues which they are studying within the wider environment of the research literature and through the case studies before continuing their studies in more depth. Indeed, the case studies are based on our own consultancy and research areas, although the names have been changed to protect the 'guilty'.

The case studies in this book represent the development of teaching approaches at the University of Glamorgan and are one of a number of innovative approaches used in the delivery of accounting modules in the Business School at the University. They contributed to the HEFCW/QAA 'excellent' rating received by the accounting teaching team. The cases have been well received by students and managers both locally and internationally (see Coombs et al., 2000) and are aimed at developing the 'graduateness' skills of critical and analytical appraisal in decision-making situations. We are grateful to the University of Glamorgan and colleagues for the encouragement we have received to develop and expand this approach.

In today's competitive world, managers from whatever background need an understanding of the tools of management accounting when making financial decisions, yet they must also be aware of the qualitative issues affecting such decisions. Furthermore, they need to be aware of what is happening through research into their competitors. In this context we believe managers and students will find this book of value.

Hugh Coombs
Dave Hobbs
Ellis Jenkins
March 2005

ACKNOWLEDGEMENTS

We would wish to thank Shane Johnson for his advice on aspects of this book and the Teaching and Learning Office at the University of Glamorgan for their support of innovative teaching methods.

Chapter 1
AN INTRODUCTION
TO MANAGEMENT ACCOUNTING

Key Learning Objectives

By the time you have finished studying this chapter, you should be able to:
- explain the meaning and nature of management accounting;
- describe the scope and content of management accounting;
- discuss the past and current issues affecting the evolution of management accounting;
- list key factors that need to be considered when designing management accounting systems.

The Nature and Role of Management Accounting

This chapter will introduce you to the world of management accounting by presenting an overview of the areas of work in which management accountants operate. It will commence by explaining the nature and scope of management accounting. You will see that management accounting is an evolving subject and that its nature and scope have changed and expanded over time, and will continue to do so. As the world of accounting has expanded, so specialities have developed, and we shall see that management accounting is one such speciality, having its own distinctive features and accepted areas of operation. You will see that, in a number of ways, management accounting is quite different from other forms of accounting.

The chapter will examine the historical beginnings and contexts of management accounting, and will consider the nature of the forces and circumstances that have shaped its development. Consideration will be given to the influences that continue to shape management accounting's current development and the likely future influences to which management accounting must respond in order to retain its relevance and effectiveness. In particular, we will consider some of the 'softer' factors that affect any area of management science, including that of management accounting, and will examine the conditions and system requirements necessary for the successful implementation and maintenance of management accounting systems. We will see that, like many areas of accounting in the current organisational environment, management accounting is not necessarily an exact, entirely reliable, science. Some of these issues will be introduced within this chapter and then developed in later chapters.

What is Management Accounting?

What is management accounting? One might think that a book devoted to management accounting would have little difficulty in answering this question. Not necessarily! A logical start is to examine the words 'management' and 'accounting' individually. Unfortunately, neither of these words has a single, universally agreed meaning. *Management* might be seen to encompass the entire range of activities involved in running an organisation, not forgetting that organisations take many forms, including businesses of many types and not-for-profit organisations, within the private or public sectors. *Accounting* may be seen to encompass any of the activities that attempt to gauge the performance of an organisation, or to plan for an organisation's future performance. Additionally it may be seen to include the traditional 'accounting' roles of stewardship, control and audit. The layman might think of accounting as being concerned only with those *financial* measurements undertaken by those with the title 'accountant' and of management as being concerned only with those activities undertaken by those with the title 'manager'. Neither is the case in real life.

In competitive business environments, and within a public sector that is increasingly focused upon effectiveness, value for money and 'best practice', all organisational participants take on a responsibility for both management and accounting. The actions of each individual within an organisation have, after all, 'trickle-down' effects on other parts of the organisation and an 'upward' effect on the eventual results of the organisation as a whole.

So, then, what is management accounting? Well, in a nutshell, management accounting is accounting (i.e. producing useful information) for management (whoever those managers happen to be and whatever their job titles). In this sense, 'accounting' includes the production of all information useful in running the organisation. Hence, such information may be:

- financial or non-financial;
- accurate, or broadly correct;
- actual (certain) or estimated (uncertain);
- based in the past or the future;
- detailed, or in a highly aggregated form;
- presented in any of a variety of spoken or written forms, such as numbers, tables, and graphs;
- related to profits/losses, costs/incomes, volumes, quality indicators, trends, etc.

Similarly, 'management' may include the activities of individuals in a number of positions, for example:

- senior managers;
- mid-level managers;
- lower-level managers;
- executive directors with management responsibilities;
- employees not usually considered to be 'managers', such as production line workers, call-centre operatives, and salespeople.

Thus, in many senses, an average person might not consider many of the areas of activity of management accounting to be accounting at all! Indeed, some writers have suggested that the term 'management accountant' should be replaced with a term such as 'information manager' in order to signify the wide scope of management accounting. Drucker (1994) has, for instance, suggested that the term 'manufacturing economics' might be a better contemporary term than management accounting, within the manufacturing environment. Obviously, a different term would be required for the public sector aspects of management accounting. Interestingly, in recent years, management accounting organisations such as the UK's Chartered Institute of Management Accounting (CIMA) have taken a more wide-ranging view of the scope of management accounting and have tended to take a more broad 'management consultancy' view of the work of their members. Perusal of a recent issue of CIMA's monthly journal *Financial Managemet* will confirm this trend. It is interesting, too, to note the recent change of name of this journal from the former *Management Accounting*. This name change and the changing emphasis of CIMA have not, however, met with the universal approval of its members, some of whom take a narrower view of what management accounting should encompass.

A selection of definitions of management accounting, from a range of books on the subject, illustrates the variety of definitions possible. Garrison and Noreen (2000: 4) state that *managerial* accounting (essentially a US term for management accounting – but see Proctor's views below) is 'concerned with providing information to managers – that is, people *inside* an organisation who direct and control its operations'. They continue that it 'provides the essential data with which organizations are actually run' and (2000: 34) that it is 'concerned with providing information to managers for use in planning and controlling operations and in decision making'. Note, here, the distinction made by Garrison and Noreen between planning, control and decision making. It is our view that planning, control and decision-making activities are inextricably interlinked. Planning, for example, can be seen as decision making for the future, and control can be seen to be ensuring that the decisions of the past are carried out (as well as ensuring that such decisions are still appropriate).

Proctor (2002: xvii) offers the following explanations of management and managerial accounting, making a distinction between the two terms:

Management accounting is orientated towards the future. It is primarily concerned with the provision of information to managers to help them plan, evaluate and control activities. It is essentially a service function; a means to an end rather than an end in itself. Managerial accounting also fits this description but the use of the word 'managerial' emphasises the service role. This may seem obvious but, for much of the twentieth century, management accounting was used mainly to serve the needs of financial accounting, rather than to assist managers in their tasks. … Managerial accounting is about improving the future performance of organisations.

Proctor emphasises that management accounting is not an end in itself. In essence, the slogan 'If it's not useful, it's not information' applies.

Wilson and Wai (1993: 15), writing about *managerial* accounting, offer the following observations:

Managerial accounting encompasses techniques and processes that are intended to provide financial and non-financial information to people within an organization to make better decisions and thereby achieve organizational control and enhance organizational effectiveness.

It is this last definition that we consider to be the most representative. Note that Wilson and Wai's definition is broad in scope, reflecting management (managerial) accounting's broad base, and that the definition incorporates aspects of many areas of study, all interrelated with management accounting:

- both *financial* and *non-financial information* – requiring management accountants to be more than just characterless 'bean-counters'. Additionally, management accountants deal in *information*, not just data, and thus must have the requisite skills to produce useful, meaningful, relevant information. Management accountants must 'add value' to *data*, processing it into useful *information*.
- the provision of information to *people* – requiring management accountants to have '*people* skills' and be able to *communicate* effectively.
- *organisational control* and *effectiveness* – requiring management accountants to have the ability to see the implications of their advice for the whole organisation and to understand how the various parts of the organisation are interrelated (i.e. the 'soft' (people) parts as well as the 'hard' parts).

Management Accounting and Financial Accounting

As seen above, management accounting has a rather broad potential coverage as compared with *financial accounting*, the latter possibly being a more generally understood term. *Financial* accounting is defined by the *Oxford Dictionary of Accounting* (Hussey, 1999) as:

The branch of accounting concerned with classifying, measuring, and recording the transactions of a business. [It is] primarily concerned with providing a true and fair view of the activities of a business to parties external to it. … Financial accounting can be separated into a number of specific activities, such as conducting audits, taxation, book-keeping and insolvency …

Thus, financial accounting can be considered to have a more narrow and specific/precise coverage than management accounting. However, the following points are worth noting:

- Although financial accounting is often considered to be a more 'exact science' than management accounting, this may not be the case, as can be seen from the recent spate of reported accounting scandals around the world. Both forms of accounting make extensive use of estimation and both may be subject to the application of 'creative accounting'. Consider, for instance, the current debate on the valuation and disclosure of organisations' pensions liabilities. The actuarial evaluations of such liabilities may justifiably take many approaches and may arrive at vastly different values for the same organisation.
- Financial accounting is no longer the relatively straightforward affair that it once was. The increasing complexity and sheer volume of financial accounting standards, designed to cope with the increasing complexity of the business world and, for instance, the explosion in financial instruments, have helped to expand the world of financial accounting. Additionally, attempts to harmonise the various systems of accounting standards across the world (e.g. the implementation of International Financial Reporting Standards by all EU listed companies' group accounts by 2005), increasing public interest in corporate governance and the increasing focus on making the public sector more accountable have all contributed to the accountant's workload. This ensures that financial accounting is a 'cutting edge' subject that can be fascinating (well, to some people, at least!). The international standard dealing with financial instruments, IAS39, is an excellent indicator of the complexity that may be inherent in a single accounting issue, and the arguments it has caused show that there is rarely a universal acceptance of any single accounting approach.
- Both management accounting and financial accounting can maintain their currency only by evolving to keep pace with changes in the organisational environment. Both types of accounting, therefore, are very much 'living' subjects.
- The boundaries of financial accounting have become more blurred as financial accountants have increasingly moved into the (more lucrative) areas of taxation advice, financial consultancy etc., raising public concerns, in recent years, about accountants' conflicts of interest.
- Both management accounting and financial accounting can only be truly useful by presenting information to the right people at the right time and in ways that are meaningful, transparent and cost-effective. There can therefore be no room in the modern organisation for information and for information-gathering methodologies that have outlived their purpose.

The History and Context of Management Accounting

So, where did management accounting come from? Who invented it? Why was it developed, and by what types of person? As with most forms of historical study, a number of partly conflicting 'stories' or paradigms exist, each claiming to give authoritative responses to such questions. Such 'stories' may concentrate, according to the slant adopted by their authors, on the commercial, organisational, cultural, sociological, political or ideological aspects of management accounting's history. The past few decades have seen an explosion in the amount and variety of research undertaken into management accounting's history, practices and trends. While some of this research might be criticised for being repetitive, unnecessary, too specialised and/or impractical, this research base at least provides a wealth of ideas to increase our understanding of the possible forces that shape management accounting. An understanding of these forces is useful in considering individual scenarios within which management accounting is applied and in analysing the likely or observed outcomes of such applications. In this book we will provide information to encourage further background reading, along with summaries of some influential and ground-breaking papers. Obviously, there is a limited amount of time available to you for such background reading, but it is often only by going back to the original papers that you can fully appreciate the worth of such contributions to the literature. Some of these papers can be surprisingly readable; others may be less so! A number of specialised texts on such papers, covering a wide variety of management accounting related subjects, have been produced in recent years, two examples being Ashton *et al.* (1995) and Emmanuel *et al.* (1995).

Excellent analyses of the history and context of management accounting, taking a variety of perspectives, have been provided by writers such as Loft (1995), Roslender (1995) and Johnson and Kaplan (1987). Some aspects of these and similar papers will be expanded upon in later chapters, although summaries of some issues are provided in the sections below.

Within such papers you will see that management accounting's past, present and future development as a profession may be dependent upon a wide range of factors. Writers of such papers may focus upon such questions as the following:

- In what ways was management accounting created and developed as a response to changes in the industrial/business/organisational environments?
- Does management accounting merely follow and react to changes in business (and other) environments, or does it take a more active role in shaping changes in those environments? To put is another way, is management accounting *passive* (reactive) or *active* (proactive)?
- To what extent do the observed changes in management accounting practice and research fit in with other schools of thought in areas such as sociology and philosophy?
- What is the significance for management accounting of areas of study such as ethics and power relationships?
- To what extent are changes in management accounting shaped by political and ideological processes?

Such questions are addressed by different writers in a variety of ways. Loft gives an overview of a number of different 'schools of thought' on management accounting's history. Roslender looks at the context of management accounting within a framework of critical theory, relating it to a number of recognised social models. Johnson and Kaplan give their own analysis of management accounting's history and apply this to their theory of why management accounting lost some of its relevance during the later years of the twentieth century. Merchant (1998) and Robson and Cooper (1989) respectively give their observations on the relationships between management accounting and theories/models of ethics and power/control.

The Scope of Management Accounting

As explained earlier, there is no single definition of what management accounting is, or of the areas of work that it includes. Additionally, as management accounting continues to evolve, some areas of its coverage may become obsolete and be discarded, and some new and initially unfamiliar areas may gradually become accepted as mainstream management accounting activities. Table 1.1 summarises some of the areas considered to be part of 'management accounting', based upon a study of contemporary management accounting textbooks. One word of warning: just because a topic is contained within a textbook, it is not necessarily part of current management accounting practice. Reasons for such a mismatch include the fact that textbooks may not be able to keep pace with changes in practice (this is not just a management accounting problem) and that textbooks may contain some 'ideal approaches' which have not yet been put into practice, or which are unlikely to ever be actioned. Some of the terms within Table 1.1 may be unfamiliar to you. Don't worry: these will be explained in later chapters. Table 1.1 concentrates on relatively 'high level' activities. Bear in mind that 'calculating the profitability of products, services and operations', for example, will involve a range of 'lower level' activities including allocating costs to products, setting inter-divisional transfer prices, and so on.

Table 1.1   Some areas of activity considered to be part of 'management accounting'

Budgeting, planning and forecasting
Calculating the profitability of products, services and operations
Measuring organisational, divisional and departmental performance
Comparing results and performance within and between organisations
Assisting in the process of increasing effectiveness and efficiency
Assessing the performance of past and future capital investments
Advising on decisions about product mix, markets to be served and selling prices
Advising on decisions on whether to outsource products, components, activities and services
Advising on decisions involving the investment of scarce funds between a range of possible alternatives
Assisting in the making of a wide range of strategic decisions

Similarly, 'assisting in the process of increasing effectiveness and efficiency' may include a range of specialised techniques such as activity-based cost management and theory of constraints.

If you browse through other texts on management accounting you will find that the authors have different ideas about what should be included within 'management accounting'. One specific area for which differences of opinion are found is that of financial management or managerial finance. Traditionally, within the syllabuses of professional accountancy examinations, and also within universities' accounting syllabuses, boundaries have been drawn between 'management accounting' and 'financial management'. This is often done as a pragmatic solution to the problems of achieving manageably-sized syllabuses for use within modularised courses. Like the boundary between financial accounting and management accounting, the boundary between management accounting and financial management is also rather blurred. Similarly, the scope or coverage of 'financial management' is not always well defined. Texts on financial management tend to have certain areas of coverage in common, such as financial theories concerning the pricing of financial instruments, the calculation of the cost of capital and the implications of gearing, dividends, the effects of risk, treasury management, and so on. The area of capital investment appraisal, that is, the appraisal of the implications of proposed investments for the value of the organisation (via the application of discounted cash-flow techniques), is usually covered by financial management texts but is also covered by many texts on management accounting. One possible reason for this dual coverage is that capital investment appraisal deals with investment decisions that have a strategically important effect upon the organisation. Thus, when the strategic aspects of management accounting are considered, such investment decisions are part of the work of management accountants. Similarly, when the strategic financing decisions related to such investments are made, these decisions form part of financial management. What is obvious, then, is that such strategic decisions cannot be made in a one-dimensional way. Their impact is such that all aspects must be considered and all interested parties (financial managers, management accountants, financial accountants, etc.) have a part to play.

For completeness, capital investment appraisal techniques will be incorporated within this text, as an understanding of these techniques and the ability to apply them competently is essential to management accountants, as is the ability to work and communicate effectively with financial managers, financial accountants and other managers. The importance of the various professional disciplines working together in order to reach decisions that have considered a broad range of issues (i.e. a *holistic* approach) is a theme that continues throughout this text.

Users of Management Accounting Information

Who uses management accounting information? As explained above, anyone who needs information to manage the organisation. Think about the people involved in managing the activities of a typical company. The following are some examples:

- A *sales manager* would require information about sales trends, profitability, stock levels, stock turnover rates, salespeople's performance (measured in a variety of ways), customer 'hit rates', sales volumes and values by customer, area, sector, product line, etc.
- A *production manager* would require information about production rates, production efficiencies, machine capacity usage, productive employee performance, quality measures and trends, stock levels, throughput rates, wastage rates, etc.
- A *human resources manager* would require information about absenteeism rates, lateness, sickness levels and trends, staff turnover rates, recruitment costs and the effectiveness of the recruitment process, training rates and success rates, comparative salary and wage levels etc.
- An *office manager*, in addition to the types of information relevant to the human resources manager, would require information about matters such as the performance of the particular office, however measured, the extent to which service level agreements with other offices had been met, the overall effectiveness of the processes carried out by the office, budgets for the office and the extent to which these are being met, the cost implications of future services to be provided by the office, comparisons between the costs of services provided by the office and those of potential external providers, etc.
- A *procurement manager* would require information about stock and procurement order levels, the effectiveness and costs of procurement processes, the cost implications of alternative procurement approaches, the comparative costs of alternative suppliers, procurement channels etc.
- A *director* or other high-level manager would require information on all of the above matters but, of course, at a more aggregated, summarised level. The high-level manager needs to be able to 'see the wood for the trees' and hence her/his information requirements will have a more strategic bias. Additionally, this type of manager would be more interested in the wider, longer-term and political aspects of the organisation's business and thus the appropriate information requirements may be broader in scope, less accurate, and more frequently exhibit a non-financial bias.

Of course, information along the same general lines will also be required by managers within a public sector organisation, or a not-for-profit organisation. The following are examples, within public sector organisations:

- A *housing department manager* will require information about occupation rates, tenant turnover rates, the capital costs of housing programmes, the comparative cost implications of different approaches to the provision of social housing, etc., as well as the types of information identified earlier relating to staff performance, budget performance, and service level agreements.
- A *hospital manager* will require information (depending upon her/his specific role) about such matters as bed occupation, waiting list trends, surgical success rates, cost effectiveness of surgical procedures, comparative costs of alternative suppliers, budgetary matters, etc.

Additionally, information of many types will be required, or at least be of interest, to employees of the organisation, whether or not they are considered to be 'managers' in the formal sense. The following are examples of such uses of management information by employees:

- Efficiency of the employee's department, production line, division, etc., as compared to that of others – particularly if the employee's monetary or other rewards are dependent upon performance.
- Comparative wage levels – particularly if wage negotiations are impending.
- The profitability and general performance of the organisation, as compared with that of competitors – particularly when job security is being considered.
- The employee's own performance, however measured, as compared with that of other employees – particularly when the employee is considering applying for promotion.

One further issue to note is that what constitutes 'management accounting information' will depend upon the uses to which such information is being put and upon the 'level' being considered. Within the public sector, for example, information that a lower-level clerical officer may consider to be 'management accounting information' may be considered by a high-level manager to be excessively detailed data. Similarly, the data that the high-level departmental manager thinks of as management accounting information would not be considered as such by a national or supranational organisation working at a sectoral, country or economic zone level. For organisations such as the International Monetary Fund, the Organisation for Economic Co-operation and Development (OECD) and the European Union, the 'detail' may consist of the total results for entire countries or states.

Issues Affecting the Evolution and Design of Management Accounting Systems

There are many versions of the 'truth' about the roots and evolution of management accounting. Some authors describe the evolution of management accounting in terms of the ways in which it can be seen to have followed, or in some cases acted as a catalyst for, changes in the ways in which organisations operate. Others describe changes in management accounting as functions of societal and other factors that have simultaneously caused changes in organisational behaviour. Some (a minority of) authors see management accounting as a symptom of perceived ills in society – as a tool of the operation of subversive forces.

An excellent account of the history of management accounting is given by Loft (1995). Loft describes a number of 'schools of thought' on the history of management accounting:

- the *traditional*, or *neo-classical revision* school;
- the *relevance lost* school;

- the *labour process* school;
- the *radical* school

A summary of Loft's account is given in the recommended further reading section at the end of this chapter. In basic terms, Loft's 'schools' have the following features:

- The 'traditional' school sees management accounting's roots in the late nineteenth century, whereby systematic costing methods evolved as a response to the problems caused by the Great Depression (1873–96). Many of the 'best methods' of management accounting are considered to have been developed during the early twentieth century as 'tools' of the manufacturer. The 'neo-classical revision' school argues that the birth of management accounting, as a way of profit maximisation and competitive defence, was as early as the late 1700s.
- The 'relevance lost' school (so called after Johnson and Kaplan's text) sees management accounting as having been a key factor in co-ordinating firms' activities over large geographical areas. Here, management accounting is seen as a necessary device that enabled the capitalism of the late nineteenth century and the rapid expansion and globalisation of companies during the twentieth century. Management accounting is seen having been a useful ally to scientific management approaches. However, the 'relevance lost' school argues that most of management accounting's main advances had been made by the early twentieth century and that it has failed since to respond to or anticipate changes in business/organisational environments, thereby losing much of its relevance during the later twentieth century.
- The 'labour process' school sees management accounting as one significant aspect of changes in the ways in which labour and processes of managing labour have been controlled, leading to a progressive alienation of the workforce. Significantly, this school sees management accounting and accountants as instruments applied by exploiters of labour – as means of reducing the power of the labour force – thereby allowing domination and 'empire-building' by the owners of capital.
- The 'radical' school has similarities with the views of the 'labour process' school and further sees the use of management accounting by organisations as part of the process of creating the 'governable person'. Here, management accounting, with its traditional focus on financial measurements and systematic surveillance of the workforce (with associated rewards and penalties), is likened to the systems of discipline and surveillance used in other institutions.

You may consider some of these views to be a little 'over the top'. Some of them may seem to have the essence of 'conspiracy theories' about them – only time will tell whether these or new alternative 'stories' are most accurate. Some things are clear from the above views. Management accounting either acts passively or as an active force for change. Where management accounting is an active force for change, this force may have been applied consciously or accidentally. There are, therefore, a number of implications for management accounting as a profession:

- If management accounting has acted predominantly in a passive way, there may be potential for management accountants to take more responsibility for creating beneficial change, rather than 'parasitically' responding to the efforts of others.
- If management accounting has acted predominantly in an active but accidental (unconscious) way, then it may have been causing unnoticed but adverse consequences for society. Maybe management accounting should face up to its responsibility to identify and consider the consequences of its actions.
- If management accounting has acted in a consciously active way and has been the cause of the adverse effects identified by, for example, the 'labour process' school, then maybe management accounting should act in a more responsible fashion and consider its ethics.

Whichever way we look at it, management accounting seems to have an important role to play within organisations and, as a profession, it should not operate in a vacuum, oblivious to the many potential offshoot effects it may cause. Among the many possible dimensions with which management accounting may interact are the dimensions of ethical behaviour, corporate governance, empowerment, agency theory, contingency theory, and so on. Additionally, the management accounting press has seen the appearance and disappearance of many 'new ideas' and 'cunning plans' over the years. Many of these ideas have turned out to be either impractical, lacking in substance or simply carefully repackaged old ideas. We will revisit some of these matters in later chapters.

The Time Dimension of Management Accounting

The *Time Focus* of Management Accounting

As you may already realise, the focus of *financial* accounting is the past. Conversely, management accounting's focus is in the *future*. Practically all of the areas of activity considered to be part of 'management accounting', as identified above, are focused upon the future. Budgeting, planning and forecasting, calculating the profitability of products, advising on short-term decisions and on longer-term major investment decisions all involve looking ahead in time. Admittedly, measuring performance and calculating product costs for previous periods involve looking backward in time, but such activities are carried out for one purpose only: to improve performance in future periods. The advice provided by management accountants can have value only if it is focused upon the future. Who would, for instance, employ a management consultant merely to pick holes in past performance? The whole point is to 'add value' by avoiding similar mistakes in the future, to learn from past experiences and to benefit from the insight of those who have 'been there before'.

The *Time* Periods (periodicity) of Management Accounting Information

Financial accounting has, as we have seen, a retrospective focus. Additionally, because of its nature and the demands placed upon it, it tends to be reported upon at regular intervals. For the purposes of publicly available financial reports, financial accounting information is produced at least annually or, in the case of listed public companies, on a biannual or quarterly basis.

Management accounting information may be produced regularly, for instance on a monthly or weekly basis, or on a more irregular, *ad hoc* basis, according to demand, purpose, circumstances and priority. Whereas many companies, particularly the more sizeable ones, organise a system of regular, standardised reporting, focusing upon such matters as performance, cost control, and marketing success, these matters are among the more backward-looking aspects of management accounting. The more strategic, more important aspects such as deciding upon the items in which to invest, which markets to enter/leave, which products to sell and which processes to adjust tend to be carried out less regularly. Such future-focused management accounting information is produced either according to immediate needs (reaction) or according to a predetermined strategy aimed at optimising organisational performance (proaction).

The *Timeliness* ('time value') of Management Accounting Information

Whichever type of management accounting information is being produced, it is only of value if it is produced within a given period of time. Regularly produced, routine, past-focused information needs to be available within a relatively short period of time after the period under review, in order to be of value in making adjustments to actions in the following period. Similarly, forward-looking, strategically focused management accounting information needs to be produced quickly in order to take advantage of the opportunities that might exist, and before competitors gain the advantage.

There are, however, relationships between the timeliness of management accounting information and other factors such as its accuracy, reliability, comprehensibility and relevance, and the cost of producing it.

The Role, Power and Responsibilities of the Management Accountant

As described in the preceding section, management accounting, and management accountants, may be in a position to have a significant influence upon the actions and strategies of organisations. With this potential influence comes the burden of ensuring that management accounting information is generated and communicated in a responsible fashion. Consider some examples of the outcomes of decisions made upon the basis of faulty or unreliable management accounting information:

- Employees may be labelled as inefficient, lazy or unsuitable and, as a result, may be subject to financial penalties or the loss of their livelihoods.
- A branch, division or department of an organisation may be labelled as ineffective or uncompetitive, resulting in the demotivation of its workforce and possibly its closure.
- Scarce financial resources may be diverted into investment projects that are unfeasible, or suboptimal, leading to adverse effects on organisational results.
- A company might decide to alter the mix of products that it produces, or to alter the geographical focus of its marketing, leading to a disastrous downturn in profitability and share price.
- A local health authority may decide to alter the range of procedures that its hospitals provide, or to close a local hospital, on false grounds, to the detriment of local health provision.
- A government department may decide to close down a service department and to use external, private sector contractors to provide the service, possibly leading to a poorer, less reliable service and escalating future costs.
- An incomplete analysis may lead to a company's outsourcing of components or services, only to find that quality and delivery suffer, with consequent effects on competitiveness, and depressing effects on the local economy and employment.

The management accountant's role is thus a responsible one which can have direct effects on people both within and outside of the organisation. As we saw earlier, the management accountant, as the provider of performance-monitoring information, acts as an important and influential link in the chain between management and employees, and between shareholders and management. The relationship between those in a position of 'power' (the *principals*) and those being managed or employed (the *agents*) is known as the *principal–agent* relationship, and the corresponding body of theory is known as principal–agent theory or *agency theory*. We will examine such theory in more detail later. It is, however, worth noting here that the management accountant is responsible for ensuring two things in respect of the principal–agent relationship:

- that any information produced to monitor the performance of the agent is as reliable and accurate as possible;
- that any system designed to enable such monitoring is *unbiased*, either in favour of the principal or the agent.

This is not easy to achieve. The management accountant is meant to be a professional, acting in an impartial fashion. At the same time, however, she/he is an employee of the principal and may feel pressure to act in favour of the principal, to the detriment of the agent. Such pressure may be applied in many ways, including the 'carrot' of enhanced remuneration for being a 'company player'. Of course, being in a position to control the destiny of others can bestow a measure of power on the management accountant, and this power must also be handled responsibly and ethically.

Later we will look in more depth at some writers' thoughts on the role of ethics, ethical codes and empowerment/disempowerment in the work of management accountants. This is an important area of study, as mishandling such matters can lead to the distrust of management accountants and the devaluation of their inputs.

Information Requirements for Management Accounting: Practicalities, Costs and Organisational Implications

An excellent coverage of the information requirements of organisations, for the purposes of planning and control, is given in the first few chapters of Emmanuel *et al.* (1995). Emmanuel *et al.* indicate a number of important considerations of information for planning and control. The following checklist below is based on Emmanuel *et al.* and is intended to act as an overview of some of the issues that should be considered when encountering any management accounting planning/control system:

- Accounting information is affected by the modern business environment. Such environments are characterised by their complexity, uncertainty and turbulence, and therefore management accounting systems must be designed to be able to cope with such environmental conditions.
- Accounting information systems must take account of the nature of control information appropriate to the particular organisation, the methods used for data and information transmission, and the culture and shared values existing within the organisation.
- Information for control may be formal or informal; quantifiable or unquantifiable; routine or *ad hoc*. The system must be designed to be able to produce appropriate control information at appropriate times.
- Accounting information systems serve as a means of control; an integrative mechanism and/or a measure of performance and viability. These multiple uses may conflict and lead to behavioural problems.
- Control is the process by which a system adapts to its environment and may have two major themes; one as a means to achieving the end of domination, and the other as a form of regulation (regulation of others or self-regulation).
- To achieve self-regulation, clear objectives are required – an internal means of achieving these objectives by measurable outputs and a predictive model of output. Any effective management control system must possess each of these. Self-regulating systems are sometimes called *cybernetic* systems.
- Control involves consideration of both operational and strategic issues and goes 'hand in hand' with planning.
- Feedback is important. There are two important terms; (i) *negative feedback* is where control action is taken to reduce deviations from the plan; and (ii) *feed-forward* is the comparison of expected outputs (predictions) with future activities, and control activities implemented. Planning is a form of feed-forward control.

- Decisions take two forms: *programmed*, where the situation is understood enough to make reliable predictions and *unprogrammed*, where no formal mechanism for prediction exists. It can be argued that a flaw of many management accounting models is that they assume programmed situations where many actual management control situations are unprogrammed in nature.
- Objectives: Emmanuel *et al.* suggest that 'individuals have objectives – collectivities do not'. One of the practical problems of designing, implementing and maintaining management control systems is that reconciling individual objectives and (assumed) group objectives may be problematic. Agreement on objectives is necessary for groups to hold together
- Some main aspects for comparison of performance, that is, performance measurement, are: current period vs. previous periods; comparisons with similar organisations; actual vs. estimates (either *ex ante* or *ex post* estimates); actual performance vs. benchmarks or necessary performance required measured against specified objectives; and so on.
- There is no 'best way' to manage an organisation, including its management control systems. Everything is contingent upon a range of factors such as the environment (its predictability; competition; product diversity; hostility and so on); organisational structure (its size, interdependencies, level of decentralisation, resource availability); and technology (nature of processes, degree of routine, clarity of causal relationships). Thus improving control systems is a continuing and iterative process requiring an enquiring mind, flexibility and an openness to change.
- Managers are limited in their capabilities in many ways. They have, for example, limited powers of understanding, a limited capability to deal with a lot of data at once and limited rationality. So, rather than undertake a full and logical appraisal of decisions (which is impossible in the practical situation) managers may jump at the first acceptable solution.
- Management control may take place at a number of levels:

    (i) *strategic planning* – information should be tailor-made, external and predictive;
    (ii) *management control* – information should be integrated, mainly internal and more historical;
    (iii) *task/operational control* – information should be tailor-made, internal and real-time.

Emmanuel *et al.* conclude that the ideal conditions for effective control systems are:

- a stable operating environment;
- a clear-cut organisational hierarchy;
- clear definitions of controllability;
- little interdependence between parts of the organisation.

Of course, in today's large, complex multinational organisations operating within an extremely competitive global marketplace, conditions are less than ideal to make life easy for the management accountant!

Conclusions

This chapter has shown that management accounting:

- is essentially the production of information for managers at all levels;
- is designed to increase organisational effectiveness;
- is forward-looking and relies upon estimation;
- has evolved and continues to evolve as organisations and society progress.

It has also argued that management accounting information:

- must be relevant to be useful and so must take account of organisational and behavioural settings;
- may have undesirable effects if used without careful consideration

Summary

This chapter has provided an introduction to the nature, scope and difficulties of management accounting. We have seen that management accounting is forward-looking in nature and is involved in assessing the implications of managerial and strategic decisions, both those decisions made in the past and those being considered at present. Essentially, we see management accounting as being interested in producing useful information to enhance organisational effectiveness.

The role of management accounting, and the definition of its scope, continues to evolve. We have seen that management accounting information is essential to most organisational players. We have also seen, however, that some management accountants must consider the effects of the information that they produce, as such information may have undesirable effects. Management accounting has an important role to play in all types of organisation, but what type of information is most useful depends upon a wide range of (contingent) factors. Finally, we note that management accounting may play a passive, reactive role or an active one. The latter approach carries with it a degree of responsibility for the organisational and possibly societal impacts it may have.

Recommended Further Reading

Loft, A. (1995) 'The history of management accounting',
in D. Ashton, T. Hopper and R. Scapens (eds), *Issues in Management
Accounting* (2nd edition). Hemel Hempstead: Prentice Hall.
Loft gives an overview of the history of management accounting, looking at the various (often conflicting) historical perspectives. Such analyses can be useful in learning from the past when negotiating current and future management accounting problems. She points to some of the problems of any historical analysis:

- the possible atypicality of early examples;
- a lack of clear evidence of how accounting records were used, and to what extent.

Loft identifies four 'schools of thought' in the history of management accounting:

Traditional School and the Neo-classical Revision

Loft explains how, as a result of the Great Depression of the late nineteenth century, there was a crucial need to calculate and be aware of product costs as competition increased. This led, she notes, to the emergence of systematic allocations, apportionment and cost/financial integration (she refers to *Factory Accounts*, by Garke and Fells (1887), in this respect). She further explains how following the nineteenth century there was a development of ideas regarding allocation to products, accounting for waste and scrap, and how standard costing methods emerged in the 1920s. Within the 'traditional' school, she explains that costing is seen as a manufacturer's tool that developed in line with manufacturing methods.

'Neo-classical revision' was, Loft observes, a similar view to that of the traditional school except it argues that *costing was a management tool as early as the late eighteenth century* and that costing methods were used to maximise profits and defend against competition. Loft mentions the work of Fleischman, Parker and Tyson as being representative of the views of the neo-classical revisionists.

In both traditional and neo-classical views, management accounting is seen as taking a *very passive and reactive* role.

'Relevance lost' school

Loft refers to Johnson and Kaplan (1991), who say that in 1962 Alfred Chandler drew attention to the importance of management accounting in the development of giant US firms. Management accounting is seen to have been a key factor in co-ordinating such firms' wide activity ranges over large geographical areas. Johnson and Kaplan argue that:

- it was the rise of the factory that led to a move away from market-exchange structures (lots of small traders/manufacturers letting the market dictate prices).
- management accounting/costing was a necessary tool of the new industrial capitalism of the late nineteenth century, developing to 'evaluate a company's internal processes' via measuring efficiency in mainly singler activity firms.
- management accounting's development *facilitated* the growth of enterprises – i.e. it was *proactive* rather than passive; a *catalyst to change* rather than an effect of it.
- as scientific management (Taylorism) developed, management accounting moved from simple records of cost (historic) into budgeting and monitoring, and financial accountants found that it was useful for simple-evaluation of stocks.
- following the turn of the twentieth century, as firms became larger and more decentralised, further management accounting measures (e.g. return on investment (ROI))

led to an increase in management accounting's role, in order to optimise the use of capital.

- most 'modern' management accounting practices had been developed by 1925 and managers have since tended to rely mainly on numbers. Therefore, management accounting's information content has lost its strategic (and sometimes most of its) relevance.

Loft points out that, although management accounting may have been slow to react to change, it was 'catching up' and that the preferred process was one of evolution rather than revolution – i.e. a series of gradual well-considered changes rather than 'fire-fighting' reactions. Although some of management accounting's key techniques and approaches were admittedly quite well established (i.e. old), this did not necessarily lessen their relevance (after all, some of the basic principles of mathematics and language, for example, have very historic origins, but they still apply today).

Labour Process Approach
Loft refers to the work of Hopper and Armstrong (1991) who:

- see management accounting's development as being one (significant) aspect of overall changes in the way in which the labour process has been controlled as capitalists have progressively alienated the process of production from the worker.
- explain the success of early factories (partly) by the way in *which management accounting was used to intensify the exploitation of labour.*
- interpret management accounting's focus in the early twentieth century as one of *reducing the power of the labour force, rather than of increasing productive efficiency*
- explain that, in order to homogenise labour via de-skilling, companies increased the percentage of unskilled labour used by reorganising the productive process. Management accounting developed rapidly in order to aid this process.
- see budgeting and the use of ROI as having been developed to increase control over managerial labour and hence, again, management accounting is interpreted as a tool used in this process of exploitation.

All of the above may explain the dominance, in the twentieth century, of accountants as senior executives in most US and UK organisations – i.e. accountants as a *dominating* force; engineers and the like as dominated managerial labour).

Radicalism
Loft explains how the writing of Foucault, Derrida and others (none of whom wrote directly about accounting) may be used to help in the interpretation of management accounting's history. Foucault (1977) wrote about the growth of disciplinary institutions (prisons, armies, schools, hospitals, *factories*) in the nineteenth and twentieth centuries, wherein individuals were arranged so that they could be watched, and discipline/punishment administered, via surveillance and record keeping.

Management accounting can thus be seen as one of these techniques of surveillance and record keeping. Such a process will lead to the prioritisation of financial factors above all others, and hence to the expansion of management accounting.

Loft points to the effects of the UK government's taking control of many factories during the world wars of the twentieth century. This led to the dominance of cost-plus pricing and a much-increased emphasis of historical costing. Therefore cost accounting expanded, as did the cost accountant's importance.

Management accounting is thus seen as part of the process of creating the 'governable person'.

Questions

1. Examine the extent to which the role and nature of management accountants might differ within the public and private sectors.
2. Critically analyse the possible effects of e-commerce on the role of the management accountant.
3. Traditionally, management accounting, financial management and financial accounting have been treated as largely separate disciplines. Discuss the extent to which such a categorisation is still valid and comment upon the implications for today's management accounting profession.
4. 'Management accountants exist to ensure that the changing information needs of managers are met.'
   'Management accountants are in the fortunate position of being the brokers and guardians of information. They may use this information to increase their own power and status.'
   'Management accountants have a duty to serve all stakeholders of their organisation and a responsibility to ensure the reliability of the information which they process.'
   To what extent are these statements contradictory or complementary?
5. Analyse the potential effects of recent developments in the business *or* public sector environments on the relevance of management accounting systems.
6. Analyse the extent to which the management accounting information system of a service-based organisation of your choice would be likely to differ from that of a manufacturing company.

Chapter 2
COST ANALYSIS AND
DECISION MAKING

Key Learning Objectives

By the time you have finished studying this chapter, you should be able to:
- describe how costs may be classified in both subjective and objective ways;
- define and identify direct and indirect costs and categorise them into their subdivisions of labour, materials and overheads;
- explain how costs behave at various levels of activity;
- classify costs for control and decision-making purposes.

Introduction

In Chapter 1 we explained the meaning and nature of management accounting, described the scope and content of the discipline, discussed past and current issues in management accounting and, finally, outlined the factors which are important when designing management accounting systems. In this chapter we begin to develop the fundamentals of cost accounting which underpin these concepts and issues. This chapter is therefore aimed at ensuring that you have a fundamental grasp of the basics as this is the bedrock upon which an ability to develop the interpretation skills of the management accountant is founded. In essence, these skills are based on the ability to understand the basis on which financial information is compiled and provided in a business environment. This applies whether the business operates in the private sector or is regarded as providing public sector services. The chapter thus contains a number of basic definitions in addition to fostering the development of analytical and critical skills.

The chapter develops what has been described as 'basic knowing' (Coombs *et al.*, 2000), in that basic concepts have to be understood before moving on to develop more advanced skills of interpretation. Hence, this explains their introduction at this stage of the text. We also introduce these concepts in a variety of organisations to show that management accounting is relevant not only to what is traditionally seen as its home in manufacturing industry but also to a wide range of other sectors of the economy, including the public sector. This move away from manufacturing industry has been highlighted by the changing nature of western economies with their reduced emphasis on heavy industry, the growth in the service sector and the almost infinite demand for public sector services despite finite resources.

Cost Management Essentials – The Basic Process and Requirements

The basic requirement in the management of the business process is for the provision of information for decision-making purposes. The nature of these decisions depends on the task in hand. Information has to be tailored to the needs and abilities of managers making decisions, but its foundation in a management accounting context is based on the attribution of costs to cost objectives. A cost objective is a purpose or activity for which a distinctly identifiable measurement of cost is desired in order that a decision can be made. In essence, the purpose is to attract the attention of managers so that they can then move into problem-solving mode. It will be noted that this emphasises the importance of information being in a format that is relevant to the decision required and the level of managers making the decision. It also implies that information, in addition to being relevant, has to be meaningful, accurate, timely and in a format suitable for use by the decision maker. This is inevitably a challenge for any accounting system or, indeed, management accountant designing the accounting information system to provide what is required by decision makers.

Fundamental in this process is the definition of the cost unit, the unit of product or service that an organisation produces. As Upchurch (1998: 35) points out, this 'must be an accurate reflection of the nature of the output to which costs are attributed', otherwise, if it is wrongly defined, then there is every chance that cost attribution will be incorrect.

It is conventional in management accounting texts to assume that all businesses aim to maximise profits as per the traditional view expressed in the neo-classical economics model. This is rather a simplistic assumption of the real world and is further discussed in Chapter 10, where agency and other theories are raised. It is presented here, however, since profit under this definition is seen as the sole function of business and is presented in many management accounting texts as somehow being self-explanatory without any attempt being made to discuss the problems of measuring 'profit'.

There are numerous definitions of what 'profit' is, as profit can be measured, for example, from an accountant's, an economist's and a taxation authority's perspective. Under these various definitions we can have a wide range of potential profit figures even in relatively straightforward companies.

Simplified definitions are as follows:

- Accounting profit is an improvement in the financial position through the excess of accounting revenue over accounting cost over a defined accounting period.

- In micro-economics economists consider the opportunity cost of capital provided by entrepreneurs (also termed 'normal profits') as a cost of production. In macro-economics the term 'profit' excludes interest on borrowed capital but not the return on the capital provided by the owners (Baring Asset Management, 1997: 217).
- Taxable profits depend on the rules set by the tax body. In the United Kingdom depreciation is normally disallowable (excluding certain intangible assets and finance leases) in computing taxable profits, being replaced by a system of capital allowances.

In the accounting context the use of various legally acceptable financial accounting techniques in stock valuation, assessing the provision for bad and doubtful debts, the treatment of an item as capital expenditure as opposed to revenue expenditure, the depreciation rates judged appropriate and applied to plant and machinery, the definition of materiality of an item and so on will have a significant impact on the financial results shown. Large-scale publicly quoted companies have been known to use these techniques to smooth profit figures (with or without the knowledge and agreement of their auditors) to manage stock market expectations, their share price and their dividend distribution policy.

As has just been indicated, a wide range of 'profits' are possible, yet profit is used as an essential measurement basis to assess the performance of a business by a wide range of commentators both internal and external to any business organisation. By using it as such a measure we are attempting to show whether it has been worth an enterprise undertaking any activity in the period of operation being measured (year, six months, week or whatever). This concept of performance measurement and the difficulties associated with measuring profit also applies to future projections of profitability and should be borne in mind when the reader comes to budgeting in subsequent chapters. It can thus be argued that the term 'profit' should carry a health warning for readers and any analyst on the figures produced.

'Profit' therefore depends on how the managers of the business define (whether actively, or passively through ignorance of accounting techniques) the profits that they wish to achieve. This will have obvious implications for the management accounting reporting system and the actions taken as a result of information produced. It may well be there is a surplus of financial benefits over financial costs in an accounting period. This would, however, be specific to the company as it defines the term 'surplus' since it expresses the financial performance the company is attempting to measure through the targets set by management. Readers should also remember that we are not talking about cash flows but about the benefits earned and costs expended in a period arising from the productive activity of the business during that period. These costs in measuring profit thus include non-cash flows such as depreciation.

In 'not for profit' organisations, as is self-evident, the organisation exists to achieve some benefit other than profit. Thus, we have charities which exist to further the cause of the specific charitable functions for which they were established and organisations such as the NHS and local government providing a national health service and local services such as education and leisure. In the case of a charity, its objective will be to maximise its revenue over its costs to maximise the achievement of its charitable functions. Thus its management accounting system will be established and run to report on how well the organisation is doing in achieving this objective. In the case of the NHS, the more economically, efficiently and effectively it use its resources, the greater the potential impact on satisfying patient needs. Where it provides services to the private health sector it will need to know the cost of those services so that it can make decisions on how it recovers those costs and at what price. Local government will have services for which it charges and may even aim to make profits (such as leisure centres), but many local government services will be provided below cost. The financial objective of local government (as with the NHS) therefore is to manage all its services on the general principles of economy, efficiency and effectiveness to reduce the calls on both local and national taxpayers who fund the majority of local government expenditure.

To turn to cost analysis, all expenditure can be divided into the groups corresponding to the activities of the concern under consideration. If we consider a manufacturing environment, the activities of the enterprise can be divided into expenditure on manufacturing, administration expenses, selling expenses and distribution expenses. For the service industry, expenditure on manufacturing can be substituted with expenditure on service delivered.

The total expenditure of a manufacturing business can be subdivided as shown in Figure 2.1. Ultimately the total cost of sales can be compared with the total income for the period resulting in a profit or loss for that period, as discussed above. A similar analysis could be performed for a service industry but excluding, of course, the manufacturing elements.

Direct labour, direct materials and direct expenses comprise *prime cost* and, together with production overheads, comprise total production costs. In more detail:

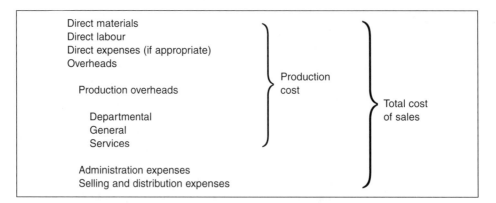

Figure 2.1　Total cost of sales analysis, manufacturing industry

- *Direct materials* comprises all material purchased for a particular job, material acquired and later issued from stores, components purchased or produced material passing from one process to another, and primary packaging materials. Items such as import duties, transport costs are also part of direct materials costs. A *de minimus* rule will also apply to items of minimal cost – meaning that there are items below which it is not worth the time, cost or effort of charging what could be regarded as the direct expenditure of manufacturing a product directly to that product. These costs will be treated as indirect expenditure (overheads). An example of direct materials where the product is a car would be the metal used to make the body shell. In essence, direct materials can be clearly observed in the product manufactured.

- *Direct labour* is the labour expended in making the product. Wages paid to skilled and unskilled workers for work rendered can be charged directly to products, hence the term direct labour. Other similar terms include process labour, productive labour and operating labour. In our car example the direct labour element would be the person who assembled the vehicle. Where the product is a service such as a taught class in a university, the direct labour is the lecturer standing in front of the class. Wages of foremen, storespersons and internal transport drivers would be regarded as indirect as they cannot be traced directly to a particular job. In the university case indirect costs would be the academic registry as it does not have direct teaching contact with students.

- *Direct expenses* are those costs other than direct materials or direct labour that are incurred in the production of a product. An example would include the hire of special tools to manufacture a particular product or deliver a specific service in the service sector.

You will have noticed that all the above costs are described as *direct*. All other costs are *indirect* – that is, overheads. While there are elements of subjectivity in the classification of direct costs, technical expertise exercised through subjective judgements plays a major part in dealing with overheads, particularly in any allocation to products. It should also be pointed out that employees working in a marketing department, for example, are a direct cost of the marketing function. In terms of the production department, however, such individuals are an overhead as they do not produce the company's product. We can further classify overheads as follows:

- *Production overheads* This category of cost covers all indirect expenditure incurred, from the receipt of the order to the dispatch of the completed goods. Other terms which describe such expenditure include 'factory overhead' and 'works overhead'. Examples are: rents, rates and insurance, excluding those that can be apportioned to the general administrative office, selling departments or warehousing and distribution areas; indirect labour, such as supervision costs, salary of the works manager, storespersons, gauging and testing, idle time of operatives, works security; consumable stores and all types of indirect material, including such items as oil and greases; depreciation of factory plant, vehicles and buildings; sundry expenses, for example, performance rights licences for factory music.

- *Administration overheads* comprise all costs and expenses incurred in the direction, control and day-to-day administration of the organisation. Examples include office lighting and heating, accountants' salaries, credit management, and directors' salaries.
- *Selling and distribution overheads* comprise the costs of selling and distributing goods to the customer or client. They therefore include the payment of salaries and commissions to sales staff, training costs, preparation of tenders, rent of sales offices, costs of transportation, packaging, despatching and so on. Selling and distribution costs can be analysed by function (e.g. warehousing or advertising) or by location (e.g. by sales territory).

The distinction between direct and indirect costs is directly related to the cost objective. If the cost objective is the establishment of the costs of selling and marketing then the salaries of salesmen and cost of promotion will be regarded as a direct cost. The costs cannot, however, be traced directly to products and are thus indirect for product valuation purposes. It should also be remembered that, for example, in a public sector organisation the cost of an accountant working in the central finance department will be a direct cost of that department. It is, however, an indirect cost of say, the education department which uses the individual to provide financial advice on the education service.

Cost Classification

Costs can basically be divided into costs for stock valuation, costs for control and costs for decision making. Stock valuation is closely linked with profit measurement and the matching concept familiar to students of financial accounting and is covered in Chapter 3. Unexpired costs are those costs that are expected to make a contribution to profit in some future accounting period and are carried forward as assets on the balance sheet. They will become an expense in some later period. Any cost consumed during a period and thus seen as having no future earnings potential is charged to revenue in the current period and is thus treated as an expired cost. In a manufacturing environment all manufacturing costs are regarded as product costs and non-manufacturing costs are treated as period costs.

Allocating costs for control is concerned with responsibility accounting. Product costs in themselves are inadequate to perform this function as a product may go through several manufacturing processes. In this case it is likely that these processes would be managed by several different people. Responsibility accounting is based on the principle of recognising an individual's area of responsibility and holding that individual accountable for his/her performance for costs (and revenues as appropriate) incurred where they are under that individual's control.

Responsibility centres are divided into three types:

- cost centres where managers are held responsible for expenses under their control;
- profit centres where managers are held responsible for both sales revenue and expenses;
- investment centres where managers are normally held responsible not only for sales revenue and expenses but also for capital investment decisions.

In the previous paragraph it was stated that managers should be only held accountable for items within their control. While ultimately all costs are controllable by someone within an organisation, clearly the costs which are controllable at the highest level of management differ from those controllable lower down the organisation. This has significant implications for accountants in terms of the design of performance reports.

As a general rule, the lower down within an organisation that a manager operates the more detailed is the performance report, although again it should only contain information on costs controllable by that manager otherwise negative behavioural implications can arise (Argyris, 1953). It also leads on to the concept of exception reporting, so that management can concentrate on those items which are important and controllable by them in a given situation.

A controllable cost can be defined as a cost over which a manager has the ability to influence behaviour. If the manager has no ability to control or influence a cost it is clearly uncontrollable at that manager's level – it is beyond the manager's span of control. As an illustration, a production manager may be able to control the usage of material but contracts for that material are let through a central purchasing department which negotiates price. In any budget variance for materials the usage variance of the material is controllable by the production manager, but any price variance is the responsibility of the purchasing arm of the organisation. Responsibility has thus been identified with the power to control.

While cost accounting is concerned with cost collation and the calculation of product costs for profit measurement, management accounting is concerned with the proactive generation of financial and non-financial information for decision making. In the public sector, costing information (to simplify) is concerned with creating budgets for agreed policy goals and monitoring those budgets. Costing information is accumulated via the accounting system of an organisation. Management accounting information is accumulated both within and outside the standard cost-gathering system with the objective of helping managers evaluate alternative courses of action to reach a decision. By its very nature, management accounting information is non-standard and decision-specific. The more complex the decision, the more complex the probable information set although managers need to be aware of the danger of being overwhelmed by the volume of data (Simon, 1953).

This leads into the discussion of various costs classifications for decision making:

- cost behaviour by volume of activity;
- sunk costs;
- relevant and non-relevant costs;
- avoidable and unavoidable costs;
- opportunity costs;
- marginal or incremental costs.

Cost Behaviour by Volume of Activity

Costs can vary by the level of activity, and this has important implications for decision making. A manager therefore has to be aware of how costs will behave in a specific situation. Typically managers might ask:

- What will happen to material costs if output rises?
- What sales level of units do we need to sell to cover our costs and at what price?
- If we expand production, what will happen to labour costs?
- How do energy costs behave at various levels of production?

These questions raise issues about how accountants estimate costs and revenues for a variety of activity levels and how they present that information to managers.

The traditional terms used in this respect are fixed costs, variable costs, semi-variable costs and stepped or semi-fixed costs. Figure 2.2 illustrates these how these categories of costs behave in relation to output changes.

- *Fixed costs* remain constant over a wide range of activity levels for a specific period of time. Examples of fixed costs include depreciation of buildings, rent and rates, and management salaries.
- *Variable costs* are assumed to vary in the short term directly in proportion to output. These costs are thus assumed to be linear and can thus be represented by a straight line. Examples of variable costs include fuel for motor vehicles (directly variable with mileage covered), sales commissions (directly variable with product sold), piecework labour costs (directly variable with produced units) and direct material costs (directly variable with product manufactured).
- *Semi-variable costs* can be illustrated by activities such as photocopier rental. Under such agreements there may be a fixed rental change followed by charge per copy made. The rental is thus fixed but total cost will depend on the addition of the variable element. A similar cost pattern exists for any utility bill which has a standing charge element.
- *Stepped* or *semi-fixed costs* remain constant within a band of activity. Here we find that over a band of productive activity there is no change, but if production levels fall or rise we may need to either lay off or employ extra labour thus progressing to the next step up or down.

It will be noted from Figure 2.2 that it is assumed that all costs exhibit straight-line behaviour. In the economist's model the economist assumes that the average unit cost declines on the basis, for example, that a firm obtains discounts for bulk buying of material and can also benefit from the division of labour as it expands. These are regarded as economies of scale. At the other extreme, as the firm becomes too large it suffers diseconomies of scale. These factors inevitable lead to a different cost function for the economist from that of the accountant. The key factor to remember, however, is that the accountant is interested in representing costs over the range of output that a firm reasonably expects to correspond to the reality of its operating environment. This is the concept of *relevant range* and also broadly represents the output levels over which the firm has gained experience of operating and for which cost data are available from the business's accounting records.

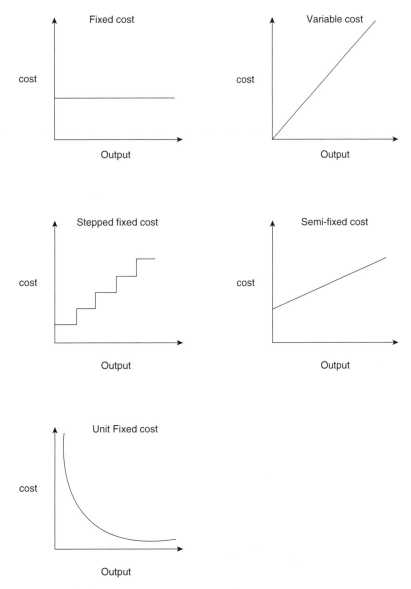

Figure 2.2   Cost behaviour against output change

Sunk Costs

These are costs which are the result of previous decisions of the enterprise and which will be unaffected by any future decision as they have already been incurred. An example is expenditure on materials that were bought in anticipation of a contract which never came to fruition. The materials are still in store and the decision to buy cannot be undone.

Relevant and Non-Relevant Costs and Revenues

In making decisions managers, in whatever enterprise they work, are primarily concerned with those costs and revenues which will be changed by their decisions. They are not interested in costs and revenues which will be unchanged by their decisions. In the short term not all costs and revenues are relevant for decision making. Costs which will be unaltered in the short term are fixed costs and include such items as rents and rates. When considering a decision on transporting goods the road tax and insurance already paid on a vehicle are fixed. Consequently, the only costs that will be altered by a decision to transport goods by road by the company's own vehicles will be any variable costs that the firm will incur (e.g. extra fuel costs, and possible bonuses paid to drivers).

Avoidable and Unavoidable Costs

These are effectively an alternative perspective on relevant and non-relevant costs. Avoidable costs are those costs that have to be incurred if a particular course of action is taken. Unavoidable costs cannot be saved.

Opportunity Costs

These measure the cost of an opportunity forgone to pursue a particular course of action. By their nature, opportunity costs are not based on past payments but are an estimate of the costs of following or not following a particular course of action. The cost arises because of the scarcity of resources and because there is competition for the use of these resources.

Marginal or Incremental Costs

These are additional costs or revenues that arise as a result of following a particular course of action. Incremental costs may include fixed costs depending on the nature of the decision being taken. Suppose an estate agent is considering increasing the size of the office accommodation available to the business by renting premises next door. Rent, while a fixed cost for the current premises, will increase on signing the contract for the new office and thus constitute an incremental cost to the business.

Unit Costs

Unit costs are widely used across all sectors of the economy to compare and control financial performance. At its most basic a unit cost is simply the total cost of producing a number of units divided by the number of units produced. If, for example, a restaurant produced

Table 2.1   Example of a unit cost statement: comparative food costs for four schools providing school meals, March–December 2004

	School A		School B		School C		School D		TOTAL	
	Cost (£000)	Unit cost (p)	Cost (£000)	Unit cost (p)	Cost (£000)	Unit cost (p)	Cost (£000)	Unit cost (p)	Cost (£000)	Unit cost (p)
Food	16.00	35	31.50	40	27.50	45	10.00	28	85.00	38
Energy	3.60	8	4.10	5	2.00	3	3.00	9	12.7	6
Kitchen staff										
Cooks	9.00	20	18.00	23	18.00	29	9.00	26	54.00	25
Asst. Cooks	12.00	27	6.00	8	12.00	20	12.00	35	42.00	19
Maids	13.50	30	13.50	17	13.50	22	13.50	39	54.00	24
Cleaners	3.00	7	7.00	9	6.00	10	5.00	14	21.00	10
Overheads	3.75	8	4.45	6	4.95	8	3.95	11	17.10	8
Supervisor	5.00	11	5.00	6	5.00	8	5.00	14	20.00	9
Capital charges										
Depreciation	10.00	22	9.00	12	9.00	15	7.00	20	35.00	16
Interest	4.00	9	2.00	2	2.00	3	2.50	7	10.50	5
Admin charge	9.00	20	15.60	20	12.24	20	6.97	20	43.81	20
Total	88.85	197	116.15	148	112.19	183	77.92	223	395.11	180
Meals provided	45,000		78,000		61,200		34,850		219,050	
No. of pupils	400		650		550		320		1920	

10,000 meals at a cost of £20,000 during an accounting period the unit cost of a meal would be £2. If all meals had been sold for £4 we would have made £20,000 profit. If we are looking forward the £2 unit cost could be the benchmark against which to measure and control future performance.

Table 2.1 is an example of a unit cost statement. The objective is the provision of school meals, and we are interested in the cost per meal provided. The categorisation of costs into their individual elements such as pay, food and energy is the subjective element of the statement. In such public sector examples the objective is defined as the service being provided (e.g. education), while the individual categories of expense represent the subjective elements as a decision has to be made on how to code items of expenditure. This example has been developed as many readers will be familiar with the provision of school meals through personal experience (good or bad!) and it could obviously be extended to a restaurant or even a hotel with relatively minor changes. Indeed, in the school situation depicted we could add in the income received from the sale of meals and work out the profit or loss on the provision of school meals.

In Table 2.1 it is evident that the provision of meals in kitchen B is considerably more efficient in cost terms than in A, C or D. Its cost per meal provided, 148p, is 75% of A, 81% of C and 66% of D. No income per meal has been shown for each kitchen to simplify the example, but it could be common across all three kitchens, given the subject of the example. Examination of the individual cost components reveals that kitchen B's lower unit costs are the result of a variety of factors. Food costs are the highest of all four kitchens but the unit costs for staff are the lowest. Managers would be interested in establishing the reasons for these variations and in doing something about them. It might be possible to direct any savings in the kitchens to the provision of further teaching support.

Food costs vary considerably. This might be caused by:

- overstocking, leading to waste;
- overprovision of portions, indicating a lack of menu and portion control;
- fraud and theft;
- buying from local suppliers rather than cheaper contractors;
- quality of food in the meals varying between the kitchens;
- special dietary needs of certain pupils (e.g. diabetic meals).

Note that we have no answers, but managers are in a position to raise questions.

Energy costs per meal vary between kitchens but judgementally are rather low when compared to total cost. It may not be possible to influence these costs other than by relatively simple measures, such as encouraging staff to turn off lights and gas when the kitchens or equipment are not in use.

Further analysis of Table 2.1 reveals cooks are paid £9,000 per annum, assistant cooks £6,000 per annum and kitchen maids £4,500 per annum. This gives the ability to produce a workload analysis, as set out in Table 2.2. The table does not tell us which kitchen is the most efficient, but it demonstrates considerable variation in workloads between staff and kitchens. This would require further study to see if the solution was to relocate staff or make staff redundant. This might be achieved via work study analysis.

Table 2.2 Workload analysis of meals per worker

Staff	Kitchen A	Kitchen B	Kitchen C	Kitchen D
Cooks	45,000	44,000	30,600	34,850
Asst. cooks	22,500	78,000	30,600	17,425
Kitch. maids	15,000	26,000	20,400	11,617

Cleaning costs vary per meal (although no mention has been made of floor area). It might be possible to contract out the cleaners if this has not already been done.

The original table/report can also be designed to highlight responsibilities. The upper part of the table focuses on costs directly incurred in the preparation of meals and presumably within the control of the cook. Kitchen staff are appointed by someone – the question is who? The employment of staff generates overheads on wages and salaries. These overheads (pension and national insurance) may be outside the direct control of the supervisor if he/she did not appoint but will depend on the number of staff employed. The supervisor line itself will also be the responsibility of a higher-level manager who may be the head teacher but is more likely to be based at a central office running the school meals service for the organisation. It should be noted that the statement is a nine-month analysis, implying that this type of data is gathered regularly. It could be used to project expenditure forward to compare against projected costs and income to act as a budgetary control statement. It is clearly meant to stimulate action or at least identify that action may be required.

The administration charge represents a fixed charge and in the example is aimed at recovering in the cost of the meal a set contribution (20p) towards the administration costs of the scheme. It thus assumes a central administration function somewhere within the organisation. This cost can only be reduced by questioning the value for money provided by that function.

It should be noted that the emphasis in Table 2.1 is on unit costs; nothing is said about the quality of meals. This is an emphasis on throughputs as opposed to outcomes. In compiling any report on the provision of meals the views of users of the service should be sought to present a more rounded picture when considering how well the provision of meals is going.

Unit cost statements broadly contribute to the management of an organisation in three main ways. First, they serve as an indicator of efficiency relative to other similar functions or providers within an organisation or between organisations. For the school meals service, they allow it to compare its cost with other internally generated data for any other kitchens or possibly those of other school meals organisations if it is part of a trade association. In the UK public sector, where data are readily available on comparative performance, the Audit Commission in England and Wales makes considerable use of unit costs for this purpose, generating batteries of comparative statistics which it can use as a starting point for analysis.

Second, unit costs can be used as an indicator of efficiency over time as data builds up on performance. This allows us to measure and compare the outputs (and outcomes) of the same function from year to year. This can show whether efficiency is increasing or decreasing over the period being measured. It also hopefully will enable us to judge if the outcomes (including qualitative factors) are also improving. Over time inflation will tend to create a problem as it increases the costs of providing a service. In order, therefore, to make costs (and income) truly comparable, the effects of inflation will need to be considered and removed from the calculation such that the 'real' picture may be understood. This is done by using price index data which are specific to the cost element, such as pay awards for salaries and wages and the utility cost index for such services as gas and electricity.

Third, unit costs can be used to set unit cost standards against which actual performance can be monitored. They thus allow managers to develop an understanding of cost behaviour and facilitate cost control.

Unit cost measures need to be used with considerable care. Some of their limitations are outlined below:

- Rather than outcomes, they emphasise throughputs.
- The quality of performance maybe be ignored in a simplistic analysis.
- They may not recognise case mix differences (e.g. open plan offices as opposed to traditional offices would distort any analysis).
- Comparisons need to be made against best practice if efficiency gains are to be maximised.
- Overheads may be charged in different ways between comparators, thus distorting any comparisons.
- Alternative depreciation techniques may affect costs and thus comparisons.

There is a danger that throughputs can be taken as a proxy for outcomes. This assumes (dangerously) that there is a linear and direct relationship between throughputs and outcomes. It also implies the assumption that all outcomes can be proxied by the throughput indicator (e.g. the number of meals in Table 2.1), but this is simplistic and significant extra information is therefore required to inform management decisions.

Throughput provides no indicator concerning the quality of performance; as indicated above, the meals may be provided to different standards of quality in each of the four kitchens, and this may explain all or part of the variations in, say, food costs. If differences in standard are laid down by the school meals service, then such differences may be acceptable. If they are not, and differences in meal standards are observed, then action needs to be taken.

This could be related to the problem of case mix. If we now turn to another example, the cleaning of offices, one cannot usefully compare the costs of three offices where one is a modern office block but not open plan (A), one is modern and open plan (B) and the third is old-fashioned and cramped (C). No information is available on best practice, so even if one office achieves greater efficiencies and cost reductions it may still be operating suboptimally. Office C will require more time to clean and possibly a higher cleaning staff ratio than either A or B. What the cost statement and attendant commentary should do for managers is to reinforce the need to recognise qualitative factors in any cost analysis.

While overheads are discussed in a subsequent chapter, in the school meals example the cost of the supervisor is an overhead and his/her costs have been allocated equally to the kitchens. This distorts the cost of each kitchen as the allocation could have been done on a variety of other bases, for example, the number of staff supervised, the number of meals provided by each kitchen, or even floor area. While these bases for allocation have varying technical merits, the total cost of the supervisor has to be borne by the business and it is only the subjective allocation of cost between the kitchens in this case that could change since the total cost of the supervisor is fixed at £20,000. Similarly, if cooks, assistant cooks or kitchen maids were reallocated between the three kitchens there would be a transfer of costs (including staff-related overheads) between kitchens. No savings would be incurred unless some staff were made redundant and this could incur a one-off redundancy payment in the year of the redundancy. This could cause the budget to overspend in that year but in the longer term should lead to savings.

Capital costs in Table 2.1 represent depreciation (the wearing out of an asset) and interest on the assets employed in the service. This concept of effectively an 'asset rent' was recently introduced in the public sector. Here, to simplify, many government assets had been acquired through paying cash and as such no cost appeared other than in the year of account when the assets were acquired. In effect, they became regarded as 'free' goods by managers. In this context public sector assets were revalued and then depreciated (where appropriate). In addition an interest charge was added to reflect the cost of capital for assets employed in the public sector based on this current value. The combined depreciation and interest charge then forms the asset rent which managers are required to cover in, for example, their pricing policies (for a fuller explanation of asset rents see Coombs and Jenkins, 2002: 26–7). The interest charge of the asset rent effectively represents the opportunity cost of tying up money in the school meals service. Asset rents are fixed costs to managers. In this example of the school meals service the greater the number of meals served by each of the four kitchens the lower the unit fixed costs per meal. A similar logic applies to the supervisor, who also is assumed to be a fixed cost.

For a fuller explanation of unit costing in the public sector, see Coombs and Jenkins (2002).

Service Costing

As mentioned in the introduction to this chapter, the UK economy has seen a growth in the service sector. In this 'industry' there is the same need to cost and price activities as in the manufacturing sector. The service sector can include elements of the public sector and services provided within organisations to other parts of the same organisation at an internal price, as with service level agreements (see the discussion of Coombs and Evans in the recommended further reading section at the end of this chapter, and Chapter 3). The latter might include the provision of IT services within a supermarket, or financial advice from the finance department of a government body. The provision of advice raises special characteristics in that each piece of advice is unique unlike, for example, a manufactured product which tends to be uniform. Advice may need to be provided instantly and once given is intangible as it cannot be undone. Advice may expire virtually instantly or have a very limited 'shelf' life, unlike a product which may have a long production cycle – although with technological advancement and consumer changes in taste, product life cycles tend to be shorter today.

In the case of a service industry, such as accounting or the provision of financial services such as investment advice, it is not realistic to attempt to cost every job or individual piece of advice. In such cases it is normal to use a cost unit based on time – cost per client hour. In this case, the more complex the case, the more time is likely to be spent with the client. In the public sector costs may be attributed to a number of different categories of work. In the NHS the cost per in-patient day may be calculated, while additional information will be provided on the cost of different surgical procedures. These costs are often related to quality measures such as patient waiting time for a specific operation such as a hip replacement. In a university the cost per student will be available and information will also be provided on the cost per subject studied. Quality data, for example, on retention rates or examination success will also be available. Inevitably, in both of these cases there may be an element of overlap between the cost data being provided, but the financial information is being provided for different purposes and decisions.

Conclusions

This chapter has:

- considered the issue of profit and problems of its definition;
- developed an understanding of cost definitions and cost behaviour and shown that it is essential that managers understand these concepts when making decisions;
- shown that costs behave differently at various levels of activity, depending on whether they are fixed or variable;
- stated that all costs in the long run are variable;
- demonstrated that cost allocation can be subjective and therefore there is no such thing as a 'true' cost;
- indicated that all costs are controllable at a certain level within an organisation, but managers should only be allocated costs over which they have specific control under responsibility accounting;
- shown that cost data say little about performance or the non-quantitative factors that are increasingly vital in decision making.

Summary

This chapter has set out the important definitions of cost and demonstrated how costs behave in different circumstances. It has also stressed that an understanding of cost and cost behaviour is essential for managers if they are to make the right decisions. Important in this is that management accounting information is presented in a format that is understandable to the manager, relevant to the decision being taken, as accurate as is relevant to the decision and timely with respect to the decision horizon.

Cost classification was shown as a fundamental requirement of this process, with costs identified with a cost objective. The cost objective is a separate measure for which the measurement of costs is desirable. Classification into period and product costs was outlined for stock valuation purposes. Costs for decision making were classified into various cost behaviour patterns and also whether they were regarded as sunk, marginal, incremental, opportunity or irrelevant costs. Finally, for cost control purposes costs were identified as controllable or not controllable and fixed or variable.

It has been stressed that cost alone tells the decision-maker little about the quality of the product or service. With unit costs it was shown that the provision of unit cost data can be seen merely as a measure of the resources devoted to an activity but gives no information on the quality of such output, and is therefore in itself a measure solely concerned with throughput.

<table>
<tr><td>

**EXHIBIT
2.1**

</td><td>

Cost Classification

</td></tr>
</table>

David Green is the newly appointed management accountant for a small manufacturing company which until now has not been particularly efficient at cost control or classifying its costs. The business is under severe financial pressure and as part of an efficiency drive is beginning the process of improving cost classification as an initial stage of improving its financial systems.

As part of his initial review of the business, David has identified the following costs:

- lubricant for machines;
- holiday pay of machine operatives;
- carriage on purchase of raw materials;
- raw materials;
- factory security guards;
- wages of store keeper in raw materials store;
- audit fees;
- salaries of administrative staff;
- rent of finished goods warehouse;
- salaries of sales staff;
- factory floor supervisors' wages;
- sales commissions;
- licenses with performing rights society for music played in factory;
- road fund licenses on delivery vehicles;
- wages of forklift truck drivers in materials store;
- fees to advertising agency;
- direct marketing campaigns;
- insurance of company's premises;
- protective clothing for machine operatives;
- depreciation of factory plant and equipment;
- interest on bank overdraft;
- royalties payable on units of production;
- trade discounts given to customers;
- production operatives' wages.

Table 2.3   Illustration of cost classification

Direct labour	Production operative
Direct materials	Raw materials Carriage on purchase of raw materials
Direct expenses	Lubricant for machines Protective clothing Depreciation of factory plant and equipment Royalties on units produced
Indirect production overheads	Wages of storekeeper Performing rights licences Holiday pay of machine operatives Forklift drivers' wages Factory insurance Security guards Supervisors' wages Rent of finished goods warehouse
Selling and distribution costs	Advertising fees Trade discounts Direct marketing campaigns Road fund licences Salesperson salaries Salesperson commissions
Admin. costs	Audit fees Admin. staff salaries
Finance costs	Interest on bank overdraft

Table 2.3 shows the subsequent classification for the costs identified. It should be remembered that this is based on David's definitions. As such it is subjective, and there may be other definitions that are equally sound. Whatever categorization is used, it should be technically sound and produce information relevant to the decision-making needs of the company.

EXHIBIT
2.2

Fixed and Variable Costs

Compass Limited is a small building company that tenders for work on a regular basis. One element contained within its tenders is for the provision of transport to carry building materials and labour to construction sites. Compass owns one lorry and bases this cost in its tenders on the estimated cost per mile of operating the lorry before adding in the cost of the driver. These calculations are done prior to the start of Compass's financial year. This coincides with the calendar year.

It is now December, and Compass wishes to calculate the estimated cost of operating its lorry fleet for the next year. Base data for the purposes of this calculation for the vehicle are as follows:

F-C ~ Cost of purchasing vehicle £20,000
Life of vehicle 4 years
Residual value £5,000
F-C ~ Insurance cost £500
F-C ~ Road fund licence £400
Annual estimated mileage 25,000
Set of tyres – replacement after 12,500 miles £600
Fuel per 5 litres £3.50
Average mileage for 5 litres 20
Estimated vehicle inflation over life 5%
F-C ~ Maintenance (5 times per year) £350

For the purpose of this exhibit we are required to calculate the cost per vehicle mile for the following year.

The *fixed costs* include the purchase price, insurance costs, road fund licence and regular maintenance. The cost of the vehicle was £20,000, and Compass assumes that vehicle inflation will be 5%, giving a replacement cost of £21,000. With a predicted resale value of £5,000, this results in an annual charge for capital consumption of £4,000 (£16,000/4). Compass could wish to recover the anticipated cost of a new vehicle rather than the historic cost as a means of attempting to ensure that it has sufficient funds to replace the vehicle at the end of its useful life. Some organisations might also build in a charge for interest based on the capital value of the asset. This is to ensure that the asset gives a return that is at least equal to that which could be earned by investing funds elsewhere. This is particularly relevant in the public sector where recent changes in central government accounting have extended this concept from the NHS and local government (H.M. Government, 1994).

	£
Cost of capital consumption	4,000
Vehicle licence	400
Insurance	500
Maintenance	1,750
Annual fixed cost	6,650
Unit fixed cost per mile (£6,650/25,000 miles)	£0.266

The variable costs are as follows:

	£
Tyres replaced after 12,500 miles (2 × 600)	1,200
Fuel (25,000/20 × £3.50)	4,375
	5,575
Variable cost per mile (£5575/25,000)	£0.223
Cost per mile	£0.489

Compass Ltd has data through this exercise that enable it to monitor and control the cost of transport. The fixed costs will not change as the vehicle undertakes more miles, but the costs incurred will be spread over more miles thus reducing the unit cost per mile. Variable costs, on the other hand, will change in direct proportion to the changed activity level.

This information is useful to Compass in that when tendering for work if the company has used the vehicle up to the budgeted figure of 25,000 miles it will have covered the fixed costs of operating the vehicle. In any future tenders, therefore, it need only build in the variable costs of operating the vehicle. Obviously Compass would be well advised to monitor costs and usage of the vehicle in order to maintain up-to-date financial information so that it can take corrective action should its financial projections prove to be inaccurate. It should also be remembered that there are other ways of calculating the costs of vehicle use. As an alternative to cost per mile, Compass might choose to use an hourly charge-out rate.

EXHIBIT 2.3

Incremental Costs and Revenue

Coral Limited is a medium-sized company based in South Wales. It has had a number of years of relative success but, being conservative by nature, it has tended to serve the local market only. This market has shown signs of a decline and the directors are now considering whether to expand the operation from its South Wales base into the West of England. They are attempting to judge how successful this strategy will be over the next six months.

The following figures are an extract from the company's existing budgeted profit and loss account for the next six months.

	£
Sales (20,000 units at £20 per unit)	400,000
Selling costs:	
Marketing	60,000
Salaries of sales personnel	20,000

Commission costs (1% of sales)	4,000
Travelling expenses of sales personnel	1,000
Sales office costs	10,000
Telephones	9,000
Stationery	5,000

The company accountant has calculated that marketing expenditure will need to double in order to achieve penetration of what has historically been a difficult area for the company to achieve even modest sales. Two new sales staff will be employed at a cost of £20,000 on six-month contracts, plus there will be the need to train them at a cost of £2,000. If the operation is judged a success the salespersons' contracts will be extended. A new office will be opened up at a rental cost of £5,000 for six months. Additional telephone equipment will cost £1,000 and existing telephone costs are projected to rise by 50%. Stationery costs will increase by £2,000. Travelling costs will rise by £1,500. An additional office assistant will be required in the finance department to process orders and monitor commissions at a salary of £8,000 for six months. Estimated sales will rise by 1000 units per month for the first two months and revenue per unit will fall to £18 per unit in order to achieve initial market penetration. It is anticipated that this discount will only be necessary for two months and that sales from month 3 will rise to 2000 units per month. The variable cost of producing each extra unit is projected to remain at the current cost of £6.

Table 2.4   Incremental analysis of proposed expansion

	Existing budget for next six months		Projected budget for next six months		Incremental costs and revenues	
	£	£	£	£	£	£
Sales		400,000		596,000		196,000
Marketing	60,000		120,000		60,000	
Sales salaries	20,000		60,000		40,000	
Commission	4,000		5,960		1,960	
Travelling	1,000		2,500		1,500	
Sales office	10,000		15,000		5,000	
Telephones	9,000		14,500		5,500	
Stationery	5,000		7,000		2,000	
Admin. asst.	0		8,000		8,000	
Training	0		2,000		2,000	
Variable production costs	120,000	229,000	180,000	414,960	60,000	185,960

The decision requires an incremental analysis of the impact on Coral to give the estimated financial position first. It should always be remembered that these are financial projections only and other issues will be relevant to any proposed new strategy. These issues are touched upon after the calculations have been demonstrated.

It will be seen from Table 2.4 that the effect of the expansion is to increase incremental revenue by £185,960 and, as such, on a financial basis the expansion is justified.

It should be remembered that the projections are simply estimates and may prove incorrect. Coral would have to consider the impact of reducing the selling price of its product on existing markets and indeed whether in its new market it will be able to raise prices as easily as is suggested. We already know from the above that Coral has struggled in this new market before and as such there is a doubt over the potential market. We are also aware that there has been a slowdown in the 'home' market that may indicate that there is a more fundamental problem with the product. There is, however, a large margin for error within the results obtained. It can also be seen in this exhibit that both fixed costs and variable costs have been subject to incremental changes.

Recommended Further Reading

Coombs, H.M. and Evans, A. (2001) 'Managing central support costs in local authorities', *Journal of Finance and Management in Public Services*, **2(1): 9–20.**
How to treat central overheads in local government is not a new issue. Since 1979, with the greater competitive pressure local authority services have been under, it has become vital that overheads be allocated on a basis which is transparent, flexible and real. Coombs and Evans first look at the definitions of central overheads in local government, dividing them into corporate costs such as council meetings which are regarded as the cost of democracy and not allocated, specialist costs such as back funding pensions which are again not allocated, and the essential central support functions essential to run the 'business' which are fully allocated to services. Under a traditional approach these costs would have broadly been allocated to services primarily on a timesheet basis. Administrative building costs would be allocated on a floor area basis.

As an alternative to these arrangements the paper looks at service level agreements (SLAs) which are seen as written internal 'informal contracts' specifying the responsibilities of and the relationships between a client or service department and the support service provider. The written agreement:

- identified the providers and users of the service;
- clarified the responsibilities between both parties over quality and costs of services delivered;
- enabled users and providers to monitor what was happening;
- clearly identified the costs and charging mechanisms.

In terms of the practice of SLAs the research discovered that typical charging mechanisms included:

- payroll/salary systems – per employee, per transaction, cost per payslip processed;
- internal audit – rate per hour, rate per person day, fixed charge plus time element;
- revenue accounting – rate per hour, charge per person day;
- cash management – per transaction, per posting;

- creditor payments – per payment, per invoice raised;
- insurance – on-cost to premiums, rate per hour.

Drawbacks of SLAs were seen as the bureaucracy associated with the agreements and procrastination by the overhead service providers. This was seen as a deliberate attempt by the providers to sabotage the initiative as it was not in their interests to pursue this policy. Other issues related to the question of under- and over-recovery of the costs of providing the central support. In addition, many managers in service departments felt they did not have the experience to negotiate with, for example, the finance department which to them held all the 'aces' in any negotiation.

In the conclusions the traditional system of apportionment of overheads to service departments without attention to the costs and quality of those services given by central support departments was seen as increasingly at odds with the pressure on resources faced by local government (and, indeed, all public sector services). There was also a discovery of variations in the type of overhead apportionment systems used in the survey, although the basic system was staff time based. Resources realised by the proper management of central services overhead costs can potentially result in these resources being redirected into frontline service delivery. Service level agreements were seen as having the potential to improve service delivery by support departments to service departments and improve the quality of delivery of overhead services. They lead to emphasis on the customer given the central component of quality at a cost the service department is willing to pay. The survey used revealed that of the 31 authorities who responded 29 had either introduced, were developing or considering introducing SLAs. While two authorities had rejected the principle of SLAs on the basis of the potential additional bureaucratic burden, they had recognised that their current systems of charging for central support services were in need of review. Discussions with employees of the local authorities showed that on balance there was support for the idea of SLAs and that in some cases poor-quality service and price had meant that potential clients to the local authority had been lost in the area of education. It was pointed out, however, that the stimulus for these developments was statutory regulation and not the result of internal pressures. Interviewees felt that in some cases the delay in introducing SLAs was the result of central departments procrastinating.

The paper also pointed out that as well as the existence of actual SLAs it is the spirit in which those agreements are operated that is equally important if any such system is to operate effectively. Thus whether SLAs are a solution to a problem, a bureaucratic nightmare or fall somewhere in between in terms of their ability to meet the needs of local government service managers, only time will tell. They are clearly not suited for many small support services as the costs of setting up and maintaining such agreements would outweigh any benefits, although there may be benefits in establishing a small-scale memorandum of understanding between providers and users setting out quality standards for service delivery. However, if implemented and managed correctly, they do appear to have considerable potential to improve the quality of services delivered by larger-scale central support departments at a price and quality that service managers are prepared to pay. This can only benefit the community the local authority is supposed to serve as extra resources are released, or protected, for frontline service delivery.

Ezzamel M., Morris J., and Smith J.A. (2004) Accounting for New Organisational Forms. Research Update, 8–9 September, CIMA.
At the time of writing this is an ongoing project which aims to identify the ways in which management accounting is informed by developments of new organisational forms which are emerging because of increased business competition and developments in IT. The project methodology was to use face-to-face interviews to build a limited number of case studies across a range of organisations and postal questionnaires to widen the sample base. Provisional results (pending publication of the final research study) indicate that change was evolutionary and incremental rather than revolutionary or transformational. Important factors as change agents were new management teams and general market conditions. There was also a desire to reduce the staff base and fixed costs. In the public sector new cost centres were found to have been created and there had been the development of non-financial measures. An increase in outsourcing was also noted. In terms of the supply chain this had evidenced itself by contracting out non-core services such as cleaning, IT and recruitment and training. Overhead costs were thus reduced as opposed to the creation of service level agreements. The role of management accounting was discovered to have changed from broadly recording to one of financial analysis and the provision of advice.

Case Study: SHB

SHB is a retailing company which has numerous retail outlets distributed throughout the United Kingdom selling a wide range of goods to the public. These goods include furniture and food, although primarily it sells clothes. It has also diversified its functions to include financial services such as credit cards and loans and insurance. Stores vary in size, with a number of medium-sized central town developments and 20 superstores nationwide. It has also, as part of its expansion programme, opened a number of new outlets in Europe. In the UK it has recently begun to develop smaller stores on out-of-town 'discount' shopping parks which it uses to sell last season's fashions and designs at reduced prices. This strategy has so far proved very successful as demand for product is high, rents relatively cheap in comparison with many of its traditional stores located in town centres and staffing costs low. It is also currently looking at establishing more of these outlets but selling food.

The stores operate with a managerial framework which gives considerable local autonomy to managers, allowing them to make local decisions appropriate to local needs. It retains a number of head office functions for such activities as purchasing, accountancy and audit, legal services and human resources management. Store managers deal with the recruitment and dismissal of store staff but consult with central head office on corporate human resource policies and complex issues such as trade union matters. The head office is responsible for corporate decision making. Store managers are expected to have worked in head office and at store level before they can manage a superstore.

The corporate head office is sited in Birmingham as it represents the best location given the distribution of the company's stores. There are, in additon, a number of satellite offices which provide local contacts with the stores on a number of central support issues, but excluding corporate strategy, IT and legal advice. The continental operation is managed directly from Birmingham in terms of central office functions although store managers on the Continent have the same roles and responsibilities as those in the United Kingdom. The head office deals with all financial services and related products.

The cost of the head office and regional support offices in the last year (2004) was as follows:

Category of cost	Budget for year £	Revised budget June 2004 £	Actual expense for year £
Accountancy and audit	2,850,000	2,555,000	2,750,000
IT	5,575,000	5,850,000	5,650,000
Legal	4,500,000	5,750,000	6,950,000
Human resources	1,850,000	1,950,000	1,975,000
Corporate strategy	1,110,000	1,111,000	1,116,000
Corporate governance	9,255,000	8,260,000	8,760,000

Head office expenditure in the previous two financial years was £23,400,000 and £22,000,000, respectively. The major overspend on the legal budget in 2004 is concerned with a legal case against the Inland Revenue over the interpretation of tax legislation under European Union law.

The staffing compliment for each section was last formally agreed in January 2002. These numbers are as follows:

	Agreed establishment (January 2002)	Actual numbers in post (December 2004)
Accountancy and audit	45	48
IT	120	118
Legal	25	31
Human Resources	47	55
Corporate Strategy	198	200
Corporate governance	60	80

The majority of the staff over the agreed establishment are on fixed term contracts expiring in September 2005. Head office management staff at team level can employ these staff without formally increasing the establishment and with limited need for higher authorisation.

The central office is supposed to be driven by the needs of the stores, but costs have to be recharged. At the moment these are done simply on a staff time analysis based on 'actual' time spent on each location by each function when the accounts are being closed in readiness for publication. 'Actual' time is recalculated every three years when a staff timesheet for a section is completed by the manager of a section. These section returns are ultimately aggregated by function (e.g. Human Resources). This detailed information is not disclosed to the shareholders but is used by managers after the year end to monitor store performance. No information is provided during the course of the year, although head office costs are supposed to be controlled within the annual budget. Some stores have started to employ their own specialists such as in accountancy and audit under their discretionary budget powers. Store managers have also expressed some concern over the company's central buying policy as the quality of clothing has deteriorated and styles are seen as old-fashioned. Store managers are held responsible for any unsold stock and not central buying. Central buying is done by the Corporate Strategy division at head office. Finally, the costs of financial services and related operations are separately identified together with the income on those products and allocated to the regional superstore nearest to the client's home address to give a geographical picture of where business is generated. Marketing campaigns, for example, are then directed based on such information.

1. Critically assess the above system of allocating head office costs to stores from both a head office and store manager's point of view. Discuss the advantages and disadvantages of the system from both points of view.
2. Discuss any possible alternatives available, including their advantages and disadvantages, from both the head office and store manager's perspective.
3. What are the main features of any alternatives and how would you go about implementing them? Cover both qualitative and quantitative issues.
4. Prepare a report for management incorporating your critical analysis with recommendations on a way forward.

Questions

1. The Tuba Company commenced business on 1 April 2004 and during its first production period produced 200,000 identical units of a product termed 'the valve'. The company sold 175,000 units of 'the valve' during this period. As this was the company's first period of operation there was no opening stock at the start. The 25,000 units unsold are closing stock.

The costs for this period were as follows:

Manufacturing costs	£
Direct labour	800,000
Direct materials	400,000
Manufacturing overheads	150,000

Non-manufacturing costs amounted to £175,000.

(i) Prepare the profit and loss account for the period.

(ii) Explain what you understand by 'period costs' and discuss your treatment of them in the calculations you have carried out. Explain fully why you have treated them as you have.

(iii) The company believes that in period 2 it will only sell 50 per cent of the items left in stock at the end of period 1. What implications do you think this has for the Tuba Company.

2. Euphonium Ltd. has an opportunity to obtain a new contract for the production of a new valve. The valve requires 200 hours of processing on machine A, which is already working at full capacity on the production of another product. There is thus no way in which production of the valve can be accommodated unless production of the other product is reduced. The lost contribution from the displaced product amounts to £500. In addition, the variable costs of the new valve amount to £1500.

(i) What price is the minimum that should be accepted?

(ii) What implications are there for the company, in both the short term and the long term, of accepting this special order?

3. Where would you allocate the following costs (e.g. selling and distribution, production, etc.) and who would you hold responsible for incurring these costs for control purposes? Would you regard them as fixed, variable, semi-variable or stepped fixed costs? Are they direct or indirect costs?

Raw materials used in the manufacture of a company's main product
Security services for the warehouse
Performing rights payments for music piped to the factory floor
Direct labour payments
Oil used to lubricate productive machinery
Costs of a sales promotion campaign
Depreciation of factory machinery
Contract price for raw materials
Overtime payments on the factory floor
Supervision costs on the factory floor
Forklift truck driver

Rent where at production above 5000 units additional workspace is required to be contracted

Audit fee

Food costs in the works canteen

Photocopy rental in sales office with additional costs incurred by use

Fire insurance costs for factory

Power used in the factory

Supervision of production operatives

Royalty payments

Factory rental

Indirect materials

Quality audit engineer

Accountancy office staff

Research and development

Membership fee to the CBI

Company's pension contributions for factory workers

Company's pension contributions for office staff

Delivery vehicle expenses

Wages to factory temporary production operatives

Television marketing campaign

Maintenance mechanic's wages

Foreman wages

Office stationery

Managing director's salary

Cost of board meetings, including non-executive salaries

Payments to focus groups for comments on new products

Payments for trade magazines

Annual awards dinner for factory employees

Head of marketing's salary

Storeman's wages

Petrol costs for salesmen

4. David is thinking of setting up a new van hire business. He has no experience of this business and is not financially qualified, but has had a go at estimating the costs he will incur. Initially he will start with one van and has come to you for financial and business advice as his financial adviser with the figures he has managed to obtain.

David's figures are set out below:

	£
Purchase cost of van	15,000
Service maintenance cost (twice per year)	500 per service

Spares/replacement parts per 2000 miles	100
Insurance per year	1,500
Vehicle licence	250
Tyres (after 30,000 miles), four at £75 each	300
Trade in value (after 3 years or 120,000 miles)	1,000
Diesel per gallon	2.80
Average mileage per gallon of diesel is 25 miles	
Estimated annual mileage 40,000	
MOT cost after 3 years	30
Maintenance and service costs after 3 years	4,500 per annum

The average mileage per gallon of diesel is 25 miles and the estimated annual mileage is 40,000.

(i) Prepare a schedule for David of the costs of operating the van over annual mileages of 20,000, 30,000, 40,000 and 50,000 miles. This schedule should clearly identify: total fixed costs; total variable costs; total costs; fixed costs per mile; variable costs per mile; total costs per mile. Critically assess your results and prepare a report for David in which you clearly explain what you have done and any assumptions you have made in your calculations. Your report should clearly advise David an the factors he should consider in his decision as to whether or not to set up this business.

(ii) You have completed task (i). David has just rushed in to your office to advise you he has discovered he can lease the van over the three years at a cost of £150 per week. This cost covers all service and maintenance charges and includes tyres. David would, however, be responsible for any damage caused by neglect of the vehicle. As a safety measure he thinks he should set aside £500 per year for this factor. What are the implications of this alternative for David and his business idea?

(iii) 'The unit costs of operating a business fall as output increases'. Assess this statement critically.

5. There are numerous classifications of cost available. These might include, for example, classification by type, by decision relevance, and by controllability. The objective of management accounting is to assist managers and decision makers in an organisation. Discuss the relationship between cost classification and the needs of managers and decision makers in a critical context.

6. You are working for an NHS Trust. The Trust manages three hospitals. Two of these, Triumph and BSA, are district general hospitals, while the third, Norton, is a small cottage-style hospital. The cleaning service contract for these hospitals is managed in-house by the Trust's own cleaning services. The target for the cleaning contract is the breakeven of revenue and expenditure. The contract was let two years ago and is due for renewal on 1 April 2005 so has one year to run.

At the request of your section head you are monitoring the performance of the contract for the financial year ending the 31 March 2004 and have obtained the following information.

(1) Financial data: payments 2003/04

	Triumph £	BSA £	Norton £
Cleaning staff – pay	66,320	79,500	39,000
Employment taxes	2,750	3,650	1,600
Pension costs	3,750	7,240	1,250
Travelling expenses	880	720	180
Cleaning materials	42,250	56,530	36,390
Window cleaning contract (external)	6,160	5,680	9,000
Other contract services	800	1,210	1,980
Miscellaneous	1,350	850	1,680
Equipment purchased (revenue)	760	820	930

(2) Statistical data

Floor area (square metres)	110,000	125,000	27,250
Average number of available staffed beds	590	720	130

(3) Additional Information

(a) Sundry creditors were:

	31 March 2003 £	31 March 2004 £
Triumph		
Equipment	180	120
Cleaning materials	1,230	1,960
BSA		
Window cleaning	2,520	1,100
Norton		
Cleaning materials	2,440	3,690

(b) Cleaning materials issued from the central stores have not been included in part (1) payments as they were issued in the last week of March 2004 and the Finance Department has only just been informed. These stock issues were: Triumph, £1,260; BSA, £1,140; Norton, £2,460.

(c) Stocks of cleaning materials in hand at each hospital at the year end were:

	31 March 2003 £	31 March 2004 £
Triumph	3,150	4,550
BSA	2,540	1,980
Norton	1,000	1,110

(d) The central stores cost for managing cleaning materials is to be apportioned to the three hospitals and has been calculated for 2003/04 at £66,000. There is no agreed basis of allocation of this cost to the three hospitals.

(e) During 2003/2004 BSA hospital required that a cleaning equipment maintenance contract be negotiated for £600 per annum payable annually in advance on 1 February in each year. This payment is included in (1) under other contract services. The contract is renewable annually now it has been signed.

(f) Outstanding bonuses in respect of BSA and Norton at the 31 March 2004 are 1.5% of wages paid in the year. This has no effect on other wage related costs.

(g) The cost of management supervision by the cleaning supervisor is £18,000 including overheads.

(h) Staff time for finance services provided by the Finance Department has yet to be charged to the cleaning contract and is to be allocated to each hospital on the basis of floor area. The costs calculated by the finance department are £20,000 for these services. This is in part based on the work that this year went into preparing a bid for the renewal (£10,000) of the contract on 1 April 2005. There will be significantly more work in the next financial year to prepare for the retendering exercise.

(i) Cleaning the hospitals requires no capital equipment.

(j) The value of the cleaning contract is £530,000. It is not broken down by individual hospital.

As a management accountant working for the Trust you have been requested to prepare a report on the cleaning service.

(i) Include a statement showing the cleaning costs for each hospital in comparison with the tendered price.

(ii) Discuss the relative cleaning costs for each hospital and outline the possible reasons for variations between them.

(iii) Comment on any qualitative factors you believe are relevant.

(iv) Make appropriate recommendations based on your analysis in the context of 2003/04 and the retendering exercise due in 2005/06.

Chapter 3
COSTING PRODUCTS
AND SERVICES

Key Learning Objectives

By the time you have finished studying this chapter, you should be able to:

- implement the allocation and apportionment of overhead costs by traditional means;
- determine overhead absorption rates;
- make use of such rates in determining the costs of products and services and the value of closing inventory;
- critically evaluate such costs;
- evaluate the contribution of activity-based costing to the costing of products and services;
- utilise the marginal cost approach to the costing of products, services and inventory.

Introduction

Initially in this chapter we will concern ourselves with total absorption costing (TAC). This is a system for determining the full cost of products and services. The full cost of a product is made up of direct costs and a share of indirect costs (or overheads). In order to achieve full cost, a number of stages have to be undertaken, as follows:

1. All costs are subdivided into direct costs and indirect costs. Direct costs (primarily direct materials and direct labour) are traced directly to individual products.
2. Factory indirect costs are apportioned to cost centres.
3. The totals of the costs of service department cost centres are reapportioned to productive cost centres.
4. Budgeted overhead absorption rates are calculated for each of the production cost centres.
5. The budgeted absorption rates are applied to products and services in order to assist in calculating the full cost of the products or services.

Table 3.1   Examples of production and other overheads

Production overheads	Other overheads
Foremen's salaries	Marketing costs
Factory manager's salary	Head office salaries
Depreciation of factory equipment	Bad debts
Cost of heating for factory	Finance costs
Factory rent	Head office rent

Allocation and Apportionment of Overheads to Cost Centres

All costs can be subdivided into direct and indirect costs. Direct costs can be traced to each unit of output, and include items such as direct materials, direct labour and direct expenses. Indirect costs represent all other costs. They are also known as overhead costs. They may relate to production or they may be of a more general nature. Examples are shown in Table 3.1.

We will be concerned only with direct costs and production overheads in calculating the full cost of products and services as these costs specifically relate to production. The other overheads are not charged to each product but are, instead, charged to the profit and loss account for the year.

Production costs are allocated and apportioned to production cost centres. Examples of production cost centres are the machining department, assembly department, finishing department, production administration, and maintenance. Allocation of costs occurs when there is a clear link between a specific overhead and a specific department. Apportionment occurs when a clear link is absent and each department is charged with a fair share of overhead. For example, if the assembly department leases a specific machine, then the costs of the lease can be allocated directly to the assembly department. Contrast this with the costs of heating the factory; the costs of heating the assembly department cannot be separately identified. In this situation, the heating costs are apportioned to departments and the assembly department will be charged with a share of the total heating cost. Examples of apportionment bases are provided in Table 3.2.

We can now consider the application of such thinking to cost information. Table 3.3 gives information relating to a factory that manufactures desks. The factory contains four cost centres. The desks are physically worked upon in two of these cost centres, the assembly department and the finishing department. These are termed 'production cost centres'. The other two cost centres provide services for these two production cost centres. These are the maintenance department and the factory administration department. These are termed 'service cost centres'. As the service cost centres provide benefits to the

Table 3.2   Examples of overhead bases

Production overhead	Possible basis for apportionment
Foreman's pay	The number of employees in each cost centre, because the foreman's workload is likely to be influenced by the number of employees in each cost centre. Alternatively, a foreman may be required to make an estimate of the amount of time taken up by each of the cost centres.
Depreciation of equipment	This could be based upon the cost, or written-down value, of each item of equipment in the different cost centres. The reason for doing this is that depreciation is generally related to the cost of assets. Other things being equal, the more costly the asset, the greater the depreciation charge.
Factory heating	This apportionment may be based upon the floor area or volume of each cost centre as these factors are likely to determine the amount of heating required by each cost centre.
Factory rent	This is usually apportioned on the basis of the floor area of each cost centre.
Factory power	This could be apportioned on the basis of the number of machines in each cost centre, but a more sophisticated approach would be to take account of the power requirements of each machine and allow for this in apportionment.
Indirect wages	The apportionment could be related to the number of direct labour hours in each cost centre, or the number of indirect employees in each cost centre. If there are any part-time indirect employees, it will be necessary to take account of full-time equivalent employees.

production cost centres, the latter will in turn be required to bear the costs of the service cost centres.

The table shows the costs incurred by the factory and provides financial and statistical information relating to the cost centres that will allow us to allocate and apportion the production overheads to the four cost centres. As may be seen in Table 3.3, the total costs of the service cost centres are to be reapportioned equally to each of the two production departments.

We have now established the indirect costs and also the bases that should be used to allocate and apportion them to the four cost centres. This is carried out by means of an overhead analysis sheet. A completed overhead analysis sheet for 2005 is shown in

Table 3.3   Apportionment data

Indirect costs	Costs £	Apportionment basis	Production departments		Service departments		Totals
			Assembly	Finishing	Maintce.	Admin.	
Factory manager	35,000	No. of employees	15	10	5	5	35
Foremen	70,000	No. of employees	15	10	5	5	35
Indirect wages	56,000	Allocation	£37,500	£16,250	£8,000	£8,000	£56,000
Depreciation	25,000	Book values of plant and machinery	£200,000	£30,000	£20,000		£250,000
Heating	15,000	Floor area (sq. metres)	50	50	20	30	150
Power	8,000	Number of machines	6	1	1		8
Factory rent	7,500	Floor area (sq. metres)	50	50	20	30	150
Service departments		Equally to each production dept.					
Total	216,500						

Table 3.4. It may be seen that the indirect costs of £216,500 have been apportioned to the four cost centres, with the total of each cost centre's overheads shown at the foot of each column. At this stage one should check that the totals add up to the total of costs in the second column. A secondary apportionment is then carried out with the costs of the two service cost centres reapportioned to the production cost centres.

We have now completed stage 3 and apportioned the budgeted factory overheads to the two production cost centres, assembly and finishing. In this case, the service departments carry out work solely for the production departments, assembly and finishing, so the costs of the service departments are reapportioned directly. There will be cases when service departments carry out work for each other, and this increases the complexity of analysis.

At the next stage, stage 4, budgeted overhead absorption rates are calculated for each of the production cost centres. In this company, as Table 3.5 shows, the main factor of production in assembly is machinery, whilst the main factor in finishing is direct labour. Accordingly, machine hours will be used to absorb overheads in assembly and direct labour hours (DLH) in finishing. Each absorption basis is chosen because of the relative

Table 3.4   Budgeted overhead analysis for 2005

Cost	£	Apportionment bases	Production cost centres		Service cost centres	
			Assembly	Finishing	Maintenance	Admin.
Factory manager	35,000	Factory employees	15,000	10,000	5,000	5,000
Foremen	70,000	Factory employees	30,000	20,000	10,000	10,000
Indirect wages	56,000	Allocation	23,750	16,250	8,000	8,000
Depreciation	25,000	Book value	20,000	3,000	2,000	
Heat	15,000	Floor area	5,000	5,000	2,000	3,000
Power	8,000	Machines	6,000	1,000	1,000	
Rent	7,500	Floor area	2,500	2,500	1,000	1,500
Sub-totals	216,500		102,250	57,750	29,000	27,500
Reapportionment of maintenance		Equally	14,500	14,500	−29,000	
Reapportionment of admin.		Equally	13,750	13,750		−27,500
Totals	216,500		130,500	86,000		

Table 3.5   Budgeted annual activity

Assembly	Finishing
2,500 DLH	6,500 DLH
6,000 machine hours	200 machine hours

importance of machine hours or labour hours in each cost centre. The budgeted annual activities given in Table 3.5 will now form the basis of overhead absorption rates in each cost centre, as shown in Table 3.6.

At stage 5, the overhead costs of the departments will be incorporated into products using these budgeted absorption rates. As we saw at the start of this chapter, a product's costs are made up of direct costs and indirect costs. Information about two products is shown in Table 3.7. Using this information, we can calculate the full cost of each product by adding to the direct cost a share of factory overhead by utilising the budgeted absorption rates and the information regarding hours for each product. This is summarised in Table 3.8.

Table 3.6   Overhead absorption rates

	Machining	Assembly
Budgeted overheads £	130,500	86,000
Budgeted activity (hours)	6,000	6,500
Budgeted absorption rate	£130,500/6,000	£86,000/6,500
per hour	= £21.75 per machine hour	= £13.23 per DLH

Table 3.7   Direct costs and production times

	Product A	Product B
Direct costs	£23.50	£14.75
Machine hours (Machining)	4	4
DLH (Assembly)	6	3

Table 3.8   The full cost of products A and B

	Product A £	Product B £
Direct costs	23.50	14.75
Overheads		
Machining		
4 hours at £21.75 per hour	87.00	87.00
Assembly		
6 DLH at £13.23	79.38	
3 DLH at £13.23		39.69
Totals	£189.88	£141.44

The Over- and Under-Absorption of Overheads

We saw above that the calculation of budgeted overhead absorption rates for both the assembly and finishing departments was a key step in the calculation of 'full cost'. As we saw, this is calculated as:

$$\frac{\text{Budgeted overhead department costs}}{\text{Budgeted departmental activity (machine hours or DLH)}}$$

Absorption rates are normally calculated before the start of the accounting year. As you can see, this requires an estimate of costs and an estimate of activity and it aims to absorb all costs by applying the budgeted absorption rate to production during the year. However, this will only occur if actual figures are the same as budgeted figures. However, such equivalence between budget and actual is not guaranteed. It is more than likely that actual costs will differ from budgeted costs and/or actual activity will differ from budgeted activity. Using the machining department for illustration, the effect of differences between budget and actual is illustrated below.

As we have seen, the budgeted absorption rate in the machine department for 2005 is £21.75 per machine hour. During January 2005 for the machine department we have:

Actual machine hours: 480 hours
Actual overhead costs: £10,875

We can now consider the effect of this on the absorption of overheads in January (see Table 3.9).

Table 3.9   Overhead absorption in January

		£
Overhead absorbed into production	480 hours × £21.75 per hour	10,440
Actual overhead cost		10,875
Under-absorption of overhead		475

The under-absorption (also termed under-recovery) can either be carried forward to the next month, or written off to a monthly profit and loss account. During the year, some months will experience under-absorption and others over-absorption so that, hopefully, they will cancel out by the year end. If, at the end of the year, the cumulative figure is a under-absorption then this means that the company's profit will be reduced as these under-absorbed overheads that cannot be charged to products will be charged as an expense to the profit and loss account of the business. The opposite applies if there is an over-absorption, which will offset costs in the profit and loss account.

Reasons for the Apportionment and Absorption of Overheads

Stock Valuation

The TAC technique ensures that all production, including work in progress, incurs a share of production overhead. For work in progress, the amount of overhead will reflect the degree of completion of the products. Closing stock is valued at full cost, including direct costs and a share of production overhead. One consequence is that a share of the overhead costs of one accounting period is transferred via closing stock into the following accounting period. This technique is accepted by taxation authorities and is accepted in financial reporting as an acceptable methodology for the valuation of closing stock and work in progress.

Product Costing

The process identifies the full cost of a product and this itself permits the calculation of product profitability by comparing selling price with this full cost, ignoring the non-manufacturing costs of the company. The product cost can also act as a floor when setting the price of the product.

Cost Control

Cost apportionment and reapportionment are initially carried out at the budgeting stage. They thus make production and service cost centre managers aware of the budgeted costs at an early stage. Indeed, the process of budgeting overheads forces managers to review these costs before they are integrated into the budget for the company. Thus it should assist managers in controlling their own budgets.

Justification for Reimbursement of Costs

Some government grant-funded activities relate the ceiling of grant to the full cost of the activity being funded. The process for calculating the full cost needs to be verifiable and capable of exposure to audit inspection. To its credit, the apportionment/absorption system lays a clear audit trail from the collection of costs through to the absorption of costs into products. It is an accepted and well-understood process.

Production Overheads are Product-Related

It is argued that products cannot be manufactured unless overheads are incurred. Indeed, the underlying assumption is that production overheads are regarded as product costs just as direct costs are. Indeed, the only reason to incur overheads is in order to manufacture products that mat be sold and earn a profit.

Criticisms of Apportionment and Absorption

We identify the following four criticisms:

1. The accuracy of product costs calculated under absorption costing is highly suspect. This is a consequence of the rather arbitrary apportionment of costs to cost centres. Changing the apportionment basis of any one overhead cost would change

a department's total costs and, therefore, its budgeted absorption rate and, of course, the full cost of products. It follows that the practice of using the product cost as a basis for constructing a product price is flawed because the product cost itself results from a more or less arbitrary cost apportionment process.

2. In the illustration above, we have used different methods for absorbing overheads in assembly and manufacturing, respectively. This is more accurate than, say, using one overall rate; for example, apportioning total production overheads on the basis of direct labour hours so that:

$$\frac{\text{Overhead costs}}{\text{Direct labour hours}} = \frac{£216,500}{9,000} = £24.05 \text{ per DLH}$$

The revised rate per DLH of £24.05 represents a significant increase over the assembly department rate of £13.23 per DLH. A study by Drury and Tayles (2000) found that a very small percentage of firms in the UK used a single plant-wide rate for absorbing overheads.

3. The system uses broad averages to spread costs over products. The arbitrariness in the process can lead to product undercosting or product overcosting. In undercosting a product consumes a relatively high level of resources but is reported to have a relatively low total cost. Overcosting implies that a product's consumption of resources is far lower than its reported cost. Next in this chapter we discuss activity-based costing, which may offer a way of refining the costing system.

4. In the short run many of the factory overheads will be fixed, and marginal costing offers a way of dealing with short-run decisions involving costs; this is considered later in this chapter.

Activity-Based Costing

The system of absorption costing has evolved from the cost accounting thinking and systems that were established in Victorian times. The conceptual basis and the systems allied to this were established in an industrial environment in which the following features were endemic: direct labour costs and direct material costs were the dominant factory costs; overheads were relatively small; information processing costs were high; there was an absence of intense global competition; there were low levels of automation and a relatively limited product range. The cost accumulation system, which was developed in order to assemble product costs in the nineteenth-century environment, was total absorption costing. As we have seen, it attaches traceable direct costs (labour and materials) directly to products and then apportions factory overheads to products in a systematic but rather arbitrary fashion, with the proportion of overheads usually following the volume of direct labour activity in a product. The underlying philosophy is that products cannot be produced without incurring overheads so they must bear their share of overheads; most overheads are time-related (e.g. factory rent and foremen's salaries) so the apportionment is usually linked to the time taken by labour to produce output.

However, during the late twentieth century absorption costing was increasingly criticised by academics, for example Zimmerman (1979). During the last 20 years, the following criticisms have been made:

- There has been a systematic distortion of product costs caused by the perpetuation of convenient but inappropriate volume-based methods of production overhead apportionment.
- There has been a lack of visibility and transparency given to increasingly important areas of overhead consumption.
- Non-factory overheads have been neglected even though these compromise significant elements of overhead expense.
- Decision making requires variable cost information, which traditional cost systems have been unable to provide.

In 1987, Johnson and Kaplan published a seminal work, *Relevance Lost: The Rise and Fall of Management Accounting*. They indicate two major environmental changes which traditional management accounting thinking had failed to address. The first of these was the phenomenal growth in the value of production overheads caused by factors such as investment in automation and research and development. As the overheads had grown in significance, the direct labour costs had dwindled and were commonly only a small proportion of overhead costs. It was now more evident than ever that direct labour represented an inadequate basis for the apportionment of overheads. The second factor was the increasing competitiveness of the world economy. In order to compete effectively, firms often adopted practices with which traditional product costing was unable to work. For example, firms commonly met niche needs with short production runs and the same production line was commonly reconfigured for a different model. The traditional methodology was simply incapable of producing accurate and representative product costs in this environment. Yet the penalty for incorrectly costing and thereby incorrectly pricing products in this marketplace was very severe. Johnson and Kaplan (1987) proposed a different way of thinking about costs and advanced a methodology termed *activity-based costing* (ABC),which would address many of the weaknesses of the traditional system.

The work was extremely well received in academic circles. Additionally, the environmental changes in the world economy were such as to raise hopes that the practitioners responsible for developing and implementing systems in the corporate world would accept it. In the past academic criticism of industrial accounting practice has often been ignored because of the perceived irrelevance of academic research by practising accountants. However, in this case, the commercial connections of the academic home of Johnson and Kaplan (1987) were such as to place the proposals at the centre of corporate thinking. Both are based at Harvard Business School, which has been associated with strategic developments in some of the largest companies in the United States. Additionally, many of the ideas of ABC may be linked to the universally accepted strategies of corporate comparative advantage developed and articulated by Michael Porter (1985) at Harvard.

Absorption costing

Total overhead costs e.g.	Apportionments to factory departments	Departments	Absorption by DLH or machine hours	Product cost
Rent	→	Machining	Machine hours	→
Power etc.	→	Assembly	Labour hours	→

ABC

Total overhead costs e.g.	Collected according to activities	Activity cost pools e.g.	Cost driver rates e.g.	Product cost
Staff costs	→	Purchase of raw materials	Cost per purchase order	→
Equipment costs	→	Machine set-up	Cost per set-up	→
Power etc.	→	Machining products	Cost per machine hour	→

Figure 3.1   Absorption costing and ABC compared

Overview

Some of the key differences between traditional absorption costing systems and ABC are highlighted in Figure 3.1.

In absorption costing, as we have seen, overhead costs are apportioned to production departments. There will usually be few of these. In ABC, on the other hand, activities that contribute to production are first defined; there will be a number of these. The costs of each activity are collected into an activity cost pool that represents the costs of undertaking the specified activity for a year. Activities include: machine set-ups (concerned with setting up machinery for production); purchase order costs (the costs of ordering raw materials); and inspection (the costs of quality control). Costs may be classified into support activities and production process activities. The former activities include inspection and purchase order costs. The latter activities include assembly, machining and finishing, and these may be synonymous with production departments. Within absorption costing the costs of support services are normally apportioned to production departments and amalgamated with all other costs, whereas in ABC they stand alone and are separately allocated as product costs.

Absorption costing normally uses one or two bases for absorbing overheads, namely DLH or machine hours. In ABC, on the other hand, there will be a range of different cost drivers. Cost drivers are factors that cause costs of the activity to increase; the direct cause–effect link is not present in absorption costing. Examples of cost drivers are shown in Table 3.10.

Table 3.10 Cost pools and cost drivers

Activity cost pool	Cost driver
Purchase of raw materials	The number of purchase orders
Machine set-up costs	The number of set-ups
Cost of machining products	The number of machine hours
Inspection costs	The number of inspections carried out

Each cost driver will be associated with a cost driver rate that will be used to calculate the amount of activity pool resource cost to be charged to each product line. A cost driver rate is calculated by:

$$\frac{\text{The costs of the activity cost pool}}{\text{Number of cost drivers for the activity}}$$

Illustration

Eiger Ltd. makes two different models of ice axe using the same factory and equipment. They are the Popular, a mass market axe, and the Expert, for the very experienced mountaineer. The annual production overhead of £92,000 has been analysed over five activities as is shown in Table 3.11. The cost drivers have been identified and counted and the cost driver rates have been calculated.

Table 3.11 Annual production overhead for Eiger ice axes

Activity	Activity Cost Pool £	Cost driver	Number of cost drivers	Cost driver rates £
Production scheduling	15,000	The number of production runs	50	£300 per production run
Buying raw materials	16,500	The number of purchase orders	110	£150 per purchase order
Material set-ups	18,000	The number of set-ups	180	£100 per set up
Machining products	24,000	Machine hours	8,000	£3 per machine hour
Quality control	18,500	The number of inspections	370	£50 per inspection
Total costs	92,000			

During the year Eiger Ltd. plans to make 3000 of the Popular model and 1000 of the Expert. Production of the Expert is much more complex and it is produced in smaller batches and in shorter production runs. The Popular requires 1 hour and 40 minutes of machine time per product, whilst the Expert requires 3 hours. Direct costs per ice axe are as follows:

	Popular £	Expert £
Direct Labour	8	12
Direct materials	<u>12</u>	<u>15</u>
	<u>20</u>	<u>27</u>

The annual number of cost drivers is split between the two product lines as shown in Table 3.12.

Table 3.12 Cost driver breakdown

Cost driver	Total	Number of cost drivers	
		Popular	Expert
Production runs	50	20	30
Purchase orders	110	60	50
Set-ups	180	70	110
Machine hours	8000	5000	3000
Quality control	370	120	250

We can now use the information about cost driver rates and the number of cost drivers in each product line to calculate the activity-based cost for one Popular and one Expert ice axe (see Table 3.13).

Overcosting and Undercosting of Products

In our criticisms of absorption costing we outlined that it may result in some products being overcosted relative to their resource consumption and others undercosted. ABC is likely to reduce the likelihood of this because it is a much more refined system. With regard to Eiger Ltd., absorption costing systems would have used a machine hour rate and this would have been:

$$\text{Production absorption rate} = \frac{£92,000}{8000 \text{ machine hours}}$$
$$= £11.50 \text{ per machine hour}$$

Table 3.13 Activity-based cost per ice axe

Activity	Cost driver rate	Popular Number of cost drivers	Popular Total cost £	Expert Number of cost drivers	Expert Total cost £
Production scheduling	£300 per production run	20	6,000	30	9,000
Purchasing raw materials	£150 per purchase order	60	9,000	50	7,500
Machine set-ups	£100 per set-up	70	7,000	110	11,000
Machining products	£3 per machine hour	5000	15,000	3000	9,000
Quality control	£50 per inspection	120	6,000	250	12,500
Total cost			£43,000		£49,000
Number of ice axes produced			3,000		1,000
			£		£
Overhead cost per ice axe			14.33		49.00
Add direct costs			20.00		27.00
Total costs per ice axe			34.33		76.00

The total product costs utilising absorption costing and their comparison with ABC product costs are shown in Table 3.14. This under- and overcosting is referred to as cross-subsidization. Popular ice axes are cross-subsidizing Experts as they are bearing some of the costs of the latter, amounting to £2.92 per Popular. If the company uses product costs for decision making, for example as a basis for determining a product price, then under absorption costing Experts may be sold too cheaply.

Types of Activity Cost Pools

Cooper (1990) classified manufacturing activities into four distinct levels:

1. *Unit-level activities*. These are performed each time a unit of the product or service is produced. They consume resources directly in proportion to production output.

Table 3.14   Product costs

	Popular £	Expert £
Overhead		
Popular £11.50 × 1.667 hours	17.25	
Expert £11.50 × 3 hours		34.50
Direct costs	20.00	27.00
Product cost using absorption costing	37.25	61.50
Product cost using ABC	34.33	76.00
Absorption overcosting of Popular	2.92	
Absorption undercosting of Expert		14.50

An example is given by machine running costs with a cost driver of machine hours as the increase or decrease in costs is caused directly and proportionately by changes in production.

2. *Batch-level activities.* These are performed each time a batch of goods is produced – for example, each time a machine is set up for a different production run. Batch-level activities are fixed for all units within the specific batch and must be averaged over the number of units produced to produce a cost per unit.

3. *Product-sustaining activities.* These are performed so that production of a specific product can take place, for example, maintaining or upgrading product specifications, or product design. These costs will be incurred irrespective of the number of batches or units that are produced.

4. *Facility-sustaining activities.* These are incurred in order that, for example, the factory can engage in manufacture, and this includes things like the plant manager and factory rents. Such costs cannot be traced to individual products and, in ABC, they are shown as a deduction from the total gross profits of production.

The Benefits of ABC

Product Costing

As we have seen, the costs obtained under ABC are likely to be more accurate in reflecting underlying resource consumption than is absorption costing. This is particularly important in a complex organisation, with many products operating in a range of competitive markets. Bhimani and Piggott (1992) found that factory managers found ABC information to be valuable in allowing them to identify overhead cost reduction opportunities. There is a summary of this article at the end of the chapter.

Decision Making

It can be argued that the product costs are valuable for decision making. Although the costs include overheads, such overheads are calculated using cost drivers that are based upon a cause–effect relationship between activity cost pool and the associated cost driver.

Activity-Based Management

ABC, through the processes of pooling of activity costs and the identification of cost drivers, can lead to a range of applications. These include the identification of spare capacity and the fostering of cost reduction by comparing the resources required under ABC with the resources that are currently provided. This provides a platform for the development of activity-based budgeting in which the resource relationships identified by ABC are used to project future resource requirements. A study by Innes and Mitchell (1995) in the United Kingdom reported that the cost management applications of ABC by firms outweighed the product costing applications.

Service Organisations

These organisations, such as banks, hospitals and government departments, have very different characteristics than manufacturing firms. Service organisations have almost no direct costs, most of the costs are overheads and they do not hold stocks of service as the service is consumed when it is produced. Absorption costing has generally been considered inappropriate for these organisations, whereas ABC offers the potential of benefits from improved decision making and cost management. Drury and Tayles (2000), in a UK survey, found that 51% of the financial and services organisations surveyed had implemented ABC, compared with only 15% of manufacturing organisations.

An Improved Role for the Management Accountant

ABC and activity-based management allow the management accountant to play a key part in maximising value from resources because of the level of understanding of key activity and cost information.

The Problems with ABC

1. Batch and product sustaining activities will need to be averaged over all units produced in order to arrive at product costs. This may give the false impression that there is a direct relationship between marginal changes in output and these costs.
2. These systems are more complex than absorption costing and are more expensive to operate. They also take a number of years to develop. All firms should consider the costs and benefits of ABC, and for small companies in particular the costs may outweigh the benefits.

3. Hopper *et al.* (2003) warn of the dangers of implementing western management accounting practices in less developed countries. There is a summary of the article at the end of this chapter.

Marginal or Variable Costing

Marginal costing is based upon the segregation of costs into two groups, variable costs and fixed costs. As you learned in Chapter 2, variable costs are assumed to vary directly in proportion with output in the short term. Examples include fuel for motor vehicles and direct material costs. Fixed costs remain constant over a wide range of activity levels for a specified period of time, and they are not affected by changes in output. Examples include rents of buildings and managers' salaries.

Marginal costing assumes that: variable costs are product-related because they vary as production is increased or decreased, and that fixed costs are time-based as they relate to a specific accounting period.

Contribution

The concept of *contribution* is central to marginal costing. Contribution is defined as selling price less variable costs. If production and sales are both expected to be 5000 in a period and selling price is £15, variable costs are £9 and fixed costs are £24,000 then:

	Per unit £	Totals £
Sales	15	75,000
Variable costs	9	45,000
Contribution	6	30,000
Fixed costs		24,000
Net profit		6,000

As can be seen, the contribution does not represent profit as we have to consider the fixed costs of the operation. We can regard the contribution as contributing to the fixed costs and net profit of the organisation. In order to make a profit, the contribution must exceed the fixed costs of the period.

Break-Even and Target Contribution

The unit contribution can be used to identify the break-even output of the company. Break-even is a situation in which a company makes neither profit nor loss. At break-even total contribution will exactly equal total fixed cost and we can find the break-even sales level quite easily by means of the following formula:

$$\text{Break-even} = \frac{\text{Fixed costs}}{\text{Contribution per unit}} = \frac{£24,000}{6} = 4000 \text{ units}$$

When 4000 units are sold, contribution will amount to (4000 × £6 =) £24,000, which is equal to total fixed costs.

In an extension of this, unit contribution also allows the identification of the number of sales units required to earn a target profit. In this case total contributions must fully cover fixed costs and earn the target profit. If the company in this case desires a net profit of £12,000 then the number of units that it must produce and sell is given by the following formula:

$$\text{Required units} = \frac{\text{Fixed costs and target profit}}{\text{Contribution per unit}} = \frac{£24,000 + £12,000}{6} = 6000 \text{ units}$$

The following statement demonstrates that the target net profit of £12,000 will be earned if 6000 units are produced and sold:

	Per unit £	Totals £
Sales (6000 units)	15	90,000
Variable costs (6000 units)	9	54,000
Contribution (6000 units)	6	36,000
Fixed costs		24,000
Net profit		12,000

Margin of Safety

The margin of safety is the difference between the budgeted (or actual) output and the break-even output. Thus, at 6000 units of output the margin of safety is 2000 units. Output can fall by 2000 units before it falls to break-even at 4000 units.

The margin of safety can also be stated in percentage terms:

$$\frac{\text{Margin of safety}}{\text{Budgeted output}} \times 100 = \frac{2000 \text{ units}}{6000 \text{ units}} \times 100 = 33\%$$

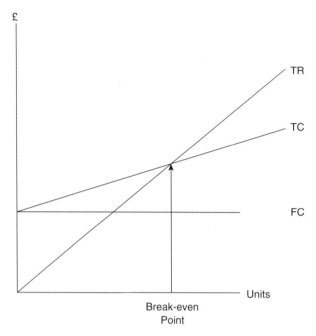

Figure 3.2   Break-even chart

Break-Even Charts

The relationship between revenues, variable costs and fixed costs can be summarised in a break-even chart, as is demonstrated in Figure 3.2. It shows the break-even point where total revenue (TR) is equal to total costs (TC, at 4000 units in our example). Total costs represent the sum of variable costs and fixed costs (FC) at all levels of output.

There are some key assumptions underpinning the construction of a break-even chart. The most important of these is the linearity assumption, which is that variable costs and sales revenue are constant per unit of output and can be represented by straight lines. In Figure 3.2 it also assumes that fixed costs are at the same level throughout the range of activity. The previous chapter discussed stepped fixed costs, and these can be easily accommodated within the diagram.

The assumption of linearity of the cost and revenue functions may be considered to be the Achilles' heel of the break-even chart. However, the concept of the 'relevant range' is important here. It states that a manager will not be interested in the whole range of the break-even chart but in a relevant area, possibly from break-even to the budgeted level of output and sales, and as long as the lines are linear within that range, that is sufficient for purposes of decision making.

One benefit of the break-even chart for managers is that they can easily assimilate the information presented and the relationships between the key variables. It is also useful for displaying the range of profits and losses and it may be much easier for non-financial managers to understand than tables of data.

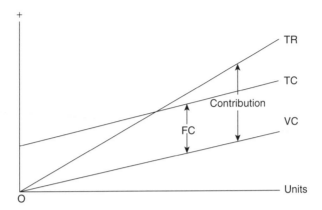

Figure 3.3 **Contribution chart**

A contribution chart is shown in Figure 3.3. This chart shows the total contribution as the difference between the total revenue and the variable cost (VC) lines. Fixed costs are represented by the difference between the variable cost and total cost lines. Break-even is at the junction of total revenue and total cost.

Marginal Costing as a Cost Collection System

The basis of marginal costing as a cost collection system is as outlined above. First, costs are broken down into fixed costs and variable costs. Secondly, fixed costs are regarded as period costs and not as product costs and are not carried forward in closing stock. In consequence, the value of closing stock will be less than under absorption costing, in which closing stock contains a share of factory costs, irrespective of whether they are fixed or variable. Marginal costing is relatively infrequently used as a cost collection system.

Illustration

McCarthy & Sons produce wicker baskets, and the firm uses marginal costing as a cost collection system. Data for the first month of production are as follows:

Unit selling price	£4	Production	6,000 baskets
Unit variable cost	£1.50	Sales	5,000 baskets
Fixed production overhead	£9,000	Closing stock	1,000 baskets
Fixed selling costs	£3,000		
	£		
Sales (£4 × 5,000)	20,000		

Costs of production		
Variable costs (£1.50 × 6,000)	9,000	
Less closing stock (£1.5 × 1000)	(1500)	7,500
Contribution		12,500
Fixed costs		
Production costs	9000	
Selling costs	3000	12,000
Net profit		500

As may be seen, closing stock is valued at the variable costs of production. By contrast, the closing stock valuation in absorption costing would, as well as the variable costs, also have included a proportion of the fixed production overheads. This amounts to (1000/6000 × £9000 = £1500) because the closing stock of 1000 units is one-sixth of production and should therefore bear one-sixth of fixed costs. This would increase closing stock from £1500 to £3000 and increase this period's profit from £500 to £2000. However, in the next period the absorption costing profit will be lower than the marginal costing profit because the former is carrying forward a higher cost to the next accounting period.

Conclusions

This chapter makes the following points:

- Absorption costing is an accepted method of costing products and inventories. There is a well-established multi-stage process to apportion and absorb overheads into production.
- It has advantages, but is flawed from a decision-making perspective.
- ABC offers improved product costing and an opportunity to improve decision making and cost management.
- ABC is complex, expensive and time-consuming. It is unlikely to be suitable for small businesses but is suitable for service sector organisations.
- Marginal costing can be used in decision-making, emphasising cost behaviour and contribution. The relationships between variables can be summarised in a break-even chart or a contribution chart. Marginal costing can also be used as a cost collection system.

Summary

The chapter has examined three approaches to product costing: absorption costing, activity-based costing and marginal costing. Absorption costing is widely used in practice, but its crude approach to costing means that it has significant weaknesses. Activity-based costing uses the ideas of cost pools and cost drivers and offers a way of overcoming some of the weaknesses of absorption costing. Marginal costing, the third approach, may be used in two ways: in decision making and in cost collection. It emphasises cost behaviour, the importance of differentiating between variable and fixed costs, the concept of contribution and that of break-even.

Recommended Further Reading

Bhimani, A. and Pigott, D (1992) 'Implementing ABC: a case study of organisational and behavioural consequences', *Management Accounting Research,* **3: 119–132.**

The authors carry out field study research within a pharmaceutical manufacturing company, Evans Medical. The company manufactures vaccines, pharmaceuticals and 'over the counter' products; in total the company manufactured 350 products and had a turnover of £50 million. In the study the authors make use of interviews and document analysis and the study was conducted over an eight-month period.

The aim of the research is to explore the behavioural and organisational consequences that can arise in a company upon the implementation of ABC and to examine such consequences from the perspective of predefined expectations about a change in an accounting system. The study commenced with the company's decision to introduce ABC and ended at a stage when the new accounting system was running in parallel with the old.

The study examines the company's rationale for installing ABC. The company had come to the conclusion that its existing cost accounting system was inadequate in terms of product costs and in the production of broader management information. The aims of implementing ABC were to produce more accurate product costs, to produce regular cost and volume reports and to identify those activities that were driving costs to permit more effective cost control and product improvement.

The article goes on to document the results from introducing the system. In summary, the new system appeared to produce more accurate product costs that were also in line with management expectations. Moreover, the ABC system provided information enabling management to reduce costs and obtain improvements, again in line with expectations.

The article then goes on to discuss the behavioural and organisational consequences that followed the implementation of ABC. The first of these relates to the perceived legitimising of the accounting function. ABC requires accountants to gain 'an appreciation of manufacturing processes, operational issues and production activities and had created the perception among factory and head office managers that the accounting data emanating … was now more firmly grounded in organisational processes' (Bhimani and Piggott, 1992: 127). Secondly, ABC information was capable of being used by managers to support their own efforts to derive economies at the factory level. The previous system had been unintelligible to them, but ABC information was intelligible and was used by factory managers to legitimise their decisions; it also improved communication by providing line managers and accountants with a common language. Finally, it raised understanding of product profitability among factory managers, and their enhanced understanding produced a broad shift in the balance of power from sales to factory. Sales managers had played no part in the introduction of a new system and did not understand the significance of the information that was being produced.

Hopper, T., Tsamenyi, M., Uddin, S. and Wickramasinghe, D. (2003) 'The state they're in', *Financial Management*, **June: 14–19.**

Hopper *et al.* consider the relevance of western management accounting trends and ideals in the context of less developed countries (LDCs). They argue that the effective internal and external financial controls that are assumed by policy makers (e.g. those within countries granting aid to LDCs) often do not occur in practice. They claim that often the market-based reforms insisted upon by policy makers may frustrate rather than facilitate appropriate development. This, in turn, is likely to facilitate a lack of transparency, poorer employment conditions, fraudulent activity, etc.

Hopper *et al.* argue that, rather than requiring specifically designed management accounting systems, the LDCs should manage well with 'imported' technology. The real problem, they argue, is not that effective management accounting systems are not available or in place, but that they are either ignored or applied in unintended ways. Hopper *et al.* continue that the special types of risk and uncertainties specific to developing economies can lead to short-termism, compounded by political volatility. They explain that the problems of obtaining sufficiently rich information systems, and skilled, committed employees may be beyond the reach of LDCs, and unskilled personnel may be required to carry out a wide variety of tasks simultaneously. Effective and honest corporate governance cannot be assumed in all such environments, the instability of government, and the level of corruption within officials often being crucial factors.

The valuation of companies (and the use of associated management accounting methods) is not a straightforward matter where stable markets do not exist and where regulation is not complied with. Additionally, Hopper *et al.* question whether the various fashionable theories regarding the interface of culture and management accounting apply in such LDC environments, as the basic theoretical assumptions of such theories are unlikely to be relevant.

Hopper *et al.* suggest a 'package' of possible areas for future research and development to overcome the problem of the lack of 'fit' of recognised mainstream management accounting ideas within LDC environments. Amongst these areas, Hopper *et al.* include:

- the relationships between management accounting, auditing and external regulation;
- the study of types of enterprise that are uncommon or poorly researched within western management accounting (e.g. plantations, small family-run firms);
- ways of measuring performance according to criteria such as poverty reduction, rather than profit maximisation, shareholder value maximisation, etc.;
- budgeting within LDC governments;
- the effects of cultural, political and ethnic issues particular to LDC economies;
- the roles of transnational bodies such as the World Bank.

Case Study: Billy Griffiths

Billy Griffiths is the newly appointed management accountant for Hopeless Ltd. The company has an appalling history in terms of its budget procedures and processes, with widely fluctuating results over the three years of its existence. This situation led to Billy's appointment, and his key initial task is to sort out these problems.

The company manufactures double glazing, making three products – windows, doors and UPVC garage doors. These products are manufactured in three production departments which are supported by two service departments – a canteen and a maintenance unit.

Billy has had some success in his first three months with the company, having been able to calculate direct material costs and direct labour costs per unit. He is willing to admit, however, that some of the basic data on which he worked is rather dubious, although sufficiently robust to make a start.

His next task is to turn to the allocation and apportionment of overheads and the calculation of appropriate hourly rates to serve as a basis for pricing. He has obtained the following information to make his judgements:

	Windows	Doors	Garage doors
Production (units)	5,000	2,500	1,250
Prime Costs (£ per unit)			
Direct materials	50	75	150
Direct labour			
Machine shop	12	22	45
Assembly	26	40	64
Machine hours per unit	3	5	10

	Machine shop	Assembly shop	Canteen	Maintenance unit	Total
Budgeted overheads (£)					
Allocated overheads	35,000	17,650	21,000	15,500	89,150
Rent and rates					32,450
Depreciation					25,000
Book value of machinery	250,000	350,000	50,000	45,000	
Number of employees	12	25	5	3	
Floor area (sq. metres)	4,500	5,500	1,500	500	

It is estimated that 65% of the maintenance section's time is spent in the machine shop, and the balance in the assembly shop.

Billy is too busy to do the actual calculation and, as his assistant, the task has landed on your desk.

1. (a) Compile the spreadsheet for the above data, ensuring total flexibility if figures change.
    (b) Calculate a machine hour rate for the machine shop.
    (c) Calculate an overhead rate based on a percentage of direct wages.
    (d) Calculate the budgeted overhead cost of a unit of each of the products.

2. Flex the model by increasing all costs by 10% and see what happens to your results. What impact will this have, should this situation arise?

3. Management are aware that Billy is undertaking this process and are concerned about the new process of apportioning overheads and the use of spreadsheets. Advise them of the advantages and disadvantages of the new methods by specifically contrasting the new process with the historical methods of managing overheads.

Case Study: Jim Davies

Jim Davies is the manager of one of six large distribution warehouses for Mars & Spars, a multinational clothing and footwear chain store. Jim's warehouse operates as a profit centre whereby purchasing officers based within his warehouse buy in items under appropriately negotiated contracts and 'sell' them on to the company's UK-based stores, although occasionally the goods can be exported. These are his 'customers'. Suppliers are both UK and overseas companies.

Goods issued by Jim's warehouse are charged to his 'customers' at the agreed contract price plus variations for agreed factors such as inflation. Any cost outside the contract price plus agreed variations are borne by the supplier. The charge to Jim's customers is the cost charged to Jim plus 5%. This is thus effectively Jim's performance measure as at the end of the year his warehouse must show a 5% 'profit' after allowing for all costs. This profit margin determines not only Jim's performance-related pay bonus but also that of every person who works in the warehouse and Jim's distribution network. It also is a factor in determining Jim's promotion chances.

Jim is feeling aggrieved. Every year for the past three years his operating surplus has failed to achieve the necessary 5% target. This has resulted in little or no performance-related pay and he is under pressure from his senior managers to explain why he is failing to perform – particularly as the other five warehouses have all achieved their targets (and more in some cases). Jim conjectures that the way in which the company allocates and apportions overheads to his warehouse causes the failure to achieve targets.

The following summary figures indicate the position for the last three years:

	2004 £000s	2003 £000s	2002 £000s
Sales	10,000	9,500	9,250
Cost of sales	7,500	7,020	6,950
Gross profit	2,500	2,480	2,300
Expenses			
Operating costs	1,800	1,780	1,700
Central overheads	400	350	200
Net profit	300	350	400
Percentage return	3	3.7	4.3

At present the company uses the following definitions of overheads:

- Corporate overheads – costs of board meetings, secretarial staff, board members salaries and expenses, etc.
- Technical support – financial, legal and personnel support, including such functions as business planning, financial advice on budgets, equal opportunities policy advice, etc.
- Buildings – costs for every building owned or occupied by the company.

All these overheads are charged to a trading account for each section – legal, finance, personnel, IT etc. – and then charged to a frontline service such as Jim's warehouse on the basis of a staff time analysis for each division. Staff in the support departments fill in an individual timesheet every three years. They are asked to estimate the amount of time they spend on each activity of the company and then these time sheets are analysed and used as the basis to apportion costs in the appropriate trading account. The last time sheet analysis was completed in 1990.

With buildings, all costs for all buildings are allocated to one central building account. These are then apportioned to all departments and functions on the basis of floor area occupied. For central overhead departments, the final costs are apportioned to all front-line services such as warehouses on the basis of the staff time analysis.

The net result of this process is that all costs of the overhead departments are fully apportioned to frontline departments such as warehouses.

Having read and analysed the above case:

(a)   Do you think the issue of overhead allocation is important to companies?
(b)   Why do you hold your point of view?
(c)   Identify what, if anything, is wrong with the above system.
(d)   What alternatives do you think might exist to the above?
(e)   Do you agree with Jim that overheads are the cause of all his problems?
(f)   How would you go about implementing any alternative?

Questions

1. Spot Ltd. produces three products, X, Y and Z in three production departments: Moulding (Dept. M), Assembly (Dept. A) and Finishing (Dept. F). It also has two service departments responsible for repairs and maintenance (Dept. R) and for development and research (Dept. D).

   Employees in Dept. R are paid total salaries of £24,000 per annum and complete timesheets to account for their time. Departments M, A, F and D utilise its services in the ratio 70:20:8:2 respectively.

   Dept. D studies improvements in working practices and product designs. The salary costs of this department total £20,000 per annum, and its work is expected to benefit the three production departments equally.

   The management accountant has estimated that the following factory overheads (excluding the salaries described above) will be incurred in the coming year:

	Note	£000's
Rent and rates		240
Electricity	1	75
Establishment costs		200
Plant insurance		60
Plant depreciation		600
Materials handling	2	12
Supervisors' salaries	3	60
Other overheads	4	72

Notes

1. Electricity costs are split equally between heating and lighting (50%) and power for production machines (50%).
2. Materials requisitions during the year are expected to average 20 per day for Dept. M, 15 per day for Dept. A, and 2 per day for each of Departments F and R.
3. There are two supervisors who cover the whole of the production and service operations of the country. It is estimated that a production employee requires three times the supervision of a service employee.
4. Other overheads are incurred 90% on production and 10% on servicing. The individual production and service departments are treated as equally responsible for their share of such costs.

The following information is relevant to the company and its departments:

		Departments			
	M	**A**	**F**	**R**	**D**
Floor space (sq.m.)	100,000	71,000	25,000	3,000	1,000
No. of employees	15	8	5	2	2
Plant value (£000s)	2,200	500	250	40	10
Budgeted machine hours	56,000	6,000	500		

The budgeted production details for the coming year are expected to be as follows:

	X	**Y**	**Z**
Direct materials per unit (£)	£3.70	£6.40	£8.90
Direct labour per unit (hours):			
Dept. M (paid at £5.00 per hour)	0.4	0.6	0.7
Dept. A (paid at £4.50 per hour)	0.3	0.3	0.3
Dept. F (paid at £4.25 per hour)	0.1	0.2	0.3
Moulding machine time per unit (hours)	0.8	1.0	1.4
Expected output (units)	10,000	20,000	20,000

(a) Given that Dept. M is machine-intensive and Departments A and F are labour-intensive, calculate the total absorption cost per unit for each of the company's three products using the most reasonable overhead absorption rates.

(b) The managing director has heard that using overhead absorption rates based on estimated figures can result in the under- or over-recovery of overheads. Write a brief memorandum to the managing director explaining the advantages of using estimated OARs, the situations in which under- or over-recovery of overheads may occur and the accounting treatment of such items.

2. A friend of yours is about to set up in business manufacturing and selling virtual reality jogging machines that will give users the perception that they are jogging through the countryside. The following information relates to the costs of producing 3500 jogging machines per year:

Although these figures are based on the production of 3500 machines, production capacity is 4000 machines per annum. The budgeted selling price is £280 per machine.

	£
Material costs	260,000
Labour costs	320,000
Production overhead	160,000
Selling and distribution overhead	150,000
Administration overhead	60,000

Following discussion with your friend, you ascertain that £207,000 of labour costs, 100% of administration overhead, 30% of production overhead and 50% of selling and distribution overhead are fixed in nature. All other costs are variable with the level of production.

(a) Calculate the unit contribution of a jogging machine and the total contribution of the budgeted level of production and sales.
(b) Calculate the amount of profit at the budgeted level of production.
(c) Construct a break-even chart, clearly showing the break-even point in units, the margin of safety and the budgeted level of production.

3. Ontario PLC manufactures three products, X, Y and Z. The following table includes information relating to the manufacture of each product

Product	Budgeted output	Material cost per unit £	Direct labour per unit (hours)	Machine time per unit (hours)	Labour cost per unit £
X	6000	15	0.25	0.25	2
Y	8500	24	0.4	0.25	2
Z	4800	18	0.4	0.50	4

The draft production overhead budget for next year contains the following departmental budgets:

Machine-oriented overheads	£16,500
Set-up costs	£38,920
Material ordering	£24,630
Material handling	£32,480

The budget absorbs these overheads into production using a budgeted machine hour rate of £18.68 per hour. This is budgeted to produce overhead costs per product as follows: X = £4.67, Y = £4.67, Z = £9.34. However, it has been proposed that the overhead budget be recalculated using activity-based costing. The following information has been provided for this purpose:

Product	Number of set-ups	Number of material orders	Number of times material is handled
X	1	1	3
Y	4	3	10
Z	2	2	3

(a) Recalculate the production overhead budget per product using activity-based costing, tracing costs to products by cost drivers.
(b) Discuss the assertion that activity-based costing is likely to produce a fairer unit product cost than total absorption costing.

4. The Dreamwheel Cycle Company is considering manufacturing a new bicycle and has prepared the following estimates of cost and selling price:

	£
Unit labour cost	20.00
Unit material cost	15.00
Unit packaging cost	5.00
Proposed selling price	80.00
Budgeted fixed cost per period	
0–7000 units	150,000
7001 units and above	320,000

Fixed overheads have been estimated by the company and represent both the apportionment of the company's existing fixed overheads to the new bicycle and the additional fixed costs incurred in the event of manufacture. Expansion beyond 7000 units will require the rental of additional premises and further additional fixed costs as shown above. Maximum production and sales are estimated at 9,000 units.

(a) Prepare a break-even chart for the bicycle identifying clearly the break-even points, and identify the profits (or losses) that would be made with sales of 6000 units and 8500 units.

(b) Comment on the results shown by the chart and interpret the key points shown by the chart for management together with any limitations in your analysis.

5. An airline catering company produces three standard meal packs about which the following information is available for next year:

Pack	Expected output (numbers of packs)	Production staff time per pack (minutes)	Total material costs £
X	90,000	10	247,500
Y	70,000	12	250,000
Z	40,000	15	180,000

For next year the production staff budget is £187,200 with a pay rate of £4.80 per hour. Apart from production staff and material costs, overheads are estimated at £1,010,000 and are made up as follows:

	Notes	£000
Ordering materials		300
Production run set ups		110
Quality control	1	90
Packing & dispatch of orders		60
Negotiation with customers		200
Central management costs	2	250
Total		1010

Notes:

1. The quality control costs are related to testing a random sample of orders dispatched.
2. The central management costs are not attributed to any activities and are to be absorbed on the basis of production staff hours.

In the coming year, the activity volumes are expected to be as follows:

	X	Y	Z
Set-ups	35	35	30
Orders for materials	85	110	105
Orders dispatched to customers	160	200	140

In the current year and in previous years the company has absorbed overheads with productive staff hours as the absorption base. Prices have been based upon full cost plus 20%. In recent years prices have been steady using this approach. The costs and prices for the current year are as follows:

Product	Full Cost	Price (Full cost + 20%)
X	£7.80	£9.36
Y	£9.50	£11.40
Z	£12.10	£14.52

(a) Determine the full cost of each pack for next year using:

    (i) an absorption approach with direct production staff hours as the absorption base.

    (ii) an activity-based approach using the information given above.

(b) Comment on the results of your calculations and indicate the advantages and disadvantages of moving to an activity-based approach.

Chapter 4
MANAGEMENT ACCOUNTING
AND THE PLANNING PROCESS – 1

Key Learning Objectives

By the time you have finished studying this chapter, you should be able to:
- discuss the relevance of an organisation's objectives to its budgeting processes;
- describe the planning process for a number of different organisation types;
- prepare master and subsidiary budgets for a number of different organisations.

Missions, Objectives, Aims, Goals, Targets and Plans

Accounting and business textbooks often use terms such as *missions, objectives, aims, goals, targets,* and *plans* interchangeably. It is a good idea to consider the meanings of these terms in order to avoid misunderstanding and/or ambiguity. The definitions given below are not the only possible ones. In the practical accounting/business situation, it is important that users of such terms come to a common understanding of their meanings within the context in which they are used. Many organisations will produce their own glossaries or 'controlled vocabularies' for these purposes.

The definitions given in Table 4.1 have been obtained from a number of dictionaries and are chosen for their everyday meanings, thereby avoiding any organisation-specific slant. A number of features are evident in Table 4.1. Firstly, the different terms may mean different or similar things and so we should avoid using terms with different meanings synonymously and, in the practical situation, be precise about what we mean by a term. Secondly, each term has an everyday meaning and ideally this should be the one allocated to the term to maximise understanding across a broad range of users. Thirdly, some of the terms have a number of possible meanings, depending upon context and upon whether the term is used as a noun, an adjective or a verb. Again, precision should be sought when using such terms within a given context.

So, within our management accounting context, let us select the bits contained within Table 4.1 that are most useful. We will probably end up with a collection of definitions

Table 4.1   Some dictionary definitions of common business terms

Term	Definition
Mission	(Noun)
	1. A specific task or duty assigned to a person or group of people: *their mission was to irrigate the desert.*
	2. A person's vocation (Collins, 2000).
	Mission statement
	1. An official statement of the aims and objectives of a business or other organisation (Collins, 2000).
	2. An explicit written statement of an organisation's long-term aims and objectives. Mission statements are designed to give substance to the perceived purposes of the organisation and provide all employees with an indication of what they are attempting to achieve through their collective endeavours (Pass *et al.*, 1995).
Objective	(Noun)
	1. Something which you try to do: *the company has achieved its objectives; we set the sales forces certain objectives.* Long-term or short-term objective – Aim which you hope to achieve within a few years or a few months (Collin *et al.*, 2001).
	2. What one intends to do or achieve: aim, ambition, design, end, goal, intent, intention, mark, meaning, point, purpose, target, view (Roget, 1995).
	(Adjective)
	1. Considered from a general point of view, not from that of the person involved: *you must be objective in assessing the performance of the staff; to carry out an objective survey of the market* (Collin *et al.*, 2001).
	2. Free from bias in judgement: disinterested, dispassionate, equitable, fair (Roget,1995).
Strategy	(Noun)
	Plan of future action: (e.g.) *business strategy; company strategy; financial strategy* (Collin *et al.*, 2001). A plan or method devised to meet a need: (e.g.) strategies for dealing with dissatisfied customers (Penguin, 2000).
	Long-term planning in the pursuit of objectives, or the art of this (Penguin, 2000).
	Business strategy
	The formulation of long-term plans and policies by a firm which interlocks its various production and marketing activities in order to achieve its business objectives (Pass *et al.*, 2000).

(Continued)

Table 4.1   (Continued)

Term	Definition
Aim	(Noun) Something which you try to do: *one of our aims is to increase the quality of our products* (Collin *et al.*, 2001). (Verb) To try to do something: *we aim to be No. 1 in the market in two years' time* (Collin *et al.*, 2001).
Goal	(Noun) 1. Aim, something which you try to do: *our goal is to break even within twelve months* (Collin *et al.*, 2001). 2. The aim or object towards which an endeavour is directed. The terminal point of a journey or race (Collins, 2000).
Target	(Noun) 1. Thing to aim for: *monetary targets, production targets, sales targets* (Collin *et al.*, 2001). 2. An object or area aimed at the object of an attack or takeover bid. A fixed goal or objective, etc. (Collins, 2000). (Verb) 1. To aim to sell. To target a market – to plan to sell goods in a certain market (Collin *et al.*, 2001). 2. To make a target of. To direct or aim (Collins, 2000).
Tactics	(Plural noun, treated as singular or plural) 1. (a) The science and art of disposing and manoeuvring forces in combat. (b) The art or skill of employing available means to accomplish an end. (c) A system or mode of procedure (Penguin, 2000). 2. The manoeuvres used or plans followed to achieve a particular short-term aim (Collins, 2000).
Plan	(Noun) 1. Organised way of doing something: *contingency plan, government's economic plans* (Collin *et al.*, 2001). 2. A detailed scheme, method etc., for attaining an objective. An outline, sketch etc. (Collins, 2000). (Verb) 1. To organise carefully how something should be done: *to plan for an increase in bank interest charges, to plan investments* (Collin *et al.*, 2001). 2. To form a plan (for) or make plans (for). To have in mind as a purpose; intend (Collin *et al.*, 2001).

Table 4.1   (Continued)

Term	Definition
Budget	(Noun) 1. (Business) Preliminary financial plan for the future needed to effectively and efficiently function. It may be short-term (1 year or less), intermediate-term (2–3 years), or long-term (3 years or more). The shorter the time span, the more accurate the budget because there are fewer uncertainties. Short-term budgets are more detailed and specific so they are more meaningful for everyday operations. Intermediate-term budgets are most concerned with tracking the success of projects undertaken and to be undertaken. Long-term budgets are broad goals and are translated into short-term plans. The budget period varies depending on objectives, use, dependability, risk, instability and manufacturing cycle (Shim and Siegel, 1995). 2. An estimate of income and expenditure for a future period, as opposed to an account, which records financial transactions after the event (Bannock and Manser, 1999). (Verb) To plan probable income and expenditure: *we are budgeting for £10,000 of sales next year* (Collin *et al.*, 2001).

such as those in Table 4.2 (these are only the authors' attempts at definition; many other variations are possible).

So what can we learn from all this? Well, as we can see from Table 4.2, the differences in meaning between the terms can be quite subtle. Sometimes the definitions (e.g. for objectives, aims, targets and goals) are just about identical. Generally though, in practice, the terms tend to be differentiated in terms of their time horizons and specificity. For example:

- *Missions* tend to be long-term and laid out in broad terms, without attempts being made to quantify them specifically.
- *Objectives and aims* tend to be medium-term and more specific in terms of what is intended to be achieved. Again, the positions to be reached may be expressed in mainly non-quantitative terms.
- *Goals and targets* tend to be medium-term or short-term and may be expressed in terms of specific levels of achievements and tend to involve more specific quantification and deadlines.
- *Plans* tend to be quite specific (the shorter-term they are, the more specific they tend to be) and are usually quantified in some detail. They will, in order to ensure that they are complied with, lay out specific deadlines for each key stage. They may also involve the analysis of priorities and constraints.
- *Budgets* tend to be expressed mainly in monetary terms, although they may focus on the amounts of physical resources (materials, labour time) required.

Table 4.2   Some attempts at defining some common terms used in management accounting

Term	Management accounting meaning
Mission	An important task that an organisation believes it is its duty to do.
	Mission statement
	An explicit statement of the aims and objectives of a business or other organisation – providing employees with an indication of what they are attempting to achieve through their collective endeavours.
Objective	Something which an organisation intends to do or achieve; a result that the organisation intends to make happen.
Strategy	A plan of future action, usually long-term, in the pursuit of objectives.
Aim	A result that an organisation's plans or actions are intended to achieve.
Goal	An organisation's aim, objective or purpose.
Target	A level or situation which an organisation intends to achieve or aim at.
Tactics	The plans followed to achieve a particular short-term aim.
Plan	A set of decisions about how an organisation intends to do something, or to ensure that an event or result should happen in the future.
Budget	A financial plan, which may be short-term or longer-term, showing probable (planned) income and expenditure.

As was stated earlier, in the practical situation, an effort should be made to use terms carefully so that confusion is avoided. We cannot, however, avoid the subtle variations of meaning produced by the richness of language.

Let us use the analogy of a football team to illustrate how these terms might be used. The football team has a mission – 'to be the best team in the country' or something similar. You may disagree with the team's idea of what its mission is; indeed, there are a large number of missions that might be suggested. It is therefore important that the team should be explicit in what its mission is, in order to avoid ineffective actions by its members. Notice also that we are considering the *team's* mission rather that the missions of the individual team members.

How can the team achieve its mission? Obviously, it needs to determine how it will know when it has achieved the mission. The team may decide that one indicator of being the country's best team would be to come top of the country's premier football league. Another possible indicator, a more exacting one, would be to come top of the league for several years consecutively.

Assuming the team chooses the indicator of topping the league for the current year, its ambitions are now becoming a little more 'concrete' – the team now is agreed on what it must do to consider itself successful. The team could, of course, achieve its ambition in a number of ways, including 'fixing' matches, but let us assume that it has honourable intentions. Also, let us assume that the mission agreed by the team is also agreed by its manager, financiers and supporters. The issue of identifying missions, objectives and plans that all affected parties can agree to is a particularly difficult issue in practice.

In this analogy, then, the team has identified its mission (being the best football team in the country) and an indicator of when it will have achieved that mission. This indicator (winning the league for this year) can be considered to be the team's objective. This objective (following our general description of an objective) is specific (you either win the league or you do not) but non-quantitative (there are no numerical values involved in the statement of the objective). Additionally, the objective (winning the league *this year*) has a specific time limit.

How will the team achieve its objective of winning the league this year? Obviously it needs to win matches. It may not have to win them all, however; much will depend upon the scoring/points system in place. A *strategy* for achieving the objective might involve making the most of the way in which the points system operates, to the team's advantage. It would be ideal, of course, to win all matches, but this may be both unrealistic and unnecessary.

Looking at team ambitions at a lower level, the team needs to maximise its success during matches. It needs to win most of its games. It may therefore set itself a shorter-term *target* of winning a particular game, or of scoring a certain number of goals in a match, or of scoring from a certain percentage of penalties. It will *plan* how to do this by considering and forming *tactics* for each game (and these tactics may change as each game develops). An important point here is that each game may require different tactics and the team must to able to respond flexibly to changing conditions.

Finally, we cannot resist observing that, in any particular football match, the *goal* is a very specific *target* at which the ball must be *aimed*!

The Organisational Planning Process – An Overview

All of this applies equally well to the 'games that businesses play'. A business will have a mission that may be expressed in a formally written mission statement (at least in the case of larger, formally managed businesses). Such mission statements might include, for example, 'to provide world-class products to a world market' or 'to be market leader in logistical services provision'. The longer-term strategy of the business should, logically, be closely focused on achieving the ambitions expressed in the mission statement. Management texts suggest that a business may 'lose its way' if the mission, objectives and lower-level targets are not co-ordinated.

In order to put its longer-term broad strategy into place, the business will set more specific strategies for marketing, production, human resources, procurement and the like. Each of these strategies will be put into effect in the short term by means of specific plans, performance targets and budgets. Obviously, all of these are forward-looking. The business also needs to ensure that such plans and targets are adhered to and, if necessary,

Figure 4.1   The strategy and planning process

modified to cope with actual conditions. This is where performance monitoring, feedback and reporting come into the equation. These processes are discussed in Chapters 7 and 10. Figure 4.1 illustrates the processes described above. Other versions of this diagram may be found in most business management texts.

The planning process, then, takes place at many levels – strategic, tactical, operational, etc. and the financial aspects of each type of planning may be known as *budgets*. Budgets may be applied at any level, although at the higher levels of strategic and tactical planning, the term *financial planning* tends to be used in preference to 'budgeting'.

The Users and Uses of Budgets

As we have seen above, budgets and budgeting may be applied at any level of management. The higher levels of financial planning are covered in texts devoted to financial management and investment appraisal such as those by Samuels *et al.* (1999) and Brealey and Myers (2002). Here we will be concentrating on medium- to short-term, lower-level processes, generally with a time horizon of one year or less. In practice, the management accountant's work is likely to encompass both short-term budgeting and the longer-term financial planning activities.

What is a Budget?

As we have seen, a budget is often thought of as a *financial plan*. A budget may, however, be expressed not only in financial terms but also in quantitative terms (e.g. budgets for labour hours, material purchases, or units of sales). Each of these will, however, have obvious implications for financial outcomes and may be seen as a subset of, or 'working paper' towards, the related financial budget.

" A budget will describe, as a minimum, estimated *amounts* (financial and/or non-financial) which will be incurred or earned as the result of a planned course of action and consider the *timing* of the incurrence/earning of these amounts."

Who uses Budgets?

Not everyone, of course, is responsible for preparing budgets, but everyone within an organisation will be affected by them, sometimes without realising it consciously. A manager will be required to set budgets for her/his area of responsibility and to manage the processes within her/his remit in order to ensure that the budget is achieved. Thus, the manager's subordinates will each bear an individual responsibility to ensure that a specific area of activity complies with the values and expectations expressed within the overall budget.

Budgets are, of course, *internal* to the organisation and, like most management accounting information, do not form part of the organisation's published financial statements. Nevertheless, such budgetary information can be of great use to competitors if they can obtain it (usually by foul means!).

What are Budgets Used For?

As well as the obvious uses of budgets (to quantify the planning process and to form a basis of performance monitoring) they may have a number of associated, subsidiary uses. These are listed in Table 4.3. Again, a common organisational problem is co-ordinating the range of uses/users of budgets in such a way that processes such as pay negotiations and cash collection do not result in actions that are contrary to the higher-level objectives/mission upon which the budget is based – organisational coherence.

Table 4.3   **Uses of budgets**

Primary uses	• quantifying planned resource usage (materials, labour, etc.) • quantifying income generation • quantifying resource procurement (materials, outsourced components, subcontractors)
Secondary uses	• quantifying payment for resources (cash budgeting) • quantifying collections of cash (from debtors, etc.)
Tertiary uses	• telling people what they are meant to achieve • basis of negotiation • means of communication • component of reward/payment systems

The Budget Preparation Process – General Principles

As we have seen already, budgeting takes place at many levels, although here we will be considering a one-year time horizon. Let us consider the yearly budget preparation process for a manufacturing organisation. What would be the main questions to be addressed for an annual budget? An attempt is made to put together some reasonable questions in Table 4.4.

Obviously, the budget for even a small manufacturing firm can be quite complex. A separate 'mini-budget' could be prepared for each of the items in Table 4.4, the size and timing of many items being dependent or related to a number of other items. For example, when we pay for materials depends upon the sources from which we purchase them and the characteristics of their credit terms. What materials must be purchased depends

Table 4.4 Some questions to be asked when preparing a manufacturing firm's annual budget

---

What products are we going to sell?
How much of each product are we going to sell?
When will we sell the products?
Where will the products be sold?
If we buy in the products for selling on:
- When will we buy them?
- Who will we buy them from?
- How much will we pay for them?

If we make the products:
- Materials:
    - How much of each material will we need?
    - Where will we get the materials and when?
    - How much will we pay for the materials and when?
    - How much will we buy and how much will we keep in stock?

- Labour:
    - How much labour will we use?
    - How many people of each type will we need?
    - When will we employ them?
    - When will we pay them?

- For each type of cost (salaries, insurance, rents/rates, administrative expenses, stationery, phone, heating, lighting, etc.)
    - How much will we need?
    - When will we need it?
    - Who will supply it?
    - When will we pay for it?

upon on stock policies and usage requirements, which depend, in turn, on production plans.

Ideally, therefore, budgets at the detailed level should 'cascade down' from the higher-level budgets which are closely dovetailed into the organisational objectives. In real life, of course, there will also be an element of 'bottom-up' planning. Although the organisation might wish to produce X units of a product, constraints on the materials or labour may prevent the required number of sales units being produced. An iterative process therefore ensues in which constraints, objectives and priorities are considered in order to produce the optimal effect.

Let us use a simple example to illustrate the budgeting process. Exhibit 4.1 demonstrates a budgetary process in a simple manufacturing firm.

EXHIBIT 4.1	**Illustration of Budgeting Within a Small Manufacturing Firm**

Buddy Ltd has the following basic plans for the forthcoming year:

Products	Sales units	Selling price £/unit
A	240	1000
B	360	800
C	120	1500

It is likely that sales of products A and C will be even throughout the year, whereas product B will be sold in four equal consignments taking place at the end of each quarter.

All sales will be made on credit terms of 30 days and the opening trade debtors' position at the start of the budget year is expected to be £50,000.

All of the company's products will be manufactured in-house and they have the following resource requirements:

	Material X		Material Y	
Product	Units of material required per unit of production	Cost per unit of material (£)	Units of material required per unit of production	Cost per unit of material (£)
A	3	50	4	60
B	2		3	
C	4		5	

At the start of the budgeted year, the following material stocks will be available:

Material	Units	Unit cost £	Total cost £
X	200	45	9,000
Y	100	55	5,500

Note that the unit material costs given in the table above are those for the opening stocks, that is, costs relating to the year before the budget period. Thus they will not necessarily be the same as the unit material costs relating to the budget period. It is intended to reduce direct material stocks by 20% by the end of the budgeted year.

Buddy Ltd's products have the following direct labour requirements per unit of production:

Products	DLH
A	20
B	15
C	40

Direct labour employees are paid at £5 per hour for a 40-hour week. After taking into account illness, leave etc., these employees work, on average, for 45 weeks of the year. Ten direct labourers are employed and any hours in excess of those normally available will be paid at an overtime rate of 'time and a half' (i.e. 50% above the normal rate). It is intended to maintain a constant number of direct labour employees throughout the budget year.

In addition to direct costs, the following monthly regular indirect costs are planned: salaries and indirect labour, £10,000; Administration, £8,000. Advertising campaigns are planned for months 4 and 8 at a cost of £15,000 each.

Suppliers of materials are paid 2 months after the materials are delivered. The opening trade creditors' position at the start of the budget year is expected to be £40,000.

Wages and all overheads are paid one month in arrears. Creditors for wages and overheads are expected to be £25,000 at the start of the budget year.

At the start of the budget year, Buddy Ltd will have the following stocks of its finished products:

Product	Budgeted opening stocks of finished goods (units)	Prime cost per unit £	Total cost £
A	50	500	25,000
B	60	350	21,000
C	80	650	52,000

Note that the unit prime costs given in the table above are those for the opening stocks, that is, costs relating to the year before the budget period. Thus they wil not necessarily be the same as the unit prime costs relating to the budget period. Buddy Ltd intends to increase its finished goods stocks to 100 units of each product by the end of the budget year.

Let us follow the process of preparing Buddy Ltd's budgets for the forthcoming year. The basic approach is illustrated in Figure 4.2.

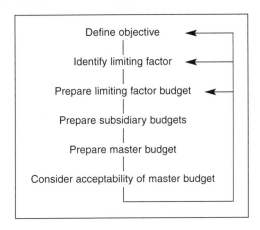

Figure 4.2   **Buddy Ltd's budgeting process**

Buddy Ltd's budgeting *objective* here is to make and sell the budgeted quantities at the budgeted selling prices. We will assume that demand is sufficient for the budgeted sales quantities at the budgeted selling prices, but we will need to check that the company has sufficient resources at its disposal to make the required units of the products.

Before we calculate the required resources, we need to calculate how many units of its products the company needs to make, given the information we have about its opening and closing budgeted stock levels. The following table may be called a *Production budget*.

	Product		
	A	**B**	**C**
Budgeted sales units	240	360	120
Budgeted closing stocks of finished goods	<u>100</u>	<u>100</u>	<u>100</u>
	340	460	220
less Opening stock available	<u>(50)</u>	<u>(60)</u>	<u>(80)</u>
= Required units of production	290	400	140

Next, now that we know the quantities of each product that Buddy Ltd will have to manufacture, we can turn our attention to the materials that will be required to produce the products. What are Buddy Ltd's materials requirements?

		Product		
		A	**B**	**C**
Budgeted units of production		290	400	140
Units of material required per unit of production:	X	3	2	4
	Y	4	3	5
Budgeted total units of each material required:	X	870	800	560
	Y	1160	1200	700

We can see now that Buddy Ltd needs (870 + 800 + 560 =) 2230 units of material X and (1160 + 1200 + 700 =) 3060 units of material Y. We can therefore calculate the amounts of each material that Buddy Ltd needs to purchase, taking into account its budgeted opening and closing stock levels:

		X	**Y**
	Units of material needed for production (see above calculations)	2230	3060
add	Budgeted closing stock (taking account of the intended 20% decrease)	160	80
		2390	3140
less	Opening stock available	(200)	(100)
	Therefore, material purchases required (in units) =	2190	3040

For the purposes of this illustration, we will assume that Buddy Ltd can find adequate supplies of these materials and hence that materials availability is not a limiting factor. If it were a limiting factor, Buddy Ltd would need to rethink its budget and consider issues such as:

- Should fewer units of both products (or a different mix of products) be made?
- Should it buy in finished products in order to make up for the shortfall of available materials?

- Should it redesign the products in order to utilise different, but readily available materials?
- Would Buddy Ltd be able to obtain more materials if it was prepared to pay a higher price for them, or pay for them more quickly?

We can also now calculate the cost of purchasing the required materials:

	X	Y	Total
Purchase requirements (units):	2190	3040	
Purchase cost per unit	£50	£60	
Purchase cost	£109,500	£182,400	£291,900

The second stage in the budgeting process (Figure 4.2) was identifying the *limiting factor*. We have assumed that demand is sufficient to allow Buddy Ltd to sell its budgeted sales quantities and that sufficient materials supplies are available. What about labour availability? Well, we are informed that if insufficient labour hours are available within normal hours, Buddy Ltd will be able to use overtime hours to make up the shortfall. So, it appears that there are no limiting factors here. Demand, materials availability and labour capacity can all be dealt with.

There are, however, practical limits to such capacity. Should demand for Buddy Ltd's products surge, then sufficient materials may be difficult to obtain. Similarly, there are obvious limits to the extent to which the labour force can work overtime, including social and legal implications. Of course, materials shortages can often be overcome by substituting materials or by outsourcing, as outlined above. Labour shortages might, in the longer term, be overcome by product redesign or by the recruiting of further employees.

In the present example, given that there are no obvious limitations on materials or labour, then the budget is driven by how much is produced, which in turn is driven by the level of demand. Effectively, sales demand is the limiting factor and hence the sales budget is the budget out of which all the other budgets are constructed.

Let us check on the requirements for direct labour:

	Product			
	A	B	C	Total
Budgeted production units	290	400	140	
Labour hours required per unit	20	15	40	
Total labour hours required	5,800	6,000	5,600	17,400

Note that we are assuming that Buddy Ltd has only one type of direct labour working in only one department. If there was a mix of different labour types, operating within a number of different departments, each having its own limitations, then this example would be somewhat more complicated – and a lot more like real life!

Does Buddy Ltd have enough capacity within normal hours to produce the required units? This can be ascertained easily. Buddy Ltd's available direct labour capacity is 10 direct labourers × 38 hours per week × 45 weeks per year = 17,100 direct labour hours. So we can see that Buddy Ltd has a shortfall of (17,400–17,100=) 300 direct labour hours. This shortfall can, however, be made up for by overtime working and these overtime hours will be paid at the overtime rate of 1.5 × the normal hourly rate. Therefore, the budgeted direct labour cost will be 17,400 × £5/hr = £87,000.

A additionally, there will be an overtime premium overhead cost of 300 hours × 50% × £5/hr = £750. Note that the budgeted overtime premium cost is treated as an *overhead*, rather than as a direct labour cost, as it is not a regular feature of the production process. Should there be a continued and increasing need for overtime working, it is likely that the company would review its direct labour requirements.

We have already identified one budgeted overhead cost, an overtime premium cost of £750. What other overheads does Buddy Ltd have? The only other overheads identified within this example are:

	£/month	£/year
Salaries and indirect labour	10,000	120,000
Administration costs	8,000	96,000
Advertising campaigns: 2 at £15,000 each		30,000

Now that we have done most of the 'hard thinking', we can now start to put together the budgets for Buddy Ltd. As production, and most other factors, are even throughout the year, we shall produce a budget for the year as a whole. Although sales of product B take place at the end of each quarter, this will merely have an effect on stock levels within the budget year.

In real life, it is likely that a number of matters would make this simple scenario unlikely and hence require budgeting on a monthly (or other periodic basis):

- Labour capacity will tend to vary throughout the year, for example during traditional holiday periods and because of sickness. Stocks would therefore need to be built up to compensate for lack of production during those periods.
- Demand may be seasonal.

Let us now put together the budgets in the order suggested by Figure 4.2. First, the sales budget:

		Product A £	Product B £	Product C £	Total £
Sales	240 × £1,000	240,000			
	360 × £800		288,000		
	120 × £1,500			180,000	
					708,000

Next, the production budget:

	Product A	Product B	Product C
Budgeted units of production =	290	400	140

Finally, the materials usage budget:

	Product A		Product B		Product C	
Units of production (see production budget)	290		400		140	
	Units Material per unit of prod'n	Units of material required	Units Material per unit of prod'n	Units of material required	Units Material per unit of prod'n	Units of material required
Material X	3	870	2	800	4	560
Material Y	4	1,160	3	1,200	5	700

What about the cost of these materials? We know, from the materials usage budget, what the material quantities required are. Where will these materials be obtained? Some, obviously, will be obtained as new purchases. Buddy Ltd will also have a quantity of opening materials stocks at the beginning of the budget period. Let us assume (as we are not told) that these opening stocks are used equally between products A and C and that (following a first-in, first-out assumption) they are used up before the newly purchased materials. Thus, the cost of the materials consumed in production will be a mixture of the cost of opening stocks (which have a different unit cost) and new purchases:

	Product A	Product B	Product C	Total
Material X:				
Required units of material	870	800	560	
	£	£	£	£
Cost of opening stocks used				
100 units × £45	4,500			
100 units × £45			4,500	

(Continued)

(Continued)

	Product A	Product B	Product C	Total
Costs of new purchases				
Used (balance)				
770 × £50	38,500			
800 × £50		40,000		
460 × £50			23,000	
Subtotal	43,000	40,000	27,500	110,500
Material Y:				
Required units of material	1,160	1,200	700	
	£	£	£	
Cost of opening stocks used				
50 units × £55	2,750			
50 units × £55			2,750	
Costs of new purchases				
Used (balance)				
1,110 × £60	66,600			
1,200 × £60		72,000		
650 × £60			39,000	
Subtotal	69,350	72,000	41,750	183,100
Total	112,350	112,000	69,250	293,600

Here is the materials purchases budget:

	Material X	Material Y	Total
Purchase requirements (units):	2,190	3,040	
Purchase cost per unit	£50	£60	
Purchase cost	£109,500	£182,400	£291,900

Finally, here is the direct labour budget:

	Product A	Product B	Product C	Total
Direct labour hours required:	5,800	6,000	5,600	
Direct labour cost per hour	£5	£5	£5	
Direct labour cost	£29,000	£30,000	£28,000	£87,000

Note that here we have not included the usual 'add-ons' of employers' national insurance, pension contributions, and so on, that are often treated as part of the labour rate in practice (as we are not supplied with the requisite information here).

We saw, when producing the direct labour budget, that Buddy Ltd had no spare labour capacity. The budgeted total cost of the direct labour force to the company is 52 weeks × 38 hours × £5/hr × 10 employees = £98,800 (assuming that employees are paid every week, even if ill, on holiday, etc.). But we have calculated that the direct labour cost of production is only £87,000. The difference of £11,800 represents the cost of holiday pay, sick pay, and so on, and is usually treated as an *overhead* cost. Another labour-related overhead cost is the overtime premium of £750 that we calculated earlier. So Buddy Ltd's overhead budget looks like this:

		£ per year
Labour-related overheads:	Holiday and sick pay	11,800
	Overtime premium	750
Salaries and indirect labour	£10,000 per month =	120,000
Administration	£8,000 per month =	96,000
Advertising	2 campaigns at £15,000 each =	30,000
Total overhead cost budget		258,550

The *master budget* is simply a summary of all the other budgets and often takes the form of set of budgeted accounts. It has little use for control purposes at the detailed level but does, at least, show the overall budgeted position (to tell us whether we will make a profit) and allows a check on whether the various detailed budgets come together as a coherent whole.

As explained earlier, if the overall outcome indicated by the master budget does not meet with approval, adjustments will be made and a process of iteration will ensue until the budget is 'right'. Of course, there is a limit to how many times this process can be carried out before the budget is finalised, but the power of modern software and hardware facilitates the process well.

Although all of the above calculations might, in practice, be undertaken using spreadsheet software, the larger firm is more likely to apply more systematised software, probably integrated with its other financial and non-financial systems. Such software, used by multinational organisations, is sometimes known as enterprise resource management software and is rapidly becoming more sophisticated.

Buddy Ltd's Budgeted Profit & Loss account

		Product A	Product B	Product C	Total
Sales	Units	240	360	120	
		£	£	£	£
	Revenue	240,000	288,000	180,000	708,000
Cost of sales					
Units of *production*		290	400	140	
		£	£	£	£
Cost of materials used (see materials budget)		112,350	112,000	69,250	293,600
Direct labour cost (see direct labour budget)		29,000	30,000	28,000	87,000
Prime cost of production		141,350	142,000	97,250	380,600
add Opening stocks of finished goods, at prime cost (given)		25,000	21,000	52,000	98,000
less Closing stocks of finished goods, at prime cost*		(49,000)	(35,500)	(70,000)	(154,500)
Cost of sales		117,350	127,500	79,250	324,100
Gross profit					383,900
less Overhead costs					(258,550)
Budgeted net profit					125,350

* <u>Calculation of prime cost per unit of stock produced during the budget period.</u>
Assuming a FIFO basis:

			Product A	Product B	Product C
			£	£	£
Materials:	X	3 × £50	150		
		2 × £50		100	
		4 × £50			200

Y	4 × £60	240		
	3 × £60		180	
	5 × £60			300
Labour	20 × £5	100		
	15 × £5		75	
	40 × £5	___	___	200
Prime cost per unit		490	355	700

The budgeted closing finished goods stock of each product is 100 units, so value of closing stocks is:

	£
Product A	49,000
Product B	35,500
Product C	70,000
Total	154,400

As we are not given details of Buddy Ltd's opening balance sheet at the start of the budget period, other than for stocks, debtors and creditors, we cannot produce its budgeted balance sheet. We can, however, calculate the *effects* on Buddy Ltd's balance sheet during the budget year. First, though, we need to produce a *cash* budget for the year.

	£	£
Inflows		
<u>Cash from sales:</u> we know that Buddy Ltd intends to make £708,000 of sales during the year. We also know that the opening trade debtors will be £50,000.		
Opening debtors (will be received during the budget year)	50,000	
+ Sales made	708,000	
−Closing debtors (not received until after the end of the budget year) = 1/12 × £708,000 =	(59,000)	
= Cash received from sales during budget year		699,000

Outflows
Material purchases

Opening trade creditors =	40,000	
+ Materials purchases (all on 2 months' credit)	291,900	
− Closing trade creditors = 2/12 × £291,900 =	(48,700) [approx]	
= Cash paid for materials during budget year		283,200

Direct labour and overheads

Direct labour cost	87,000	
Total overhead cost	258,550	
Total labour and overhead cost	345,550	
+ Opening creditor	25,000	
− Closing creditor = 1/12 × 345,550 =	(28,800)	
= Cash paid out during budget year		341,750

Thus the change in cash resources during the budget year is:

Total inflows − Total outflows = 699,000 − (283,200 + 341,750) = £74,050

Let us now look at the effects of the budget year on Buddy Ltd's balance sheet:

			£	£
Assets:				
Increase in cash			74,050	
Increase in trade debtors				
(59,000 − 50,000)			9,000	
(Decrease) in materials stocks:				

		Closing stocks (calculated) £	Opening stocks (given) £	
Material X	160 × £50 =	8,000	9,000	
Material Y	80 × £60 =	4,800	5,500	
		12,800	14,500	(1,700)

Increase in finished goods stocks:

		closing stocks (calculated) £	opening stocks (given) £		
Product A	100 × £490 =	49,000	25,000		
Product B	100 × £355 =	35,500	21,000		
Product C	100 × £700 =	70,000	52,000		
		154,500	98,000		
				56,500	
					137,850

Liabilities:
(Increase) in trade creditors
  (40,000 – 48,700) =   (8,700)

(Increase) in creditors for
  wages and overheads:

         = (25,000 – 28,000) =   (3,800)

                                                  (12,500)

∴ Total effect on balance
sheet (a net increase in
assets) =   125,350

Note that, as we would expect, this increase in budgeted balance sheet net assets is equal to the budgeted net profit that we have calculated.

So, we have produced the main budget statements for Buddy Ltd as required, but how realistic has this example really been? A few (!) matters that may go towards complicating things for Buddy in real life are given in Table 4.5.

Toll Processing or Contract Manufacturing

Toll processing is a recent trend in manufacturing industries, particularly multinational groups. Previously, a company might have manufactured products or components, or carried out a production or refining process, using materials that it has purchased from another company within the group. Under a toll processing arrangement, the same operation or processing is undertaken but the materials being worked upon do not change ownership: the processing company undertakes work on materials provided by the customer company, and returns the processed materials to the customer. Thus, instead of the previous situation where the materials are purchased from and the processed output sold back to the customer, under toll processing the processing company simply charges the customer a 'tolling fee' for the services provided.

Table 4.5   Some possible complicating factors in real-life budgeting

Possible complications	Solution approaches
Vast range of products and a need for careful allocation of resources to products	Strategic approaches to product portfolio analysis and application of mathematical approaches such as linear/integer programming
Non-linear relationships between sales price and demand	Some mathematical approaches possible. Multi-scenario modelling using advanced software
Changing goals, targets, tactics, etc., and/or unexpected changes in resource availability.	Need for a more flexible, less detailed approach to budgeting. Extensive use of computer modelling
Multinational buying and selling leading to complex effects upon profits, depending on the geographic mix of resources and customers	Need for a co-ordinated modelling approach involving input from, and negotiation between all relevant parts of the multinational group
Changes and/or differential effects in inflation rates	Need to take a more flexible approach; potential for 'what if' analysis
Potential for reducing labour costs by outsourcing or relocating operations overseas	Budget model to build in various possibilities for location, etc., including potential implications for other non-labour related factors, e.g. communications, logistics, treasury
Potential changes in corporate structure because of take-overs, etc.	Incorporate potential effects (where foreseeable/quantifiable) into higher-level models
Changes in pricing/stocking/profit structures because of move to a contract manufacturing (toll processing) organisational set-up	Ensure that alternative budgeting models produced. Budgeting approaches used will be basically the same but the emphasis may change to focus on the characteristics of the new set-up, including increased focus on overheads, transfer pricing, service fee structures
Wish to calculate profits at a more detailed product level	Application of a form of absorption costing (either traditional or activity-based) to overhead costs, being careful that the extra 'information' produced is reliable/useful

The reasons behind toll processing are varied, ranging from economic effectiveness (in terms of specialisation, decentralisation, or risk management) to tax avoidance/ evasion.

Toll processing may take place within any manufacturing or processing industry, and may take place within groups (e.g. to minimise taxation by taking advantage of differential local tax rates/rules) or between 'arm's length' parties. It is found noticeably within oil, chemicals, pharmaceuticals and computer industries.

Organisational Contexts and Budgeting Requirements

We have considered the basic budgeting requirements of the manufacturing sector in the passages above and have examined some of the complications that may arise. Of course, in some countries the services sector has grown rapidly. Similarly, in many 'advanced' countries, the public sector, measured in terms of employment figures, is larger in size than any industrial or other sector. It may therefore appear that the traditional emphasis of management accounting texts upon *manufacturing* businesses may have an inappropriate bias. This is true to an extent, but there are a number of 'extenuating factors':

- Many of the features of manufacturing and service organisations are similar. Both sectors, for example:
  - use materials (manufacturers to a larger extent)
  - may outsource resources or processes
  - use labour, although the 'admin' activities will be a higher proportion within service organisations. The meaning of 'direct labour' will vary, though, between service and manufacturing organisations.
  - make sales. There is also a degree of cross-over in that, increasingly, in certain sectors such as metals, pharmaceuticals and chemicals, manufacturers may process goods for others. Such toll manufacturers or contract manufacturers may therefore manufacture goods in their own right or provide a processing service (or both).

- The processes of setting objectives, aims, goals, etc. and of planning, budgeting, etc. are similar in principle for both manufacturing and service sectors. Any differences lie in the detail and emphasis within the budgets and plans of each sector.
- The public sector is vast and covers a broad range of organisations. Many of these organisations will apply similar approaches to planning/budgeting to those used in the manufacturing and service sectors. Indeed, in the search for 'best practice', UK public sector bodies often turn to the manufacturing/service sectors for inspiration. Recently acquired approaches include activity-based costing and balanced scorecard approaches to performance management.
- The public sector (particularly the various forms of government) contains specialised, publicly owned, forms of service organisation.

There are, of course, also significant differences between the public sector and other sectors. As stated above, the public sector is 'publicly owned' in that it is financed by public contributions. Hence, its objectives and goals should reflect public wishes. It is thus inappropriate for public sector organisations to follow an overall objective of profit maximisation to the detriment of social objectives and considerations. The budgeting models illustrated above still apply, but the objective is more likely to be framed in terms of such matters as minimising cost, optimising service provision, and optimising quality. Profit (or, more precisely, cost reduction) becomes more of a *limiting factor* than an objective in itself.

One further significant factor of some public sector organisations is that of *incrementalism*. Incrementalism is a name given to the public sector's tendency to take a short-term, year-by-year approach to budgeting (see Coombs and Jenkins, 2002). Basically, because of a government's need to control costs within the framework of long-term social and economic objectives, there may be a tendency to impose top-down 'caps' (i.e. upper limits) on expenditure. This in itself is not necessarily a problem (except that it may result in a rather short-term bias). However, in some public sector organisations, a failure to use (i.e. spend) the allocate budget limit will lead to a reduction in the following year's allocation of funding to that part of the organisation, resulting in a gradual and continuous upward 'creep' in spending. A failure to allow a department to benefit directly from its cost savings or income-generating activities can lead to similar consequences.

In the public sector (but not only in the public sector – similar characteristics may be exhibited in many large companies) over-formalisation of planning systems often occurs. This may lead to a high degree of bureaucracy whereby:

- expenditure may not be committed to a project /service unless it has been planned and approved well in advance;
- over-rigid rules are enforced regarding the reallocation of budgets from one project/ service to another;
- it may be easier to obtain authorisation for smaller-scope projects than for more meaningful/strategically important projects.

Such features may lead to ineffectiveness creeping into the organisation, with an increasing emphasis on short-term and less strategic issues. Limiting factors are often imposed from within the organisation rather than from without it. Labour availability, for example, may be more a matter of limits imposed on the maximum size of a department than of how much labour is available in the external labour market.

Having said all of this, things are changing and successive governments have made efforts to become more effective, efficient and economical, though not always successfully. Recent years have seen much criticism of efforts to improve effectiveness of sectors such as public health, public transport and education. Moves are also afoot in the UK public sector to align accounting practice with the 'best practice' of the private sectors, although much of this emphasis (e.g. via the *Resource Accounting Manual*, maintained by the Financial Reporting Advisory Board) is on financial rather than management accounting issues.

Behavioural Consequences of Budgetary Control Systems

Obviously, planning and control systems are linked inextricably to the ways in which people behave. Such systems consider and deal with what people are meant to do (missions, objectives, goals, etc.), how they should do it (plans), what they should allocate resources to (budgets) and how well they do it (budgetary control mechanisms). As this was such an obvious area for research into the social aspects of budgeting, it was one of the first 'growth areas' in management accounting research, leading to a wealth of later research. Some of this research is outlined below and covered more extensively in the recommended further reading section.

Amigoni (1978) attempted to prepare a conceptual framework for the design of management control systems which was tailored to corporate and environmental characteristics. He claimed that there were two main factors for consideration, the degree of complexity and the degree of discontinuity that existed within the business system/environment. He suggested that management control systems research should concentrate on how to deal with complex companies in highly turbulent environments. Effectively, Amigoni argued that, as regards budgeting and control systems, it was not a case of 'one size fits all'. The control system, the plans that it contains, and its degree of flexibility must all be carefully tailored to have optimal relevance to the particular organisation and its current and future environment. This does not mean that every aspect of a budgetary system must be complex, at least not more complex than is necessary to achieve the intended outcomes.

Otley and Berry (1980) argue that many of the theories of accounting control and organisation are outdated and that several issues need to be resolved before the cybernetic (closed-loop feedback) control model can be applied confidently to accounting information systems. They argue that control and organisation are unclear concepts and that objectives may change over time. Otley and Berry draw attention to how the different types/natures of organisation (normative, instrumental, coercive) may impact on the required nature and information of control systems. They draw attention to the role of power relationships within organisations and the impact that these may have on the nature and outcomes of control systems. Otley and Berry argue that most management accounting information systems fail to produce predictive information for problem-solving because of difficulties in obtaining data. They therefore argue for a contingent approach to systems design. They identify the practical problems of identifying the conditions for control (objective, measuring device, predictive model, choice of alternative actions) and the need for compromise or consensus in the real world. They conclude that a holistic approach to control is optimal. In essence, Otley and Berry make a similar case for 'tailored' systems to that of Amigoni.

Briers and Hirst (1990) provide an extensive review of the literature in this area and attempt to assemble an analytical framework using supervisory style as the key independent variable. They point, particularly, to the piecemeal, selective and method-driven nature of previous studies and to these studies' overdependence on statistical analysis and subsequent inference. They argue that, while a contingency theory underpinning (see Chapter 7) is common in this area, they have some concerns about contingency theory's lack of conceptual clarity and the ambiguity of constructs such as 'environmental uncertainty', 'job performance' and 'budget performance' and their interrelationships. They argue that the effects of the choice of supervisory style are 'neither a simple nor inevitable consequence of a particular supervisory style'. Briers and Hurst then attempt to identify possible factors upon which the optimal control system design would be contingent. They make reasonably clear that the application of a 'tailored', contingency theory approach is neither easy nor obvious.

Conclusions

This chapter has:

* reviewed terms such as strategy, mission, objectives, goals and aims, and emphasised the need for clarity of meaning;
* shown that effective budgeting depends on setting clear objectives, reliable monitoring and feedback systems and effective reporting;
* argued that budgets affect everyone in an organisation, whether they are involved in setting or being assessed by them;
* stated that budgetary practices may vary depending upon the organisation and environmental setting;
* shown that budgets may have unintended consequences if used inappropriately.

Summary

In this chapter we have focused on the budgetary control aspects of management accounting. We have considered the scope for confusion that may arise from the use of words such as strategy, goals, aims, missions and target, and urged the management accountant to specify meanings where possible. Budgeting is an activity that links these terms and permeates all levels of all organisations.

We have seen that budgetary control depends upon clear objectives and the implementation of effective monitoring systems. We looked, in some depth, at the typical activities involves in producing a master budget for a typical organisation. Budgets were seen to have a wide range of uses, from control to communication. Finally, we observed that a variety of views exist upon the nature, requisites and possible outcomes of budgetary practices.

Recommended Further Reading

Amigoni, F. (1978) 'Planning management control systems', *Journal of Business Finance and Accounting*, 5(3): 279–292.
Amigoni attempts to prepare a conceptual framework for the design of management control systems which is tailored to corporate and environmental characteristics. He claims

that there are two main factors for consideration: the degree of complexity and the degree of discontinuity. The former takes into account:

- independent variables, such as the company's structural complexity and degree of environmental turbulence;
- distinctive features, such as detail, relevance, formality and control style;
- control tools, such as financial accounts, ratios, management accounts, and budgets.

The degree of discontinuity is concerned with the adaptability of the system: if the assumptions about the economic scenario are wrong, or change frequently, the system will be unable to adapt.

Amigoni argues that the distinctive features of management control systems are as follows:

- degree of detail in management accounting information, e.g. product/divisional analysis;
- degree of relevance (to individual managers);
- degree of selectivity – the greater the selectivity, the higher the ratio of relevant to irrelevant information, i.e. the better the system is;
- degree of formal responsibility;
- degree of procedural rigidity – 'standard' v. 'contingency' systems;
- style of control – tight v. loose (socially/individually aware managers);
- quickness (between event and management response);
- orientation (to the past or to the future).

He suggests connections between environmental variables and management control system features. A stable environment has

- lots of business units and communications, therefore more detailed systems and output orientation;
- more complex organisational structures, therefore more system relevance, selectivity and degree of detail at lower levels;
- a higher degree of formal responsibility and procedural rigidity, and a tighter control style.

A turbulent environment, on the other hand, is a more discontinuous one, with systems oriented to future and a high degree of quickness.

According to Amigoni:

- cost accounting increases the relevance of information and increases formal responsibility;
- budgeting (with responsibility accounting) increases formal responsibility, increases procedural rigidity (often with 'tight' style) and has limited orientation to the future (although the use of NPV analysis increases future orientation).

He suggests that management control systems research should concentrate on how to deal with complex companies in highly turbulent environments (see also Preston, 1995).

Otley and Berry (1980) 'Control, organisations and accounting', *Accounting, Organisations and Society*, 5(2): 231–244.

Otley and Bory argue that many of the theories of accounting control and organisation are outdated and that several issues need to be resolved before the cybernetic (closed-loop feedback) control model can be applied confidently to accounting information systems. They make some suggestions for research in this respect.

Control is an unclear concept, argue Otley and Berry. They discuss the various possible motivators for control systems, such as domination vs. regulation, monitoring vs. taking action and so on. Additionally, the idea of the 'organisation', they maintain, is unclear. Organisations are 'social constructs' continually evolving and modifying to adapt to their situations and that even organisational objectives may change over time. Otley and Berry explore the concepts of planning and control. They suggest that planning may be seen as 'future control' or that 'control' may, in fact, be seen to contain both the components of planning and control.

Otley and Berry further discuss the types of organisational nature that may exist, referring to the earlier work of Amitai Etzioni, who established that organisations may have several natures – normative, instrumental or coercive. The nature of the organisation has, of course, implications for the required control systems and the information to be produced. Additionally, the role of power within the organisation would need to be accounted for within the control system's design. Otley and Berry refer to the work of Stafford Beer who criticised the naïve ideas of causality accepted by many observers, i.e. to what extent can organisations/control be modelled by mathematical models or replicated in human organisms? They argue that most management accounting information systems fail to produce predictive information for the 'problem-solving' function of management because of obvious difficulties in obtaining the data. They argue for a contingent approach to designing management accounting information systems and that little research has been carried out in this respect.

They refer to Keith Tocher's four conditions for control – an objective, a measuring device, a predictive model, and a choice of alternative actions – but ask how easy is it to define/design these in practice. (They also refer to Vickers' more detailed control process model.) Such models, they comment, pay little attention to notions of compromise or consensus as found in the real world (or domination, power, encouragement or agency aspects) and the accountant's role/position in all of this.

They go on to look, in more depth, at Tocher's four conditions for control, examining the problems involved, for example:

1. *Objectives* – problems of defining, deriving or clarifying,
2. *Measuring devices* – necessarily simplistic/reductionist – but representative surrogates?
3. *Predictive models* – are they ever complete/reliable? Accounting measures are only a small part of the whole, and
4. *Choices of action* – identification and persuasion to change are both prerequisites.

Otley and Berry conclude that a holistic approach to control would be best and that accounting procedures, although presently inadequate, may prove to be the best basis for such development.

Briers, M. and Hirst, M. (1990) 'The role of budgetary information in performance evaluation', *Accounting, Organisations and Society,* **15(4): 373–398.**
Briers and Hirst provide an extensive review of the literature in this area and attempt to assemble an analytical framework which, using supervisory style as their key independent variable, categorises other variables involved into those which are:

- *antecedents* – having a causal effect upon supervisory style;
- *moderators* – where supervisory style is thought to depend on their value;
- *intervening* – if they are both affected by supervisory style and also have a causal effect on the dependent variable of interest (e.g. dysfunctional behaviour, job performance, budgetary performance).

They argue that, while their literature review indicates the complexity of their area of study and that, generally, a contingency approach seems to have found favour, previous writing has demonstrated failings conceptually and methodologically. They point, particularly, to the piecemeal, selective and method-driven nature of previous studies and their overdependence on statistical analysis and subsequent inference.

Briers and Hirst also point to the conflicts between earlier analyses and make some suggestions as to possible causes of such conflicts. They draw attention to the difficulties in identifying the nature/interrelationships and significance of the variables identified in earlier studies, which include:

- technical features of systems;
- styles of use;
- implications of participation/pseudoparticipation;
- economic conditions;
- environmental uncertainty;
- degree of multidimensional communication;
- degree of existence of informal information systems;
- the nature of interpersonal relationships;
- the time focus of performance management systems (short or long term);
- the degree of task uncertainty;
- business strategy (defender, prospector, analyser);
- business culture/philosophy;
- the role of technology;
- budget emphasis and budget pressure, etc.

They argue that, while a contingency theory underpinning is common in this area, they have some concerns about it:

- a lack of conceptual clarity (what exactly is contingency theory?);
- a lack of clarity in the understanding of the nature of change;
- the ambiguity of constructs such as 'environmental uncertainty', 'job performance' and budget performance' and their interrelationships.

They conclude that 'the use made of accounting information in performance measurement is neither a simple nor inevitable consequence of its availability' and that the effects of the choice of supervisory style are 'neither a simple or inevitable consequence of a particular supervisory style'. Whilst their study is intellectually demanding, it does provide a useful checklist of the factors which may impact on performance evaluation.

Case Study: Budget Preparation

SIG PLC manufactures two types of crampon: peaks and grips. The current factory manager, E. Whymper, formed the company in 1986. The company uses a standard cost system and fully absorbs factory overheads into the cost of production. Closing stocks of finished goods are valued at the standard cost of production. Production and sales are planned to be at the same monthly level throughout the year 2002.

The estimated balance sheet for the year ended 31 December 2001 is as follows:

SIG PLC
Balance Sheet as at 31 December 2001

Assets employed	£000	£000	£000
Fixed assets	Cost	Depn	Net
Plant and machinery	700	140	560
Current assets			
Stock			
Raw materials	53		
Finished goods	80	133	
Debtors		30	
Cash		109	
		272	
less Current liabilities			
Creditors	12		
Proposed dividend	60		
Provision for taxation	13	85	
Working capital			187
			747

Financed by	
Share capital	646
Retained profit	<u>101</u>
	<u>747</u>

The following information has been obtained for the purpose of preparing the budget for the year ending 31 December 2002:

Sales Forecast	Peaks	Grips
Planned selling price per unit	£110	£130
Forecast sales volume (units)	6,400	4,200

Direct Costs

The following standard costs have been estimated for the year 2002.

Materials	£
Teal (per kilogram)	9
Spake (per litre)	5
Direct labour	£/hour
Machining department	6
Finishing department	5

The standard direct material and standard direct labour content of each unit of the finished product is as follows:

	Peak	**Grip**
Teal	4 kg	4 kg
Spake	3 litres	3.5 litres
Machining direct labour	3 hours	4 hours
Finishing direct labour	2 hours	3 hours

The following numbers of direct employees work in each of the production departments: machining, 22; finishing, 10. All employees work a 38-hour week and receive paid leave for 5 statutory bank holidays and 15 additional days per year. The normal working week is five days. Any overtime is paid at time and a half.

Factory overheads are fully absorbed into production, using direct labour hours. At the planned output levels the following costs are forecast:

	£000
Indirect labour	30
Indirect materials	22

Repairs	11
Rates	22
Canteen	16
Depreciation	70
Heat and light	3
Power	6
Factory management	49

The factory has three cost centres: machining department, finishing department and a general service department. Data relating to these three cost units for 2002 are as follows:

Data	Machining dept.	Finishing dept.	General service dept.
Indirect labour hours	3500	1000	300
Indirect materials	£13,000	£5,000	£4,000
Repairs	£5,000	£4,000	£2,000
Factory managers	£16,000	£19,000	£14,000
Plant and machinery values	£600,000	£100,000	0
Floor area	2000 sq.metres	500 sq. metres	500 sq. metres
Machine hours	5500	1500	0
Canteen employees			2

The following stock forecasts are available:

Raw materials	Teal (kg)	Spake (litres)
Opening stock	5000 (£46,000)	1400 (£7,000)
Closing stock	4900	2300

Finished goods	Peaks	Grips
Opening stock	90 (£5000)	920 (£75,000)
Closing stock	700	520

Forecast selling and administrative expenses (in thousands of pounds) are as follows:

Selling expenses	
Salaries	43
Advertising	20
Administrative expenses	
Office salaries	34
Sundry expenses	10
Professional fees	5

The costs of raw materials purchases, direct labour, factory overheads, selling and administrative expenses will be met in full in cash. At 31 December 2002 it is estimated that outstanding debtors and creditors will stand at £23,000 and £21,000, respectively. Tax owing at 31 December 2001 will be paid by 1 September 2002 and proposed dividends will be paid in the first three months of 2002. Machinery purchases during the year are estimated to cost £45,000 and will be paid for.

Any profits are taxed at the rate of 23%.

You are required to produce the following budgets and working papers for 2002.

Sales Budget (1)

Product	Units	Selling price £	Revenue £
Peaks			
Grips			
Budgeted revenue			

Production Budget (2)

	Peaks (units)	Grips (units)
Forecast sales		
Planned finished goods closing stock		
Total units required		
Less finished goods opening stock		
Budgeted production		

Direct materials used budget (3)

Raw material	Peaks Content per Peak	Peaks Output of Peaks	Peaks Usage of raw material	Grips Content per Grip	Grips Output of Grips	Grips Usage of raw material	Total usage
Teal							
Spake							
Total	–	–	–	–	–	–	–

Cost of Direct Materials Purchases and Cost of Usage Budget (4)

	Teal (kg)	Spake (litres)	Totals
Planned closing stock			–
Production requirement (3)			–
Total required			–
Less: opening stock			–
Purchase requirement			–
	£	£	£
Cost per unit			–
Budgeted purchases			
Add o/stock raw mats.			
Less c/stock raw mats.			
Cost raw mats. used			

Direct Labour Budget (5)

Dept./ Product	Labour hrs per unit	Units of output	Total labour hours	Wage rate per hour	Total labour costs
				£	£
Machining					
Peaks					
Grips					
Finishing					
Peaks					
Grips					
Totals	–	–		–	

Overtime/Idle Time Working Papers

Hrs.

Dept.	Peak hrs	Grip hrs	Total hrs	Available Hours	Idle time hrs	Overtime hours
Man						
Fin						

£

Dept.	Wages	O/T	Total	T Labour	OT Prem	Idle T
Man						
Fin						

Factory Overhead Costs Budget (6)

	Apportionment basis	Total costs £	Manufacturing department £	Finishing department £	General service department £
Canteen					
Depreciation					
Heat and light					
Indirect labour					
Indirect mats.					
Management					
Power					
Rates					
Repair					
Overtime prem.					
Idle time					
Total cost					
Reapportionments					
Total costs					
Planned activity (hrs.)					
Rate per hour					

Standard Manufacturing Cost (7)

	Cost per unit (DLH, litre or kg) £	Peak		Grip	
		Units in one peak	Cost per peak £	Units in one grip	Cost per grip £
Direct materials					
Teal					
Spake					
Direct labour					
Machining					
Finishing					
Unit prime cost					
Factory overhead:					
Machining:					
Finishing					
Unit production cost					

Closing Stock Budget (8)

	Units	Unit cost £	Total cost £
Raw materials			
Teal			
Spake			
Total cost			
Finished goods			
Peaks			
Grips			
Total cost			

Cost of Goods Sold Budget (9)

	£
Direct materials used (4)	
Direct labour (5)	
Factory overhead (6)	
add Finished goods opening stock	
less Finished goods closing stock	
Budgeted cost of goods sold	

Selling and Administrative Expenses Budget (10)

Selling Expenses	£	£
Salaries		
Advertising		
Administrative Expenses		
Office salaries		
Sundry		
Professional fees		
Totals		

Budgeted Cash Flow (11)

	£	£
Opening cash balance		
Add receipts		
Total cash available		
Payments		
Purchases (4)		
Direct labour (5)		
Factory ohead (excluding dep'n) (6)		
Selling and admin (10)		
Tax		
Machinery purchase		
Total payments		
Budgeted closing cash balance		

Budgeted Trading Profit and Loss Account Year Ended 31 December 2001 (12)

	£
Sales (1)	
less Cost of sales (9)	
Budgeted gross profit	
less Selling and admin. expenses (10)	
Budgeted net profit before tax	
Taxation	
Budgeted net profit after tax	

Budgeted Balance Sheet as at 31 December 2002 (13)

Assets Employed	£000	£000	£000
Fixed assets	Cost	Depn	Net
Plant and machinery			
			(Continued)

Budgeted Balance Sheet as at 31 December 2002 (13) (Continued)

Assets Employed	£000	£000	£000
Current assets			
Stock			
Raw materials			
Finished goods			
Debtors			
Cash			
Less Current liabilities			
Creditors			
Provision for taxation			
Working capital			
Net assets employed			
___*Financed by*___			
Share capital			
Retained profit: at 31.12.01			
add Year to 31.12.02			
Capital employed			

Questions

1. The production manager of the company for which you are an assistant accountant has recently sent you the following memorandum:

    To: Assistant Accountant
    From: Production Manager
    Date: 1 September 2004

    Subject: Accounting Terms

    I have, as you know, been attempting recently to gain a better understanding of the financial side of our business, particularly in the management accounting area. I should therefore be grateful if you would explain to me (in simple language) the following matters:

    1. *Budgets, forecasts and plans*: I am unsure as to the differences (if any) between these terms. Would you please explain these differences and the significance these differences would have for me.
    2. *Budgets and standards*: Is a budget the same as a standard? I have always worked on the assumption that it was.
    3. *Cash budgets*: What is the point of producing cash budgets when we already spend an enormous amount of time on producing profit-based budgets? Producing cash

budgets seems superfluous when we are in a profit-making position. Surely cash budgets are only relevant when a bank overdraft situation is likely?

4. *Production budgets*: I see that you have once again instructed managers to prepare their budgets. Is the production of budgets not your department's responsibility? Line managers have enough of a problem managing without the further burden of having to produce budgets.

Perhaps you could let me have your comments.

Respond to the production manager's points. Your answer should be in the form of a memorandum.

2. The company you work for has asked you to write an introductory section to its budget manual. Some managers have complained that they do not really understand the reasons for spending such significant resources on producing budgets.

Write an introductory section for a budget manual entitled 'The Reasons for Preparing Budgets'.

3. CZD Ltd supply records, tapes and CDs to retail outlets. You are presented with the following financial information and are required to complete the cash budget for the three months ending 31 December 2005.

Opening cash 1/10/05 is £16,000.
Creditors give one month's credit.
Salaries are paid in the same month as they are earned.
Other expenses are paid one month in arrears and include £2000 depreciation each month.
Credit sales are settled 30% in the month of the sale and the remainder one month following the sale.

Month	Cash sales £	Credit sales £	Purchases £	Salaries £	Expenses £
September	25,000	40,000	70,000	6,000	7,000
October	28,000	45,000	68,000	6,000	7,000
November	28,000	40,000	59,000	6,000	7,000
December	30,000	38,000	60,000	6,000	7,000

(a) Prepare a cash budget for the months of October, November and December 2005.
(b) Prepare a schedule of outstanding debtors at the end of each of the months of October, November and December 2005.

4. The Amplifying Manufacturing Co Ltd issued £300,000 of share capital for cash on 1 January 2004, the date of its incorporation. In the following two weeks it raised an additional £50,000 by way of a loan from its local bank and spent £200,000 on machinery. The machinery is expected to last 10 years. The company rents a factory at a cost of £10,000 per month, paid on the last day of each month. Additional fixed costs (excluding depreciation) of £10,000 are paid monthly.

During its first six months of trading the company expects to sell the following numbers of amplifying widgets: January, 1000; February, 3000; March, 5000; April, 7000; May, 9000; and June, 12,000. Of these sales 10% each month will be cash sales; the remainder are on credit, with debtors paying 40% in the month following the sale and 60% in the month following that. The selling price of each amplifying widget is £12.

The company will produce the following number of widgets each month: January, 4000; February, 5000; March, 7000; April, 9000; May, 12,000; June, 15,000. Materials cost £3 per widget and are purchased in the month of production on one month's credit. Labour costs at £3 per widget are paid in the month of production, as are other variable overhead costs of £1 per widget.

(a) Prepare monthly budgets for production, cost of materials and direct labour for the first six months of trading.

(b) Prepare a monthly cash budget for the Amplifying Manufacturing Co Ltd for its first six months of trading. Show clearly the closing cash balance each month and the total cash flows over the period.

5. Belt plc sells men's and boy's belts that are cut to order. Each foot or fraction thereof sells for £2. Small belts average 2 feet and large belts average 3 feet in length. The leather is purchased from a local tannery at 90 pence per foot. The buckles are purchased at 50 pence for the small size and 75 pence for the large size.

Direct labour requirements are 10 minutes for a small belt and 15 minutes for a large belt. Skilled labour costs £5 per hour.

Machine requirements are 5 minutes for a small belt and 6 minutes for a large belt. Machine time costs £6 per hour.

Sales are expected to be 10% more than last year. Last year, the company's sales during October and November were as follows:

	October	November
Small belts	3000	2600
Large belts	1400	1500

The inventories at 30 September 2004 are as follows: leather, 1800 ft; small buckles, 2000; large buckles 1200.

In future the company desires month's end inventories as follows:

Finished goods:	10% of current month's sales
Leather:	40% of current month's production requirement
Small buckles:	30% of current month's production requirement
Large buckles:	30% of current month's production requirement

(a) Prepare a production budget for small and large belts for October and November 2004.
(b) Prepare a purchases budget for October and November 2004.
(c) Prepare a wages budget for October and November 2004.
(d) Comment on the difficulty of obtaining data when production budgets are being prepared.

Chapter 5
MANAGEMENT ACCOUNTING AND THE PLANNING PROCESS – 2

Key Learning Objectives

By the time you have finished studying this chapter, you should be able to:
- use and understand specific non-quantitative techniques to estimate costs;
- use and understand relevant quantitative techniques to estimate costs;
- interpret the results of your analysis and advise management accordingly;
- discuss advances in budgetary techniques and their influences in new organisational environments;
- outline a selection of contemporary management accounting approaches and techniques;
- appreciate the role and philosophy of just-in-time production as a means of stock control.

Cost Estimation

It might be assumed that it is reasonable to suggest that the identification of cost behaviour is relatively straightforward in the business world. This is, however, far from the case, but determining how cost will change with output, or other measures of activity associated with, for example, service delivery, is essential. To give a few examples of the problems encountered:

- Direct labour is often treated as a variable cost. For companies, however, which retain a static workforce because of the skills possessed and who thus cannot be simply hired and fired, direct labour is treated as a fixed cost.
- Depreciation of assets is suggestive of being a fixed cost yet certain assets are more likely to be exhausted by production level changes than by time.

- Time has an impact on cost classification, as the longer the time period the more likely the cost is to become variable.
- Tight budget control systems with positive management intervention are more likely to keep costs under control than weaker systems.

The first section of this chapter is thus concerned with developing an understanding of these issues given their actual and potential impact on managerial decision making. We begin with relatively straightforward techniques before moving on to discuss techniques using more quantitative analysis.

Engineering Methods

Under this system of estimating cost behaviour a study is undertaken of the technological relationships between outputs and the inputs required to achieve those outputs. Various techniques are used associated with work study and time and motion methods. By their nature they are more practical where there is a significant repetition of a manufacturing productive process, although they can be applied equally well to administrative and selling functions. The disadvantages of using engineering methods, however, are associated with attempting to measure overhead costs. In addition, in recent years as UK manufacturing has gone into decline, such techniques may not be as relevant. Those large-scale manufacturing businesses which remain in the UK are no longer huge employers of labour but are likely to have highly automated production techniques with a major emphasis on the identification and controlling of overheads for which the engineering method is not ideally suited.

Inspection of Accounts

Under this system the accountant and manager classify each item as wholly fixed, wholly variable, semi-variable or semi-fixed. This process is clearly subjective and different individuals might get different results even if the technical reasons for the alternative choices can be fully justified. This analysis might well be based on historical data; however, in decision making managers are dealing with the future, with all its complexities and uncertainties. In summary, inspection of accounts methods leads to arbitrary decisions and a consequent potential for lack of precision. As such its approach cannot be recommended for use in managerial decision making.

High–Low Method

This method consists of looking at the period of highest and lowest volumes of productive activity and comparing the cost changes that result from the two levels. This is illustrated by the following example:

	Lowest	**Highest**
Volume of production	10,000	20,000
Cost (£)	25,000	37,500

For these data

$$\text{Variable cost} = \frac{\text{Change in cost related to change in output}}{\text{Change in activity level}}$$

$$= \frac{£12,500}{10,000}$$

$$= £1.25 \text{ per unit}$$

and

$$\text{Fixed cost} = \text{Total cost} - (\text{Number of units} \times \text{Variable cost per unit})$$
$$= £25,000 - (10,000 \times £1.25)$$
$$= £12,500$$

This method assumes a straight line relationship between costs and output levels lying between the two observations. This may of course be incorrect as by taking extremes (the highest and lowest) these production levels and their associated cost behaviours may be atypical and thus unrepresentative. While the method may have the advantage of simplicity, it cannot be recommended.

Mathematical Methods

These methods centre on the technique of regression analysis. In their simplest form, the relevant costs and the related cost driver data can be plotted on a graph and a 'line of best fit' drawn in by eye. While this method is simple to use and provides a visual indicator of how costs depend on their driver, the process is subjective and can thus give different results.

The most appropriate method therefore is one involving mathematical equations, although today the development of packages such as Microsoft Excel makes it easier to manipulate the numbers. The process involves deriving a regression equation which is used to identify the relationship between cost (the dependent variable) and cost driver (the independent variable). This driver is an activity measure (number of direct labour hours, number of machine hours, etc.). The model can be adopted for use with a single independent variable (simple regression) or where there are two or more independent variables (multiple regression).

Table 5.1 shows maintenance costs and direct machine hours for the last 10 accounting periods for a company. It is assumed for the purpose of this exercise that maintenance costs are correlated with machine hours. Maintenance costs are the dependent variable (Y)

Table 5.1   Total maintenance costs and direct machine hours for the past
10 accounting periods

Accounting period	Direct machine hours X	Maintenance costs Y
1	990	2060
2	920	1980
3	690	1650
4	770	1710
5	860	2020
6	550	1750
7	450	1650
8	320	1660
9	250	1570
10	290	1680

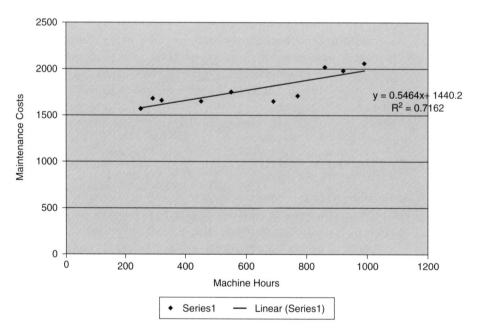

Figure 5.1   Graph of maintenance costs against direct machine hours

and machine hours the independent variable (X). While the graph based on the information
in this table in Figure 5.1 has been produced using Excel, what follows is the detail of the
calculation to show how the technique may be applied. Table 5.2 shows the regression calculations that would be performed by Excel to ultimately produce the graph discussed
later in this section.

Table 5.2   Regression analysis calculations

Direct machine hours X	Maintenance costs Y	X^2	XY
990	2,060	980,100	2,039,400
920	1,980	846,400	1,821,600
690	1,650	476,100	1,138,500
770	1,710	592,900	1,316,700
860	2,020	739,600	1,737,200
550	1,750	302,500	962,500
450	1,650	202,500	742,500
320	1,660	102,400	531,200
250	1,570	62,500	392,500
290	1,680	84,100	487,200
6,090	17,730	4,389,100	11,169,300

The regression line is the 'line of best fit' and is that line which when compared with other possible lines is that one which minimises the square of the vertical deviations from the observed points. The equations used are:

$$\Sigma y = na + b\Sigma x,$$

$$\Sigma xy = a\Sigma x + b\Sigma x^2.$$

In the above formula n is the number of observations, in this example 10. Substituting the data in Table 5.2,

$$17,730 = 10a + 6,090b,$$
$$11,169,300 = 6,090a + 4,389,100b.$$

Solving these equations results in an answer of $b = 0.55$ and $a = £1,440$, which naturally agrees with the result obtained using Excel.

This gives us an indication that at 770 hours of activity, maintenance costs are estimated at £1,863 (£1,440 + 0.55 × 770). In fact they were £1710 and, since the equation is based on an average, they do not match exactly and it is essential that managers in making a decision based on these data realise how reliable they are.

An indication of reliability is given by (amongst other possible measures) the coefficient of determination (r^2). This has been calculated by Excel at 0.7162. This means that we can explain 71.62% of the relationship between the two variables. The measure of the association between the two variables is referred to as correlation. The square root of the coefficient of determination is the correlation coefficient (r). The lower the value of the coefficient of determination the less the linear relationship. The closer to 1 the stronger the linear relationship. In this case 28% of the relationship is unexplained by the independent variable used. Managers would need to consider this when reaching decisions on how to use this relationship between the variables discovered by the analysis.

Other possible methods include the standard error of the estimate and the standard error of the coefficient (for a fuller explanation see Drury, 2004).

In the example above there was one dependent variable and *one* independent variable. In reality, a number of variables are likely to influence costs. In the case of machine maintenance it might include the frequency of the servicing intervals and not just hours of operation. Thus what is required is the identification and analysis of all variables which can affect cost. This leads to a multiple regression equation of the form

$$y = a + b_1 x_1 + b_2 x_2 + b_3 x_3 \ldots.$$

Again, various computer programs exist to solve such equations and report the degree of reliability managers can place on the results in terms of decisions based on the answer obtained. One further complication is that multiple regression assumes no correlation between the independent variables. This condition is called multicollinearity and prevents the availability of sufficient information to enable the regression coefficients to be determined, although writers such as Kaplan (1982) suggest this problem can be ignored in certain circumstances. To explain further, an example might include a company which manufactures a range of closely-related products where each product's output is treated as a separate variable, yet in reality, the demand for these products is highly correlated. In this situation, the regression coefficients would be meaningless and any predictions, based on the results obtained from a multiple regression analysis where such relationships exist, would be misleading and potentially dangerous as the wrong decisions could be made.

Finally in this section, we turn to the conditions for applying the techniques above, although they are common to any similar activity:

- Cost and activity data are matched so that they relate to the same period, otherwise we are not comparing like with like.
- Sufficient observations of cost behaviour are made to support the statistical analysis.
- When using data under conditions of inflation the observed costs should be adjusted to place them on the same price basis.
- Any technology changes should also be taken into account. This is known as the learning curve phenomenon.
- Known changes that will take place in the period for which the forecast is being made should be taken into account.
- Recognition should be given to those accounting policies which have the potential to distort the results. This particularly applies where fixed costs are allocated to production departments and as such may appear variable when it is known they are fixed.

Advances in Budgetary Techniques

In the previous chapter we looked at the general principles of the budget preparation process and the impact of the organisational context on budgeting requirements. In this section of this chapter we turn to look at advances in budgetary techniques.

Zero-Based Budgets

Traditional methods of budgeting have taken the current level of operating activity (the base) as the starting point and then adjusted this starting point for expected changes. As these changes are normally made at the margin of the existing budget and do not involve a fundamental review of the base budget, the term *incremental budgeting* is used to describe this process. In this context it can be seen that any inefficiencies in the base can be overlooked. Again we would, however, point out that many industries are under severe cost pressure so this may present a somewhat simplistic view of the world, and probably considerably more work goes on reviewing the base budget from the previous period than many textbooks appear to suggest.

The alternative solution presented to the problem of inefficiency in the base is termed zero-based budgeting (ZBB) or sometimes *priority-based budgeting*. As can be imagined, under this system each manager in charge of an authorised programme has to justify each item of expense as if the programme was totally new to the organisation. This solution would thus reject the concept of an existing base and raise issues over whether the function should be performed at all, how it should be performed, how much should it cost to perform and so on. Managers are thus constantly questioning the way in which an activity is delivered and if it is to the benefit of their organisation. Advantages of ZBB are as follows:

- ZBB allocates resources according to priorities which managers decide are essential or less essential.
- As budget allocations are related to business objectives, this results in resource allocation being improved.
- Managers, in having to defend their budgets, are forced to plan ahead and justify activities.
- Managers feel a greater sense of ownership as a result of the process.
- ZBB creates a questioning and critical attitude to processes and procedures amongst managers.
- Resources are allocated on the basis of need and benefits received in line with the objectives of the organisation.

The disadvantages of ZBB are:

- Other than in the smallest organisations, it is not possible from a time basis to constantly be reappraising activities.
- The organisation could lose sight of its strategic goals if its gets obsessed with 'navel gazing'.
- The bureaucracy of meetings and reports can overwhelm managers.
- In government organisations managers are locked into delivery of certain programmes by law, although this should not stop them questioning the methods of delivery to seek efficiencies.
- In some organisations activities are highly interlinked and difficult to separate. In a university, for example, staff could teach on a variety of courses, so closing one course may not achieve a great deal or may be completely impractical.

As a way of mitigating some of the disadvantages the organisation could target certain activities for a full review, such that over time it covers the organisation as a whole. This may work in certain cases. However, in complex organisations such as a university a decision to zero-base the budget of one school or department while ignoring others in forecasting a particular budget year sounds straightforward, but there can be many complex relationships with other schools or departments which again overwhelm managers in terms of the detail to be considered.

It should also be remembered that there are benefits to the incremental budgeting approach which can be ignored if a manager focuses on a single technique such as ZBB. One major advantage of incrementalism is that it can minimise conflict as it facilitates the consensus-produced bargain. It may trade some inefficiencies in that type of budget process for the greater benefit of goal congruence amongst managers. As can be imagined, a core feature of ZBB is the conflict between managers in the fight to gain scarce resources built in as a fundamental principle especially when people's behavioural characteristics are brought into consideration. Thus the qualitative gains of incrementalism in the areas of company harmony could outweigh any minor inefficiencies sacrificed through not using ZBB.

Option Budgets

A variation on ZBB that may add to the efficiency with which it can be made to operate is the use of option budgets. Under this system managers are required to consider how their department/service would respond to a 5% or 10% cut in expenditure (increases are equally possible). These options are designed to force managers to think through their policies and operating procedures by again forcing them to question what they do and how they do it.

Planned Programme Budget Systems

This is a public sector technique which gained some credence in the 1970s as a way forward. It is intended to be a fully rational and corporate system. In essence, it attempts to identify the goals and objectives of the organisation in each area of activity and analyse the results of activities against objectives within programmes. Activities are multidimensional and cross traditional departmental boundaries. They are also extend beyond the time period of a year. Thus the concentration is on programmes which encompass all organisational endeavours to achieve the specific outcomes that the programme is set up to deliver. Programmes are broken down into objectives, subobjectives and activities to make a coherent whole. A programme with an objective of delivering care and support for the elderly, for example, could have health care activities, accommodation activities, educational activities and so on with a range of complex objectives which together should add up to the overall programme objective.

As can be imagined this results in very demanding programme structures which cross traditional departmental boundaries. It is difficult to allocate activities to programmes, as some activities will contribute to objectives across a number of potential programmes. Coombs and Jenkins (2002: 93) point out that financial information is equally complex and leads to the allocation of joint costs over a number of programmes with a wide variety of allocation bases available. As a result of these issues, interest in the technique has faded.

Formula Budgets

Under the 1988 Education Reform Act in the UK the process of delegating budgets to schools was begun. After taking account of mandatory and discretionary retentions, the local authority is required to distribute what remains to schools through the use of a formula to give the individual school budget. The elements which the local authority can retain have been reduced over time, thereby transferring more of the education budget to schools.

The elements contained in the formula distribute money on the basis (as appropriate to the level of education provided by the school) of pupil numbers, sixth-form provision, school meals activities and the provision of nursery education. It is the job of the school and its governors to balance their expenditure against the funding distributed by the formula. It is this requirement to balance which places significant budget pressure on schools. It also impacts on quality in that if a school can, for example, drive up its examination results it can attract pupils in, and with extra pupils come more resources. This effectively introduces to some effect an element of the market system in the budget process for schools. There may, however, be a time lag between attracting any extra pupils and gaining extra resources, as the school still operates within the local authority budgeting time framework. Control at the local level is increased as the school has its own bank account and therefore increased ownership and control of its delegated budget.

Activity-Based Cost Management

In contrast to the traditional ways of reporting budgets, activity-based cost management attempts to critically assess costs by activity and to provide managers with information on why costs are incurred in any process (see also the discussion of activity-based costing in Chapter 3). It also aims to look at the output from that activity. The process concentrates on cost drivers and divides activities into value-added activities and non-value-added activities. By concentrating on non-value-added activities it is possible in the budget process to reduce these without impacting on the customer's use of the product or service. Managers are thus able to prioritise where they should be reducing waste and inefficiency.

Under the traditional approach to budgeting, costs are allocated against subjective (i.e. judgemental) headings – payroll, premises costs, transport and so on. As has been stated above, there is no information linking costs with outcomes from the expenditure. Under activity-based budgets major activities are linked to the resource inputs. In summary, the process is as follows:

- Identify and define activities and activity pools.
- Directly trace costs to activities and cost objects where possible.
- Assign costs to activity cost pools.
- Calculate activity rates.
- Assign costs to cost objects using the activity rates and activity measures.
- Prepare necessary reports.

The organisation is now in a position to focus on managing activities as a way of eliminating waste and reducing delays and defects. This information can be used to directly improve the budgeting and budgetary control processes.

Benchmarking provides a structured approach to identifying the activities with the greatest room for improvement. In the public sector, for example, many organisations have formed 'benchmark clubs' as a source of information to identify waste and inefficiency. In the private sector trade associations exist to help ensure that efficiency gains can be achieved but within a confidential information-gathering process. This is not to ignore the information that a company can itself generate over time and can access at a particular point in the budget decision cycle. By examining the number of times a particular activity is set up or the number of engineering changes, attention is focused on areas where a detailed study may reduce the volume of such activities and consequently costs.

Within this process, value chain analysis, which links sets of activities from the beginning of the production process through to the end use of the product or service, is becoming the increasing focus of attention. If each activity in that process is viewed as a customer–supplier relationship all opinions can be used to improve that process so that budgets reflect optimum opinions. It should be recognised that we are stressing cost management as being the key, rather than cost imposition on products and services.

Balanced Scorecard

The objective of the balanced scorecard is to express an organisation's strategy and mission in a comprehensive set of range of performance measures which provides a framework for implementing strategy. It inevitably provides a framework against which performance against those measures can be tested over time. It is important to recognise that such a framework is based on measures other than financial. The balanced scorecard is made up by setting four key perspectives – finance, customers, internal business processes, and learning and growth, although variations are possible. Figure 5.2 shows the balanced scorecard performance matrix for an administrative unit and defines the key areas as: people, to develop and enable people to progress; processes, to aim for continuous improvement; resources, to use them wisely; and, service, to respond to the needs of customers. The concept is relatively straightforward to implement:

- Staff from each frontline unit identify the goals that are most critical to their unit's success.
- They then devise a measure ('metric') to track the unit's performance at achieving each of these goals.

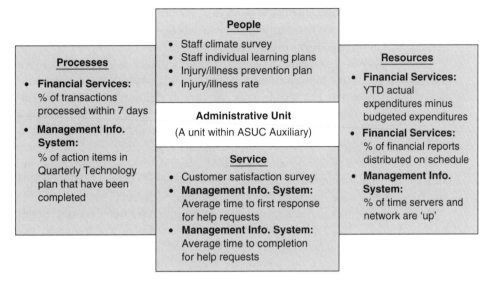

People
- Staff climate survey
- Staff individual learning plans
- Injury/illness prevention plan
- Injury/illness rate

Processes
- **Financial Services:**
  % of transactions
  processed within 7 days
- **Management Info.
  System:**
  % of action items in
  Quarterly Technology
  plan that have been
  completed

Administrative Unit
(A unit within ASUC Auxiliary)

Service
- Customer satisfaction survey
- **Management Info. System:**
  Average time to first response
  for help requests
- **Management Info. System:**
  Average time to completion
  for help requests

Resources
- **Financial Services:**
  YTD actual
  expenditures minus
  budgeted expenditures
- **Financial Services:**
  % of financial reports
  distributed on schedule
- **Management Info.
  System:**
  % of time servers and
  network are 'up'

Figure 5.2   Balanced scorecard (University of California – Business and Administrative Services)

- The result is staff have created a set of metrics under each of the core values which is referred to as the unit's balanced scorecard.
- Finally staff assess progress over time and revise as necessary.

In this example it is these core values which drive the organisation and, taken together, they point out virtually all things the organisation must do to be successful. Each of the work units is seen as achieving success by putting the organisation's core values into practice and tracking achievement through the metrics.

The term 'balance' arises from the desire to balance quantitative and qualitative performance measures in both the short term and long term. The scorecard is an attempt to reduce managers' concentration on short-term changes by emphasising the longer-term consequences. An emphasis on expenditure in a particular function in the short term is planned to lead to improvements in non-financial measures such as customer satisfaction which will lead to growth in long-term sales and income.

Let us examine the four elements in more detail. The *financial* perspective could examine the profitability of following a particular strategy. Many businesses aim to reduce costs in comparison with their competitors, or to utilise spare capacity. Target performance would be set in financial terms for each of these strategies to measure their effect on the bottom line, with initiatives to achieve the strategies. This would be expressed in financial terms so that actual performance can be compared with plan.

The *customer* perspective identifies the target market segments and measures the company's success in each area. An objective might be to increase market share. For a multi-product company this could be expressed in terms of increasing a particular segment. For a company such as Sony this might be to increase the share of the plasma TV market. Target performance could then be expressed as a percentage increase in market share as measured against actual performance in due course.

The *business processes* (internal) would be identified, such as improving the yield from the raw materials input into a particular manufacturing process. Specific initiatives would be identified to do this and a percentage increase in yield set as a target. Again actual results could be compared with the target. Targets could be set by benchmarking against competitors. Improvements in the operational process could benefit customers through better quality or improved delivery times, while the bottom line would also improve.

The *learning and growth* perspective would include developing skills through measures such as improved training, with target numbers set to benefit from the training. This could be extended to include improved manufacturing processes and enhanced IT.

While presented above as separate paragraphs, each of the processes is linked as improved training could improve operational business practices which leads to better customer relationships and finally to a better financial position. It should also be remembered that each company, even if operating in the same industry, would have a different scorecard depending on its own strategy and assessment. Finally, by invoking a balanced scorecard process we should be involving more people in the company, potentially improving motivation and a feeling of 'belonging' to the process.

The balance scorecard is equally appropriate for use in the public and not-for-profit sectors and is discussed further in Chapter 10.

Business Process Re-engineering

This area concentrates on making substantial changes (or re-engineering) to the business processes which operate within an organisation. Within the business process will be a series of activities which make up that process. The objective is to concentrate on improvement such that the business sees cost reduction, quality improvement and increased customer satisfaction. This can be seen as one element of a balanced scorecard or an activity in its own right.

Economic Value-Added Analysis

Economic value-added analysis aims to measure the value created for shareholders by a business unit or company. The objective is that these have an ability to earn more than the cost of capital, and the framework provided allows firms to assess various options to increase value to shareholders. Trade-offs between reinvesting in existing businesses, investing in new businesses and returning cash to the shareholders can be compared. In this process the cost of capital is highly visible to managers and attention can be focused on making investment decisions which are in the best interests of stockholders. This means that attention is also focused on the disposal of or, improvement in the use of, underutilised assets.

The elements of the technique are the following:

- Determination of income generated by a new business and the extra value created by the potential investment opportunity.
- Estimation of the return required by shareholders. This requires a calculation of the cost of capital.
- Determination of the economic value added of each business. This is achieved by deducting the expected return to the shareholders from the value created by the firm or business unit by the new project. This return has to be above that required by shareholders for the investment to take place. This analysis is claimed by its proponents to be suitable for one-off major investment decisions or everyday decision making in an enterprise.

Beyond Budgeting

A view is emerging that annual budgeting tends to fix a company's thinking and response to events when the world is changing. This limits flexibility in responding to these events. There is an argument that the budget in effect reflects the previous year's reality, and this is what locks companies and managers into the past rather than thinking about what is happening to the business in the present. Rolling or perhaps monthly forecasting and budgets focus thinking on current and future realities and contexts. This is not seen as managing change as this is outside the control of the organisation, but rather as an attempt to be ahead of change or more in control of the response to the challenges facing the organisation. This importance may be emphasised in the knowledge-based economies that the western world has increasingly developed. Knowledge-based companies face competition which detracts from any innovation made particularly in respect of the time horizon for the life of products, which is becoming shorter and shorter. Prices are also falling and quality rising. Firms need to be operating at the excellent end of the quality spectrum if they are to continue to flourish and be close to their customers. Managers are also talented people in short supply. This type of individual seeks freedom, challenge and responsibility. Traditional time-consuming and 'legalistic' budget processes can be off-putting for such persons. The rapid production of new solutions to constantly changing issues in the competitive environment and strategies also depends on attracting and retaining such individuals.

In this view of the world the traditional budget is seen as the fixed point around which all management processes are based and aligned. This determines how managers behave and the activities and objectives on which they focus. Annual budgeting is seen as absorbing considerable management time, and the monthly budget actual comparisons as primarily about control. Managers will not exceed their budgets by perhaps spending necessary resources outside the planned budget cycle to react to events because their bonus or even their jobs will depend on it. This, in a globally competitive world where, when the budget was set, circumstances were entirely different from those pertaining when any comparisons are being made and decisions required. Inflexibility is thus seen as the key failing of traditional budgeting and companies are being urged to move towards continuous rolling forecasting to enable speedy and co-ordinated adaptations to actual and anticipated changes in the business environment.

Under rolling monthly forecasts of financial performance and for other non-financial value drivers, managers are forced to confront current and future opportunities and risks. In essence, the beyond budgeting model calls for devolving managerial responsibility where power and responsibility go hand in hand. The system:

- creates and fosters a performance climate based on competitive success. Goals are agreed external benchmarks and not internal negotiated fixed targets. The focus is on beating the competition not other managers for a slice of resources.
- motivates people by giving them challenges, responsibilities and clear values as guidelines. Rewards are team-based, recognising that no single person can act alone to achieve goals.
- devolves performance responsibilities to operational management closer to the 'coal face'. This uses know-how from the individuals and teams at the customer front to adapt quickly to changing market needs.
- empowers operational managers to act by giving them the capability to do so by removing resource constraints. Key ratios are set rather than detailed line by line budgets. Local access to resources is thus based on agreed parameters rather than on line by line budget authorisations. This is aimed at speeding up the response to changing threats and exploiting new opportunities as quickly as possible.
- establishes customer-orientated teams that are accountable for profitable customer outcomes. Frontline units agree resource and service requirements with service units and standards of service from these departments (service level agreements).
- creates transparent and open information systems throughout the organisation. The information system should provide fast, open and distributed information for multi-level control. The IT system is crucial in flexing the key performance indicators as part of the rolling forecasting process.

It can be seen that the above represents a private sector view of the world; the legal framework of public sector organisations would probably prevent such a system being extended to them. As with all alternatives, the success of a particular process depends on the needs of the individual organisation. The alternative of 'beyond budgeting' places considerable emphasis on organisational and managerial cultural changes, and without these it is doomed to failure.

Just-in-Time Stock Control and Production Systems

It will have been gathered from what has just been said that there have been tremendous changes in the business environment. These changes show no sign of slowing down – if anything, the pace of change is quickening. Companies have had to react or cease trading. One of the reactions to change has been to use just-in-time (JIT) stock (inventory) control systems. An example of a company which use such methods is Toyota, although it is common among other car-producing companies. In this type of organisation the management view is that holding stock is a waste of a resource and should be minimised through careful planning throughout the supply chain. One obvious saving is the gains in interest earned (or saved on the bank overdraft) through not having money tied up in stock. Other benefits include reduction in handling costs, reduced risks of obsolescence of stock, increased production space available and reduced stockholding-related security costs. There may be a reduction in suppliers, saving in paperwork and time, although often there will be a substantial time commitment invested in the supply chain to ensure everyone is fully aware of the objectives of each party.

JIT production systems are systems where each component is produced immediately it is needed in the next stage of production of a product. Production is thus triggered by demand. At the end of the line is the customer asking for finished product, and it is the request for supply which triggers everything back to an order for raw materials. Traditional systems tended to be push-through systems in that the budget would predict that a certain level of sales and production occurred, thus building up stocks of raw materials, work in progress and finished goods.

Features of JIT include:

- production organised in work units or cells;
- multi-skilled workers who can perform a variety of tasks and operations;
- emphasis on total quality management (TQM) to eliminate defects as such defects disrupt the planned time cycles and even shut down production altogether;
- reduced lead and set-up times;
- careful selection of suppliers who deliver on time and to the required quality;
- a claimed reduction in paperwork.

TQM, referred to above, is a system designed to continuously improve quality through focusing on customer needs and systematic problem solving through teams involving frontline workers. If a worker in a production unit or cell discovers a quality problem the production line is halted until the problem is solved. JIT creates an urgency to solve the problem as delays are now costly as there are no (or minimal) buffer stocks to call on. Energies are thus concentrated on:

- identifying in a systematic manner what has gone wrong and planning to avoid it happening again (planning stage);
- implementing corrective action (perhaps on a small scale first) to prevent it happening again (doing stage);
- evaluating the results of the change in practice (checking stage);
- assessing that the problem has now been solved and, if relevant, extend the agreed solution to the whole system (action stage).

It should be remembered that JIT is not confined to manufacturing industry but is relevant to hospitals and even accounting practices (service sector) through the focus on the customer. In terms of a service industry such as accounting, an important element of TQM is the customer satisfaction survey.

Conclusions

This chapter has:

- used and developed specific non-quantitative techniques to estimate costs;
- examined the quantitative techniques used as a way of estimating costs;
- discussed the interpretation of the results of analysis in the context of advice to management;
- outlined advances in budgetary techniques and their influences in new organisational environments;
- reviewed a selection of contemporary management accounting approaches and techniques;
- developed an appreciation of the role and philosophy of just-in-time systems in the modern business environment.

Summary

The first part of this chapter pointed out that while the identification of cost and cost behaviour appears to be relatively straightforward in theory, it is far more complex in reality. Various methods were explored to help managers identify how costs behave, although each has its limitations. The second part of the chapter explored various advances in budgeting techniques to indicate how the forces of change unleashed by an increasingly competitive world were compelling a variety of responses in both private and public sector organisations. A range of these techniques were explored to allow the reader to gain a broad understanding of the key issues associated with the techniques.

Recommended Further Reading

Burns, J. (2000) 'The dynamics of accounting change – interplay between new practices, routines, institutions, power and politics', *Accounting, Auditing and Accountability,* **13(5): 566–596.**

In this paper the author looks at a small chemicals manufacturer (Becks) located in the North of England. The company had suffered severe cash-flow problems and consequently needed to move towards a results-orientated approach to decision making and control. This approach was supported by new accounting practices imposed by the managing director and locally developed accounting solutions by financially aware departmental managers. There were still issues about the adoption of the approach particularly in the product development department (PDD); which was widely seen as doing science simply for its own sake and not for the benefit of the organisation. There were weak, or non-existent, controls in this department over product development and innovation. The primary focus of the paper is how the dynamics of accounting change in a unique organisational setting interacted with organisational culture. Thus the paper is concerned with how and why accounting change evolves in the way it does, through time and within the organisational context.

The company was established in the 1970s; by 1995 there were 150 employees and turnover was £20 million. The economic recession of the late 1980s saw demand fall significantly, and productive capacity became considerably underutilised. Bankruptcy loomed. This cash-flow crisis, which was caused by primarily external factors, created recognition for and stimulated the need to change. Much of the company's traditional business was in so-called 'captives' companies locked in by period contracts. As the external market for chemicals changed these organisations failed to renew contracts, creating considerably underutilised capacity. The bank was unwilling to extend the overdraft, forcing the company to seek alternative sources of finance. The marketing department stated the experience was 'like a Siberian wind blowing straight through you' making the company realise that 'it was a small and very vulnerable business' (p. 575).

In addition to revising other strategies, greater emphasis was placed on developing new products internally. This affected the PDD in that it had to develop more products which could be sold successfully within more acceptable timescales. The board felt, given legal issues, that product costs could not readily be reduced and an alternative sales and market focus was needed. Production costs had already been cut as much as possible.

Becks wished to see the PDD recognising its profit role. New accounting techniques were introduced to increase awareness of profitability and to prioritise new products which could be brought to market faster. Scientific expertise was thus supplemented by attempting to develop accounting ways of thinking about profit and cost. This required new reports and reporting processes. Analysis was thus required to establish the basis from which the results-orientated approach could be developed. The initial investigation revealed that about 50–60% of time was spent on research (primary tasks) and 40–50% on administration (secondary tasks). Only one product which had been developed in the period of study was seen as making an acceptable return. The change in approach saw chemicals, yields and products being expressed in terms of 'pound notes' (p. 578). This included emphasis on start and finish dates, hours devoted to the project, costs, technical difficulty of the process, and so on. A target of 75% of scientific time on primary tasks was set. In this process the managing director drove change through the exercise of power within the company. This was backed by his accounting expertise. The essence of such challenges to the PDD was to translate technical scientific feedback at board level into recognition of what the PDD was contributing to profit and results. The paper claims that through the skilful manipulation of accounting terms the board was convinced of the need for and desirability of new accounting.

In the context of this chapter the paper illustrates that the mobilisation of power is needed to effect change, even where such change is essential for the survival of the organisation. Such power was mobilised following a crisis caused by external factors. Interestingly, despite this process the PDD still maintained its traditional ways of thinking, although presumably in a more questioning, results-orientated environment. In this context, as the paper concludes, accounting change is not 'the end' but part of the process.

Case Study: Tuba Accessories

Tuba Accessories produces a standard navigation system for motor vehicles. Its assembly department is largely mechanised and most of the costs of the department are produced by the two overhead support centres – assembly support and machine service.

You are the assistant to the manager of the assembly department, Charlie Cregan.

Each department is evaluated by comparing its actual costs with its flexed budget. This comparison is effected on a monthly basis through the year. The differences between the actual expenditure and the flexed budget are referred to as 'operational cost variances' by the company. Each department is responsible for investigating its own operational cost variances and, each month, the manager of each department has to make a presentation of findings and remedial action in a senior management meeting that is chaired by Alastair Graham, the company's managing director.

During the past 12 months the assembly department's cost variances have been negative in most months and its manager has regularly attributed this to the inaccurate budgeting of overhead costs. However, Alastair Graham has not been convinced by this argument because Charlene O'Donaghue, the management accountant, has stressed that the method of predicting overheads is based on the current methodology used in manufacturing companies.

The assembly manager is very keen to establish whether there is a better basis for projecting the overhead budgets for the next 12 months and, knowing that you have studied accountancy at university, has asked you to undertake an investigation of the current system and to examine alternative approaches.

Month	Units produced	Assembly support costs (£000)	Machine service costs (£000)
1	8000	37.9	70
2	7400	33.8	66.9
3	7000	30.5	65.1
4	6500	33.9	63.2
5	6200	32.4	61.2
6	8000	39.3	70.1
7	5000	28.2	56.2
8	4300	26.6	53.5
9	6200	33.8	61.2
10	8200	39.4	71.1
11	8000	38.1	70.3
12	9200	41.5	76.5

Your first step was to collect data for the last 12 months for the assembly department and the machine service department. These data have been summarised on page 142.

Your next step was to speak to Charlene O'Donaghue about the method used by her department for predicting overheads. A summary of her response is as follows:

> The predicting of overheads in manufacturing companies such as Tuba is difficult and also very important because overheads constitute a high proportion of total costs. We have considered an activity-based cost (ABC) approach and employed a consultant to conduct a feasibility study for us. However, his recommendation was that there would be little positive financial return compared with the costs of installing, implementing and updating an ABC system. The single-product nature of Tuba's output strongly influenced his recommendation, with which I concur.
>
> I have also considered an engineering approach to determine the overhead component of product costs. Discussion with our engineers has shown this to be a practical and highly accurate method of budgeting the direct cost elements of our navigation system. However, they can see no way of transferring this approach to overheads within the company.
>
> The approach that we have adopted for the past three years is as follows. We treat each overhead department separately. For each department we identify the highest and lowest monthly output and cost for the previous year and we use this information to estimate the fixed cost and variable cost per measure of output for each department. We do this by simply comparing the change in cost with the change in output which allows us to calculate the variable cost per unit of output. It's a short step to calculate the fixed cost. If necessary, we then apply inflation in order to uplift the costs. This has the advantage of simplicity and can be readily understood by all managers. We regard this as very important, not least because the managers are being evaluated by comparing the budgets (based on cost estimation) with the actual expenditure incurred by their departments.
>
> I am pleased that you are interested in this problem and I would be happy to discuss any further issues with you.

From your university studies you recall that regression can be used in cost estimation. You are also aware that it need to be used with care. Consequently, you decide to investigate whether regression analysis can make a contribution to cost estimation within Tuba Accessories.

(a) Carry out a regression analysis, for each department and summarise your results.

(b) Explain the main features of the regression analysis output and, making use of the output, explain the relevance to cost estimation of each of the following: correlation coefficients; R^2; standard error; 95% confidence limits; residuals.

(c) Using graph paper for each pair of dependent/independent variables, draw scatter graphs and also draw in both regression lines using the regression results from your output in (a) above.

(d) For the next month (month 5) the predicted output is 6800 units. Provide a forecast of the predicted costs of both assembly support and machine service at a 95% confidence level.

(e) Carry out a high–low analysis for both departments. Predict costs using this approach and compare your results with the results of the regression programme in (d) above.

(f)   Explain the major limitations with regard to the use of regression analysis in cost estimation in Tuba Accessories.

(g)   You are to make two presentations of your results: first, to the company's management accountant; and second, to a group of senior managers which is chaired by the managing director. What alternative approaches might you adopt in presenting your results to these two parties?

Questions

1.   Trent PLC produces a single product. Currently, the company is attempting to improve the way it estimates its manufacturing overheads. The following information has been collected for the last 12 months, and one independent variable has been identified as a key cost driver – direct labour hours (DLH):

Month	Overhead (£000s)	DLH (000s)
1	10	4
2	12	6
3	14	7
4	11	6
5	9	4
6	8	3
7	8	3.5
8	9	4
9	10	5
10	11	5
11	12	6
12	15	7

The following calculations are provided:

$$\Sigma Y = 129, \quad \Sigma X = 60.5, \quad \Sigma XY = 682, \quad \Sigma X^2 = 325.25, \quad \Sigma Y^2 = 1441.$$

Using regression analysis, estimate, for manufacturing overheads, the fixed cost and variable cost per direct labour hour. Use your model to estimate the cost at 4000 direct labour hours.

2.   Extra Accessories produces a navigation system for motor vehicles. Its assembly department is largely mechanised and most of the costs of the department are produced by the two overhead support centres – assemby support and machine service. Each department is evaluated by comparing its actual costs with its flexed

budget. During the past 12 months, the assembly department's cost variances have been negative in most months and its manager attributes this to the inaccurate budgeting of overhead support costs. The assembly manager is very keen to establish a better basis for projecting the budgets for the next 12 months and has asked you to undertake a cost investigation as a basis for improved budgetary preparation.

Your first step was to collect data for the last 12 months for the overhead support departments:

Month	Units produced	Assembly support costs £000	Machine service costs £000
1	8000	37.9	70
2	7400	33.8	66.9
3	7000	30.5	65.1
4	6500	33.9	63.2
5	6200	32.4	61.2
6	8000	39.3	70.1
7	5000	28.2	56.2
8	4300	26.6	53.5
9	6200	33.8	61.2
10	8200	39.4	71.1
11	8000	38.1	70.3
12	9200	41.5	76.5

You have carried out regression analysis on each pair of dependent/independent variables and the results are as follows:

Dependent variable	Independent variable: Units produced	
	Assembly support costs	Machine service costs
R	0.939	0.998
R^2	0.882	0.996
a	£12,830	£32,608
b	£3.11	£4.69

(a)   For next month the expected output is 6800 units. Provide cost forecasts for both departments at that level of output.

(b)   Using the high–low method, determine the fixed costs and unit variable costs for both overhead support departments and project total costs for both departments when 6800 units are produced.

(c) Explain why the estimates obtained in (a) and (b) above are different.

(d) Discuss three limitations with regard to the use of regression in cost estimation.

3. Carveri Brown is a leading manufacturer of navigational fins. It currently adopts a subjective approach to classifying overheads into their fixed and variable elements for purposes of cost estimation. It is not entirely satisfied with its current approach and is looking for a more scientific way of estimating costs.

For each of the last 12 months it has collected the following data: monthly production overhead costs; monthly machine hours; and monthly output. The data have been input into a computer package which has produced the following regression statistics:

- Using *monthly machine hours* as the independent variable and production overhead costs as the dependent variable:

$$y = -500 + 1.2x, \qquad r^2 = 0.96, \qquad n = 12.$$

- Using *monthly output* as the independent variable and production overhead costs as the dependent variable:

$$y = 500 + 4.9x \qquad r^2 = 0.94, \qquad n = 12.$$

(a) Calculate each independent variable's estimate of production overheads in a month when 5000 machine hours will be used to produce 1000 fins.

(b) Comment on the relative value of each of these independent variables to cost estimation in this case.

(c) Identify five limitations of regression in cost estimation and explain carefully why each is a limitation.

4. Explain why a standard costing system may be less useful in the following manufacturing environments:

(a) just-in-time manufacturing.

(b) total quality management.

5. The use of incremental budgeting processes may lead to the carry-forward of inefficiencies in organisations. Examine the contribution of each of the following in improving efficiency in such organisations:

(a) zero-based budgets.

(b) planned programme budget systems.

Chapter 6
MANAGEMENT ACCOUNTING AND THE CONTROL PROCESS – 1

Key Learning Objectives

By the time you have finished studying this chapter, you should be able to:
- explain the nature of organisational control;
- understand the key nature of control information;
- prepare flexible budgets for control;
- calculate standard costs and variances for purposes of control;
- examine the interpretation of variances and other control data.

The Nature of Organisation Control

This section looks at two aspects of control: the control process itself and feedback concepts.

The Control Process

You have seen in the previous two chapters that all organisations need to engage in planning. Planning is essential in order to achieve the objectives of the organisation. These objectives can be very diverse, and examples are: to achieve a target profit for the year, to manufacture 25,000 items in a year, and to teach 300 students in the period from September to June.

Plans that are stated in money or financial terms are called budgets. Therefore a company will have a profit budget, a factory will have a production budget and a school will have a teacher budget.

Many organisations will also have a multi-year budget, say a three-year budget. The detailed annual budget will form the first year of this three-year period. The budget rolls forward through time, with the second year becoming the first year as another year is added in to make the third year.

The budget sets out in financial terms what the organisation plans to achieve in the forthcoming year. It is essential if the organisation is to succeed and represents an important first step on the road to success. The organisation should follow this up by checking on progress regularly in order to achieve its goals by the year's end. This process of regular checking is termed *management control*. Management control has two important aspects:

- There must be a regular (e.g. monthly) comparison of the budget against what is actually achieved.
- Having made such a comparison, managers must make the necessary changes to ensure that any underachievement can be corrected and the budget achieved.

Feedback Concepts

The process of comparing plans against actual output and expenditure is termed *feedback*. It has two different dimensions. *Feedback control* is the process of looking back in time and comparing the budget against actions. This is a regular and recurring process so that every month, say, the budget is compared with actual outcomes. An example of a feedback statement is shown in Table 6.1. This statement is for the third month in the university's financial year, which commences on 1 August. It shows in the second, third and fourth columns the cumulative figures for the first three months of the year. The variance shows the difference between budget and actual; as actual expenditure exceeds budget, this is signified by the letter A for 'adverse'. The last three columns show the figures for the month of October; October is the third and most recent month. Of the cumulative variance of £10,400 adverse, £2000 was generated in October. As you can see, the statement looks backwards and is an example of feedback control; by informing the head of department of the significant overspending on salaries, it should lead to investigation of the problem and to steps to correct the situation.

For a feedback system to operate effectively there is a need for:

- objectives for the period that can be quantified;
- outputs for the period that can be compared with the objectives;
- a reporting system that effectively compares the objectives and the outputs;
- the capacity to take action if objectives and outputs are not the same.

Table 6.1   Expenditure control statement for a university department

Expenditure head	Cumulative budget £	Cumulative expenditure £	Cumulative variance £	October Budget £	October Exp. £	October variance £
Salaries	150,000	160,400	10,400 A	50,000	52,000	2000 A

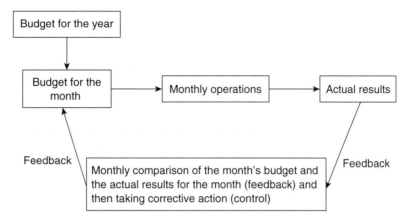

Figure 6.1   Feedback control loop

The feedback control loop in Figure 6.1 illustrates this diagrammatically:

- The budget for the month is derived from the budget for the year so that the annual objective is broken down into monthly objectives.
- Feedback involves monitoring the actual results for the period by comparing them against the budget for the period and identifying differences.
- If the differences require action then control involves carrying out that action. It may be necessary to take action to improve operations so that they are more effective next month. Alternatively, action on the budget itself may be required if, for example, material prices have increased significantly since the start of the year, rendering the budget out of date.

Feed-forward control involves trying to predict outputs against desired outputs. An example is the monthly cash budget. If this shows that a negative cash balance is likely to occur in a specific month, it alerts management who can then try to take preventative action by rephasing expenditure or by ensuring that overdraft facilities will be in place. So, feed-forward control is about trying to take action before an event occurs in order to influence the sequence of events.

Feed-forward control attempts to take corrective action before an event, whereas feedback control takes corrective action after the event. But, sometimes it will prove impossible to predict problems, however refined the forecasting process. It has been pointed out by Lyne (1995) that the development of a predictive model requires more than technical proficiency. He argues that in order to get the individuals to perform at a predicted level of activity, it is necessary to know how those individuals are motivated. Lyne's article is summarised at the end of this chapter. We will return to the issue of motivation later in this chapter and in the next.

Information for Control

This section considers the issues of summarising information and qualities of control information.

Summarising Information

The control system consists of layers of feedback systems, each of which involves summarising lower-level reports. In this process, information is lost. Figure 6.2 illustrates this process, showing how information is summarised or filtered. The head of the Machine Department sees a detailed performance report for that department as this is the manager's responsibility. However, the factory manager has to oversee the management of the factory and the three production departments. In consequence, the factory manager sees a summarised report of each department's performance. At a higher level of summary, the managing director is responsible for three factories, finance and marketing and receives a summarised report on each factory. The information has to be summarised in this fashion in order to make it manageable. However, at each stage of summarisation, information is lost; one consequence of the system may be to conceal important detailed information from top management.

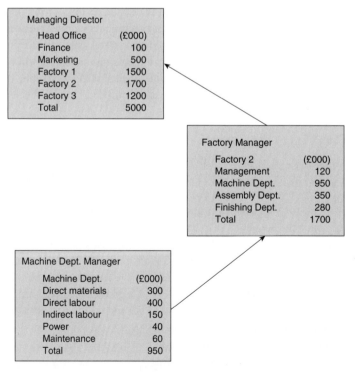

Figure 6.2   The information summarising process

Qualities of Control Information

The summarised reports in Figure 6.2 would form the focus for the preparation of control information. For such information to be effective and be valuable to the user, it should meet the following criteria:

- *Timeliness*. The information should be made available by a certain date. For example, the monthly control statement should be provided by, at most, a week after month's end in order to give the appropriate manager time to use the information in the most effective way.
- *Clarity*. The user should be able to read and assimilate the information quickly. The information should be clear and unambiguous, avoiding unnecessarily complex technical terminology. Clarity is assisted by the use of subtotals, totals and the use of graphs. Superfluous detail may be sacrificed.
- *Succinctness*. Information should not be excessive as this will waste the manager's time. There should be communication between providers and users of information to determine what the latter require.
- *Relevance*. The information should be relevant to the requirements of the user. Although the information should be succinct, it should also be complete so that the user does not need to access other sources of information. The provision of irrelevant information is unhelpful to the user.
- *Accuracy*. If the statement lacks accuracy, this may embarrass the user and lead to a loss of confidence in the information. However, not every manager needs the same level of accuracy. In Figure 6.2, the assembly manager will need much more detailed information about the different elements of the Assembly Department than will the managing director.
- *Cost-effectiveness*. The benefit to the user manager must exceed the cost of providing the information.

If these criteria are followed, user managers will gain confidence in the control information and this may assist in raising the profile and prestige of the management accounting function.

Fixed and Flexible Budgets

This section considers:

- the different objectives of fixed and flexible budgets;
- the benefits of flexible budgets;
- the preparation of flexible budgets;
- the calculation of variances from flexible budgets.

Fixed Budgets

Chapters 4 and 5 introduced you to budgets and budgeting. The budgets discussed were fixed budgets. A fixed budget is one that is based on one level of output; it is not usually changed after it is agreed. The fixed budget is used for planning purposes. The budgeted profit and loss account, budgeted balance sheet and cash budget constitute the highest level of fixed budgets and together may be termed the master budget. The master budget, including the budgeted net profit, will be discussed by and approved by the board of directors. Once approved by the board, the master budget becomes officially the company's target for the forthcoming financial year.

Flexible Budgets

A flexible budget is designed to change as the underlying volume of activity changes. It does this by considering the factors that cause costs to change as the volume of activity changes. Flexible budgets have two principal benefits:

- They allow the firm to project outcomes, including key variables such as profit, at different levels of activity. This is useful if the firm is unsure about some key issues, such as the potential sales for the year. A firm may also engage in 'what if' or sensitivity analysis in order to determine the impact on profitability and cash of changes in key variables such as sales, production and costs.
- They can be used for feedback control after the actual costs for a specific period have been determined. There can be valuable control information if the actual costs for a period are compared with the flexed budget for the period rather than with the fixed budget. The following illustration demonstrates this.

	Fixed budget for June	Actual data for June
Output	3,000 units	3,500 units
Production costs		
Variable costs (£, at £3 per unit)	9,000	10,400
Fixed costs (£)	10,000	10,000

First we will consider the comparison of the actual data with the fixed budget and then with a flexible budget. Comparison with the fixed budget for June gives the results shown in Table 6.2.

The cost variance is calculated by subtracting the actual costs from the budgeted costs. If the actual costs exceed the budget, this is termed an adverse variance as it increases costs over budget. On the other hand, if budget exceeds actual, this is termed a favourable variance. In this case, we have an adverse variance of £1,400. However, as can be seen,

Table 6.2   Comparison with a fixed budget

	Fixed budget	Actuals	Variances
Output	3,000 units	3,500 units	
Costs			
Variable costs (£)	9,000	10,400	1,400 Adverse
Fixed costs (£)	10,000	10,000	0
Totals (£)	19,000	20,400	1,400 Adverse

Table 6.3   Comparison with a flexible budget

	Flexible budget	Actuals	Variances
Output	3,500 units	3,500 units	
Costs			
Variable costs (£, at £3 per unit in the flexible budget)	10,500	10,400	100 Favourable
Fixed costs (£)	10,000	10,000	0
Totals (£)	20,500	20,400	100 Favourable

the variance arises because output is 500 units more than the budget; it would be expected that the variable costs of producing 3500 units exceeds the budgeted variable cost of producing 3000 units. In this situation, a better comparison is between the actual costs and a flexible budget. The flexible budget restates the fixed budget for June, making allowance for the actual output of 3500 units and the actual costs of producing 500 more units. This is demonstrated in Table 6.3.

Comparison with a flexible budget for 3500 units demonstrates that in June the actual costs are less than the flexed budget, and this is reflected by the £100 favourable variance.

The Development of Flexible Budgets

In order to develop flexible budgets, we need to understand the way that costs behave. Direct costs (direct labour and direct materials) will often have a linear relationship with output, so that costs double as output doubles. At the other end of the cost spectrum, fixed costs such as rent and managerial salaries are unlikely to change as volume changes. You read in Chapter 2 that some fixed costs increase in a step cost fashion. An example is foremen's salaries that double when a factory moves from a single-shift system to a two-shift system. Other indirect costs such as power may be semi-variable in nature, reflecting an annual standing charge and a variable cost element that is related to the amount of power consumed.

We will now give an example to demonstrate the construction of a flexible budget. Using the following information, we will produce flexible budgets for the production of 3000, 6000 and 9000 units:

Variable costs
Direct material A   £4 per unit of output
Direct material B   £1.50 per unit of output

Semi-variable costs:	Output	Costs (£)
	3,000	13,000
	5,000	19,000
	8,000	28,000
	10,000	34,000

Fixed overhead:	Output	Costs (£)
	0–4,000	25,000
	4,001–8,000	35,000
	8,001–12,000	47,000

The first task is to segregate the different elements of the semi-variable overheads. This involves the use of the technique termed the 'high-low' method, which you met in Chapter 5. It involves the selection of the lowest and highest levels of output and costs, calculating the differences between them, and uses this information to identify the variable costs.

	Output	Costs (£)
High	10,000	34,000
Low	3,000	13,000
Change	7,000	21,000

The costs that change must be variable, and the variable cost per unit is £21,000/7,000 = £3. The variable cost information can now be used to calculate the fixed cost element:

	£
Total costs at 3000 units	13,000
Less variable cost at 3000 units = 3000 × £3 =	9,000
Therefore, fixed costs	4,000

We are now able to prepare the flexible budgets, as shown in Table 6.4. These demonstrate how total costs behave at the different levels of output shown. Also of interest are the total variable costs, which can be calculated by multiplying the output by the unit cost. As the fixed costs have also been identified, flexible budgets can be prepared for any level of output.

Table 6.4   Flexible budgets at different levels of output (£)

	Unit cost	Output 3,000	Output 6,000	Output 9,000
Variable costs				
Direct material A	4	12,000	24,000	36,000
Direct material B	1.50	4,500	9,000	13,500
Direct labour	6	18,000	36,000	54,000
Semi-variable overhead: variable costs	3	9,000	18,000	27,000
Total variable costs	14.50	43,500	87,000	130,500
Semi-variable overhead: fixed costs		4,000	4,000	4,000
Fixed costs		25,000	35,000	47,000
Total costs		72,500	126,000	181,500

Calculating Budget Variances

We can use the power of the flexible budget to generate variances. Let us assume that in the month of May, output was 5560 units and the costs were as shown in the 'actual' column in Table 6.5. The flexible budgets for the variable costs are calculated by multiplying the unit costs by May's output. The fixed costs are taken from the data in the previous illustration. The last column contains details of the variances between the flexed budget and actual costs. As has been indicated above, if the flexed budget exceeds the actual cost, this generates a favourable (F) variance, while if the actual cost exceeds the flexed budget, this results in an adverse (A) variance.

Table 6.5   Calculating flexed budget variances

Cost element	Output: Cost per unit £	5560 units Flexed budget £	Actual costs £	Variances £
Variable costs				
Direct material A	4	22,240	22,220	20 (F)
Direct material B	1.50	8,340	8,440	100 (A)
Direct labour	6	33,360	33,550	190 (A)
Semi-variable	3	16,680	15,040	1,640 (F)
Total variable costs	14.50	80,620	79,250	1,370 (F)
Fixed costs				
Semi-variable		4,000	3,920	80 (F)
Fixed 4001–8000		35,000	35,050	50 (A)
Total fixed costs		39,000	38,970	30 (F)
Total costs		119,620	118,220	1,400 (F)

The variances in the final column show that in total the actual cost is £1400 less than the flexible budget cost. Examination of the individual variances shows that to a large extent the overall favourable variance is largely due to the semi-variable favourable variance of £1,640.

Standard Costing and Variance Analysis

This section considers:

- the definition of a standard cost;
- the construction of standard costs, including behavioural issues;
- the advantages of standard costing;
- the concept of standard time;
- the use of standard costs in variance analysis;
- the interpretation of variances;
- performance ratios.

The Definition of a Standard Cost

A *standard cost* is the planned unit cost of a product or service. It normally has a physical and a financial component. For example, a bicycle factory has a wheel-building department and within this the standard costs of a wheel are shown in Table 6.6.

Table 6.6 Standard cost statement for one wheel build

Item	Quantity	Price (£)	Standard cost (£)
Wheel rim	1	7	7.00
Spokes	36	0.15 each	5.40
Hub	1	3.30	3.30
Labour	0.75 hours	6 per hour	4.50
Variable overhead	0.75 hours	2 per hour	1.50
Fixed overhead	0.75 hours	4 per hour	3.00
Total			24.70

The Construction of Standard Costs

There are two methods for setting cost standards: the analysis of past costs and functional analysis.

- Analysis of past costs. Companies with a history of production experience will have a record of past costs, and these can provide a reliable basis for generating standard costs. Where these are used, adjustments to past costs will need to be made to reflect changes in price levels and wage costs. However, even where historical data are available, their use may be invalidated by technological change. Of course, this approach cannot be used for new production methods.

- Functional analysis. This requires the involvement of engineering and work study staff. Engineers will be required to specify material requirements and calculate how much should be used to produce the product. The purchasing department will be required to determine the price of raw materials and components. Work study experts and engineers will work together to determine the labour time required, whilst representatives from human resources will advise on rates of pay for the grades of labour stipulated. However, the overhead element of the standard cost may be difficult to estimate. The figure may simply be related to labour hours or, preferably, will be related to cost driver consumption in an activity-based costing environment.

The level of difficulty of standards should be considered when they are set. It is possible to distinguish between 'ideal' and 'attainable' standards. Ideal standards assume that employees work at 100% efficiency as they make no allowance for wastage or inefficiency. They assume ideal technological conditions, and it is invariably impossible to do better than the standard. They are unlikely to be used in practice as they may be expected to demoralise workers due to an expected preponderance of adverse variances.

Attainable standards are set at high but achievable levels. They assume a brisk level of working. They also assume normal working conditions and make allowance for idle time and breakages. There are opportunities for workers to do better than attainable standards so that they generate a mix of favourable and adverse variances. The combination of standards that are attainable and favourable variances that result from effective working is likely to motivate employees. Preston (1995) argues that budgetary systems risk stifling creativity within organisations. The article is summarised at the end of this chapter.

Argyris (1953) raised awareness of the dangers of setting impossible standards over 50 years ago. He observed that such standards led to the formation of informal anti-company subgroups amongst workers whose objective was to frustrate attainment of the standard. He also pointed out the intolerable pressure felt by supervisors caught between the demands of senior management and the workforce. Argyris proposed that budget holders should participate in the budget-setting process (the term budget holders refers to managers who are responsible for controlling budgets). He argued that participation was likely to produce more realistic budgets and lead to feelings of ownership and commitment as the budget was internalised by participants. Participation can also improve communication in a company; the act of participating spreads knowledge about the company's objectives and activities. Additionally, it allows an opportunity for managers to input their detailed knowledge into the budgeting process.

Ouchi (1979) discusses several types of control; the article is summarised at the end of this chapter.

However, other writers have indicated that participating managers may seek to build in 'budgetary slack' so that the budget is set at a slightly lower level, making it easier to achieve. To guard against this, it may be necessary to establish reference points such as past performance or performance in another part of the company. Even so, senior managers have the responsibility for achieving profit targets that may have been agreed by the board of directors, and as such targets will invariably override the results of participative budgets, many companies impose budgets but allow managers a certain amount of freedom in achieving them. For example, a report in the *Daily Telegraph* on 22 January 2004 on the UK telecom company mmO_2 quotes its chief executive, Dave McGlade, attributing a large part of the company's success to 'setting managers from one end of the business to the other a few clear, simple targets then giving them the freedom to get on with their jobs and make decisions on the spot'.

Advantages of Standard Costing

- They are of help in building up costs for budgeting. They also provide a significant input to flexible budgeting to assist with decision making and control.
- They lead to a detailed comparison of standard and actual costs. This forms a very important feedback control function. The size of variances alerts managers as to the costs that are most in need of attention and corrective action.
- They assist in evaluating managerial performance by highlighting fixed and variable variances.
- They provide targets for managers and employees to aim at and to achieve. By achieving or improving on standard costs, they are more likely to achieve the budget.
- A standard costing system simplifies inventory valuation as goods are taken into closing stock at the standard cost of production made up of direct material, direct labour, variable production overhead and fixed production overhead.

The Concept of Standard Time

Standard time refers to the quantity of output that should be produced in a specific period. Thus, a standard minute refers to the amount of work that should be produced in a minute and a standard hour the amount of work to be produced in an hour. Standard time is not an input measure. It does not refer to the actual time worked. Instead it refers to the amount of time represented by the output of the period.

For example, the standard amount of time to build a cycle wheel in Table 6.6 is 0.75 hours or 45 minutes. In a six-hour period, a wheel-builder completes seven wheels. The standard time represented by the production of seven wheels is 7×45 minutes = 5 hours 15 minutes. As can be seen, the wheel-builder has taken 6 hours to complete 5 hours 15 minutes of output and would be regarded as inefficient.

As well as a measure of efficiency, standard time also offers a way of adding together different products or different types of activity as the following examples illustrate.

Different Products

A factory produces three types of office furniture, and the standard times for the production of one of each are as follows:

Product	Standard time (minutes)
Chair	30
Stool	20
Desk	70

Table 6.7   Standard times of output

Product	Standard time (minutes)	Units	Total standard time (minutes)
Chair	30	25	750
Stool	20	49	980
Desk	70	25	1750
Total			3480

In a week the factory produces 25 chairs, 49 stools and 25 desks. The total standard time represented by this output is shown in Table 6.7.

This demonstrates that the different products can be added together through their standard times of production. From a control perspective, the 3480 standard minutes (= 58 standard hours) of output of Table 6.7 could be compared with the budgeted total of standard hours.

If actual hours worked exceeded 58 hours, it would indicate the workforce was inefficient.

Different Types of Activity

In a garage the standard times shown in Table 6.8 have been established for different tasks. These form the basis of charges to customers so it is important that mechanics keep to them. Table 6.8 also shows the activities completed in a 37.5-hour week.

As can be seen, the mechanic has completed 39.5 standard hours of work, which exceeds his 37.5 hours of actual input. For the company there is a monetary benefit

Table 6.8   Standard times of activities

Activity	Standard time (hours)	Activities completed Number	Activities completed Standard Time (hours)
Short service	0.75	10	7.5
Long service	1.5	14	21
Clutch change	2	5	10
Wheel bearing change	0.5	2	1
Total			39.5

Table 6.9   Standard costs per unit and annual budget

| | Standard costs per unit | | |
Cost element	Components of standard cost	Standard cost per unit (£)	Annual budget for 120,000 units (£)
Direct materials	2 kg at £1 per kg	2.00	240,000
Direct labour	30 minutes at £5 per hour	2.50	300,000
Variable overhead	30 minutes at £3 per hour	1.50	180,000
Fixed overhead	30 minutes at £4 per hour	2.00	240,000
Totals		8.00	960,000

because it is able to charge out to customers an additional 2 standard hours over and above the 37.5 hours that it has paid the mechanic for.

The Use of Standard Costs in Variance Analysis

To illustrate the use of standard costs in control, we now consider the calculation and interpretation of cost variances. In order to illustrate this, we will consider the example of a company that manufactures a single product and has established a system of standard costing. The standard costs and annual budget for the current year are shown in Table 6.9.

The overhead costs, both variable and fixed, are charged to the product via the direct labour time. As can be seen, the product consumes 30 minutes of both overhead cost elements, the amount of labour time required to produce one unit. The total budget for the year is calculated by multiplying each standard cost by the annual output of 120,000 units.

It is planned to produce the annual output of 120,000 units evenly through the year, with 10,000 units produced each month. The fixed overheads are planned to amount to £20,000 per month.

During October, actual output and costs were as shown in Table 6.10. The total cost variance for the period is calculated by comparing what it should cost to produce 8,000 units (the standard cost of 8,000 units) with the actual costs as follows:

Table 6.10   Actual output and costs for October

Output: 8000 units	
Costs	**£**
Direct materials: 16,300 kg at £0.98 per kg	15,974
Labour: 3950 hours at £5.06 per hour	19,987
Variable overhead: 3950 hours at £3 per hour	11,850
Fixed overhead	20,400
Total	68,211

$$\text{Total cost variance} = \text{Standard cost of output} - \text{Actual costs}$$
$$= (8000 \text{ units} \times £8) - £68,211$$
$$= £64,000 - £68,211$$
$$= -£4,211.$$

As the actual costs exceed the standard costs, there is an adverse variance of £4,211. The variances for each of the costs can be calculated using the same formula and the variances can be set up in a table as shown in Table 6.11.

Table 6.11   Variances for October (£)

Cost element	Standard cost per unit	Standard costs of 8000 units	Actual costs	Variances (standard cost – actual)
Direct materials	2	16,000	15,974	26 (F)
Direct labour	2.50	20,000	19,987	13 (F)
Variable overhead	1.50	12,000	11,850	150 (F)
Fixed overhead	2	16,000	20,400	4,400 (A)
Totals	8	64,000	68,211	4,211 (A)

As may be seen in the table:

- Direct materials, direct labour and variable overhead all show favourable variances.
- Fixed overhead shows a large adverse variance that swamps the three favourable variances and produces a large adverse total cost variance.
- The bottom row shows the make-up of the total cost variance, which comes to £4,211 adverse.

Subvariances

The next stage is to analyse each variance further. We will use the data in Tables 6.10 and 6.11 to calculate the subvariances described in Table 6.12.

The material price subvariance is given by

$$(\text{Standard price per kg} - \text{Actual price per kg}) \times \text{Actual kg}$$
$$= (£1 \text{ per kg} - £0.98 \text{ per kg}) \times 16,300 \text{ kg}$$
$$= £326 \text{ F.}$$

This variance is favourable because the actual price paid per kilo is less than the standard price of £1 per kilo, Material price variances may be caused by: purchasing in favourable market conditions, price increases since the budget was set, taking advantage of quantity discounts or purchasing non-standard quality materials.

Table 6.12   Subvariances

Variance	Subvariance 1	Subvariance 2
Direct materials	This is the materials **price** subvariance and is calculated by comparing the standard purchase price of raw materials with the actual price paid	This is the materials **usage** subvariance and is calculated by comparing the standard quantity of raw materials used (for the output achieved) with the actual quantities used
Direct labour	This is the **rate** subvariance and is calculated by comparing the standard wage rate with the actual wage rate	This is the **efficiency** subvariance and is calculated by comparing the standard number of labour hours (for the output achieved) with the actual labour hours
Variable overhead	This is the **expenditure** subvariance and is calculated by comparing the standard variable overhead based on actual hours worked with the actual variable overhead. That is, it calculates what the variable overhead should be for the hours worked and compares this with the actual overhead	This is the **efficiency** subvariance and is calculated by comparing the standard hours of production with the actual labour hours. That is, it compares the standard hours of output with the actual hours of input
Fixed overhead	This is the **expenditure** subvariance and is calculated by comparing the fixed overhead budget with the actual fixed overhead	This is the **volume** subvariance and is calculated by comparing the overheads absorbed by the actual output and the fixed overhead budget

Material usage variance is

(Standard material use − Actual material use) × Standard price per kg
  ((8000 units of output × 2 kg per unit) −16,300 kg) × £1 per kg
  = (16,000 kg − 16,300 kg) × £1 per kg
  = £300 A.

In this case the variance is adverse because we have used 300 kg more than the standard use of 16,000 kg for the output of 8000 units. Material usage variances may be caused by excessive waste due to a poorly trained workforce or due to substandard materials. It may also be caused by poor storage or machine breakdown resulting in damage to raw materials. In this case, there is a favourable price variance that may have been due to the purchase of slightly lower-grade materials. The adverse use variance may reflect higher waste associated with the purchase of poor quality materials.

The two materials subvariances of £326F and £300A sum to the materials variance of £26F calculated in Table 6.11.

The wage rate subvariance is given by

> (Standard rate per hour − Actual rate per hour) × Actual hours worked
> (£5 per hour − £5.06 per hour) × 3950 hours
> = £237 A.

The variance is adverse because the actual rate of pay per hour is greater than the standard hourly rate. Wage rate variances can be caused by recruiting the incorrect grade of labour, by inadequate supply of the right grade of labour in the labour market, by unplanned overtime working and by an increase in wage rates since the start of the year.

The wage efficiency sub-variance is calculated as

> (Standard labour hours − Actual labour hours) × Standard wage rate
> ((8000 units × 0.5 hours per unit) − 3950 hours) × £5 per hour
> = (4000 hours − 3950 hours) × £5 per hour
> = £250 F.

This variance is favourable because the actual hours worked are 250 hours less than the standard of 4000 hours. Efficiency subvariances may also be caused by recruiting the wrong grade of labour or by inadequate training. They may also be caused by machine breakdown or by wasting time dealing with poor-quality materials. Low levels of motivation in the workforce may also be a contributing factor, and this might be attributed to a range of things including levels of pay, stress levels and poor working conditions. In this case the rate variance is adverse as the rate paid was £5.06 rather than £5.00 and this may have led to the favourable efficiency variance.

The two wage rate subvariances of £237A and £250F sum to the wages variance of £13F calculated in Table 6.11.

The variable overhead expenditure subvariance is given by

> (Standard variable overhead rate per hour × Actual hour worked) − Actual cost.
> (£3 per hour × 3950 hours) − £11,850
> = £11,850 − £11,850 = 0.

Causes of the overhead variable expenditure subvariance would depend on the constituent elements of variable overheads, For example, there could be an increase in the costs of power (a variable overhead).

The variable overhead efficiency subvariance is calculated as

> (Standard hours of output − Actual hours of input) × Standard variable
> overhead rate per hour
> = ((8000 units × 0.5 hours) − 3950 hours) × £3
> = (4000 standard hrs − 3950 hours) × £3 per hour
> = 50 hours × £3
> = £150F.

This variance is favourable because we have produced 8000 units in 50 hours less than the standard time of 4000 hours. The causes of this variance are similar to the causes of the labour efficiency variance listed above.

Again, it can be seen that when the variable overhead variances of £0 and £150F are added together they equal the variable overhead variance in Table 6.11.

The fixed overhead expenditure subvariance is given by

$$\text{(Budgeted fixed overhead} - \text{Actual fixed overhead)}$$
$$= £20,000 \text{ per month} - £20,400$$
$$= £400 \text{ A.}$$

This variance is adverse because actual expenditure is £400 more than the budgeted fixed overhead for the month. As these are fixed overheads, we would expect that actual overheads would equal budget overhead. For the precise causes of fixed overhead variances we would need to examine the constituent elements of the fixed overhead cost. For example, it may be that we have (erroneously) paid next month's rent as well as this month's.

The fixed overhead volume subvariance is calculated as

$$\text{(Standard fixed overhead cost per unit} \times \text{Output)} - \text{Budgeted fixed overhead}$$
$$= (8000 \text{ units} \times £2 \text{ per unit}) - £20,000 \text{ per month}$$
$$= £16,000 - £20,000$$
$$= £4,000\text{A.}$$

This variance is associated with the total absorption costing system dicussed in Chapter 2. The standard overhead cost per unit is the same as the fixed overhead absorption rate per unit. Therefore, in this case the variance is adverse because our output of 8000 units absorbs only £16,000 of fixed overhead whereas the fixed overhead budget for the period is £20,000. We have failed to recover all the budgeted fixed overhead from the month's production. The budget for the month planned for the production of 10,000 units, each of which would have absorbed £2 of fixed overheads, amounting to £20,000. As we have produced 2000 units less than the budget, this means that we have failed to recover 2000 units × £2 of fixed overhead. The adverse variance is the result of failing to produce at the budgeted level. However, the underproduction may be the result of either or both of the following factors:

- The failure of the labour force to work sufficient hours. In this case 3950 hours were worked, but budgeted hours were 30 minutes per unit × 10,000 units = 5000 hours.
- Inefficient working by the labour force in their working hours. In this case 3950 hours were worked and 4000 hours of output (8000 units) produced. Therefore, the labour force was efficient and the failure to produce 10,000 units is due to working 3950 rather than 5000 hours in the month. The reasons for this need to be investigated.

When the expenditure variance (£400A) is added to the volume variance (£4,000A), they sum to the total fixed overhead variance of £4,400A in Table 6.11.

Table 6.13   Reconciliation of standard and actual costs of production

	£	£
Standard costs of production*		64,000
Direct material variances		
Price subvariance	326 F	
Use subvariance	300 A	26 F
Direct wages variance		
Rate subvariance	237 A	
Efficiency subvariance	250 F	13 F
Variable overhead		
Expenditure subvariance	0	
Efficiency subvariance	150 F	150 F
Fixed overhead		
Expenditure subvariance	400 A	
Volume subvariance	4000 A	4400 A
Actual costs		68,211

*See Table 6.11.

The variances may be summarised as in Table 6.13 in a statement that reconciles the standard cost of production to the actual costs, showing the subvariances in detail.

Interpretation of Variances

The individual variances described in the previous section may have one or more causes, which may or may not be clear. Before we can correct such variances, we need to understand the reasons for them. Only then can we identify what steps should be taken to address them. Five types of causes may be identified:

- *Inefficiency in operations*, for example, purchasing raw materials at an uneconomic price, leading to an adverse price variance; productive inefficiency by labour, so that actual hours worked exceed standard hours of output, or the recruitment of the wrong grade of labour.
- *Incorrect plans or standards*. These include plans that were originally incorrect, such as the incorrect price per litre for materials, and plans that were originally correct but have been invalidated by environmental changes.
- *Poor communication of standards*. Standards may contain errors, may arrive after work has started, or may be set out in such a way as to cause confusion.
- *Interdependence of variances*. One variance may be influenced by another. For example, the employment of unskilled labour may give a favourable rate variance, but if the work is skilled it will probably result in a unfavourable efficiency variance;

a favourable material price variance may be the result of buying poor-quality materials and this may lead to an adverse material use variance (as more waste is likely to result) and an adverse labour efficiency variance as workers take longer to process substandard materials.

- *Random fluctuation around standards.* Humans are not machines and cannot be expected to work as consistently as machines. Efficiency will fluctuate. Consequently, a labour standard, for example, may be viewed as a long-run average that performance will conform to. In this situation, one must accept that in some periods performance will be better than the standard and at some times worse.

Performance Measures

There are three non-financial performance measures that provide a perspective on factory operations. The *production volume* (PV) ratio, given by

$$\text{PV ratio} = \frac{\text{Standard hours of actual output}}{\text{Budgeted standard hours}} \times 100,$$

expresses actual output as a percentage of budgeted output. If actual output is more than budgeted output the ratio will be more than 100% and if lower than budgeted output it will be less than 100%. Using the data in Tables 6.9 and 6.10, we can calculate the PV ratio for the factory:

$$\text{PV ratio} = \frac{4000 \text{ std. hours}}{5000 \text{ std. hours}} \times 100$$
$$= 80\%.$$

Standard hours of actual output is 30 minutes per unit multiplied by actual output of 8000 units. Budgeted standard hours is 30 minutes per unit multiplied by the budgeted output of 10,000 units. This ratio reflects the fact that output was only 8000 units compared with the budget of 10,000 units.

The efficiency ratio,

$$\text{Efficiency Ratio} = \frac{\text{Standard hours of actual output}}{\text{Actual hours worked}} \times 100,$$

expresses output as a percentage of hours worked. If the workforce is as efficient as the standard, the ratio will be 100%. If the workforce is less efficient, standard hours will be less than hours worked and the percentage less than 100%. Using the data in Tables 6.9 and 6.10:

$$\text{Efficiency ratio} = \frac{4000 \text{ standard hours}}{3950 \text{ hours worked}} \times 100$$
$$= 101\%.$$

The workforce has thus been more efficient than the standard – something that we knew from the variance analysis.

Finally, the *capacity usage* ratio

$$\text{Capacity Usage Ratio} = \frac{\text{Actual hours worked}}{\text{Budgeted working hours}} \times 100,$$

as its name implies, measures to what extent factory capacity has been used in the period. It expresses actual hours as a percentage of budgeted working hours. If actual hours are less than budgeted hours, this produces a percentage below 100%, signifying that capacity was not used fully. Using the data in Tables 6.9 and 6.10,

$$\text{Capacity usage ratio} = \frac{3950 \text{ hours worked}}{5000 \text{ budgeted hours}} \times 100$$
$$= 79\%.$$

In this case we used only 79% of the planned working hours in the month; in itself this would lead to the failure to achieve the month's planned output.

Conclusions

This chapter has demonstrated that:

- budgets are an essential tool of control. Control can be feed-forward or feedback.
- control information should possess various key qualities if it is to be effective.
- flexible budgets are useful for projecting different outcomes and also serve as a basis for control. They allow the calculation of variances.
- a standard cost represents the planned unit cost of a product or service. They can form the basis of cost systems and they are also used to generate a wealth of variance information.
- generating the variances has to be followed by their interpretation in order to make managerial use of the control information.

Summary

All organisations need to engage in planning, but in order that planned outcomes are achieved it is essential that organisations engage in control. Control information alerts managers to deviations from plan and allows them to take action to change the course of events. The master budget is of little value for monthly control. Instead, flexible budgets may be used; they flex budgeted costs to reflect actual outputs. Variances are then generated by comparing the flexed budget costs with the actual costs.

Standard costs are developed relating to one unit of output or one unit of a service. It is important to set standards that are achievable but challenging. If standards are set at too difficult a level they may lead to a demoralised workforce. In a standard cost system, closing stocks are valued at standard cost of production. Standard costs themselves can be used to generate a range of variances; these include direct materials, direct labour, variable overhead and fixed overhead. The interpretation of each of these variances is important. Finally, we examined three performance ratios (production volume, efficiency and capacity usage) and saw how they were related to the variances.

Recommended Further Reading

Ouchi, W. G. (1979) 'A conceptual framework for the design of organisational control mechanisms', *Management Science*, 25(9): 833–848.
Ouchi describes three mechanisms to cope with evaluation and control:

- *markets*, precisely measuring and rewarding individual contributions;
- *bureaucracies*, relying on a mix of close evaluation and social acceptance of common objectives;
- *clans*, relying on relatively complete socialisation to remove incongruent objectives.

He uses a case based in a large organisation's parts division to show how an organisation can use control mechanisms to move towards achieving its objectives.

In the warehouse, the supervisor uses a mix of formal authority and the trust and respect of the workers for him (i.e. formal and implicit informal agreements).

In the purchasing department, the relationship of supervisor and workers is more at 'arm's length' (i.e. a 'market' mechanism), purchasing agents needing only market/price information to make purchasing decisions. Markets are not perfect, however, therefore a degree of bureaucratic control over purchasing officers is needed (i.e. a mix of market and bureaucratic controls).

Where bureaucratic control is used, administrative costs will be high if qualitative as well as quantitative control measures are needed. In the warehouse, he points to the problems of using a market-based mechanism to control and explains that, if teamwork is required, the allocation of rewards may be problematic. He demonstrates that trying to set up an internal market will often result in over-bureaucratisation. Bureaucratic control is preferred where frictionless markets do not exist.

He concludes that where objectives are clear but tasks are often uncertain, complex and involve teamwork, the formation of clans removes much of the need for close bureaucratic control.

Ouchi provides a model that tries to relate the control type used (market, bureaucracy or clan) to the social and information requirements of such control systems. Hence, depending upon the control type used, prices, rules or tradition will have varying degrees of legitimacy. This model also assumes the existence of the self-interest of all participants.

He points to the problems of obtaining perfect transfer prices and hence the need for a layer of imposed bureaucratic control, which in turn requires acceptance of authority, to work. He criticises existing organisational theory (Simon, March, Parsons, etc.) for concentrating on the bureaucratic form and overlooking the others' importance.

Ouchi compares the costs of obtaining the 'right' people and using (simpler/cheaper) results (market) controls, with having to use the more expensive action (bureaucratic) controls. He suggests the former results in a higher level of staff commitment, whereas the latter may alienate employees. He proposes another model that interrelates three factors – people treatment, form of commitment and control type – and suggests that the degree of employee commitment is related directly to the type of control required. He describes how the type of control used may lead the organisation to become coercive, with associated ethical issues.

The bureaucratic control type, argues Ouchi, may be unsuitable for many organisations. In order for the organisation to make rational decisions, it must be able to measure relevant information. He gives examples of conditions affecting the measurement of behaviour and output. In some organisations, such as research laboratories, schools and government agencies, outputs and behaviour are both difficult to measure, thus the clan approach may work best, along with careful selection of employees – a *loose coupling* approach.

He points to two main underlying issues affecting the form of control – the degree of clarity with which performance can be assessed, and the degree of goal incongruence – and to the fact that, to enable co-operation in organisations, people must be able to trust each other.

Lyne, S. (1995) 'Accounting measures, motivation and performance appraisal', in D. Ashton, T. Hooper and R. Scapens (eds), *Issues in Management Accounting*, pp. 237–257. Hemel Hempstead: Prentice Hall.

Lyne's article attempts to produce a compendium of recent ideas in control system and motivation theories. He defines control as the 'regulation and monitoring of activities' and regulation as ' fulfilling what has been laid down' and as 'adapting to requirements'. He comments that control has two aspects – motivation and performance measurement.

Lyne refers to Hopwood (1974) who identifies four classes of control – *administrative, organisational, social* and *self* – each having an effect on motivation. He notes the limited application/value of accounting controls. He quotes Otley and Berry's (1980) ideas of prerequisites for effective control systems (i.e. clear objectives, output measure related to objectives, good predictive models and the ability to take action). He comments on the need for *dual-loop feedback* and *feedforward* and notes that organisations often seem to lack the flexibility to consider altering objectives.

He goes on to give an overview of four recognised groups of theories of motivation:

- *needs-satisfying* theories – Maslow's hierarchy of needs;
- *achievement* theories – McClelland's hierarchy of motivators;
- *motivation/hygiene* theories – Herzberg;
- *equity* theories – based around the demotivating dissatisfaction arising from a sense of inequity.

Lyne next discusses *expectancy theory* (Ronen and Livingstone, 1975) in some detail. Such theories are based on ideas from psychology and incorporate a wide range of internal and external factors in an attempt to predict/explain motivation in terms of expected utility. He does not, however, suggest that such ideas have great practical applicability.

Lyne comments on the need to use realistic targets in order to maintain motivation and avoid reducing aspiration levels – see Stedry and Hofstede (1968) and Locke's (1968) questionable lab-based experiments. He also argues that flexible budgeting with regularly adjusted targets is necessary for effective motivation.

In discussing the relationship between accounting measures and performance evaluation, he refers to the usefulness of *ex post* measures (e.g. planning and operational variances) as a way of improving the validity of performance monitoring. He also identifies the problem of budgetary *slack* as a 'predetermined attempt to manipulate the objective or target'. He argues that it arises when two conditions exist – incongruent personal and organisational goals; and information asymmetry. He relates the latter idea to those prevalent in *agency theory* and cites the work of Walker and Choudhury (1987).

In terms of the effects of the style of use of budgets (in order to optimise their motivational effects), he notes the work of Hopwood (1972) who identified four different styles:

- budget constrained;
- budget profit style;
- profit conscious;
- non-accounting.

He also refers to Otley (1978) who looked empirically at the effects of such styles on managers in various degrees of task uncertainty.

He refers to Kennis's (1979) study of *participation* on job satisfaction, job tension and job attitudes and how such work relates to Hofstede's improved model of participation and other models which focus on intervening variables which affect performance, such as personality types, organisational attitudes, motivation, uncertainty, and role ambiguity. In this respect he outlines, and criticises as unrealistic, the attempts which have been made at 'management by objectives'.

He concludes that motivation and performance appraisal, whilst involving accounting measures, have a much wider context.

Preston, A. (1995) 'Budgeting, creativity and culture', in D. Ashton, T. Hopper and R. Scapens (eds), *Issues in Management Accounting* (2nd edition) pp. 273–298. Hemel Hempstead: Prentice Hall.

Preston explores ways in which budgeting contributes to or impedes the creative process. He looks at two models of creativity: the rationalist model and the social constructionist model.

The rationalist model represents the view that the 'natural order' is knowable if all relevant variables are identified, along with their relationship rules. Therefore, with perfect information, perfect prediction is possible. In this view, creativity is a mysterious factor, not yet understood but ultimately understandable.

The traditional response of management accounting has been to try to improve quantitative techniques to deal with uncertainty (on the basis that systems work to a predetermined, predictable order), although practical people appreciate that perfect information is not likely and that creativity plays a part. Creativity is seen here in the forms of adaptability and flexibility, and these are enhanced (and creativity promoted) when organisational structure and leadership style are 'got right', although different combinations of such factors may be possible.

Preston argues that organisational structure and budgetary style are closely related and that traditional (textbook) budgeting seems to assume mechanistic rather than 'organic' structures. He quotes Mintzberg (1975) who criticises budgetary systems for concentrating on easy-to-measure events; providing out-of-date, historical information; oversimplifying or reducing information; and concentrating on internal rather than external factors. This, Preston argues, often leads to managers 'ignoring traditional budgeting systems' outputs. Therefore, information is hardly likely to contribute to the essential organisational creativity. Traditional budgeting is based on highly authoritarian systems of management.

Preston refers to Otley (1980) who argues for budgetary systems which (while still essentially rationalist) are tailored around contingent environmental factors, that non-financial, qualitative information often will enhance a system's outputs and that, by participation (cf. Ouchi's 'clans'), the more organic organisational structure can be adapted to by the budgetary system. He argues that organisations and environments reciprocally create each other and that organisational boundaries are difficult to define. Budgetary activities may affect the external environment, for instance, Within organisations, it is the interactions of individuals that 'construct' the organisation, therefore the idea of predetermined order is flawed in that it ignores or overlooks the self-determination of individuals. (The rationalist view effectively says that individuals will react in predetermined ways to known stimuli.)

In the *social constructionist* model, behaviour is seen as the product of creative processes. An individual's response to a stimulus, situation or event depends on the individual's interpretation of the stimulus; that is, meanings are constructed by social interaction. These meanings are then internalised and shared between individuals. Therefore budgets, accounts and formulae have constructed meanings which can change and which are only symbolic representations of reality, The source of creativity/adaptability is the redefinition of constructed meanings (see his example concerning the NHS on p. 283).

Preston argues that 'creativity … rests upon the potential in individuals to look at the world anew and to interpret what they see differently'. This reinterpretation is bound, however, to be affected by social interaction and shared meanings. Preston argues (a little like Ouchi) that 'shared beliefs' and values lead to the organisation as a 'constructed order', but points to the organisation as a set of interrelating individuals. Organisations *are* thus the shared meanings/values/beliefs of the individuals within them. The rules of such systems are not like those in the rationalist model, but rather are 'rules in process', continuously changing and reinterpreted.

The meaning of budgets within this social contructionist perspective may not necessarily be the same to all organisational participants. Preston cites NHS budgets as a way of making more informed decisions to optimise the use of resources, or as a cost-cutting tool. Hence doctors' refusing to participate in the 'Trojan horse' of budgeting. Often, Preston notes, managers may go along with budgeting because they think it makes them look good/rational managers, even though they have no faith in budgets. If budgets are interpreted as a pernicious form of control, this may lead to stifled creativity (apart from creative accounting maybe!).

Budgets, states Preston, may not be a neutral process in that they may shape individuals' interpretations by, for example, narrowing focus and hence stifling creativity. Excessive budgeting may change the nature of an organisation's culture from aesthetic to hard-nosed.

Budgets may be seen as a 'political bargaining process' where those with budgets get the allocations they want and big allocations give power (a self-perpetuating process?) – thus budgets are both an *instrument* and *reflection* of power.

Budgeting, Preston argues, may lead to a culture of rationality and consistency, and this, in turn, may limit creativity and promote unidirectional behaviour (as specified in a rigid budget). To create a more appropriate budgeting system, participation is needed and should allow for improved solutions to problems as they arise.

Preston identifies the work of March (1976) who suggests the following ideas to deformalise/destandardise budgeting systems:

- treating goals as hypotheses (where uncertainty is high);
- treating intuition as real;
- treating hypocrisy as transitory, for example, using semi-confusing information systems to provide the inconsistencies necessary to stimulate creativity;
- treating memory as an enemy – breaking the link between the past and the future;
- treating experience as a theory – the past 'reality' can be reinterpreted to have another meaning.

Formalised systems, like budgeting, may eradicate the creative behaviour essential to an organisation's survival.

Case Study: Budget Preparation and Variance Analysis

Eiger PLC manufactures two types of high-quality ice axe, M1 and M2. The current managing director, C. Chaplin, formed the company in 1996. Your position is that of management accountant and you normally report to the finance director; occasionally you are required to report to the managing director.

The company uses a standard cost system and fully absorbs factory overheads into the cost of production. Closing stocks of finished goods are valued at the standard cost of production. Production and sales are planned to be at the same monthly level throughout the year 2004.

The estimated balance sheet for the year ended 31 December 2003 is as follows:

EIGER PLC
Balance Sheet as at 31 December 2003

Assets employed	£000	£000	£000
Fixed assets	Cost	Depn	Net
Plant and machinery	600	120	480
Current assets			
Stock			
Raw materials	54		
Finished goods	79	133	
Debtors		200	
Cash		79	
		412	
less Current liabilities			
Creditors	40		
Proposed dividend (payable March 04)	30		
Provision for taxation (payable Sept. 04)	10	80	
Working capital			332
			812
Financed by			
Share capital			750
Retained profit			62
			812

The following information has been obtained for the purpose of preparing the budget for the year ending 31 December 2004. First, the sales forecast is:

	M1	M2
Planned selling price per unit	£125	£180
Forecast sales volume (units)	6,500	6,300

Next, direct costs:
Materials (£)

Carbon steel - per kilogram	25
Key rubber- per kilogram	13
Direct labour (£/hour)	
Machining department	6.50
Finishing department	5

The standard direct material and standard direct labour content of each unit of the finished product is as follows:

	M1	M2
Steel	2 kg	3 kg
Rubber	1.5 kg	2 kg
Machining direct labour	3 hours	4 hours
Finishing direct labour	2 hours	3 hours

Turning now to the direct labour force, the following numbers of direct employees work in each of the production departments: machining, 22; finishing, 10. All employees work a 38-hour week and receive paid leave for 5 statutory bank holidays and 15 additional days per year. The normal working week is five days. Any overtime is paid at time and a half.

Factory overheads are fully absorbed into production, using direct labour hours. At the planned output levels the following costs (in £000) are forecast:

Indirect labour	30
Indirect materials	22
Repairs	11
Rates	22
Canteen	16
Depreciation	70
Heat and light	3
Power	6
Factory management	49

The factory has three cost centres: machining department, finishing department and a general service department. Data relating to these three cost units for 2004 are as follows:

Data	Machining dept.	Finishing dept.	General service dept.
Indirect labour hours	3500	1000	300
Indirect materials	£13,000	£5,000	£4,000
Repairs	£5,000	£4,000	£2,000
Factory managers	£16,000	£19,000	£14,000
Plant & machinery values	£600,000	£100,000	0
Floor area	2000 sq. metres	500 sq. metres	500 sq. metres
Machine hours	5500	1500	0
Canteen employees			2

The following stock forecasts have been made:

Raw materials	Steel (kg)	Rubber (kg)
Opening stock	1900 (£46,000)	620 (£8,000)
Closing stock	2000	900

Finished goods	M1	M2
Opening stock	90 (£5,000)	920 (£74,000)
Closing stock	700	520

Selling and administrative expenses have been forecast as follows:

Selling expenses (£000)

Salaries	43
Advertising	20

Administrative expenses (£000)

Salaries	79
Sundry expenses	12
Professional fees	5

The costs of direct labour, factory overheads, selling and administrative expenses will be met in full in cash. Raw materials are purchased on one month's credit and the amount outstanding on the balance sheet at 31 December 2003 will be paid in January 2004. All sales are made on a two-month credit basis so the debtors in the balance sheet will make their payments in January and February. Tax owing at 31 December 2003 will be paid on 1 September 2004 and proposed dividends will be paid in March 2004. Machinery purchases during the year are estimated to cost £30,000 and will be paid for in June. Rates are paid quarterly in January, April, July and November.

Profits are taxed at the rate of 23%.

The budgets for 2004 are shown below.

Sales Budgets

Product	Units	Selling Price £	Revenue £
M1	6,500	125	812,500
M2	6,300	180	1,134,000
Budgeted Revenue			1,946,500

Production Budget

	M1	M2
Planned sales	6,500	6,300
Planned finished goods closing stock	700	520
Total units required	7,200	6,820
Less finished goods op. stock	90	920
Budgeted production	7,110	5,900

Direct Materials Used Budget

Raw material (kg)	Content per M1	Output of M1	M1 usage of raw material	Content per M2	Output of M2	M2 usage of raw material	Total usage
Steel	2 k.g.	7,110	14,220	3	5,900	17,700	31,920
Rubber	1.5 k.g.	7,110	10,665	2	5,900	11,800	22,465

Direct Materials Purchase Budget

	Steel kg	Rubber kg	Total £
Planned closing stock	2000	900	
Production requirement	31,920	22,465	
Total required	33,920	23,365	
less Opening stock	1,900	620	
Purchase requirment	32,020	22,745	
Cost per unit (£)	25	13	
Budgeted purchase (£)	800,500	295,685	1,096,185
add Opening stock			54,000
			1,150,185
less Closing stock	50,000	11,700	61,700
Cost of raw material used			**1,088,485**

Direct Labour Budgets

	Labour hrs per unit	units of output	total labour hours	wage rate per hour £	total labour costs £
Machining					
M1	3	7,110	21,330	6.5	138,645
M2	4	5,900	23,600	6.5	153,400
Finishing			**44,930**		292,045
M1	2	7,110	14,220	5	71,100
M2	3	5,900	17,700	5	88,500
Totals			**31,920**		159,600

Overtime/Idle Time Working Papers (Hours)

Dept	Total hours required	Available Hrs.	Idle time Hrs.	Overtime Hrs.
Manufacture	44,930	40,128	0	4,802
Finishing	31,920	18,240	0	13,680

(£)	Total Direct Labour.	Overtime Premium	Idle Time	
Manufacture	292,045	15,606.5	0	
Finishing	159,600	34,200	0	

Holiday Pay Working Paper

Dept	Employees	Days/year	Hours/year	Cost £
Manufacture	22	440	3,344	21,736
Finishing	10	200	1,520	7,600
			Total	29,336

Factory Overhead Costs Budget

	Apportionment Basis	Total Costs £	Machining Dept. £	Finishing Dept. £
Canteen	GSd employees	16,000		
Depreciation	P&M Valn.	70,000	60,000	10,000
Heat and light	Floor area	3,000	2,000	500
Indirect labour	ILH	30,000	21,875	6,250
Other ind. Labour		49,807	15,607	34,200
Holiday pay		29,336	21,736	7,600
Indirect materials	Direct	22,000	13,000	5,000
Management	Direct	49,000	16,000	19,000
Power	M/C Hrs.	6,000	4,714	1,286
Rates	Area	22,000	14,667	3,667
Repair	Direct	11,000	5,000	4,000
Total Costs		308,143	174,598	91,502
Reapportion GSD			24,579	17,462
Revised Totals			199,178	108,965
Planned Activity			**44,930**	**31,920**
Rate/dlh			4.43	3.41

	Cost per unit of input £	M1 units in one M1	COST £	M2 units in one M2
Steel	25	2	50	3
Rubber	13	1.5	19.5	2
Direct labour				
Machining	6.5	3	19.5	4
Finishing	5	2	10	3
Unit prime cost			99	
Factory overhead				
Machine	4.43	3	13.30	4
Finishing	3.41	2	6.83	3
Unit production cost			119.13	
Selling Price			125	
Budgeted margin			5.87	

Closing Stock Budget

	Units	Unit Cost	Total Cost
Raw Materials			
Steel	2000	25	50,000
Rubber	900	13	11,700
Total Cost			61,700
Finished goods			
M1	700	119.13	83,388.60
M2	520	169.97	88,386.13
Total cost	1220		171,774.73

Costs of Goods Sold Budget

	£
Direct Materials used (3)	1,088,485
Direct Labour (5)	451,645
Factory overhead (6)	308,142.5
Add: Finished goods opening stock	79,000
	1,927,273
Less: Finished goods closing stock	171,775
Budgeted cost of goods sold	1,755,498

Selling and Administrative Expense Budget

Selling Expenses		£
Salaries	43,000	
Advertising	20,000	63,000
Administrative Expenses		
Office sals.	79,000	
Sundry	12,000	
Prof.fees	5,000	96,000
Totals		159,000

Budgeted Cash Flow

	Total
Cash inflows	
Receipts from debtors	1822.1
Total receipts	1822.1
Cash outflows	
Payments to creditors	1044.8
Wages	451.65
F Overheads	216.14
Rates	22
Selling & admin.	159
Dividends	30
Taxation	10
Machinery	30
Total Payments	1963.6
NCF	−141.5
Balance b/f	79
Balance c/f	−62.54

Balance Sheet as at 31 December 2004

Assets Employed	£000	£000	£000
Fixed Assets	Cost	Depn	Net
Plant and machinery	630,000	190,000	440,000
Current Assets			
Stock			
Raw materials	61,700		
Finished goods	171,775		
Debtors	324,416.7		
Cash	−62,540.42		
		495,351	
Less Current Liabilities			
Creditors	91,348.75		
Provision for taxation	7,361	98,709	
Working capital			396,642
			836,642
Financed by			
Share capital	750,000		
Retained profit	86,642		**836,642**

Budgeted Trading Profit and Loss Account 2004

	£
Sales	1,946,500
less Cost of Sales	1,755,498
Budgeted Gross Profit	191,002
Less Selling and admin. Expenses	159,000
Profit before int. & tax	32,002
Interest	0
Budgeted net profit before tax	32,002
Taxation	7,361
Budgeted net profit after tax	24,642

Having prepared the budgets for 2004, you are now required to deal with the following issues.

You have already been informed that planned outputs and costs will be incurred evenly through the year. The actual output and costs for the first quarter of 2004 were as follows:

Production
Products: M1   1400
            M2   1150

Costs:
Direct materials usage: 6255 kgs. of Steel at a total cost of £156,375.
                                     4444 kgs. of Rubber at a total cost of £57,772

Direct labour costs:
Machining Department 9032 direct labour hours at a direct wages cost of £60,966.
Finishing Department 6255 direct labour hours at a wages cost of £31,275.

The fixed factory overheads for the period are appended below. They include an apportionment from the service department.

	Machining £	Finishing £
Depreciation	15000	2500
Heat and light	530	130
Indirect labour	5468	1563
Idletime/overtime premium	6500	3655
Holiday pay	5434	760
Indirect materials	2970	1105
Management	4000	4750
Power	1002	289
Rates	3667	917
Repair	1250	1000
Reapportion General Service Department	6145	4366
Total overhead costs	£51,966	£21,035
Notes:		
Overtime hours		1462
Idle time hours	1000	
Holiday hours	836	152

Write a memorandum to the managing director of Eiger PLC in which you interpret the key results of the first quarter. Your objective is also to provide any key recommendations that result from your analysis and interpretation. You should attach to your memorandum a statement of ratios and variances that you have calculated from the information for the first quarter.

Questions

1. Drum Ltd. makes a single product, using a process involving stamping a circle out from sheet steel, covering it with hide and attaching it to a sidepiece.

For 2004 the standard materials costs and requirements have been as follows: 0.4 square metres of sheet steel at £5.20 per square metre; 0.8 square metres of hide at £9.20 per square metre; sidepiece at £4.20. Price increases relating to these raw materials have been notified for the year 2005. Sheet steel will fall in price by 10%, whilst hide will increase in price by 10% and the sidepiece will cost £5.

It takes 30 minutes of labour to punch out the metal, cut the hide and complete the assembly of the product. Labour currently costs the company £4 per hour, and this will increase by 4% with effect from 1 January 2005.

Semi-variable overheads measured at different levels of output in 2004 were:

Output	Costs (£)
30,500	20,225
45,560	27,002
63,620	35,129
81,040	42,968

For the year ended 31 December 2004 fixed factory costs were as follows:

Management	£35,600
Depreciation	12,500
Insurance	5,600
Rates	11,000

With the exception of depreciation, all fixed and semi-variable overheads will increase by 5% with effect from 1 January 2005.

(a) Prepare flexible budgets for monthly output levels of 55,000 and 65,000 units for the year ended 31 December 2005.
(b) Explain the principal benefits that firms obtain from the preparation of flexible budgets.

2. Great Lakes Co. is about to commence the final quarter of activity for the current financial year. The results for the first three quarters of the year have been as follows:

	Q1	Q2	Q3
Sales volume	12,000	20,000	18,000
Production volume	15,000	25,000	18,000
Costs (£000)			
Direct materials	150	250	180
Direct labour	130	190	148
Depreciation of plant	12	12	12
Other production overheads	50	70	56
Administration costs	30	30	30
Selling and distribution costs	38	50	47
Total costs	410	617	473

Notes:

(i) The variable elements of production costs are related to the volume of production. The variable element of selling and distribution costs is related to the volume of sales.

(ii) During the fourth quarter of the year sales volume is expected to range between 18,000 and 24,000 units; production will be set equal to sales in the quarter. The company has been informed that the unit price of materials will increase by 8% in the fourth quarter.

(iii) For the whole of the year the selling price is £30 per unit.

Prepare flexible budgets for the final quarter at production (and sales) levels of 18,000 and 24,000 units. Forecast the profit at these sales levels.

3. Omega PLC manufactures a product for which the standard cost data are as follows:

	Units of input	Cost per input unit (£)	Cost per unit of output (£)
Direct materials	3 kg	5	15
Direct labour	2 hours	4	8
Variable overhead	2 hours	2	4
Fixed overhead	2 hours	10	20
Standard cost			47

The budget for the month of April was set at an output of 5000 units and a total cost of £235,000.

The actual output and costs for the month of April were as follows:

Actual output	4800 units
Actual costs (£)	
Direct materials (14,480 kg)	73,656
Direct labour (9700 DIH)	38,800
Variable overhead	18,960
Fixed overhead	99,000
Total costs	£230,416

(a) Calculate the following variances and associated subvariances for April: total cost; Direct material; Direct labour; Variable overhead; Fixed overhead.
(b) Interpret the information provided by the fixed overhead variances in this case.

4. Trimtone Limited' is a company that manufactures the Trimouse. At the start of the year the budgeted costs per unit of the Trimouse were as follows:

Direct costs

Direct material:	4.5 kg at £12 per kg
Direct labour:	Skilled: 3 hours at £14 per hour
Fixed overheads:	Overheads are budgeted to be £47,250 per annum
	Overheads are absorbed on a basis of total labour hours
Budgeted production:	1,500 units

During the period the following costs were actually incurred:

Direct materials:	7,100 kilograms were used, costing £74,550 in total
Skilled labour:	4,275 hours worked at a total cost of £70,110
Fixed overheads:	Overheads incurred were £52,025
Actual production:	1,450 units

The production manager has expressed concern that the total costs seem to be running at too high a level against budgeted costs forecast at the start of the year. You work in the finance department, and the production manager has approached you to see if you can analyse the causes of the problem.

(a) Calculate the budgeted standard cost of one Trimouse.
(b) Prepare a statement analysing the high level of costs that are worrying the production manager using appropriate materials, labour and overhead variances.

(c)   Making use of your results in (b) interpret for management the key features of the firm's performance.

5.   Wrycooder Guitars is a manufacturer of one standard type of guitar. Its recent budgetary report for its assembly department for October 2004 is as follows:

Department: Assembly Annual output: 24000 guitars		Month: October 2004 (Month 7) This month's output: 2300 guitars		
Cost element	Annual budget (£)	Month's budget (£)	Actuals (£)	Variances (£)
Labour	240,000	20,000	21,340	1,340 A
Materials	480,000	40,000	46,500	6,500 A
Power	12,000	1,000	1,100	100 A
Depreciation	96,000	8,000	8,000	0
Totals	828,000	69,000	76,940	7,940 A

Indicate the weaknesses of the cost report presented above and explain how it could be improved.

Chapter 7
MANAGEMENT ACCOUNTING AND
THE CONTROL PROCESS – 2

Key Learning Objectives

By the time you have finished studying this chapter, you should be able to:
- discuss the relevance of, and improvements which might be made to, standard costing in contemporary organisational environments;
- analyse variances in order to provide the most appropriate information;
- calculate the probable benefits of a variance investigation;
- outline the theoretical background to the control process;
- explain and apply within a management accounting context, statistical control methods.

Further Aspects of Standard Costing

In Chapter 6 we looked at the basics of standard costing techniques and noted that, although based on sound principles, the techniques had a number of limitations in certain environments. Here we will look a little further at these limitations and consider approaches that have been suggested for increasing the efficacy of standard costing.

Let us start with a look at one of the more common 'extended' applications of standard costing.

Within the field of material variances, we have already studied the calculation of materials price and usage variances. Although these are useful variances, it is likely that, in at least some cases, those held responsible for variances will want to carry the analysis further in an attempt to isolate the actual causes of the variances and to try resolving them. In the pages that follow, we will see how the various possible factors leading to the existence of a variance may be identified through analysis.

One reasonable, obvious reason why a materials *usage* variance may occur is that, where a product involves the use of a mixture of different materials, the actual proportion of materials used may differ from the standard 'mix'. It is possible to analyse the proportion of the overall materials usage variance that has resulted from using materials in non-standard proportions. Such a variance may be termed a materials *mix* variance. The principles of calculating and interpreting such variances are illustrated below.

We will also explore other avenues of analysis. Standard costs are based upon standard usages and standard unit costs. In either case the standard itself may be poorly chosen. It is therefore possible, given sufficient information, to isolate the effects of poor planning. Such analysis may establish 'planning variances' (that is, those caused by poor planning) and may go even further in attempting to establish the extent to which this poor planning was unavoidable. The principles are also illustrated in the calculations and discussion below.

Mix Variances

A company produces product X, composed of materials A and B. Standard data for product X are as follows :

$$
\begin{array}{ll}
 & \pounds \\
\text{Material A: 3 kg @ £3 per kg} & = \ \ 9 \\
\text{Material B: 2 kg @ £5 per kg} & = \underline{10} \\
\text{Total materal cost per unit of Product X} & = 19
\end{array}
$$

Actual data were as follows

Units of Product X produced = 20 units

Actual materials usage:

Material A: 55 kg costing £200
Material B: 44 kg costing £230

Analysis of materials variances:

Traditional variances:
Materials *price* variances [actual materials @ std materials price – actual materials @ actual price]:

$$
\begin{array}{ll}
 & \pounds \\
\text{Material A: [55 kg} \times \text{£3/kg]} - \text{[£200]} = & (35) \text{ adv} \\
\text{Material B: [44 kg} \times \text{£5/kg]} - \text{[£230]} = & \underline{(10)} \text{ adv} \\
\text{Total materials price variance} & = \underline{\underline{(45)}} \text{ adv}
\end{array}
$$

Materials *usage* variances (traditional):

{= [std Q allowed for actual production – actual usage] × std material price}

$$
\begin{array}{ll}
 & \pounds \\
\text{Material A: \{[20 units} \times \text{3kg]} - \text{55 kg\}} \times \text{£3/kg} = & 15 \text{ fav} \\
\text{Material B: \{[20 units} \times \text{2kg]} - \text{44 kg\}} \times \text{£5/kg} = & \underline{(20)} \text{ adv} \\
\text{Total materials usage variance} & = \underline{\underline{(5)}} \text{ adv}
\end{array}
$$

Check:

Total materials variance =

= std material cost allowed for actual production
− actual materials cost

		£
for Material A = [20 units × 3 kg × £3/kg] − £200	=	(20) adv
for Material B = [20 units × 2 kg × £5/kg] − £230	=	(30) adv
Total materials variance[= price + usage variances]	=	(50) adv (correct)

Variances focusing on mix aspects:

Materials mix variance:

By comparing the amount of materials actually used with the proportion of each material that we would expect to see in the finished product, we can isolate the effects of non-standard mixes of materials. (Note that, actually, we are examining here the proportions of each material input to the product, rather than the materials mix evident in the process outputs).

What were the standard proportions of materials A and B?

Well, in the standards the material quantities were in the proportions 3:2, i.e. 0.6 of the material content of each unit of product X should consist of material A.

We can see that, in the actual mix, there were 55 kg of material within the total of 99 kg of material used, i.e. a proportion of material A of 55/99 = 0.555r of the actual mix.

Therefore there is a mismatch between the standard and actual mixes in that there is a lower proportion of material A which has the lower standard cost of £3 per kg. Therefore this will mean that a higher proportion of the more expensive material B will be evident, leading to a higher materials cost per unit of product X.

Materials mix variance =

= [std proportion of material in actual mix − actual quantity of material] × std material price

For *Material A:*

$= \{[0.6 × 99kg] − 55kg\} × £3/kg$ = £13.20 fav

For *Material B:*

$= \{[0.4 × 99kg] − 44kg\} × £5 /kg$ = £(22.00) adv

Total Materials mix variance = £(8.80) adv

Of course, the mix variance is just one part of the explanation of the non-standard use of materials. It has isolated the effect of non-standard mix from the rest of the materials usage variance. The remaining part of the materials usage variance, i.e. the 'mix adjusted usage variance' is often referred to as the *materials yield* variance and is calculated thus:

Materials *yield* variance =
> = [std allowed usage of material
>   − std proportion of actual materials usage] × std material price

For material A = {[20 units × 3 kg] − [99 kg × 0.6]} × £3/kg = £1.80 fav
For material B = {[20 units × 2 kg] − [99 kg × 0.4]} × £5/kg = <u>£2.00 fav</u>
         Therefore, total materials yield variance   = <u>£3.80 fav</u>

Note: Mix variance + Yield variance = Materials usage variance.

Check: £(8.80)   +   £3.80   =   £(5) adverse   (Correct)

The technique of analysing mix variances separately can be extended to most situations where an element of mix exists. Practising accountants must, however, consider carefully the pay-off between cost and complexity/usefulness of information. Information overload is an evil to be avoided and indulging in it can put the accountant at a distance from his/her colleagues.

Although mix variances are used in practice (e.g. in steel and chemical processing industries) they are sometimes used selectively. Such variances may be used to highlight specific factors upon which management wishes to focus without necessarily preparing a complete network of variances. Similarly, such variances may be calculated in non-financial terms only rather than attempting to show the effects on budgeted/actual profits. Further analysis of variances could take many forms. Figure 7.1 suggests some possible avenues that could be explored, using a materials cost variance for illustration.

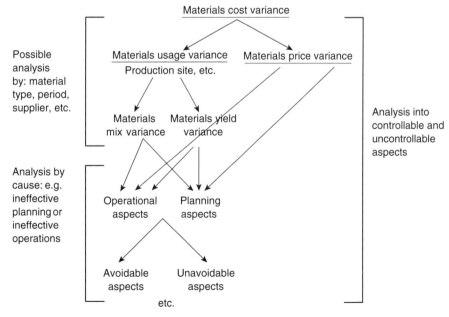

Figure 7.1   Possible avenues for exploring variances in more depth

Another possible way of visualising the richness of possible variance analysis is demonstrated in Figure 7.2, using materials variance as an example.

A numerical illustration

Now let's put some numbers to the above variances to see how they would look in practice. Exhibit 7.1 contains an illustration of the calculation of some of the variances described above.

<table>
<tr><td>**EXHIBIT 7.1**</td><td>**Illustration of a More Comprehensive Analysis of Materials Variances**</td></tr>
</table>

A company's materials data for a period were as follows:

Actual data:

Units of product produced = 110 units

Materials purchased and used:
Materials X: 230 kg costing   £720
Material Y: 280 kg costing   £500

Budget data:

Budegeted production = 100 units of product

Standard data:
               Per unit of product

Material X: 2 kg @ £3/kg
Material Y: 3 kg @ £2/kg

Ex-post ('after the event') data

With hindsight, it is realised that the person who set the materials standards should have realised that a more realistic usage standard for material X would have been 2.2 kg per unit of product.

Similarly, obvious changes in the market for material Y should have made the person who set the price standards realise that the standard price for Y should have been set at £1.80 per kg.

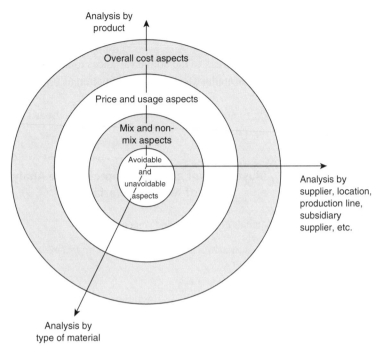

Figure 7.2   **The multidimensional aspects of (materials) variance anaylsis**

Analysing the data
Let us construct a table which presents the data available in a readily analysable way:
What is the 'standard mix'? In this example, we can calculate it as follows:

Material	Actual materials @ actual price	Actual materials @ std price	Actual materials in std proportions @ std price	Std quantities allowed for actual production, @ std price	Actual material quantities @ *realistic* std price	Std allowed quantities (at *realistic* std usage rate) @ original std price
	(i)	(ii)	(iii)	(iv)	(v)	(vi)
X	230 kg costing **£720**	230 kg @ £3 = **£690**	204 kg @ £3 = **£612**	100 units × 2 kg @ £3 = **£600**	230kg @ £3 = **£690**	100 units × 2.2 kg @ £3 = **660**
Y	280 kg costing **£500**	280 kg @ £2 = **£560**	306 kg @ £2 = **£612**	100 units × 3 kg @ £2 = **£600**	280 kg @ £1.80 = **£504**	100 units × 3 kg @ £2 = **£600**

Standard mix = 2 kg of X + 3kg of Y = 5 kg in total.

i.e. standard proportions are 40% X to 60% Y, by weight.

The total actual usage of materials was 230 kg of X and 280 kg of Y, i.e. 510 kg in total.

Therefore, the actual materials if they had been in the standard proportions would have been in the following proportions:

Material X [510 × 40%] = 204 kg
Material Y [510 × 60%] = 306 kg

Variance Analysis:

Let us start by calculating the 'traditional' materials variances (A = adverse, F = favourable)

Materials price variance (= (ii) − (i) in the table above):

$$£$$

Material X = £690 − £720   = (30) A
Material Y = £560 − £500   = 60 F
Total materials price variance = 30 F

Materials usage variance (= (iv) − (ii)):

Material X = £600 − £690   = (90) A
Material Y = £600 − £560   = 40 F
Total materials usage variance = (50) A

Now, analysing the materials usage variances further in order to isolate the effects of non-standard mix:

Materials *mix* variances (= (iii) − (ii)):

Material X: = £612 − £690   = (78) A
Material Y: = £612 − £560   = 52 F
Total materials mix variance   = (26) A

Materials *yield* variances ((iv) − (iii)):

Material X: = £600 − £612   = (12) A
Material Y: = £600 − £612   = (12) A
Total materials yield variance = (24) A

Note that the total materials mix variance [(26) A] plus the total materials yield variance [(24) A] must equal the total materials usage variance [(50) A].

Now, analysing the materials price variances – for Material Y – further, to isolate the effects of ineffective planning:

Materials price *planning* variance – for Material Y:

$$= \text{(ii)} - \text{(v)} = £560 - £504 = £56 \text{ F}$$

Materials price *operational* variance for Material Y:

$$= \text{(v)} - \text{(i)} = £504 - £500 = £4 \text{ F}$$

Note that the materials price planning variance [£56 F] plus the materials price operational variance [£4 F] must equal the materials price variance for material Y [£60 F – see above].

Taking a similar approach, we can isolate the planning variance aspects of the materials usage variance for *Material X*:

Material usage variance for Material X (see above)	= £(90) A
Materials usage *planning* variance [(iv) – (vi)] = £600 – £660	= £(60) A
Materials usage *operational* variance [(vi) – (ii)] = £660 – £690	= £(30) A

Check:
Material X usage planning variance + usage operational variance = usage variance (√).

As mentioned earlier, such analyses as those above can be taken to extreme extents. We could, for instance, have calculated the mix and yield variances at the realistic standard materials prices, or have used the realistic standard usage rates for X etc. What, however, would these 'extra' variances have told us? Well, for such variances to be useful, it must be possible for users to understand them. Let us have a go at understanding the meaning of the variances we have calculated above.

Interpreting Mix and Yield Variances

The materials usage variance is a useful indicator of non-standard usage rates but it can be distorted when materials are used in proportions that are not standard. In Exhibit 7.1, the standards assume that materials will be used in proportions 2 kg of X to 3 kg of Y. In the actual mix, these proportions are not maintained.

The adverse mix variance for X tells us that, in total, the use of a non-standard mix cost the business an extra £26. The individual mix variances indicate that the overall £26 adverse variance was caused by using more than the standard allowance of X (which is more expensive) and less of Y (which is less expensive).

The yield variance is simply a reworked usage variance undistorted by the non-standard mix effect.

While mix variances can be useful for identifying the effects of non-standard materials mix, they must be interpreted carefully. Although, for example, using less than the standard proportion of Y has 'saved' material costs, this may mean that the product becomes useless, or that labour costs increase as the product becomes more difficult to operate upon.

A similar approach may be taken to any factors which may be subject to variation in mix, so that variances such as sales mix variances and labour mix variances could be calculated. Again, the full significance of non-standard mixes for quality, marketability and efficiency must be considered carefully.

Interpreting Planning and Operational Variances

We analysed, in Exhibit 7.1, the materials price variance for material Y in the aspects caused by ineffective planning (the sales price planning variance) and by operational factors (the sales price operational variance). What can these variances tell us? Again, we must take care in interpreting them.

The sales price variance tells us the amount by which profits have been affected by the use of non-standard selling process. Of course, the sales price variance might be caused by one of two factors (or both): increases/decreases in sales price above/below the standard; and the use of an inappropriate standard. That is to say, the sales price planning variance tells us how much of the sales price variance was caused by poor planning; whereas the sales price operational variance gives us an adjusted sales price variance, undistorted by the effects of this bad planning.

Once again, questions need to be addressed when interpreting the sales price planning variance, such as:

- How should the realistic standard be established and how should subjectivity be minimised?
- Was the error in setting the standard unavoidable?

Some writers have suggested that planning variances could be split into their 'possibly avoidable' and 'unavoidable' components – but we must take care not to get too carried away! If we were to follow the route suggested by such authors, it would be possible for a manager to argue that his/her adverse planning variance was caused largely by poor planning and that he/she had not been responsible for setting the standards. Attention would then pass to the person who had set the standard who, in turn, might then 'pass the buck' by suggesting that the planning error was largely unavoidable. Splitting the materials usage variance into planning and operational aspects leads us to a similar set of considerations.

Standard Costing in Non-Manufacturing Environments

Standard costing evolved in reponse to a particular type of environment. After all, the term 'standard costing' refers to an environment in which repetitive activities lead to standardisation of resource usage (standard time, standard resource usage). Such an environment exhibited the features of the mass production of components or products over considerable periods of time.

The nature of today's business environment is rather different. Long production runs of standard products have, in many cases, given way to shorter runs of much more diverse and customised products in response to customer expectations. Wider markets, stimulated by more effective communications technologies, have also led to businesses' needing to become more flexible and responsive. Consequently, in many but not all cases, the manufacturing business environment has moved away from the fundamental characteristics traditionally associated with standard costing techniques.

Of course, the market for services and service organisations has expanded rapidly as have, in many countries, the size and range of public sector organisations. So, does standard costing still play a useful role in such environments? To an extent, yes.

In modern 'high tech' manufacturing environments, elements of standardisation will still be found. Materials will still be used within products, although the use of these materials may change more rapidly as products are redesigned more frequently and as the business responds to consumer tastes. Direct labour input to products will, however, tend to decrease in relevance as technology is increasingly harnessed. Although labour will still be utilised, this will tend to be more in the nature of a fixed overhead than a direct variable cost. Thus the nature of labour variances must change. Overhead costs will become a more significant aspect of the overall cost structure and the emphasis of overhead costs will reflect the greater effort being put into marketing, technological developments, communications, and so on. Thus, the traditional cost structures associated with standard costing have been replaced by a less standardised, overhead-heavy, more non-production-biased cost structure.

Although standard costing approaches can still be applied to such situations, several factors must be considered:

- the extent of standardised processes;
- the benefits to be gained, in terms of improved management information, by applying standard costing approaches;
- the problems associated with trying to 'force' ill-fitting techniques into an unsuitable environment.

Conversely, the 'standard' application of standard costing techniques may be replaced by a more relevant, tailored application by:

- concentrating less on extreme accuracy and detail and more on broader, more strategic issues;
- investing less in time-consuming, over-formal systems and, instead, using standard costing approaches more as a useful aid to planning and cost control;

- making increased use of flexible, user-friendly software to increase the speed with which standard costing techniques may be used and to increase the 'disposability' of the standard costs being used.

Each case must be judged on its merits and care must be taken to avoid dogged attempts to apply outdated techniques. This is, of course, a philosophy that should be followed wherever systems are in danger of becoming outdated or obsolete. Similar questions about the usefulness and appropriateness of standard costing apply to non-manufacturing and public sector environments.

Service (Non-Manufacturing) Environments

Service organisations, although they do not produce physical products, share many (standardised) characteristics with manufacturing organisations:

- They employ labour, though the relationship between hours worked and units of service provided may not always be clear.
- They incur overheads (occupy buildings, use electricity, pay for insurance, etc.).
- They need to market their services at home and overseas.

There are some differences, unsurprisingly, between service and manaufacturing organisations:

- The level of stocks in a service organisation is likely to be much lower, Although consumable materials may be stored, there can be no stocks of 'finished goods' in a service organisation. An airline cannot, for instance, carry a stock of unused travel slots, or places on chartered flights from previous periods – once they have gone, they have gone! Work-in-progess stocks may need to be evaluated, however, for example in the case of 'incomplete work' carried out by solicitors or accountants.
- There is likely to be a greater emphasis on indirect (overhead) costs, although it is feasible to treat labour costs as direct to a unit of service output when hours are recorded to jobs (e.g. in a vehicle repair workshop). Overall, however, and in the shorter term, labour is relatively fixed and is thus essentially an overhead item.
- The focus of the business may be on throughput, rather than on detailed analyses of essentially fixed costs.
- The focus may be more on the customer, or the major contract, than on repeated mass output of small-scale units.

The use of traditional standard costing under such conditions is thus questionable. Although attempts have been made to use standard costing within such environments, this may be more evidence of resistance to change than a case of applying the most appropriate solution to modern organisational issues. Not a great deal of research appears to have been undertaken on the subject of the application of standard costing techniques to non-manufacturing environments, possibly as a result of the lack of 'fit' of the techniques in such settings.

Non-manufacturing environments, with their emphasis on overhead costs, are likely to be environments in which activity-based costing approaches may be applied to advantage. Drury (2004) mentions the work of Kaplan (1994) and Mak and Roush (1994) who suggest a specialised application of standard costing to activity costs and cost drivers. The resultant variance calculations, however, give the impression of being an academic exercise with little useful application (or comprehensibility) for everyday non-financial managers.

Statistical Approaches to Variance Investigation

We have examined the use of variances to isolate the components of an overall variance. Such analysis will not tell the investigator the answers to the following questions, amongst others:

- What caused the variance?
- Was the variance the outcome of a continuing or one-off issue?
- Was the variance directly related to other variances (i.e. was the underlying cause of the variance a single factor or one of several interconnected factors)?
- How long it would take, and how much it would cost, to investigate the variance further?
- Would such further investigation be likely to identify the cause of the variance?
- Would the cost of the investigation, and any subsequent corrective action, be justified by the benefits?
- How would these benefits be identified and evaluated?

Questions such as these can be presented within a network/tree such as that in Figure 7.3. Such a diagram can be extended almost indefinitely given the number of outcomes that can occur (you might want to try this for yourself).

In Exhibit 7.2 we use some data to illustrate the general approach that might be taken to the process outlined within Figure 7.3. Again we must be careful here. The analysis described in Exhibit 7.2 would be dependent upon a great deal of estimations and it would be foolish to get too carried away with the application of such techniques.

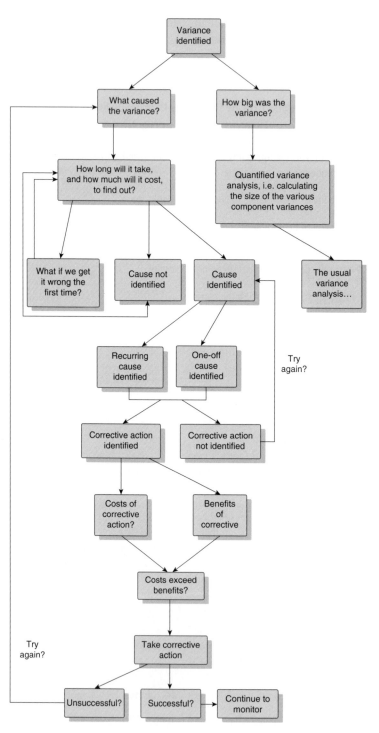

Figure 7.3　Variance investigation tree

Using the data above we can identify the costs and expected value of benefits resulting from an attempt to 'cure' the variance. Figure 7.4 displays the data in the form of a 'probability tree'. In numerical terms:

Application of Statistical Techniques to the Variance Investigation/Correction Decision

A company has identified a cost variance for a period. Experienced staff within the company have produced the following estimates:

Probability of the variance having a identifiable cause	=	70%
Probability of being able to identify appropriate corrective action	=	60%
Probability of corrective action being successful	=	80%
Probable cost of identifying the cause	=	£100
Probable cost of identifying appropriate corrective action	=	£80
Probable costs of corrective action	=	£150
Probable benefits:		
if variance is a one-off event	=	£1000
if variance is recurring	=	£5000
Probability of variance being caused by a one-off factor	=	50%

Please bear in mind that these figures have been made up! We are merely trying to illustrate a general approach here. If you think about these data you will see that, in reality, to try to assess all these factors in detail would be highly unfeasible. The likelihood is that, in the practical situation, such techniques would be applied sparingly and, even then, to one subset of the problem at a time.

Cost of successfully 'cured' variance = £100 + £80 + £150 = £330

Probability of achieving success in curing the variance = $0.7 \times 0.6 \times 0.4 = 0.168$

Probability of the variance being a recurring one = $0.168 \times 0.4 = 0.0672$

Therefore, expected value = $0.0672 \times £5000 = £336$

Probability of the variance being non-recurring = $0.168 \times 0.6 = 0.1008$

Therefore, expected value = $0.1008 \times £1,000 = £101$

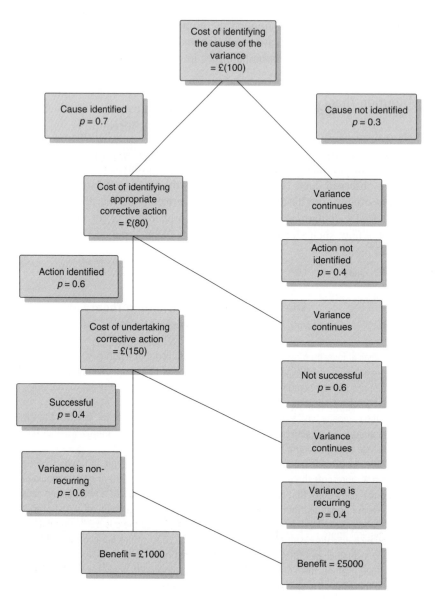

Figure 7.4   Probability tree for Exhibit 7.2 data

Therefore expected net value of the investigation and correction process = £336 + £101 − £330 = £107

Therefore the investigation and correction process has a positive value of £107 and is thus probably worthwhile.

Of course, we must bear in mind the limitations of such a statistical approach to this decision. The reliability of our conclusion is entirely dependent upon the accuracy of the estimated costs, benefits and probabilities in the data used.

Normal Distribution Theory

One of the quantities that would have to be estimated in Exhibit 7.2 is the probability that the observed variance was caused by an identifiable cause (i.e. other than random factors). Any variance can be caused by the everyday, random variations that occur in most observed data. Normal distribution theory is based upon the assumption that data are often normally distributed around a mean and that the use of standard deviation based calculations can identify the probability of an occurrence. Exhibit 7.3 illustrates how such statistical techniques could be applied to variance investigation considerations.

| EXHIBIT 7.3 | The Use of Normal Distribution Theory in Variance Investigations |

Statistical investigation of past periods has identified that a particular direct unit variance has a mean value of £100, with a standard deviation of £20. Consequently, a value of £100 has been used as the standard cost per unit for this item. In the latest period, the same cost item had an observed value of £130.

The company wishes to use normal distribution theory to decide whether the variance from standard (i.e. £30 adverse) is likely to be worth investigating – that is, whether the variance is likely to have an identifiable, non-random, cause.

We can present the data above in a normal distribution graph. In Figure 7.5 the shaded area X represents the probability that an observed cost of £130 or greater would occur under normal conditions, that is, that the adverse variance of £30 had a non-random cause.

From normal distribution tables we can see that the probability of a cost of £130 or above is only approx. 7% (i.e. a Z score of 30/20 = 1.5), hence there is a 7% probability that the variance was the result of random unassignable causes. Thus we can conclude that there is only a small chance that the variance would not have an assignable cause.

How useful is this analysis? Well, we would still need to apply some subjective judgement and the analysis is only as good as our assumptions:

- The probability of the variance's occurring is only as reliable as the data upon which the calculations have been based.
- The value calculated does not give a positive yes/no answer to the question of whether it is worth investigating the variance. Although in the research world a figure of 5% or 10% is sometimes used to indicate whether something is significant, this approach is still arbitrary to some extent.
- The likelihood that the variance has an assignable (i.e. non-random) cause does not guarantee that it has a readily identifiable cause.

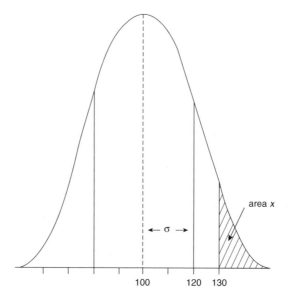

Figure 7.5   Investigation of latest direct unit variance in Exhibit 7.3

Control Systems and their Influence on Organisational Design

The interface between control systems and human behaviour has been a fertile ground for research activity. The application of accounting control systems may always lead to undesired behavioural consequences, sometimes even resulting in behaviour that is the opposite of that which was intended. All management accounting activity, whether in the area of standard costing, budgeting, decision making or control, carries with it the dangers of unintended adverse behavioural responses.

As we have seen in this and earlier chapters, enthusiasm to apply a given control technique may lead one to ignore the potential human reactions. Below are some brief summaries of some of the noted authors in this area. Fuller summaries of these articles are given in the recommended further reading section at the end of this chapter.

Principal–Agent Theory

Principal–agent or agency theory, discussed in more depth in Gietzmann (1995), considers the behavioural impacts of transactional relationships that exist within and between organisational players. In any transaction or business relationship the parties involved will have unequal amounts of power. The party in the stronger position (the principal) will attempt to enforce his/her requirements upon the weaker party (the agent) via the use of monitoring and control mechanisms. Management accounting systems may constitute such controls. The agent, whose rewards or potential penalties will depend upon being seen to behave in the manner required by the principal, will be keen to be seen to be performing well. Thus the agent may be tempted to induce a degree of bias and incomplete/misleading information into the system ('moral hazard'). The agent's ability to do this will depend on the degree to which each party has access to the 'true position'. Thus 'information asymmetry' is a significant factor in the process. Such ideas are of obvious relevance to management accounting, whose effectiveness is only as good as the reliability of the information it produces.

Gietzmann (1995) gives an introduction to the underlying principles of agency theory, discussing the inferential control problem, moral hazard, and asymmetric information. Although the principal within a principal–agent relationship can select some form of reward system (e.g. results-based wages), there is no guarantee that this will result in desirable actions by the agent. Gietzmann describes, and illustrates mathematically, the principles and assumptions behind agency cost–benefit calculations when trying to optimise the agent's or principal's utility.

Chwastiak (1999) claims that principal–agent theory is loaded with capitalist subjectivity and that it thus legitimises exploitation of weaker parties – it is in the principal's interest. Chwastiak argues that it should have the aim of human enrichment rather than material gains for the owners of businesses. Accounting is seen as being representative of this process of abandonment of human rights/needs in favour of corporate interests. Such systems, Chwastiak argues, see humans as a means to an end, and impose a cold rationality on organisational decision making and control systems. Chwastiak argues that accounting, by taking a more holistic approach, could go some way to righting the balance between the means and ends of production.

Contingency Theory

Contingency theory, as it applies to management accounting, states that no one system is ideal for all situations. The effectiveness of a control or planning system will be dependent upon the extent to which it 'fits' the environment within which it operates. Management accountants must therefore be careful to optimise the appropriateness of the systems that they produce, and to monitor these systems' response to change.

Otley (1980) attempts to construct an improved model of a contingency theory of management accounting based around organisational control and effectiveness. He criticises many models of contingent variables as difficult to monitor/measure and as oversimplistic. He says that it is often 'impossible to separate the effect of an accounting information system from other controls; they act as a package and must be assessed jointly'. He adds that a fundamental issue is to find useful and meaningful ways of measuring effectiveness.

Behavioral Impacts, the Aspects of Power and Social Groupings and the Importance of Ethical Considerations

Robson and Cooper (1989) suggest that organisational goals exist within a 'social world' and are thus 'constructions', so management control systems may be seen as 'power systems'. They identify several approaches to the idea of power. It is possible, they contend, to see power as either a positive or negative phenomenon, in the context of management accounting/control.

They examine the implications of different views of the sources/effects of power for management control systems and draw the links between their analysis and such areas as principal–agent theory and the 'received wisdom' regarding the traditionally assumed purposes of management accounting systems.

Merchant (1998) identifies the need to consider the rights, values and ethics of all stakeholders, and presents a range of socialist and capitalist views of management issues. He argues that a consideration of the ethical aspects of management issues may prevent managers/management accountants being 'unreservedly optimistic'. He discusses the differences between ethical and legal stances and explains that laws can be oversimplistic (e.g. 'do no harm', 'never lie') in a business context, although he argues that some (e.g. 'do unto others') can work quite well. He presents various models of ethics, describing how they may apply to management control issues. He suggests a framework for analysing ethical issues, which is essentially applicable in a similar fashion to many other decision-making models.

Merchant also gives an analysis of the ethical aspects of the budgetary slack/padding decision (e.g. the advantages of protecting the 'weak' against the disadvantages of inherently fraudulent practice). He provides similar, interesting analyses of the ethical issues involved in management control areas such as the 'massaging' of earnings and 'creative accounting'.

Additional commentaries on the role of power and ethics within management accounting are given by Burns (2000) – see the further reading section at the end of this chapter.

The Theory of Constraints

The theory of constraints is an idea promulgated by Goldratt and Cox (1984). Goldratt argues that commercial organisations should have only one goal – 'to make more profit now and in the future' – thus performance measures must indicate the firm's progress towards this goal.

Goldratt argues that by focusing on the 'cost world', management accountants tend to create 'local optima' which are not necessarily congruent with global optima. The theory of constraints, also known as *throughput accounting,* promotes the idea that global performance (i.e. performance of the whole organisation) may be usefully gauged (Goldratt, 1990a) in terms of:

* *throughput*, which is defined as sales less raw (direct) materials;
* *inventory*, i.e. money invested in things which it is intended to sell (including plant, property, equipment and stocks);
* *operating expense*, i.e. money spent on converting inventory into throughput

(note that Goldratt's definitions of these items are not the traditional ones). The overall aim (goal), according to Goldratt, is to 'increase throughput while decreasing inventory and operating expense'. Goldratt feels that this focus should be enough to ensure the success of the organisation and, for control purposes, suggests suitable performance measures, including:

- net profit (throughput minus operating expense)
- return on inventory (net profit divided by inventory)
- productivity (throughput divided by operating expense)
- inventory turnover (throughput divided by inventory).

Goldratt argues that, to maintain continuous improvement, management accountants should change their priorities as follows:

Priority	Cost-world orientation (focus)	Throughput-world orientation
1st	operating expense	throughput
2nd	throughput	inventory
3rd	inventory	operating expense

Goldratt argues that, although many apparent constraints exist within an organisation, only a few real constraints (*bottlenecks*) exist, and he calls the process of isolating (and eliminating) these 'focusing'.

A wider reading of Goldratt's work (which evolved and developed over time) is necessary to fully understand his proposals (see Goldratt, 1990b). Many criticisms have been made of Goldratt's work, for example regarding its potential to increase short-termism, although Goldratt has commented that a contingent/flexible approach should be taken when applying the principles of the theory of constraints within any organisation.

The Link between Control and Decision making

One thing should be relatively clear from a reading of the authors mentioned above. The various considerations of ethics, agency relationships and power all have implications for both control and planning systems. The behavioural consequences resulting from control systems set up in the past may also be observed in the future, as a result of the decisions made today. In effect, the planning systems of today lead to the control systems of tomorrow and so planning and control systems are part of a continuum, rather than separate entities. This understanding implies that management accountants should consider both aspects simultaneously within their professional activities.

Conclusions

This chapter has shown that:

- standard costing needs to be adapted in an effort to increase its appropriateness to modern business environments.

- care should be taken not to produce standard costing information that is unnecessary, irrelevant or of little value;
- variances should be analysed in the most appropriate way, to suit the user's needs;
- a significant amount of theoretical background exists to the control process which can help the management accountant to understand the context and impacts of her/his activities;
- among the most significant theories are contingency theory, agency theory and theories associated with ethics and power.

Summary

In this chapter we have considered the extent to which standard costing is still relevant in today's organisational environment. We have seen that standard costing's history is in the industrial, mass-production setting and that its significance may be less today, particularly in non-manufacturing environments. We have looked at some attempts to increase its relevance but have also realised that one should not get too carried away in trying to maintain a technique for its own sake. We have looked in more detail at some of the behavioural theories that underlie the practice of management accounting. It is important to realise that, when studying such theories, we take a critical and enquiring stance and consider the practical applicability of such theories to any given setting.

Recommended Further Reading

Otley, D.T. (1980) 'The contingency theory of management accounting: achievement and prognosis', *Accounting, Organisations and Society*, **5(4): 413–428.**

Otley attempts to construct an improved model of a contingency theory of management accounting based on organisational control and effectiveness.

He cites the contingency approach, according to which 'there is no universally appropriate accounting system'. He mentions the work of Charles T. Horngren who argues that the management accounting system and the organisation structure are inseparable, and that of J. Dermer (*Management Planning and Control System*, 1977), who argues that there is no prescribed system, only possibilities of what might be done in any particular situation. Otley's empirical results (to 1980) suggested the following contingent variables:

- the effect of *technology structure* (production technology, task complexity/variety, etc.)
- the effect of *organisation structure* (hierarchy, rigidity, style of budget use, etc.)
- the effect of the *environment* (competition types/force etc.)

Otley suggests that the earlier contingency theory of organisations led to the applications to management accounting although, since 1979, the contingency theory of organisations had been heavily criticised. He refers to the work of a number of writers in this area:

- Bruns and Waterhouse 'Budgetary control and organization structure', (1975) suggest two modes of control strategy (administrative and interpersonal) suitable for different organisational arrangements.
- In 1977 D.C. Hayes published an article, 'The contingency theory of management accounting', in which he suggests that subunit interdependence, environmental relationship and internal factors of subunits are important to subunit performance.
- L.A. Gordon and D. Miller's article 'A contingency framework for the design of accounting information systems' (1976) tried to construct a comprehensive framework of contingent variables. Waterhouse and Tiesen 'A contingency framework for management accouting systems research', (1978) propose a much simpler framework with two main variables – environment (simple/complex; static/dynamic) and technology (degree of routineness, etc.).
- Dermer suggests that management accounting information system design depends upon the objectives of the system; the differentiation and decentralisation form chosen; the nature and mix of the processes being controlled; and the managerial style of senior managers.

Otley proposes a linear framework of AIS design:

contingent variables—organisational design—type of AI system—organisational effectiveness

He criticises many models of contingent variables as difficult to monitor/measure and as oversimplistic. He says that it is often 'impossible to separate the effect of an [accounting information system] from other controls; they act as a package and must be assessed jointly'.

Otley and Berry (1980) suggest that four characteristics are necessary for effective control:

- clearly specified objectives;
- a measure of the degree of attainment of that objective;
- a predictive model of the likely outcomes (of the control system);
- the ability and motivation to act.

They add that a fundamental issue is to find useful and meaningful ways of measuring effectiveness and of gauging the effect of the accounting information system information.

Robson, K. and Cooper, D.J. (1989) 'Power and management control', in W.F. Chua, E.A. Lowe and A.G. Puxty (eds), *Critical Perspectives in Management Control*, London: Macmillan, pp. 79–114.
Robson and Cooper suggest that organisational goals exist within a 'social world' and are thus 'constructions', so management control systems may be seen as 'power systems'. They identify several approaches to the idea of power, some of which are outlined below. It is possible to see power as either a positive or negative phenomenon, in the context of management accounting/control.

Objectivist approaches have a behavioural concern with 'who has power'. Power is a negative force, denying the interests of others. Empirically:

- *pluralism* concentrates upon observing conflict as society or organisations try to influence others.
- *elitism* also looks at who decides 'what is to be decided', by focusing on observable conflicts.
- *radicalism* involves identifying the 'real interests' of those over whom power is exercised (i.e. not the artificial 'needs' into which they have socialised). This, of course, is difficult to do.

Overall, the objectivist paradigm treats power as 'an exercise and a simple relation between individuals'. Few management control/accounting textbooks mention power, its origins, forms or effects, except when conflict is at issue (e.g. in identifying who influences budgets and strategies). Very few studies of management control and power take either elitist or radical approaches. They all tend to ignore the *source* of power and tend to focus on the actions of individuals.

The *integration* approach is concerned with the 'power to do', that is, power as an 'economic medium'. In this context, power is legitimised through 'binding obligations' secured by those with the capacity to do so, via collective, normative consensus. Here, power need not be linked with conflict if societal, normative consensus exists. It recognises, however, that 'common goals' may arise via manipulation. Power is seen as a property of societies, through social conditioning, for example at school and via everyday life (a view similar in some ways to that of Foucault). Within this paradigm, the management control literature sees power as an 'enabling force' within a reasonably static and harmonious environment. It thinks of principal–agent theory as merely the principal's problem, and that if the principal is satisfied, so will be the agent. Robson and Cooper refer to work of Michael Crozier, who sees the source of power in the control of 'critical uncertainties', and to that of John French, Jr. and Bertram Raven, who identify power as having five main sources or types – reward; expert; coercive; legitimate; referent. Such ideas, similar to those of Talcott Parsons, arise out of the 'social system' concept. Some views add that power comes additionally from environmental, as well as, organisational factors (i.e. from outside as well as within the organisation).

Marx suggests that power is derived from past actions, economic practices and modes of production. *Historical materialism* looks at the social transformation and power relationships that derive from different modes of production. Robson and Cooper refer to Nicos Poulantzas who sees power as the 'capacity of a class to realise its objective interests', but denies that *class* is the foundation of power. He sees power as being an *effect* of the levels in the hierarchical order, rather than as residing within the levels (i.e. power tends to overlook the individual as a 'conscious, self-determining entity'). Robson and Cooper point to other factors affecting power, such as state exploitation, gender conflict and racial discrimination, and criticise historical materialism for adding little to our knowledge of the operation of power in everyday life, while conceding that it does recognise power's historical context.

Robson and Cooper feel that taking a historical materialist approach puts management control in a historical context and sees management control systems as dynamic and contingent, helping to produce the social world in which they operate. Management is seen as having little autonomy (i.e. it must follow the wishes of capitalists, in conflict with labour). Standard costing is, for example, seen as a means of transferring specialist knowledge to managers who can then control the work, thereby dominating labour. Return on capital employed is also seen as a tool of the domination of labour by capitalists. Much academic work has revolved around the 'labour process', the appropriation process, direct surveillance and the coercion of productive labour via formal organisation, planning, reward and training systems all in the interest of capitalists' enlarging the capital. They refer to the work of P. Armstrong, who discusses the increasing centrality of the role of accountants in industry (by taking advantage of their role in the appropriation process).

Concerning disciplinary power, Robson and Cooper also refer to Foucault (1977), who underlines the notion of progress by the delegitimising of the present. He argues that (through surveillance, regulation of the 'self', etc.), power produces knowledge. Foucault argues that power is exercised more efficiently through invisible, 'lenient' approaches to produce the human being as a 'docile body'. Discipline can be seen as a form of domination, or as a way of increasing utility. He argues that disciplinary power creates individuals, how to position/judge them and how to induce self-regulation.

Robson and Cooper discuss the implications for management control (and management accounting) of the foregoing. The surveillance of managers via cost accounting, budgets and performance reports increases the domination of (power over) managers and productive workers, and faster communications increase the ability to dominate/discipline. Much of current accounting systems (see Loft, 1995) relates to the control of industry by the military during the war years, as the idea of 'intelligence' crossed over to the industrial sector. R&C conclude that management control practices have not evolved out of a rational need to control/allocate resources. The desire on the part of capitalists and the state to dominate has, they argue, played a big part. Power (if we agree with Foucault) comes with knowledge.

Merchant, K.A. (1998) 'Management control-related ethical issues and analyses', in *Modern Management Control Systems*, Prentice Hall, pp. 697–712.

Merchant identifies the need to consider the rights, values, and ethics of all stakeholders, and presents a range of socialist and capitalist views of management issues. He argues that a consideration of the ethical aspects of management issues prevent managers and management accountants being 'unreservedly optimistic'. He suggests that senior managers (such as management accountants) have the opportunity to act as 'moral exemplars'. He discusses the differences between ethical and legal stances and explains that laws can be oversimplistic (e.g. 'do no harm', 'never lie') in a business context, although he argues that some (e.g. 'do unto others') can work quite well.

Merchant presents various models of ethics, describing how they may apply to management control issues. He explains that *Utilitarianism* judges the 'righteousness' of actions based on their consequences (and the amount of good or bad they cause). He explains that there is a need to consider group vs. individual utility giving the examples of the decisions that need to be taken wherein 'the needs of the many outweigh the needs of the few'.

Merchant considers the issues of *Right and Duties*. He poses the question of how we know what rights are or whether they actually exist. He comments on the dangers of the over-proliferation of claimed rights. *Justice*, Merchant explains, is based on equity, expressed through the introduction of systems of penalties, compensation and so on. Additionally, Merchant considers the concept of *Virtues* – integrity, loyalty, courage etc. – and he describes how such concepts are difficult to define and impose in the practical situation.

Merchant gives an example of a 'code of conduct' and the difficulties its application might cause. He suggests a framework for analysing ethical issues which is essentially similar to any other decision-making model:

- defining the 'facts';
- defining the ethical issues;
- specifying alternative courses of action;
- evaluating and choosing the best alternative.

Merchant also gives an analysis of the ethical aspects of the budgetary slack/padding decision (e.g. the advantages of protecting the 'weak' against the disadvantages of inherently fraudulent practice). He provides similar, interesting analyses of the ethical issues involved in management control areas such as the 'massaging' of earnings and 'creative accounting'.

Gietzmann, M. (1995), 'Introduction to agency theory in management accounting', in Ashton D, Hopper T and Scapens R, Issues in *Management Accounting* (2nd edition), Hemel Hempstead, Prentice Hall, 259–272.

Principal–agent theory or agency theory relates to decentralised organisations and arises out of the need for delegation. Where delegation exists, the transparency of decision making disappears. Agency theory looks at the 'costs' of delegation arising out of such unobservability of decision making at other levels.

The organisation can be seen as a set of transactions or relationships between principals and agents and controls designed (with their associated cost effects) to ensure that the agent acts in the best interests of the principal.

Gietzmann gives an introduction to the underlying principles of agency theory, focusing on the inferential control problem and on moral hazard.

The inferential control problem is that performance measurement is usually carried out by results/outputs and thus the principal can only infer what efforts/actions by the agent caused these (imperfectly measured and represented) results. Chance, for instance, will have some indeterminable effect on results. Similarly, the causal relationship of input/result is not perfectly known by the agent. Agency theory also assumes wealth-maximising and work-averse (theory X) agents.

Moral hazard concerns itself with the problem that, although the principal can select some form of reward system (e.g. results-based wages), there is no guarantee that this will result in desirable actions by the agent.

The article describes, and illustrates mathematically, the principles and assumptions behind agency cost–benefit calculations when trying to optimise the agent's/principal's utility. The illustration presented is worth following through to obtain a feel of the assumptions and quantifications, which would be necessary, if one were to attempt a practical application of the theory.

One issue to consider (again, an illustration is given) is that the effort required to produce an optimum reward for the agent may not be the highest effort level, nor that which is optimal to the principal.

Throughout the article, the idea of the asymmetry of information is identified, an idea which has implications for many areas of management accounting.

Chwastiak, M. (1999) 'Deconstructing the principal–agent model: a view from the bottom', *Critical Perspectives on Accounting,* **10: 425–441.**

Chwastiak claims that principal–agent theory is loaded with capitalist subjectivity and that it thus legitimises exploitation; that is, principal–agent theory is seen as being in the *principal's* interest. He argues that PAT should have the aim of human enrichment rather than material gains.

Chwastiak argues that principal–agent theory is legitimised by giving the appearance that it is in everyone's interest, good for the labour force as well as for the principal. It does so by equating wealth accumulation with self-realisation, thus ignoring the richer aspects of the human experience. He argues that principal–agent theory supports the growth of the economy, ignoring human needs. Accounting is seen as being representative of this process of abandonment of human interests for corporate ones. Such systems see humans as a means to an end, and impose a cold rationality on organisational decision making and control systems.

Chwastiak suggests that such exploitative systems tend to alienate agents and destroy their potential for autonomy and self-fulfilment. Additionally, such systems, he claims, will tend to have destructive effects upon the environment and world order. Chwastiak recommends that a system that supports organisational 'kinship' rather than partisan relationships (as in principal–agent theory) should be sought and that accounting, by taking a more holistic approach, could go some way to righting the balance between the means and ends of production.

The rather emotional, left-wing, revolutionary style of the article may not find much favour with accounting/finance-based readers, but this may be a result of such readers' entrenched traditionalist views (as a result of their conventional business/accounting education?).

Case study: Dayview Ltd

Dayview Ltd was established in 1975 and manufactures a range of night-sighting optical (NSO) equipment. The company was founded by two brothers, Mike and Terry Scope, both of whom had previously worked as skilled engineers in the optical instrument industry.

Until 1994, the company had produced its products entirely under contracts with the British armed forces. Since 1994, it has supplied, also via annual contracts, three overseas military customers. The new overseas contracts have required modifications to Dayview's standard product specifications and have resulted in a total range of six product variations.

The Scope brothers have recently become increasingly worried about the decline in volume of their company's sales to the military and they have been exploring new product/market possibilities. Several potential new developments have been identified, including the following:

- *Multi-purpose spectacles.* A recent discovery by a Dublin-based sunglasses manufacturer, O'Clea and Co., has made it possible to design spectacles that could provide sun protection during the day as well as enhancing vision if worn at night. It is envisaged that such a new product would appeal to both the outdoor pursuits and fashion markets. A tentative agreement has been reached whereby Dayview Ltd would develop and perfect the products and all marketing services would be managed by O'Clea and Co.
- *Extension of existing markets.* Despite the decline of the military markets, Terry Scope is convinced that the company's existing NSO products could, with some slight modifications, be made attractive to the outdoor pursuits market. Substantial cost savings would have to be made, however, in order to be able to offer such products at prices which would be acceptable to customers in the new market.

The company is quite cash-rich at present and Terry has suggested to Mike and the other shareholders that the company's surplus liquidity could be used to finance a substantial increase in the company's manufacturing equipment and storage facilities.

Hitherto, the company has utilised mainly skilled labour-based methods of manufacture, but Mike insists that the proposed product developments would require a considerable modernisation of production methods, including the introduction of highly automated production systems and the need to embrace modern ideas such as just-in-time manufacturing and total quality management. It is felt by the Scope brothers that the potential increase in the company's markets should counteract the need to make staff redundant as a result of the new technology. Rather, they hope, some of the productive staff will be moved into administrative roles in order to manage the larger and more complex company. The brothers have already earmarked some of the less efficient production staff for these roles, including a large proportion of the company's long-serving employees.

Dayview Ltd's finance manager, Iris Coffey, is worried about the future, although she has not expressed her fears to either of the Scope brothers. They are too busy, she reasons, with the technical side of the business to be bothered with problems of a general managerial or financial nature. Although Iris's official duties are financially-orientated, as the firm has expanded she has additionally become its unofficial general manager and administrative manager. Her concerns about the future are related to several areas:

- Iris is not a formally trained or qualified accountant. What financial knowledge she does have has been acquired through her employment by Dayview Ltd, which she joined nine years ago. She feels that the planned expansion of the company will place her 'out of her depth'.
- Although she has taken upon herself many additional administrative duties, Iris feels that she will not have the time for these in the future, nor does she feel that

she has the experience or skills to manage the additional (ex-production) staff resulting from Terry and Mike's reorganisation plans.

- The company's current financial systems have been developed to satisfy the requirements of Dayview Ltd's auditors. Apart from a rudimentary standard costing system (which has not been altered, since it was installed by a friend of Mike's in 1991) and a budgeted profit and loss account which is produced twice a year, there is little produced in the way of management information.

- The demands being made on Iris's time have meant that a backlog of creditors has built up this year and several component suppliers are complaining that they have not been paid for several months. Iris hopes to settle these matters soon and is keen not to let the Scope brothers know about her inefficiency in this area.

Dayview's existing production operatives have heard, from Iris, about the Scope brothers' plans. Naturally, they are worried about the security of their future employment and, because many of the operatives rely heavily on piecework bonuses and overtime pay, there is great concern about of their future roles within Dayview Ltd. Many of the company's production workers have worked for Dayview Ltd since it was established and they have become very proficient at producing the company's products well within the standard times. They fear that, even if they remain within production roles, the company's planned new products and production methods will disturb their comfortable working lives. Some operatives have started to seek similar employment elsewhere in the local area.

Dayview employs a production manageress, Ida Seymour, who is very keen to maintain the quality of the company's products. She is concerned that an expansion of Dayview Ltd's product range, combined with new technology and cost-cutting exercises, could have an adverse effect on quality. Although she has been aware for several years that the productive workforce is not over-stretched by the existing standard times, she has not relayed this information to the Scope brothers as she feels that quality would suffer under a more stringent regime. Additionally, the relaxed factory atmosphere has made it possible for her to maintain good social relationships with members of the productive workforce.

Ida is rather worried that the rumoured reorganisation plans would mean her being in control of technology and production methods with which neither she nor the workforce will have had any previous experience. She is also worried that, if staff are moved to office positions on the basis of their apparently low efficiency, she will lose the very workers who she rates as being responsible for the presently high quality standards.

Given below are examples of Dayview Ltd's existing reports.

Dayview Ltd

Budgeted Profit and Loss Account for January 2004

		£	£	£
Sales:	Military – UK		95,000	
	Military – overseas		20,000	
				115,000

Materials:	direct	20,000		
	bought-in parts	15,000		
			35,000	
Direct labour			30,000	
Factory overhead			20,000	
			85,000	
Stock adjustment			(15,000)	
Factory cost of sales				70,000
Gross profit				45,000
Non-factory overheads				(20,000)
NET PROFIT				25,000

Dayview Ltd

Budget Report December 2003

		Budget £000	Actual £000	Variance £000	%
Sales:	Military – UK	100	90	(10)	(10)
	Military – o'seas	15	20	5	33
		115	110	(5)	(4)
Materials:	Direct	20	23	(3)	(15)
	Bought-in	12	14	(2)	(17)
		32	37	(5)	(15)
Direct labour		22	18	4	18
Factory overhead		16	23	(7)	(46)
Stock adjustment		(12)	(12)	—	
Factory cost of sales		58	66	(8)	(14)
Non-factory overheads		20	18	2	10
Total costs		78	84	(6)	(8)
NET PROFIT		37	26	(11)	(30)

Dayview Ltd

Standard Cost Card Product NSO 1

Last Update: 21st Nov 1998

		Units	£ per unit of resource	£ per unit of product
Materials:				
	Matl'l A	2	15	30
	Mat'l B	1	20	20
	Mat'l C	10	10	10
				60

Components:	Comp. L	5	1	5	
	Comp. M	4	2	8	
	Comp. N	1	5	5	
	Comp. O	3	6	18	
	Comp. P	1	2	2	
	Comp. Q	1	12	<u>12</u>	
					50
Direct Labour:					
	Grade I	2	4	8	
	Grade II	5	5	25	
	Grade III	3	3	<u>9</u>	
					<u>42</u>
PRIME COST					152
Factory Overhead @ 30% prime cost					<u>46</u>
Total production cost					198
GROSS PROFIT @ 40% selling price					<u>132</u>
SELLING PRICE					<u>330</u>

1. In a management accounting information system context, identify the main behavioural problems which have occurred, and which are likely to occur in the near future, at Dayview Ltd. You should make reference to appropriate literature in discussing these problems.
2. Discuss the extent to which such problems might be overcome by making changes to Dayview Ltd's management accounting information system.
3. Analyse the extent to which Dayview Ltd's present decision-making process follows a classical decision-making model.
4. Suggest improvements which could be made to Dayview Ltd's current management accounting information system in an effort to improve the company's decision-making, at both an operational and a strategic level. Be *specific* about the information required.

Questions

1. 'The necessity for constantly increasing efficiency is a basic fact of business life. Budgets are utilised as pressure devices for that purpose. But because of the effect of budgets on people, they tend to generate forces which in the long run decrease efficency' (Argyris, 1953). Explain the ways in which budgets can in the long run decrease efficiency and examine how management can prevent this occurring.

2. A new management accountant in your company has sent to managers of the company the following memorandum:

To: Production Plant Managers
From: P. Richards, Management Accountant
Subject: Management Information
Date: April 30, 2004

The first area to which I shall be attending is the budgetary control system. In my view the main problems have been those of quantity and quality of information. You have been receiving too little information to control effectively. I intend to provide you with much more information although, of course, this will mean slight delays in its preparation.

Referring to the issue of quality of information, you have become used to receiving information that is not accurate enough. You cannot be expected to manage effectively without the backup of reliably accurate information. I shall therefore be installing new computerized systems to increase the accuracy and reliability of the control information that you receive.

As you are aware, the manufacturing process is very complex and technical. It seems that current budgetary reports are produced in a form that fails to reflect this degree of complexity. I shall ensure that in future the nature of the control information produced matches the technical complexity of the production process.

Finally, there seems to have been some slowness in preparing annual budgets in the past. In order to overcome this problem, I shall endeavour to provide you with your annual budgets in good time. Should you find that problems arise out of using these budgets, please inform me as soon as possible.

The memorandum has received an unfavourable response from plant managers. Discuss the underlying reasons that are likely to have caused the adverse reaction.

3. The production manager at Breaklack has been called to an urgent meeting by the managing director to discuss his annual performance-related bonus payment.

He has been unhappy in his job for some time, and has found it increasingly difficult to meet the production targets set for him by the sales manager, or to stay within the budget imposed by the management accountant, and has never had any input into the setting of these targets. He knows the level of his bonus payment is dependent on meeting the targets set, and is fearful that he will not receive enough to pay for the summer holiday he has just booked!

Having never had any training in budgetary control, he finds it difficult to understand the adverse variance reports that arrive on his desk every two months, or even how his cost targets are worked out in the first place. He has heard the accountant talking about 'standard costs' but has no idea what these are. Over the past six months the material price adverse variance has been increasing dramatically, but he cannot understand why, as all materials come from the central stores and are bought by the purchasing manager without reference back to the production department.

He has also often wondered why his budget for materials and labour never seems to increase, even though the sales manager regularly asks him to increase production to meet an increased level of anticipated sales. He usually manages to meet these increased targets, but his staff often have to work overtime to do so. Having discussed the matter with the production supervisor they were in agreement that increasing production was bound to lead to higher costs in some areas – so why was this never reflected in his budget?

    (a)   Discuss the underlying problems with the budgetary control system in operation at the company.

    (b)   Identify ways in which the system could be improved.

4. Discuss the key factors that would be considered in determining whether a cost variance should be investigated.

5. Examine the interrelationships of budgeting, creativity and culture and discuss the implications of such interrelationships for management control systems.

6. Contingency theory has played a significant role in the management accounting literature of the past two decades. Critically examine the role of contingency theory in contemporary management accounting thinking.

7. Various writers have commented upon the prerequisites for control, that is, the conditions and control system features that must be in place before effective control may take place. Identify and explain the prerequisites necessary for accounting control and analyse the difficulties that might be experienced in achieving them.

8. Discuss the interrelationships between principal–agent theory and performance measurement systems within multinational corporations.

9. Critically compare the interpretations of management accounting history of the 'relevance lost' and 'traditional/classical' schools of thought, commenting on the implications of such interpretations for the practice of management accountants.

10. The theory of constraints as described by Eliyah Goldratt, has generated some interest in management accounting circles in recent years. Critically examine the conceptual basis of the theory of constraints and evaluate its usefulness to management accounting practitioners.

11. The focus of management accounting research has moved, in recent years, away from a prescriptive/normative mode towards more prescriptive/analytical approaches. Identify the factors influencing this change in research focus, and assess their importance.

12. Preston (1995) suggests that relationships exist between budgeting, creativity and culture. Examine the influence of budgetary processes and styles on creativity within an organisation and explain the associated consequences for strategic management.

13. 'The management accountant's role is that of a servant of managers, assisting them by supplying appropriate information. Management accountants thus have little need to consider ethical or empowerment issues.' Give, and justify, your opinion on this statement.

14. Evaluate the significance of principal–agent theory for management accountants and outline its conceptual and practical limitations.

15. Why would anyone take the trouble to study the history of management accounting? Identify the benefits and beneficiaries of such a study, examining critically the work already carried out in this area.

16. Several writers have drawn attention to the 'contingent variables' which determine management accounting information systems. Identify, and discuss the significance of, such contingent variables and examine the practical value of the contingency theory of management accounting.

17. Various views exist on whether management accounting has been reactive or proactive in the development of western businesses. Critically analyse the role played by management accounting in shaping the evolution of businesses in western economies, and comment on the views of the 'labour process' school of thought.

18. Coad (1999) proposed that the personal orientation of management accountants might affect their choice and application of management accounting systems. Evaluate this proposition.

19. Two theories prominent in management accounting thought are principal–agent theory and contingency theory. For *one* of these theories:

    (i) analyse the main implications for management accounting within a fast-moving environment;

    (ii) critically analyse the theory's underlying assumptions.

Chapter 8
OPERATIONAL DECISION MAKING

Key Learning Objectives

By the time you have finished studying this chapter, you should be able to:
- decide how to allocate scarce resources;
- use various costing techniques to make decisions on the utilisation of scarce resources;
- interpret the results of your analysis and advise management on such decisions;
- understand the application of the marginal costing/contribution approach to management decisions;
- recognise the importance of risk in the decision-making environment;
- recognise the importance of both quantitative and qualitative factors in decision making.

Introduction

So far in this book we have looked at the basics of management accounting and costing techniques. This chapter aims to apply these techniques to reach relevant decisions in the 'real' world. Inevitably in this 'real' world of the management accountant we are dealing with both quantitative and qualitative factors in reaching decisions, although many traditional textbooks tend to concentrate on the financial aspects of any decision. Hence this chapter will also attempt to recognise those factors other than financial ones which play an important part in the managerial decision-making environment. In this context the chapter develops a 'qualitative' matrix which aims to provide a frame of reference for managers to quantify these non-financial factors as a guide to decisions. This framework is seen as relevant to both the public and private sector. The chapter also looks at the importance of an understanding of risk by managers in the decision-making and business cycle and how to respond to – or better still prepare for – these eventualities. It is also vitally important that managers are able not only to understand the information they receive but also to interpret such information to maximise the benefits of decisions. In the private sector, therefore, the general assumption of profit maximisation is taken. For the public sector such decisions are inevitably more complex due to their social, political and environmental context. It is hoped that as the chapter unfolds it will, through the techniques described and developed, provide a frame of reference to assist managers in potentially complex situations in whatever sector they work.

Marginal Cost and Marginal Revenue

As stated above, in the private sector the goal of companies has been assumed for simplicity to be profit maximisation. Other goals are possible such as sales revenue maximisation or just growing the sheer size of the company, which may be measured by such factors as the number of employees or the number of subsidiaries it controls. Profit maximisation can be achieved in the short term through perhaps setting high prices for products, or in the long term by some form of market penetration exercise. All strategies will be reflected ultimately in the amount of product to be produced and sold. In the public sector the emphasis has traditionally been on the cost of services. A greater emphasis today is being placed on increasing performance through achieving value for money, defined as economy, efficiency and effectiveness in the delivery of services. Where possible, however, more emphasis is also being placed on generating extra revenue as public sector budgets come under increased pressure due to a lack of available resources from general taxation.

In both the public and private sector the concepts of marginal cost and marginal revenue are relevant. Marginal revenue is the increase in unit revenue which corresponds to an increase in the unit provision of a service or product produced and sold. Marginal cost is the increase in cost for a unit increase in the service or product produced and sold. If marginal revenue is in excess of marginal cost then increasing the production or supply of a product or service will generate a profit on that unit. If marginal cost exceeds marginal revenue a loss will occur. In the public sector, for those services where no extra revenue can be generated because they are provided as free goods, we are dealing with the marginal cost of producing one extra unit of service. There will be no marginal revenue associated with such services and decisions would be made on the marginal benefit achieved for clients from the extra expense incurred. In the health service, for example, this can be measured by the improved quality of life that an operation can bring.

In decision making in the above context it is important to recognise the use of contribution analysis. 'Contribution' represents the difference between the selling price for a product or service and the variable costs of providing that product or service. It goes towards initially covering fixed costs, assuming that the selling price exceeds the variable cost. Once fixed costs are covered it is a contribution to profit. It is clear that in order to use this analysis we need to disaggregate costs into their variable and fixed components, making an understanding of cost behaviour essential. In this context the traditional format of the profit and loss account which essentially concentrates on a functional format – selling and distribution, administration – provides inadequate information for planning, control or decision making. This is because it does not classify costs by their behaviour.

As can be seen from Exhibit 8.1, the contribution approach divides costs into their fixed and variable elements and then deducts this from the sales figure to arrive at the contribution margin. As stated, it can be seen that this represents the contribution to cover the remaining fixed cost elements of the expenses. The development of such statements is a decision for the organisation and should be designed so as to facilitate internal planning, control and decision making. In designing the format of the statement it is also possible that it can facilitate the appraisal of managerial performance, in particular where there is segmented reporting of profit and loss data or to emphasise different elements of the budget. It should also be observed that the results achieved are identical whichever approach is adopted. All that has been changed is the classification of costs incurred by the business.

EXHIBIT 8.1

Contribution Statement Compared with a Functional Financial Reporting Type Approach

	Contribution Approach		Functional Approach	
		£		£
Sales Income		120,000		120,000
Less Variable Expenses				
Variable Production	55,000			
Variable Selling	10,000			
Variable Administrative	5,000			
		70,000	Cost of Goods Sold	59,000*
Contribution Margin		50,000	Gross Profit (Margin)	61,000
Less Fixed Expenses			**Less Operating Costs**	
Fixed Production	4,000		Selling	30,000
Fixed Selling	20,000		Administration	20,000
Fixed Administration	15,000			
		39,000		
Net Profit		11,000		11,000

*Cost of sales includes both fixed and variable costs

Assumptions of the Marginal Cost Approach

- Fixed costs remain fixed in the short term, irrespective of the level of activity.
- Fixed costs are not directly related to specific units.
- Variable costs vary directly in proportion to activity levels.
- Total costs can be split between fixed and variable elements.

Using Contribution Analysis for Decision Making

As stated in the Introduction, this chapter is concerned with decision making and therefore this section examines contribution analysis as a relatively simple but powerful technique in a decision-making context for a service industry.

Weeds R Not Us is a garden centre business of long standing operating in the Vale of Evesham in the Midlands of England. It can sell all it grows, given the rising interest in its activities following the popularity of gardening programmes on radio and television. The objective of the garden centre is to maximise revenues by growing and selling those flowers and shrubs which contribute most to that objective. It has a total of 40 acres of land that it can access.

As well as passing trade from amateur horticulturists, the garden centre supplies a stately home belonging to the National Trust. Under the terms of the contract it must supply 420 begonias, 185 fuchsias, 576 dianthuses and 110 bay trees for each of the next five years. Past experience shows that it can sell up to 4500 shrubs of any type, but these four shrubs are particularly popular and well suited to the soil and English climate.

The garden centre has considerable experience in budgeting, and Table 8.1 shows the budgeted cost for the next growing season.

Table 8.1   Budgeted cost for shrub growing

	Begonias	Fuchsias	Dianthuses	Bay trees
No. of shrubs per acre	210	185	192	220
Selling price each	£16	£19	£18	£21
Variable costs per acre				
Seedlings	£160	£220	£240	£325
Wages	£35	£30	£20	£25
Fixed cost per annum	£65,000			

Wage costs are treated as variable as gardeners are brought in and paid a daily rate per acre. This is traditional in the industry, although some of the shrubs require higher skill levels, hence the different variable costs for wages. No problems have been experienced in the past in acquiring suitable skilled labour at the budgeted rates.

Fixed costs cover management salaries, business rates on the office premises, selling and distribution costs. Since the business is classified as a farm, agricultural land is not subject to business rates.

This problem should be tackled in two stages. The first stage is this to identify the contribution per shrub per acre, as land is the limiting factor (Table 8.2). As can be seen, the greatest contribution per acre of land is from the bay trees. Table 8.3 shows the results for the growing period, taking account of the existing contract with the National Trust. It can be seen that bay trees provide the greatest contribution per limiting factor and as such should be selected to be grown in preference to the other alternatives.

Table 8.2   Contribution per acre

	Begonias	Fuchsias	Dianthuses	Bay Trees
Revenue	£3360	£3515	£3456	£4620
Variable costs	£195	£250	£260	£350
Contribution	£3165	£3265	£3196	£4270

Table 8.3   Maximum contribution and profit available

	Begonias	Fuchsias	Dianthuses	Bay Trees	Total £
Sales to National Trust	420	185	576	110	
Acres required	2	1	3		
Acres for bay trees				14	
Contribution per acre	£3,165	£3,265	£3,196	£4,270	
Total contribution	£6,330	£3,265	£9,588	£59,780	£78,963
Fixed costs					£65,000
Net profit					£13,963

In making the decision to concentrate on bay trees, however, the management would need to consider a range of other factors. Gardening is subject to changing fashions as much as any other business. As such they would need to consider market trends so the historic information for the centre on sales can only provide a guide to the future. Equally, the business needs to be aware of the competition in the area, new housing developments coming into the area or even industrial decline, as all will have a potential impact on sales in what is a discretionary purchase. It might be possible to negotiate other contracts to ensure that in the event of a change in consumer demand the centre will continue to flourish. The business is thus not immune from risk, despite having sold all it can produce in the past. In addition, given that it is a gardening business, the weather will have an important influence.

Financial Modelling using Contribution

The objective of financial modelling is to present a representation of business reality. In essence, the model should allow various assumptions to be made and then varied in order to carry out sensitivity analysis. In the context of contribution, one of the more basic financial models that maybe employed is that of break-even analysis. This, can be used to summarise the effect that sales volume changes can have on an organisation's revenues, costs and, therefore, profit. Break-even analysis is often considered under the heading cost–volume–profit analysis. The model is frequently used to present the effects on profits of various decisions as many individuals prefer a picture as opposed to a mass of figures and, consequently, find it easier to understand. It should, however, be remembered that many managers use a complex range of tools and data to forecast profits or losses and their ability to understand should not be underestimated. In that sense what follows needs to be assessed as part of the contribution to a holistic managerial decision-making process.

To build an example of this concept we will assume a company is in the business of making picnic baskets, amongst other products, for sale to the general public and has provided the information contained in Exhibit 8.2. The exhibit is structured such that we will calculate the break-even model first and then use the data in the exhibit to construct further analysis.

EXHIBIT 8.2

The Hardy Out Door Company

The Hardy Out Door Company has obtained data on its production of picnic baskets for sale to the general public. As might be expected, it is a seasonal business. The financial results for the last financial year were as follows:

Units produced and sold	5,800
Selling price	£59.00
Fixed overheads	81,000

Variable costs per unit

Wages	£25.50
Materials	£10.20
Overheads	£2.30

A budget has been prepared for the next financial year, showing the following information:

Units to be produced and sold	6,200
Selling price	£60.00
Fixed overheads to rise by	£9,000

Variable costs per unit

Wages	£26.50
Estimated material costs	£10.50
Overheads to rise by	£0.70

Fixed costs are allocated to the part of the premises used to produce the picnic baskets on the basis of floor area.

The following results were achieved during the three years prior to the last year. Thus the company has sales and cost data for the last four years.

Sales are normally made direct to the public, but a well-known retail company has just approached the firm with an order of 1000 units. They have indicated, however, that they are only willing to pay a maximum of £54 per basket.

	Last Year – 1	Last year – 2	Last year – 3
Actual sales	6,100	6,500	6,400
Selling price (£)	58	55	54
Fixed costs (£)	85,260	81,810	79,905
Variable costs (£)	278,750	247,000	249,600

Company management has just heard about the technique of break-even analysis (although you first read about it in Chapter 3) and has requested information regarding the break-even point and also the production of relevant graphs based on the predicted results for the next financial year. They also want comments on the information provided.

As stated in Chapter 3, the first step in this analysis is to calculate the contribution for the coming financial year. Contribution equals selling price minus variable costs:

$$£60.00 - (£26.50 + £10.50 + £3.00) = £20.00$$

To calculate the break-even figure we divide the fixed costs (£90,000) by the contribution (£20) which gives the break-even point in terms of the sales unit figure as 4500. Thus, once the company sells 4500 units every extra sale is a contribution to profit as fixed costs have been covered. Once the break-even figure has been achieved any additional sales represent what is termed the margin of safety. This means that the company has a 'comfort' zone by which sales can decline before it moves into a loss-making situation. It should be pointed out that sales below break-even are not termed 'the margin of danger', although in the long term all costs must be covered if any company is to survive.

Figure 8.1 shows the break-even chart. The relevant range has been assumed to be between 2000 units and 6500 units. Outside this range the assumptions of straight-line relationships might not hold. As can be seen activity levels below 4500 units represent a loss. In contrast, any activity level above 4500 units results in a profit being made.

Figure 8.2 is an alternative presentation to Figure 8.1, with the advantage of placing emphasis on the total contribution, which managers may prefer.

The third alternative method of presenting the information is shown in Figure 8.3. This graph, as the title suggests, stresses the relationship between sales volume and profit or loss. By reference to the graph it can be seen that if sales are equal to zero the total loss incurred is the amount of the fixed costs. The line representing units produced and sold allows us to read off the profit or loss at any point along that line.

These graphs allow managers to interpret what will happen to company profits under different market conditions. In addition, assumptions on price and variable cost, for example, can be varied again to assess the impact that such changes have on the business and the graphs redrawn for visual impact.

The straight lines drawn in these graphs represent accounting assumptions on cost and price behaviour and, by their nature, these differ from those made by economists. The effect of making accounting assumptions is that the functions are all linear and that, in the case of the

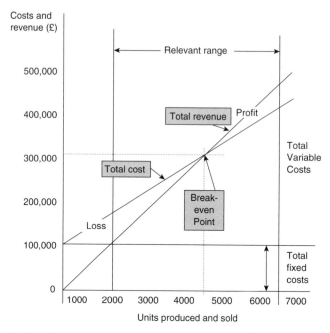

Figure 8.1   The break-even chart

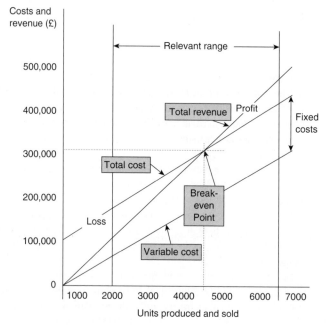

Figure 8.2   The contribution graph

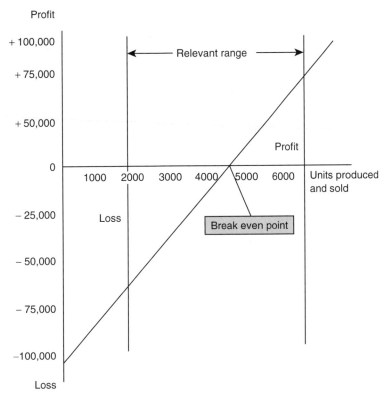

Figure 8.3   The profit-volume-graph

example shown, there is only one break-even point. The break-even chart can also be amended if stepped fixed costs were involved. All that would happen is that at the 'step-up' point the variable cost line and the sales revenue line would move up by the amount of the step to form higher parallel lines. This could result in two break-even points, one below the step and one above the step.

Setting Target Profits

While management will be interested in the break-even figure as the number of units that need to be sold to cover costs, they will be more interested in profits that can be earned from the product. To this extent a target profit figure of £10,000 could be input into the calculation. One way of doing this is to treat the target as the equivalent of extra fixed costs. In this context we would require unit sales of 10,100 to achieve a target profit of £10,000: (Fixed costs (£91,000) + target profit (£10,000))/contribution (£10). Management can now assess whether this level of sales activity can be achieved.

Table 8.4 Analysis of past performance

	Last year	Last year – 1	Last year – 2	Last year – 3
Actual sales	6,200	6,100	6,500	6,400
Income (£)	359,600	353,800	357,500	345,600
Fixed cost (£)	81,000	85,260	81,810	79.905
Variable costs (£)	235,600	228.750	247,000	249,600
Profit/(loss) (£)	43,000	39,790	28,690	16,095
Selling price (£)	58	58	55	54
Unit variable cost (£)	38	37.50	38	39
Contribution (£)	20	20.50	17	15
Breakeven units	4,050	4,159	4,812	5,327

The Model in Context

Exhibit 8.2 contains additional information to help set the decision in the real world. As can be seen, sales have declined from 6400 units four years ago to 6200 units last year, while the company is now estimating sales at 5800 for next year. Is this reasonable as the price has risen again? The projected break-even is at 4,500. Table 8.4 shows the results for the last four years and reveals an interesting picture. Unit variable cost is calculated by dividing the total variable cost by the number of units sold.

The analysis begins to reveal a picture of the company as having a rising cost base which it is attempting to cover by raising prices. The price rises undertaken have been sufficient to compensate for these cost rises and the break-even target has fallen as the contribution has risen over the period. Profits have consequently increased. A significant contribution to this rise was the fall in fixed costs in the last financial year. In the next financial year fixed costs are predicted, however, to rise by 11%.

Sales are in decline so this raises concerns as to whether the target sales figure for next year will be achieved, particularly as the price has again been increased. The break-even sales figure has been around 4000–5000 units for a while and the projection for next year lies in the middle of this range. The margin of safety at a projection of 5800 units is clearly 1300, and this may provide a sufficient cushion to absorb any lost sales due to the price rise.

Unit variable costs have remained reasonably stable over the period shown. Further rises in these costs are forecasted to occur in the next financial year.

The exhibit comments that fixed costs are allocated to picnic baskets on the basis of floor area. This suggests that other products are being made in the workspace available in the production unit. A reasonable question therefore concerns whether the rise in fixed costs results from a change in the basis of allocation and whether this is fair. Further research is needed.

Outside of financial issues the company would need to consider issues such as design as it is possible that a price rise coupled with a dated design could lead to a failure to sell product despite a history of acceptable sales levels. This would be considered in the context of competitor analysis and risk.

With regard to the potential new order for 1000 units at £54 each, as variable costs are £40 there is a contribution of £14 towards fixed costs. Serious consideration can therefore be given to the order as it represents guaranteed sales and improved cash flow (subject to financial appraisal of the retail company). The company may also see this order as compensating for any further falls in sales given the historical picture.

Assumptions Underpinning Break-Even Analysis

Relevant Range

The accounting model presented is based on the assumption of linearity over the relevant range. This is the key to understanding the model and the cost/income behaviours represented. It attempts to provide an accurate picture over the range of output and sales that the business can realistically achieve in the planning horizon envisaged. In the case of Figure 8.1 this might be a range of 2000 to 6500 as shown. Outside this range, the assumption of linearity would not hold. It is within this range that the business has reliable information on cost and cost behaviour.

Fixed Costs

The assumption for fixed costs again is related to the relevant range, here the accountant assumes that over the levels of activity envisaged the costs the business is committed to meeting are known and can be represented in a linear manner. It is possible to reconstruct the graph without too much difficulty if the fixed costs follow a stepped pattern as outlined in Chapter 2.

Revenue Line

The total revenue line again is linear. As you will be aware, if you wish to sell more product the economist would consider supply and demand and suggest price reductions to achieve higher sale volumes. Here the accountant, however, assumes that the business is operating in a market where the selling price tends to be fixed in the short term. As stated above, the figures can be redrawn with alternative selling prices (and costs) to present an alternative picture to managers. Again, however, within the relevant range the assumption of linearity for the total revenue line is assumed to hold.

Time Horizon

The assumptions hold over the time horizon envisaged. Typically, as in this example, this time horizon is one year. If we consider typical fixed costs, property taxes are normally known for a year in advance and it is possible to budget reasonably accurately for managerial salaries (including any salary increments or pay rises). Operating capacity will also be known reasonably well in advance as it takes time to plan and commission new productive capacity. In the longer term, however, there will be a need to change the assumptions on which the model is based.

Cost Split between Fixed and Variable

The model assumes that it is relatively easy to split fixed and variable costs. In practice this is not as easy as is suggested, but it has to be done as accurately as possible if the model is to work. Fixed costs are assumed to be unrelated to the level of activity. This assumption will normally only hold true in the short term.

Stock is Ignored

The model takes no account of stock. This is, however, acceptable as basically the model is trying to influence managerial decision making and as such cannot be totally representative of what will actually happen. It is thus just one of the tools for decision making by managment.

Single Product/Constant Sales Mix

The illustration used in this section has concentrated on one product. In more complex analysis it is possible to assume that sales will be in accordance with a preplanned sales mix. This is carried out by measuring sales volume using standard batch sizes based on this planned mix.

Complexity in the Production Process

Cooper and Kaplan (1987) undertook an analysis in which they suggest that firms need to be aware of the complexity of the manufacturing process where multiple products are manufactured. They suggest that many so-called fixed costs vary with the range of items manufactured as opposed to the volume of manufacture. Thus, as complexity related costs do not vary significantly, in the short term the emphasis in cost–volume–profit techniques will tend to show a growth in short-term profits as new product variants are introduced. They will, however, potentially cause a rise in fixed costs in future periods resulting in long-term disadvantage to the firm. The work of Kaplan is placed in context by Otley (2001) – see the section on further reading later in the present chapter.

Consumer Behaviour

While reducing the price of a product should in theory generate more revenue, in practice consumer behaviour is complex. A reduced price may cause consumers to question quality even if there are no grounds to do so. Fashion changes can also dictate the purchase of goods. In the case of wicker picnic baskets the market has been adversely affected by the sale of 'cool boxes' as they possess better insulating properties.

To conclude this section, Exhibit 8.3 contains an illustration of the core formulas associated with break-even analysis.

EXHIBIT 8.3

Break-Even and Related Formulas

Sales − Variable Costs = Fixed Costs + Profit (or −Loss)

Contribution = Selling Price − Variable Costs

Profit/(Loss) = Contribution − Fixed Costs

$$\text{Break-even (units)} = \frac{\text{Fixed Costs}}{\text{Contribution}}$$

$$\text{Break-even (sales value)} = \frac{\text{Fixed Costs} \times \text{Sales Units}}{\text{Contribution}}$$

$$\text{Margin of safety (units)} = \frac{\text{Profit}}{\text{Contribution per unit}}$$

$$\text{Margin of safety (sales value)} = \frac{\text{Profit} \times \text{Sales}}{\text{Contribution}}$$

Linear Programming

The earlier garden centre example concentrated on one limiting factor, which was land. In order to maximise contribution the land was allocated to production by reference to the contribution per limiting factor. In practice, decision makers find that there is normally more than one limiting factor. In the manufacturing process these might be limited to the available labour, the available machine hours and the available materials. Effectively, in our garden centre example the limited factor equivalents to the manufacturing process could be land (materials) and labour.

The technique used to solve these decision dilemmas is termed *linear programming*, and this section of the chapter explains how the technique can be applied.

EXHIBIT 8.4

Maximise Contribution

A company manufactures two products, X and Y. During the next budget period it is estimated that there will be only 4200 direct labour hours available and that the supply of the common materials used by both products is restricted to 3600 units. Machine hours available are limited to 4000.

The budget for the next period shows the following standard information per unit of each product:

Product X	£	£	Product Y	£	£
Standard selling price		40	Standard selling price		59
less			less		
Materials	6		Materials	8	
Labour	15		Labour	30	
Variable overhead	4		Variable overhead	4	
		25			42
Contribution		15			17

Product X uses 3 units of material per unit produced, while product Y uses 4 units of material per unit produced. Material cost is £2 per unit.

Product X uses 3 hours of labour, while product Y uses 6 hours. The labour rate is £5 per hour.

Variable overheads are allocated on the basis of machine hours. The rate is £1 per hour. Product X uses 4 hours of machine time, as does product Y.

The sales department estimates that the organisation can sell an unlimited number of units of product Y, but that X is limited to 550 units.

Clearly this is a much more complex problem for the manager operating in this business environment than the garden centre decision maker, and linear programming is needed to solve it. Solutions can be found both graphically (two products) and by the manipulation of mathematical formulas (more than two products). Excel can be used to perform the mathematics, and the manager must then correctly interpret the results.

As the term linear programming implies, all relationships are assumed to be linear:

- The contribution per unit produced and sold within the relevant range remains constant, and therefore are linear.
- Resources utilised are constant whatever the units produced, and are therefore linear
- Units produced and resources allocated/available are infinitely divisible.
- The objective is to maximise the contribution.
- All variables in the equation must be equal to or greater than zero.

To solve the problem we state it mathematically by setting up an objective function. Denoting the contribution by C, we must

$$\text{maximise } C = 15X + 17Y,$$

subject to:

$$\text{materials} \quad 3X + 4Y \leq 3600,$$
$$\text{labour} \quad 3X + 6Y \leq 4200,$$
$$\text{machine hrs} \quad 4X + 4Y \leq 4000.$$

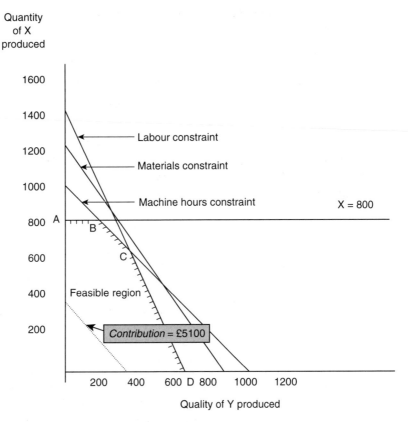

Figure 8.4   Graphical solution to contribution maximisation problem

Here the constraints have been expressed by relating the quantities of each resource used by each product against the maximum available resource for each of those elements in the production process. Taking materials as an example, the equation $3X+4Y$ means that 3 units of material are used to produce product X and 4 units of material used to produce product Y in the final solution when we know the decision as to how many units of each product will be made cannot exceed 3600 units of material. A similar logic applies to each of the other constraints.

To satisfy the final assumption outlined earlier, product X must be greater than or equal to zero but, given the maximum we can sell, be no greater than 550. As Y has no upper limit the assumption here is that product Y must be greater than or equal to zero. This assumption of non-negativity avoids getting results which are counter-intuitive. This is expressed as

$$0 \leq X \leq 550, \quad Y \geq 0.$$

Let us use the graphical method first. Figure 8.4 shows the constraints plotted for the quantities of the two products that can be produced. The only region on the graph which satisfies all four constraints is within the area ABCD. This is known as the *feasible region*. Outside this region it is not possible to satisfy all four constraints. It is still, however, necessary to find which production level for X and Y maximises contribution. If we therefore choose a random contribution line of £5,100 this would represent 340 units of X or 300 units of Y. As stated, our objective is to maximise contribution so higher-level contributions can be represented by drawing parallel lines until we reach the boundary of the feasible region. In this example the farthest we can move from the origin and still satisfy the constraints is at point C. It should also be noted that the materials constraint lies completely outside the boundary of the feasible region and it is the other three constraints which are crucial in determining production.

Reading from the graph the maximum contribution is achieved at approximately 600 units of X and 400 of Y. This is proved below:

contribution at point A is $800 \times £15 + \quad 0 \times £17 = £12,000$;
contribution at point B is $800 \times £15 + 200 \times £17 = £15,400$;
contribution at point C is $600 \times £15 + 400 \times £17 = £15,800$;
contribution at point D is $\quad 0 \times £15 + 700 \times £17 = £11,900$.

As indicated by the word 'approximately', it is obviously not always possible to measure from a graph the exact output at point C, and consequently a more accurate alternative is to solve the simultaneous equations which can be formed from the binding constraints at that point:

$$4X + 4Y \leq 4000, \tag{1}$$

$$3X + 6Y \leq 4200. \tag{2}$$

Multiply equation (1) by 3 and equation (2) by 2,

$$12X + 12Y \leq 12000,$$
$$6X + 12Y \leq \ \ 8400.$$

By a process of division $6X$ equals 3600, so X is 600. By substitution, Y is 400. This is the financial calculation result, but it cannot be divorced from the marketing information. The question in this case is that from marketing we believe we can sell an unlimited number of Y and a maximum of 550 for X. While further research may be needed into these claims the results, now that we have a potential production plan produced by solving the equation, indicate that the initial market research supports that production plan.

This can be further developed by use of Table 8.5 to show if it is worth attempting to procure more of the scarce resources. What the table shows is that we have no spare capacity in either labour or machine hours, but spare capacity in materials. If we could remove these constraints would it be worth the company paying a premium to do so. If we take labour, the equations would be revised:

$$4X + 4Y = 4000 \text{ (unchanged machine hours)},$$
$$3X + 6Y = 4201 \text{ (revised labour constraint)}.$$

Table 8.5   Shadow prices – resource table

Constraint	Total available	Constraints used at optimum (hrs per product)	Total used	Spare capacity	Shadow price?
Labour	4200	1800 X, 2400 Y	4200	0	Yes
Materials	3600	1800 X, 1600 Y	3400	200	No
Machines	4000	2400 X, 1600 Y	4000	0	Yes
Market	800	600X	600	200	No

Solving, we obtain

$$X = 599.67 \text{ and } Y = 400.33.$$

Therefore the planned production of X should be reduced by 0.33 and Y increased by 0.33. This is termed the marginal rate of substitution. The change in contribution arising from obtaining one extra element of labour is

Increase in contribution from Y is (0.33 × £17)	£5.61
Decrease in contribution from X is (0.33 × £15)	£4.95
Increase in contribution	£0.66

Therefore the value of an additional unit of labour is £0.66. This is the *opportunity cost* or *shadow price*. The company is thus able to pay up to £0.66 over and above the present cost of labour and still obtain a contribution towards fixed costs.

Obviously it is not possible to produce and sell 0.67 units of X and 0.33 units of Y. Output has to be expressed in whole numbers, but the basis of the calculation can be used to calculate the revised optimal output if extra units of labour are available.

Developing this theme, the company is advised that 50 extra units of labour are available at £5.50 per hour. This is below the opportunity cost by £0.16. The revised equations are now

$$4X + 4Y = 4000,$$
$$3X + 6Y = 4250.$$

X is now 583.33 and Y is 416.67. This makes the total contribution £15,833. At this level of production we still satisfy the material constraints as we would use only 3417 units of material. Therefore the decision that the company should take is to buy in the extra labour.

**EXHIBIT
8.5**

Cost Minimisation

The above example has concentrated on maximising contribution, but managers may also be interested in cost minimisation. This is illustrated in the following example which relates to a business manufacturing a fuel additive, Polycon, for tractors to improve engine performance. Every 10,000 litres of the product requires three elements: 600g of A, 400g of B and 450 g of C. In order to obtain these additives, it is necessary to purchase two ingredients, X and Y, which contain them. This information is set out below:

	Composition (g) of	
	X	**Y**
Additive A	3	8
Additive B	4	4
Additive C	3	5

Ingredient X costs £20 per litre, and Y costs £40 per litre.

The maximum that can be stored on site is 100 litres of each ingredient and the objective of the company is to decide how much of the ingredients should be added to every 5,000 litres of the additive to minimise costs.

$$\text{minimise } Z = 20X + 40Y,$$

Subject to

$$3X + 8Y \geq 600,$$
$$4X + 4Y \geq 400,$$
$$3X + 5Y \geq 450.$$

Note the equations are now greater than or equal to the minimum requirements. The limitations on storage are expressed by the equations:

$$X < 100,$$
$$Y < 100.$$

Finally the non-negative constraint is $X, Y \geq 0$.

Figure 8.5 shows the graph obtained by plotting the constraints. The feasible region is bounded by the points P, Q, R, S and T. Drawing in the minimum cost line $Z = 20X + 40Y$ and moving this line inwards towards the origin would give the minimum cost at the nearest point of the feasibility region that the line would touch to the origin. This is point Q

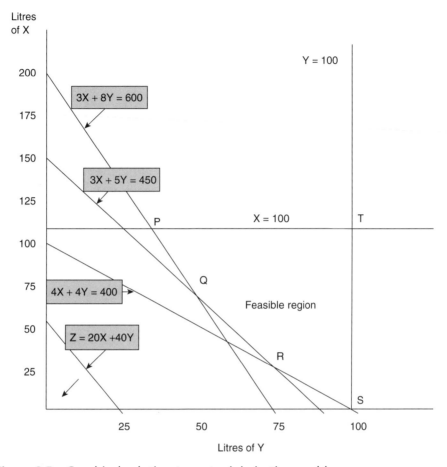

Figure 8.5   Graphical solution to cost minimisation problem

and the minimum cost is $66X + 50Y = £3,300$. This could also be solved by using the simultaneous equations for point Q: solving

$$3X + 8Y = 600,$$
$$3X + 5Y = 450.$$

gives $X = 66.67$ and $Y = 50$. Thus if the company is to achieve its decision objective of minimising the cost of the additives while satisfying all constraints, it would mix 66 units of X and 50 of Y in each batch of 5000 litres produced.

Relevant Costing

In making managerial decisions it is essential that managers recognise the importance of considering only relevant costs and benefits. This section looks at these issues. It deals first with financial costs and benefits, and then goes on to develop a technique to enable managers to consider qualitative issues in decision making. In financial terms, the relevant costs and benefits relate to the future cash flows of the organisation which would differ as a result of implementing the decision. This type of analysis thus concentrates on the incremental or differential changes that must be considered. Any cash flows that would remain the same for any alternatives that are being considered are irrelevant.

This section considers four areas:

- ceasing (or shutting down) production of a product or service;
- the make or buy decision;
- pricing;
- special orders.

Cessation of Production of a Product or Service

Managers are frequently required to consider whether a particular product, service or section is unprofitable and thus should be discontinued. It is particularly important that managers define closely what is meant by 'unprofitable'. Even if a product or service is seen as making a 'loss' if its variable costs are less than its selling price, it is making a contribution towards fixed overhead. Clearly this contribution would be lost if production or supply ceased. It may also be the case that sales of other products or services may suffer.

**EXHIBIT
8.6**

Ceasing Production

Country Limited makes three products (picnic baskets, picnic seats and picnic tables) and uses an absorption costing basis. In addition, you discover that production overheads of £333,000 consist of £200,000 which are fixed. The variable element for each of the three products is: picnic baskets, £3,000; picnic seats, £45,000; and tables £85,000. Non-production overhead is entirely fixed. There are no opening and closing stocks as all items are made to order, with just-in-time management techniques.

The information in Table 8.6 has been extracted from the budget forecast for next year. In order to reach the correct decision the above information is recast as shown in Table 8.7.

Table 8.6 Country Limited absorption budget statement

	Picnic baskets	Picnic seats	Picnic tables	Total
Sales (units)	2000	24000	6000	32000
	£	£	£	£
Sales revenue	31,000	480,000	600,000	1,111,000
Direct material – variable	18,000	150,000	80,000	248,000
Direct labour – variable	12,000	100,000	90,000	202,000
Production overhead	8,000	150,000	175,000	333,000
Non-production overhead	15,000	25,000	40,000	80,000
Profit (loss)	(22,000)	55,000	215,000	248,000

Table 8.7 Country Limited restated contribution budget statement

	Picnic baskets (£)	Picnic seats (£)	Picnic tables (£)	Total (£)
Sales	31,000	480,000	600,000	1,111,000
Variable costs				
Materials	18,000	150,000	80,000	248,000
Labour	12,000	100,000	90,000	202,000
Overheads	3,000	45,000	85,000	133,000
	33,000	295,000	255,000	583,000
Contribution	(2,000)	185,000	345,000	528,000
Fixed costs				280,000
Profit				248,000

It can be seen that in Table 8.7 the restated budget for picnic baskets neither makes a profit nor contributes towards fixed overheads. It would thus appear that the decision on a profit maximisation basis would be to close this line. However, we need to give further consideration to a number of points:

- The accuracy of the budget forecast; here we could consult historical data, for example.
- The obviously integrated nature of the product mix, as closing picnic baskets may cost the company sales. They may even be included as a loss leader or even frequently given away with the table and chair sets to further encourage sales.
- Are the figures for the variable element of production overhead accurate?
- If the decision to close the picnic basket line is to be made, managers need to consider its contribution to the long-term business plans of the organisation.
- As all stock is bought on a just-in-time basis there are no stock holding or stock pricing costs, but does the budget reflect agreed contract prices with suppliers?

- The contribution on picnic baskets is only a small negative, so could the price be increased.
- Are any efficiency gains in the use of labour and materials possible?

The above points concentrate on financial issues only and we will return in the final section of this chapter to consider the qualitative issues concerning such decisions.

Make or Buy Decisions

Where a company carries out several processes within the value chain, it is following a policy of vertical integration by controlling all aspects of production. While this may have a number of advantages for the company in terms of control of the supply process, it may not necessarily be the most cost-efficient way of managing the business. Thus a decision to make the part or buy it from an external supplier is naturally termed a *make or buy* decision. By buying from a supplier, that supplier can potentially maximise the benefits of economies of scale which may also result in better quality and not just lower prices. Obviously there are situations in which a company would never consider subcontracting production, for example, where it would put its competitive position at risk either through disclosing trade secrets or risking poor quality.

EXHIBIT 8.7

Avoidable and Unavoidable Costs

Tenby Ltd. produces product X, for which the following information is available:

Cost category	Unit cost (£)
Direct materials	10
Direct labour	5
Variable overhead	1
Section Supervisor	2.5
Depreciation	2
Fixed overhead	4
Total	24.5

An outside UK-based supplier has indicated that it can supply the 10,000 units required at a price of £20 per unit. The question for Tenby is what are the avoidable and unavoidable costs of producing product X. These costs are set out in Table 8.8.

As can be seen, the price differential in favour of in-house manufacture is £1.50 per unit – £15,000 for 10,000 units for the budget period. Depreciation is a sunk cost in relation to

Table 8.8   Avoidable costs

Cost category	Budgeted Unit Cost (£)	Avoidable Cost Per Unit (£)	
		Make	**Buy**
Direct Materials	10	10	
Direct labour	5	5	
Variable overhead	1	1	
Section supervisor	2.5	2.5	
Depreciation	2		
Fixed overhead	4		
Total Cost	24.5	18.5	
Purchase Price			20

product X and may be for special machinery to make the product, but it is ignored in the decision. The fixed overhead represents general overhead apportioned to the product and as such is unavoidable. All other costs are relevant to the decision as they vary with the production of the product; in the case of the supervisor, this cost can be avoided by redundancy.

If we assume now that the supervisor would be entitled to a redundancy payment of £12,500 on top of the above calculation, then we can see that there is still a cost differential in favour of manufacture of product X, even if now it is only £2,500. This requires further thought, however, in that if in the next budget period the alternative supplier came forward again, how would we treat this cost? In this situation the company has already effectively used the £12,500 once to make the 'make' decision and as such should only count £2,500 as being unallocated. Next year (and assuming no other changes) the decision would be to buy. A more sophisticated analysis would incorporate discounted cash-flow analysis, which will be discussed in Chapter 9.

Finally, in this section opportunity cost needs to be mentioned. It has been assumed in the above example that the capacity potentially released by a buy decision will be idle. It could, of course, be used to manufacture an alternative product. If this were possible then Tenby would need to consider the value of the opportunity forgone in reaching its decision. This has particular implications for the use of the specialist machinery mentioned above.

Relevant Costing Explored

Relevant costs and revenues are those that will occur in the future and are relevant to specific decisions. The idea of cost relevance can be illustrated as follows.

A company has 100 components in stock at a manufacturing cost of £100,000, but the prospective customer can no longer afford to pay for them and it has proved impossible to find an alternative customer for the components. Two alternative uses for the components have been identified (see Table 8.9):

Table 8.9   A conventional approach to identifying revenues and costs

	Conversion (£)	Scrap (£)
Revenue	50,000	5,000
Costs		
Manufacturing	100,000	100,000
Conversion	30,000	
Carriage	1,000	500
Total costs	131,000	100,500
Loss	81,000	96,500

Table 8.10   Relevant costs and revenues

	Conversion (£)	Scrap (£)
Revenue	50,000	5,000
Relevant cost		
Conversion	30,000	
Carriage	1,000	500
Total relevant costs	31,000	500
Net cash flow	19,000	4,500

- Convert them into garden gnomes at a cost of £30,000 and then sell them for £50,000, incurring carriage costs of £1000.
- Scrap the components for £5000. Carriage costs will also be £1000.

This approach gathers together all the costs and revenues. However, in terms of the decision whether to convert or scrap the components, not all of the costs are relevant. The non-relevant cost in this case is that of manufacturing: this is a historic or 'sunk' cost and has already been incurred, whichever decision we make. We can remove it from Table 8.9, to give the statement in Table 8.10. As the statement shows, the preferred option is conversion. Conversion will lead to an increase in future net cash flows of £19,000, whereas they will increase by just £4,500 under the scrap option.

Relevant costs have the following characteristics:

- They are *future* costs.
- They are *differential* costs (they differ between different alternatives).
- They are *decision-specific* (if you change the decision, the relevant costs will change).

We now examine the application of relevant cost principles in three cost areas: salaries and wages, materials and depreciation.

Salaries and Wages

If there is spare capacity in the workforce, the relevant cost of wages is zero if the workforce is paid whilst spare capacity exists. If there is no spare capacity, the relevant cost of labour may be represented by the following cases:

- The costs of overtime working when the existing workforce is required to work overtime to complete the project. In this situation the relevant cost is the cost of overtime working.
- The cost of bringing in new workers to cover for existing workers when this is done to take work off existing workers to allow them to work on a new project. In this situation, the relevant cost is the cost of the replacement workers.
- The contribution that is lost when workers are transferred from another project. This occurs when the labour force is fully employed and where workers must be moved away from one profitable area in order to work on another. In this situation, the relevant cost of labour is its opportunity cost.

Materials

The relevant costs of materials depend initially on whether the materials are to be purchased or are in stock. If they are to be purchased, then the relevant cost is the future acquisition cost of the materials.

If they are already in stock, then the *book value* (or the historic cost of the materials) is irrelevant, as it is a historic or sunk cost. However, materials in stock do have a relevant cost. If the materials are in continuous use within the business, then the relevant cost is equal to the replacement cost of the materials. This is because, if materials are in continuous use, once they are used they will be replaced. If, on the other hand, the materials are not in continuous use – for example, they are obsolete, ordered in error or have become surplus to requirements – then their relevant cost is their opportunity cost and this may be estimated as the greater of their net realisable value and their value in alternative use.

The net realisable value is equal to the sales proceeds less the selling costs, for example, carriage. The value in alternative use is the saving obtained by using the material elsewhere within the company, for example, in place of another material that is currently in use.

The following example demonstrates the application of these principles to the relevant cost of material. A contract requires 1000 kg of material A, 500 kg of material B and 200 units of C.

Material A is in continuous use by the company. The company currently has 400 kg in stock at a total book value of £2000. Future purchases of material A will cost £5.20 per kilogram.

There are 100 kg of material B in stock, with a total book value of £350 if used on the contract. Material B will not be replaced. It has no anticipated use other than disposal for £1.20 per kilogram. Its replacement cost is £2.80 per kilogram.

Table 8.11   Relevant cost of material, and explanations

Material A	
Material A is in continuous use and so all material to be used should be valued at replacement cost. 100 kg × £5.20	520
The book value is sunk or historic cost.	
Material B	
Material B is not in continuous use and the relevant cost of materials in stock is its opportunity cost. £1.20 × 100.	120
Additionally 400 kg. will be purchased at a cost of 400 kg × £2.80.	1120
The book value is sunk or historic cost.	
Material C	
There are sufficient items in stock. Material C is not in regular use and its relevant cost is its opportunity cost. If sold, it will realise 200 kg × £1.50 = £300.	
If converted and used in place of Y, it will save the company 200 kg × (£2 − £1.20) = £160.	
C's opportunity cost is the higher of these	300
The book value is sunk or historic cost.	
Total relevant cost of materials	£2060

There are 300 units of C in stock. This material is not in regular use by the company and would realise only £1.50 per unit if sold, whereas its original price was £2.75 per unit. Its replacement price is £2.50 per unit. However, the stock of C could be used in the business in place of another component, Y, if £1.20 were spent on the conversion of each unit of C. Y is in continuous use by the business and its current replacement price is £2 per unit.

Table 8.11 summarise the relevant costs for this example

Depreciation

Depreciation is based upon the historic cost, estimated life and estimated scrap value of fixed assets. Because deprecation is related to historic or sunk cost, it is not a relevant cost. However, the use of equipment that is owned can have a relevant cost, as is illustrated in the following situations:

- Using equipment on a project may result in a reduction in its resale value as a result of the additional wear and tear or because holding on to the asset reduces its resale value. In both cases the reduction in resale value may be regarded as a relevant cost.
- Equipment may be hired out to other companies. If such equipment is to be used on a project, then the hire charge revenue that is forgone by the company should be regarded as a relevant cost.

<table>
<tr><td>**EXHIBIT 8.8**</td><td>**Reviewing a Project**</td></tr>
</table>

EXHIBIT 8.8	**Reviewing a Project**

A project which to date has cost the company £50,000 is under review. It is anticipated that, should the project be allowed to proceed, it will be completed in one year when it will generate income of £250,000. Shown below are the additional expenses that the managing director estimates will be necessary to complete the work.

- Materials, £90,000. These have just been received and paid for. They have cost £90,000 and if not used on the project would have to be disposed of by special means at a cost of £5,000.
- Labour, £60,000. The men are highly skilled and very difficult to recruit. They have been transferred to the project from a production department and, at a recent board meeting, the works director claimed that if the men were returned to him he could earn the company each year a contribution of £80,000 over and above the cost of materials and labour.
- Project staff, £40,000. A decision has already been taken that this will be the last project undertaken, and consequently when work on the project ceases, the staff will be made redundant.
- Share of general building services, £35,000. The managing director is not very sure what is included in this expense. He knows, however, that the accounts staff apportion similar amounts each year to each department.

Table 8.12   Calculation for Exhibit 8.8

	£
Revenue	
£150,000 is future income and is relevant	250,000
Costs	
£50,000 is a sunk cost and is not relevant	
Materials. Historic cost is not relevant as the materials have been delivered and paid for. However, if the company does not proceed with the contract, the relevant cost of disposal will be saved if the company proceeds with the contract.	(5,000)
Labour. In this case the £60,000 cost of labour is a common cost as it will be incurred whether or not the company goes ahead with the project. The works director estimates that the labour could earn a contribution of £80,000. As this is is after deducting labour costs, which are not relevant, the company will loose (£80,000 + £60,000) as a result of undertaking the contract. This the opportunity cost of labour in this case.	140,000
Project staff. This is a relevant cost as it will only be incurred if the project goes ahead.	40,000
Share of building services represents an apportionment and is a common cost that will be incurred irrespective of whether the project proceeds.	
Total relevant costs	175,000
Net cash flow	75,000

Assuming the estimates are accurate, and given that Table 8.12 shows that the net cash flow is positive, the managing director is advised to allow the project to proceed.

Qualitative Factors in Decisions

The above section covered the financial analysis in make or buy decisions but qualitative factors can be important. The following applies a public sector technique known as *desiderata* to such analysis. While it is normally used on capital projects, there is no reason why it cannot be used in the private sector in this or any other type of decision.

As was seen in Exhibit 8.6, Tenby considered on a financial basis that the make decision was the correct one. We will now add an overseas supplier to the equation who has come in with an offer price of £18.00 per unit. Should Tenby thus use this supplier?

The company now needs to draw up a list of other issues (the desiderata) which affect its choice. This would be done possibly by a team of individuals to ensure all factors are considered. Table 8.13 illustrates the result of such discussions.

In terms of the factors identified for this company, we can see that the make decision scores highest. Other managers might include other factors, such as exposure to foreign exchange risk. The financial decision, while marginally favouring buying from overseas,

Table 8.13 Desiderata table for make or buy appraisal

Criteria important to Tenby	Weights in the decision	Option 1 score: make	Option 2 score: UK source	Option 3 score: Overseas
Reliability of Supply	25	25	20	10
Impact on motivation of company workforce	15	12	8	7
Customer reaction	10	5	5	5
Quality of supply	50	45	40	28
Total benefits	100	87	73	50

with the new information provided is outweighed in this instance by the qualitative factors now input into the decision. Managers would need to assess the significance of this result. The advantage of the use of desiderata is that quantitative information has now been expressed in numeric terms. Obviously such information is subjective, but it is an attempt to move the debate over such issues forward to give managers more information in a manageable format to arrive at the correct decision for their company. The technique can also be used in a variety of decision-making situations and is further explored in Chapter 9 when capital investment decisions are considered.

Pricing Decisions

There are two types of pricing decision, which relate to either internal customers or external customers. In the former case, one division of an organisation charges another for goods or services provided, and this is known as *transfer pricing*. In both the public sector and private sector such transfer prices may be subject to an internal service level agreement which is effectively an internal contract for the supply of goods or services at a set price and set quality.

Cost Plus Pricing

In simple terms, the pricing decision is about covering costs and earning a mark-up which represents profit. The problem comes in what to include in the costs. One approach could be to take prime costs (all direct costs) and add production overheads to give the full production cost. Full production cost would then form the basis for the addition of the mark-up percentage (say, 25%). By this method the firm has a cushion in the price for any budget variation, but there is no guarantee that the price at 25% over production costs will cover other non-productive costs such as selling and distribution and give a satisfactory level of profit. The alternative is to include non-production costs in calculating the unit cost of output and then to add the mark-up percentage. By this method the company would hope to reduce the failure to cover all its costs. The final alternative, cost plus, would be to calculate the variable cost per unit of production and then add on a large profit mark-up to cover all fixed costs (production and non-production), but this is a high-risk strategy as all fixed costs might not be covered. In addition, whatever price is set, the company would need to consider the marketplace and the actions of its competitors as the percentage mark-up needs to be realistic in terms of achievability.

On page 229 we looked at the issue of a special order and recognised that the company would accept the order as the price was above unit variable cost. Production and non-production overheads were unaffected by this decision and the order represented cash flow to the company. There is, of course, a danger that other customers could hear of the discounting on normal selling price and therefore expect similar treatment.

Lowering the price raises the issue of selling below costs and whether this is acceptable in any circumstances. The following suggestions are made:

- A new product is being introduced and the company wishes to create demand so it sets a price below cost in anticipation of raising the price later. There is, of course, a danger that this may not be possible.
- The market is in recession and as such a company needs cash flow. It would, of course, hope to cover variable costs at a minimum as in the short term it can ignore fixed overheads to generate cash flow.

- Product life cycles are important. In the early days of the product, when there is a desire to recover the investment costs, a high price (coupled with a positive consumer image) will be set. As the product moves through its life cycle prices may be reduced to continue to sell the product. In this context the decision maker is into life cycle costing, under which an attempt is made to track budgeted and actual costs and associated revenues through each stage of the product life cycle.
- Predatory pricing (loss leading) may be used to enter a new market and attract sales and potentially customer loyalty.
- Defensive pricing to defend the market from a potential entrant to ensure that the market is unattractive to that potential entrant.
- To use spare capacity (as with a special order) since fixed costs would be covered by the normal activities and pricing policy of the company.

Target Costing

Under this system management would set a potential target price based on capturing an envisaged share of the market. The firm will thus take direct account of market intelligence and will build the product (or provide the service) to this target price. The price obviously builds in a profit percentage, and costs are budgeted to come in below this figure. The advantages of this method are as follows:

- The price is set in advance based on specific market intelligence and requires detailed consideration of all relevant strategic information.
- Once the price has been established tight budgetary control is vital if planned profits are to be delivered. Once the price is set managers are forced to find savings if one particular element of the budget shows increased costs, otherwise the company's strategy is at risk of failure.
- It overcomes the problem of cost-based prices which can ignore the marketplace. In terms of the delivery of a service, for example, it is not unusual for public sector organisations to simply increase prices by the rate of inflation (usually from 1 April) without any demand analysis. This clearly ignores market information.

Transfer (Internal) Prices

It is quite common for larger organisations to employ an internal market system where one segment of the entity will trade with another to encourage efficiency. Under this system income for one segment is expenditure for another, although when the consolidated accounts of the organisation are compiled these transactions will cancel each other out. It is important that these internal prices are set to optimise the results for the business as a whole and not to encourage suboptimizing where the goals of a segment are seen as more important by managers in the segment than the best interests of the company as a whole. The summary of the article by Spicer (1988) at the end of this chapter places transfer pricing in an organisational context. The topic is also developed further in Chapter 10.

The objectives of a system of transfer prices should be to:

- report results for each segment which reflect the managerial performance of the segment or division;
- motivate individual managers to make sound decisions such that their results also improve the results of the company as a whole;
- support segment autonomy while not undermining decision making in the organisation as a whole.

There are a number of alternative bases for transfer pricing available including: negotiated prices, opportunity cost, total cost, variable cost, and adjusted market price.

In these decisions the role of the management accountant is to supply decision-relevant information and to interpret that information. In giving advice on setting transfer prices, whatever price is to be charged will be based around the objectives set out above.

Conclusions

This chapter has:

- used various costing techniques to make decisions on the utilisation of scarce resources;
- shown how to interpret the results of analysis to advise management on such decisions;
- developed an understanding of the application of marginal costing/the contribution approach to management decisions;
- recognised the importance of risk to the management decision making environment
- recognised the importance of both quantitative and qualitative factors in the decision-making environment.

Summary

Having read this chapter, you have reviewed the utilisation of scarce resources to maximise profits within an organisation based on an understanding of the contribution per unit of scarce resource. This was then developed to examine how break-even analysis can contribute to a manager's understanding of business behaviour. The identification of fixed and variable costs via a variety of techniques was considered and decision making examined using a method to quantify qualitative factors. Finally, the chapter looked at pricing both from an external and internal perspective. It should be remembered that there is rarely a single correct answer to the decisions required by managers. What is important is that the data available are analysed correctly and presented in a form which managers can use. It is therefore crucial that the management accountant provides that information in the form required and that managers are aware of their information needs in specific circumstances. This represents a considerable challenge to both parties.

Recommended Further Reading

Otley, D. (2001) 'Extending the boundaries of management accounting research: developing systems for performance management', *British Accounting Review*, 33(3): 243–261.

This paper opens by pointing out that by the mid-1980s the practice of management accounting was in decline, with little in the way of new developments for decades. Therefore management accounting was seen as irrelevant to contemporary organisations and, even worse, its influence seen as counterproductive to good managerial decision making. Otley points out that since 1987, when Johnson and Kaplan's book *Relevance Lost* appeared, Johnson appears to have given up on accounting to emphasise 'softer' areas, while Kaplan has pushed forward the reinvention of management accounting practices. Kaplan's work is essentially strategic management accounting, through a change in emphasis of the historic context of cost accounting to become forward-looking, to concentrate on planning, to move from an emphasis on cost to one on value, to stress marketing as well as production and recognise external clients and competitors as opposed to the internal factors. While the author feels that this emphasis perhaps undervalues the contribution of previous practice, he goes on to quote a past president of the Chartered Institute of Management Accountants as claiming this new emphasis releases 'the management accountant from the factory floor'(Bromwich and Bhimani, 1989).

Otley goes on to look at the so-called second major innovation to come from Kaplan (see Kaplan and Norton, 1996), the 'balanced scorecard', which is seen as a framework for performance measurement that includes both financial and non-financial elements in the strategic decision-making process. However, he points out that the literature on the balanced scorecard shows a lack of coverage of target setting, resource allocation, reward systems design, and the separation of tactical and strategic feedback, despite diagrams covering these items in the 1996 book. In contrast, the economic value-added technique developed by Stern Stewart Corporation is seen as putting no 'explicit' emphasis on strategy either in practice or in theory, but adherence to the principle of generating shareholder value is achieved by close attention to each stage of the management process. Performance measurement is core to the system, and rewards devised to mitigate inappropriate behaviour within feedback processes which update targets over time to achieve 'value added'. Initially these approaches were seen as in conflict, but more recently a more collaborative approach seems to be developing, taking the benefits of both ideas. In the context of the paper by Otley, what is stressed is that management accounting practices have changed radically over the past fifteen years. This is through the linking of financial and non-financial measures and presents major challenges to the discipline.

The remainder of the paper goes on to explore issues of how management accounting research has adopted to this environment. Otley's answer is 'not very well' in that the discipline seems to have become somewhat sterile, perhaps losing touch with management practices. The theme of the paper is the widening role of the management accountant in both public and private organisations. The call in the paper is to put 'management' back into management accounting; the interest in 'real' organisations in understanding and developing their systems of performance management has never been greater. Otley concludes by saying that in his opinion management accounting researchers should 'seize these opportunities'.

Spicer, B.H. (1988) 'Towards an organisation theory of the transfer pricing process', *Accounting, Organizations and Society*, 13(3): 303–22.

Spicer's article builds upon the work of Watson and Baumler (1975) relating to the behavioural aspects of transfer pricing (TP).

The classical approach makes assumptions about the firm (e.g. profit maximising) and tries to develop an optimal TP model using an analytical (linear programming) approach. The assumptions, however, limit the wider organisational analysis of the effects of TP, for example on the firm's various strategies of diversification, management accounting and control. It must be recognised, however, that the benefits of any chosen TP system are contingent upon the organisational structure of the firm.

The firm, states Spicer, can be seen as a network of transactions whose costs vary with complexity. These transactions (both internal and external to the firm) and their associated choices, have associated problems, such as bounded rationality and opportunism. Therefore moral hazard is introduced into exchange relationships (by taking advantage of asymmetric information).

Spicer refers to Watson and Baumler, who argue that authors on TP have failed to 'offer a coherent theory of decentralisation' so that the relationship between TP and decentralisation is not well thought out. The TP system should try to optimise effective *differentiation* (i.e. segmentation) and *integration* (i.e. common purpose) of the firm. TP enhances differentiation by pinpointing responsibilities and, via negotiation, can aid in the integration process. Spicer refers to Swieringa and Waterhouse (1982) and Eccles (1985) who comment that the *process* of TP (rather than the details) may be useful in furthering organisational control. They concluded that the need for (and details of) the TP process will depend heavily upon the *diversification and decentralisation strategies* of the company – the more a firm is diversified, the less likely it is to have a high level of interdivisional transfers and the less of a problem TP is.

Spicer argues that two decisions are necessary: the design of the intermediate product (standardised or specialised/unique) and whether to make or buy the intermediate product. He provides a table examining the dimensions of such decisions and states that the costs and hazards associated with such decisions are dependent upon the investments in assets necessary, the degree of uncertainty, and the extent (frequency and volume) of activity.

Spicer goes on to analyse this further, looking at a particular case where the intermediate product is made within the firm and transferred between different profit centres with different profit streams. This analysis looks specifically at: the dimensions of intrafirm transactions, internal contracting hazards (how they arise and how they can be dealt with), and the need for adaptation and co-operation (to achieve overall objectives). The analysis discusses these factors at length and also considers the factors involved in deciding the degree of managerial autonomy in the TP process.

Spicer puts forward nine hypotheses, drawn from the preceding discussion, relating to the factors likely to affect the mode and process of TP likely to be chosen by an organisation. These hypotheses deal with the effects on TP of factors such as: diversification strategy; product design; organisational structure; transaction-specific investment; frequency and volume of transactions; degree of uncertainty; degree of conflict; the need for articulation and negotiation; the bases of TP (e.g. cost- or market-based); and degree of central control.

Overall, using a contingency approach, the article attempts to place TP within a wider organisational context and prepares the ground for further empirical research.

Case Study: The Odd-Job Manufacturing Company

The Odd-Job Manufacturing Company (OJMC) produces toolboxes from plastic and metal in a single plant. The basic product is made from strong 5 mm plastic with a plastic handle and metal hinges and wheels. The company has a good reputation in the market because the standard toolbox is a high-quality item, has been well-produced and has sold well for many years.

Two years ago the company decided to expand its product line and produce bespoke boxes for the different retail outlets, usually those that specialise in do-it-yourself supplies. These boxes differ from the standard because they are produced in a range of sizes, they have a metal handle and carry the logo of the specific retail outlet. The standard one-size toolboxes are simply imprinted with the company's initials, OJMC.

In order to reduce the labour cost of the speciality toolboxes, much of the assembly work is done by automated machines. These machines are used to a much lesser degree in the production of the standard toolbox. With the lower cost of labour, the accounting department has determined that the speciality toolboxes are less costly to manufacture than the standard toolboxes. This is shown in the summary data below. Because the bespoke toolboxes are special-order items, they are priced at a higher level than the standard toolbox.

The managing director of OJMC, T.E.N. Onsaw, exploded when he saw the above figures and demanded, 'Why do we produce the standard item? It seems time to cut back, cut the standard, just produce the special lines and see if we can grow them more.'

The company's marketing director, Pierre Lasterboard, commented, 'I agree that the bespoke business is working better and there seems to be plenty of work out there,

Per unit	Standard (£)	Bespoke (£)
Selling price	9.00	10.00
Manufacturing cost	8.94	6.10
Gross profit	0.06	3.9

particularly as the competition has not been able to touch our price. Our biggest competitor charges £15 for bespoke items.'

However, the finance director, Dee Rill, is not as easily convinced. She observes that, 'Since we introduced the bespoke lines, our annual net profit has fallen by £350,000. This business has produced sales but it has also required investment and other costs.' The Managing Director responds, 'Dee, that's all very well but the unit gross profit figures tell their own story! Your argument just seems to be suggesting that neither line makes a profit – yet the company makes a profit so we must be doing something right. As chief accountant, Dee, I suggest that you sort this out as soon as possible and let me have something definitive before we move any further on this issue.'

Dee begins her investigation and first obtains a breakdown of the manufacturing cost of each of the company's product lines as follows:

	Standard	Specials
Units produced each month	10,000	5,500
	Per unit	Per unit
	£	£
Direct materials	5.00	4.13
Direct labour (at £4 per hour)	0.80	0.40
Prime cost	5.80	4.53
Manufacturing overhead (£15.69 per hour)	3.14	1.57
Manufacturing cost	8.94	6.10

Note that the manufacturing overhead is absorbed via direct labour hours and the absorption rate of £15.69 per hour is obtained from the budgeted manufacturing overhead (£40,012) divided by the budgeted direct labour hours (2550 hours).

Further investigation reveals that standard toolboxes are produced in batches of 200 units, whilst speciality toolboxes are produced in batches of 25 units. In consequence, in each month the company makes 100 set-ups for the bespoke items and 50 set-ups for the standard products. Each machine set-up requires 1 hour for the standard product and 2 hours for the bespoke product.

Each standard toolbox requires 0.5 hours of machine time but, due to its higher level of automation, each bespoke toolbox requires 2 hours of machine time.

At the end of the production process all toolboxes are inspected to ensure that quality standards are met. The standard toolbox requires little inspection time as the workers correct for any quality problems as they process the units. In total the standard toolbox requires 300 hours of inspection per month, and the speciality toolbox 500 hours of inspection time per month.

Dee also has access to results of a consultant's recent study of monthly overheads. The consultant's report includes the following summary:

Overhead activity (cost driver)	Overhead cost £	No. of events	Standard products	Speciality products
Purchasing (no. of orders)	3,000	60	48	12
Material handling (no. of receipts)	3,750	60	52	8
Production orders and set-ups (set-up time)	5,062	150	50	100
Inspection (inspection hours)	4,000	800	300	500
Frame assembly (assembly hours)	10,200	2,550	2,000	550
Machine-related (machine hours)	14,000	7,000	2,000	5,000
Total	40,012			

Complete Dee Rill's investigation and write a report to the managing director that examines the strengths and weaknesses of the existing costing system, examines the consequences for the company of continuing with it and evaluates an alternative system. You should illustrate how an alternative system should work and explain its significance for the company's production and marketing strategies.

Questions

1. Submarine Cables makes mobile telephones for underwater use. The budgeted revenues and costs for the year ended 30 June 2004 are as follows:

Revenues	£600,000
Variable costs	420,000
Fixed costs	150,000
Net profit	30,000

Capital employed will be £600,000. Budgeted output for the year ended 30 June 2004 is 30,000 units, which represents 60% of output capacity.

The management of the company are concerned about the low level of budgeted profit and return on capital employed. They have asked you to analyse and evaluate the following independent options for improving performance:

(a) An enquiry has been received from a wholesaler in Kazakhstan who has indicated that he is prepared to take 12,000 units at a price of £16 per unit, with Submarine Cables paying the carriage and customs charges estimated at £2000. Submarine Cables has never previously dealt with this wholesaler or this distant market.

(b) Reduce selling price by 10%. It is thought that this will increase demand to capacity. However, it will need to be supported by a new system of salesmen's commissions; these will be 50 pence per unit sold in 2000/2001.

(c) The managing director believes in setting targets and has announced a profit target of 10% of capital employed. The managing director wants to know what price increase is necessary to achieve the target with the current level of sales, and what sales increase is necessary to achieve the target with the current price per unit.

(d) A machine may be leased at a cost of £15,000 per annum. The machine will cause variable costs to fall by 50% per unit; it will also increase current capacity by 20%.

For each option (a)–(d), determine whether it is financially worthwhile and comment on its non-financial aspects.

2. Didcot is small company that specialises in producing virtual reality (VR) machines for large international entertainment companies. One of these has offered Didcot a contract to produce and deliver 1000 identical VR machines over a 26-week period starting on 1 June 2004.

Each machine requires the following materials:

- *2 square metres of Yalloy*: Yalloy is in continuous use by the company and 500 square metres are currently in stock at a book value of £80 per square metre. Future purchases will cost £90 per square metre.
- *1 translucent fitment*: 1500 are in stock at a book value of £10 each. However, this type of fitment will have no other use if not used on this contract, although they may be sold for scrap at £2 each. It is possible to purchase a new version of the fitment at £20 per fitment, although the type in stock is adequate for the contract.
- *2 yardarm controllers*: there are none in stock. The current purchase price is £50 per controller.
- *1 piezo control*: these will be purchased at £25 each and are specific to VR machines in the contract.

The following mixture of labour is required:

- *Skilled*: each VR machine will require 3 hours of skilled labour. Skilled labour is currently paid £4.80 per hour and will be fully employed on other work during the next 26 weeks. In order to fulfil the contract a skilled worker will be taken off other work which will be undertaken by a temporary replacement provided by a local agency at £6 per hour.
- *Semi-skilled*: each machine will require 4 hours of semi-skilled labour. The current rate for semi-skilled labour is £3.50 per hour and sufficient temporary workers can be recuited for this work.

In the case of both skilled and semi-skilled employees, national insurance adds a further 12% to the cost of employment. This is not payable by Didcot in the case of agency workers.

Supervision of the work will be carried out by a senior manager who is currently paid £25,000 per year (with superannuation and national insurance adding a further 20% to the costs of employment). In order to free her time to undertake this work, an agency will provide cover at a cost of £500 per week.

Didcot absorbs production overhead by a machine rate that is currently £40 per hour. Of this, £15 is variable and £25 is fixed. Each VR machine will require 2 machine hours. Additionally, fixed overheads directly attributable to the production of VRs are likely to increase by £15,000 over the period of the contract.

The costs of negotiating and drawing up the contract to supply 1000 VR machines have amounted to £800.

A price of £520 per machine has been agreed with the entertainment company. The entertainment company has stipulated within the contract that it will pay only £250 per machine for any that are delivered up to four weeks late. Machines delivered more than four weeks late will be delivered free of charge.

(a) Prepare a statement of the relevant costs of the contract and state whether or not the contract should be undertaken by Didcot. Provide notes to indicate why you have selected some costs and rejected others.

(b) Comment on *three* significant factors that management needs to consider before finally agreeing to take the contract.

3. Traffick PLC has been forced to close for two weeks because of supply problems. During that time the company produced no count meters. The company issued a press statement that the supply failure had cost the company £1 million. This figure was based on the loss of turnover over the two-week period.

The company's financial accountant has subsequently made a more detailed assessment of the cost, as follows:

		£000	£000
Lost revenue (40,000 units @£25 each)			1000
	Standard cost		
Costs saved	per unit (£)		
Materials	1.0	40	
Direct labour	2.5	100	
Depreciation	4.0	160	
Variable overhead	3.0	120	
Sub-contracting work	1.0	40	
Fixed overhead	5.0	200	660
Cost of the supply failure			340

The following information is available:

(i)   The direct labour was paid 75% of the normal wage during the two-week period, and this amounted to £75,000.

(ii) Depreciation is based on the straight-line method. However, there is a variable component of depreciation amounting to 50 pence per unit produced.

(iii) Fixed overhead is absorbed at the rate of 200% on direct wages.

(iv) The maintenance team was able to carry out a major overhaul of one of the machines during the period of closure. They had to purchase materials costing £5000, but a contractor would normally have performed the overhaul at a cost of £25,000 (including materials). The cost of the maintenance team is included within fixed overheads. The cost of the materials has not yet been recorded.

(v)   The sales manager has estimated that because of the closure, there will be unsatisfied demand amounting to half the production lost. This can be made up by the production workforce working overtime during the next month. Overtime is paid at an enhanced rate of 50% above the normal hourly rate.

(a) Examine points (i)–(v) and discuss the relevance of each of these costs to the identification of the cost of closure.

(b) Produce a statement indicating the net cost of the closure. You will need to explain the inclusion (or exclusion) of any items that you have not discussed in part (a) of the question.

(c) Outline *two* potential problems with the use of relevant costing in decision making.

4. Emily Wye is currently working on the production schedules for next month. Her firm manufactures two types of ceramic grids:

	Type A £	Type B £
Selling price	60	70
Material X1 (at £2 per kg)	3	6
Material X2 (at £5 per kg)	10	10
Direct labour (grade 1)	12	9
Direct labour (grade 2)	10	15
Variable overhead	5	7

Notes:

(i) Labour rates and maximum labour hours available in the next month are:

Grade	Hourly rate	Max. monthly hours
1	£6	640
2	£5	Unlimited

(ii) Both products involve machine work, type A requiring 1 hour and B half an hour. The machine is available for 400 hours per month.

(iii) Next month the company will have available 900 kg of X1. The firm can buy as much X2 as it wishes.

(iv) Fixed overheads in the coming month will amount to £1950.

(a) The company wishes to maximise contribution. Set out the objective function and the constraints.

(b) Determine the optimum output of each product next month using the graphical approach to linear programming. Calculate the optimum profit for the month.

(c) Calculate the amount of spare capacity available next month.

(d) Discuss three limitations of linear programming.

Jane Lane is the management accountant of a small manufacturing company. Jane normally gets involved in the production scheduling of the firm. She is currently working on this for the last three months of 2004, making use of her management accounting and linear programming skills.

The company manufactures components for rock climbing, including two types of ice axe, the X1 and the X2. During the last quarter of 2004, each X1 will have a selling price of £67 and each X2 a selling price of £78.

The cost of each axe is made up as follows:

	X1 (£)	X2 (£)
Materials: STX2 at £12 per metre	15	18
Labour: at £4.50 per hour	9	18
Variable overhead: at £5 per mc/hr	10	15

In addition, monthly fixed manufacturing overheads are budgeted to be £2000 per month and fixed non-manufacturing overheads are budgeted to be £5000 for the three-month period.

The company will have the following resources available to it for the last quarter of the year: 800 metres of STX2, 2000 hours of labour and 1800 machine hours. The firm wishes to supply its retailers with no less than 150 of each type of axe during the final quarter.

(a) The company wishes to maximise contribution. Set out the objective function and the constraints.

(b) Determine the optimum production of each product over the final quarter using the graphical approach to linear programming and calculate the optimum net profit for the final quarter of 2004.

(c) Calculate the shadow price of STX2 and explain how Jane may use it.

Chapter 9
STRATEGIC DECISION MAKING

Key Learning Objectives

By the time you have finished studying this chapter, you should be able to:
- understand the concept of discounting;
- calculate net present value and internal rate of return;
- apply non-discounting methods;
- understand the importance of taxation and inflation to strategic decision making;
- apply sensitivity analysis.

The Nature of Strategic Decision Making

Strategic planning and strategic decision making look ahead to several years into the future. They are concerned with the organisation's major products and services and related aspects of marketing, manufacturing, service delivery, and research and development. Strategic decisions almost invariably result in long-term financial costs and benefits and may require significant investment.

Examples of strategic decision making from a range of organisations are as follows:

- A university is located in an area with a declining and ageing population, with the result that its potential student base is declining. It is looking at several ways of dealing with this problem, one of which involves building on-campus student accommodation in order to attract students from more distant locations. This would require significant investment by the university in constructing the accommodation, but it is expected that this would result in future rental income and an increase in its student population.
- An airline has a long and profitable history of flying long-haul routes. Due to the growth in world terrorism, it is considering moving into the European short-haul market by leasing a fleet of aeroplanes. This market has grown significantly in the last decade, and looks as if it will continue to grow. However, the airline is aware that this sector is highly competitive, highly efficient and operating in a low-cost way that is alien to it.

- An engineering company is assessing the profitability of producing a new product. This will involve acquiring a new machine. The company will need to take account of the cost of the machine, the projected operating costs, the projected revenues from the sale of the product, and the expected lives of the machine and the market for the product.
- A company currently pays mileage travel allowances to its staff. It is evaluating leasing a fleet of cars and requiring its employees to use these cars for company business. In this case, the company will need to collect the costs of mileage allowances, estimate the annual leasing and operating costs of a fleet of vehicles, and estimate the additional costs or savings of the venture.

As can be seen, strategic decisions are long-term in nature and usually involve investment, costs and revenues. This chapter will focus on the appraisal of these investment decisions.

Steps in Project Appraisal

The first step is to specify the scope and objectives of the project. Scope relates to the breadth and coverage of the project. Its objectives should be directly related to the strategic decisions taken within the company. Each of the examples of strategic decision making listed above directly leads to a clearer definition of a project's scope and objectives.

The second is to identify the relevant cash flows for project appraisal. Chapter 2 introduced the concept of relevant cost (see also Chapter 8). Recall that relevant costs may be distinguished by the following three characteristics:

- They are decision-specific in that if the decision changes the costs change.
- They are future costs. From a decision perspective, past costs are sunk costs and they should have no influence on the current decision. Sunk costs include past expenditure on machinery, the book cost of materials held in stock and the depreciation of past capital expenditure.
- They are differential costs. Common costs, that is, costs that would be incurred in any event, should have no influence on the decision. Examples of common costs include fixed overheads, fixed overhead apportionments and labour costs when there is spare capacity.

Relevant cash flows include the following:

- Incremental costs and revenues that are attributable to the decision that has been made.
- Financing costs: in order to undertake capital expenditure such as the construction of student accommodation, the organisation will need to obtain finance. The costs of finance, in the form of interest costs, represent a relevant cost. Alternatively, if the organisation finances the project from its own resources, the interest forgone due to the financing activity represents an opportunity cost and is relevant.

Table 9.1 Data for projects A, B and C

Project	Project A		Project B		Project C	
	Cash flows	Net profits	Cash flows	Net profits	Cash flows	Net profits
Years hence	£	£	£	£	£	£
0	−1000		−1000		−2000	
1	600	350	500	250	600	350
2	400	150	400	150	600	350
3	300	50	600	350	600	350
4	300	50	700	450	1600	350
Other information						
Residual values	0		0		1000	
Annual depreciation over 4 year's life of each project	= investment/4 = £1000/4 = £250 per year		= investment/4 = £1000/4 = £250 per year		= net investment/4 = £(2000 − 1000)/4 = £250 per year	

- The timing of returns that arise from the project is also relevant. Returns that arise at an early date are worth more than the same returns received at a later date.
- Working capital changes should be brought into the appraisal if these change as a result of the project. For example, the project may require an increase in debtors or a build-up in stocks of raw materials, and these represent relevant cash flows.
- Taxation effects: the investment may attract tax allowances that have the effect of reducing the taxation paid by the company. Any additional profits generated by the project will be subject to taxation.
- Future inflation is likely to affect costs and revenues in different ways and will need to be taken into account.

The third stage is to select and apply at least one method of appraisal. We will consider the following four methods: net present value; internal rate of return; pay back; and accounting rate of return. The first two are discounted cash flow methods; the second two are non-discounting methods.

In order to help explain and demonstrate these four methods, we will use the data contained in Table 9.1. As may be seen, there are three projects, A, B and C. The first column indicates the number of years hence. Year 0 always represents now and this is often when the initial investment in the project occurs, year 1 is 1 year after, year 2 is 2 years after and so on.

For each project there are two columns. The first column represents the project's cash flows. The second represents the annual net profits, which differ from the cash flows because they allow for depreciation on the original investment. The table indicates that there is no residual value in the case of project A and B and the annual depreciation is £250, with the result that the annual profits are £250 less than the cash flows. Project C has a residual value of £1000 so its annual depreciation is also £250. In year 4, project C's cash flows include the £1000 residual value.

After applying one or more of the investment appraisal techniques, the fourth step is to make sense of the results. In order to do this, one needs to understand the basis, the strengths and limitations of each technique and any limitations in the underlying data.

Finally, the decision maker needs to make a decision based on the above information. At this point, qualitative issues will also be considered and possibly tactical and strategic issues relating to the organisation's planning processes.

Project Appraisal Using Discounted Cash-Flow Methods

Compounding, Discounting and Present Value

Both compounding and discounting involve the use of an appropriate rate of interest or rate of return. Generally, keeping the rate of interest constant, the longer you invest, the greater the total accumulated interest will be. We will now look in more detail at the use of the rate of interest, first dealing with compounding and then with discounting.

Compound interest occurs when the interest is applied to the principal (the sum invested) plus the accrued interest. At the end of the first period, the interest is calculated on the principal only. At the end of the second period, interest is calculated on the principal plus interest earned in the first period. Thus, if £100 is invested at 10% compound, at the end of the first year the interest earned is £10, and the principal becomes £110. At the end of the second year, the interest earned is $10\% \times £110$, and the principal is now £121. This can be generalised so that one can calculate the future value, if there is a constant interest rate, by the following formula:

$$FV = P(1 + r)^n$$

where FV is future value, P is the principal, r is the rate of interest per period, and n the number of periods. So, if we invest £100 at 10% for 5 years, it will be worth

$$FV = 100(1 + 0.1)^5 = 100 \times 1.6105 = £161.05.$$

Discounting is the opposite of compounding. Discounting involves finding the present values of future cash flows. We have just seen that, when invested at 10% compound interest, £100 at year 0 produces £110 in one year's time. We can say that an investor is indifferent between receiving £100 now (year 0) or £110 in one year's time or £121 in two years' time and so on, because he can invest £100 at 10% to produce each of these amounts. The person who invests £100 at year 0 will require more than £100 in future, the exact amount depending on the time period and the rate of interest. The concept that £1 in the future is worth less than £1 today is termed the *time value of money*. In project appraisal, this is an important concept as, typically, projects will have cash flows that continue well into the future. In these situations, future cash flows cannot simply be added together. They must first all be discounted to present values.

In order to discount future cash flows to present values, we first rearrange the future value formula to obtain the present value (PV):

$$PV = FV \times \frac{1}{(1 + r)^n}.$$

Here $1/(1+r)^n$ is termed the *discount factor* and r is termed the *discount rate*. In Table 9.2 we demonstrate the use of the formula to find the present value of future cash flows when the discount rate is 10%.

As can be seen, discounting is the inverse of compounding. To save calculating the discount factor every time, they are precalculated and appear in Table 9A.1 in the Appendix at the end of this chapter. An extract from Table 9A.1 is presented in Table 9.3

Looking at Table 9.3, we can read off the appropriate discount factor once we know the periods hence and the discount rate. So, the discount factor for 5 years hence when the discount rate is 7% is 0.713. The present value of the sum of £4500 to be paid or received in 5 years' time with a discount rate of 7% is 0.713 × £4,500 = £3208.

Net Present Value

Net present value (NPV) is a discounted cash-flow method of investment appraisal. It involves discounting future cash flows to present values. The sum of the present value of

Table 9.2 Present value calculations for a discount rate of 10%

	Year 0	Year 1	Year 2	Year 3
Discount factor	Present values	Future values		
$1/(1 + r)^n$	$FV \times 1/(1+r)^n$			
$1/(1 + 0.1)^1 = 0.909$	$110 \times 0.909 = 100$	110		
$1/(1 + 0.1)^2 = 0.826$	$121 \times 0.826 = 100$		121	
$1/(1 + 0.1)^3 = 0.751$	$133.1 \times 0.751 = 100$			133.1

Table 9.3 Discount factors for one to five periods and discount rates up to 10%

Periods	1%	2%	3%	4%	5%	6%	7%	8%	9%	10%
1	0.990	0.980	0.971	0.962	0.952	0.943	0.935	0.926	0.917	0.909
2	0.980	0.961	0.943	0.925	0.907	0.890	0.873	0.857	0.842	0.826
3	0.971	0.942	0.916	0.889	0.864	0.840	0.816	0.794	0.772	0.751
4	0.961	0.924	0.888	0.855	0.823	0.792	0.763	0.735	0.708	0.683
5	0.951	0.906	0.863	0.822	0.784	0.747	0.713	0.681	0.650	0.621

future cash flows less the initial investment gives the NPV of the project. If the discount rate represents the company's cost of finance, then the NPV represents the returns to the company's shareholders over and above the costs of finance; in consequence, we may say that a positive NPV contributes to the wealth of the shareholders.

The decision rule in the case of NPV is to accept only those projects providing a positive NPV. (A negative NPV indicates that the project is not even covering the costs of finance.) If a number of competing projects have positive NPVs, and only one can be selected, these are termed mutually exclusive projects. For example, there may be an area of land and one can build either a school or a sewage farm on the site! In the case of mutually exclusive projects, the rule is to select the project with the highest positive NPV.

Table 9.4 shows the calculation of the NPVs of projects A, B and C using the data from Table 9.1. NCF stands for the net cash flow in each year. This is the cash receipts for the year less the cash payments. PV stands for present value. The discount rate is 10% and the discount factors have all been obtained from Table 9.3.

All cash flows have been discounted to year 0 by multiplying the annual NCF by the discount factor in the second column. For example, for project A, 2 years hence, the annual NCF of £400 has been discounted by multiplying it by the year 2 discount factor 0.826.

As can be seen, the NPV for project A is £305. The investment at year 0 represents a negative cash flow and the figure of £305 is the net total allowing for the negative cash flow of £1000. All projects have positive NPVs and should therefore be accepted. If only one project can be chosen, this would be project B as it has the highest NPV.

Annuities

An annuity is a series of equal and consecutive cash flows. They may be flows of payments or flows of receipts. In Table 9.4, Project C's net cash flows in years 1, 2 and 3 represent an annuity of £600. There exist discount tables for annuities and these are contained in Table 9A.2 in the Appendix at the end of this chapter. An extract is provided in Table 9.5.

Table 9.4   Project net present values

Years hence	Discount factor	Project A NCF	Project A PV	Project B NCF	Project B PV	Project C NCF	Project C PV
0	1.0000	−1000	−1000	−1000	−1000	−2000	−2000
1	0.909	600	545	500	455	600	545
2	0.826	400	330	400	330	600	496
3	0.751	300	225	600	451	600	451
4	0.683	300	205	700	478	1600	1093
NPV			305		714		585
Select					B		

Table 9.5 Present value of annuity

Periods	1%	2%	3%	4%	5%	6%	7%	8%	9%	10%
1	0.990	0.980	0.971	0.962	0.952	0.943	0.935	0.926	0.917	0.909
2	1.970	1.942	1.913	1.886	1.859	1.833	1.808	1.783	1.759	1.736
3	2.941	2.884	2.829	2.775	2.723	2.673	2.624	2.577	2.531	2.487
4	3.902	3.808	3.717	3.630	3.546	3.465	3.387	3.312	3.240	3.170
5	4.853	4.713	4.580	4.452	4.329	4.212	4.100	3.993	3.890	3.791

Annuity tables enable us to take a short cut when calculating NPVs. The PV of an annuity is the amount of the annual net cash flow × the annuity factor. For example, a project is expected to produce net cash flows of £2000 per year for each of the next five years. The discount rate is 6%. The present value of this annuity will be: 4.212 × £2000 = £8424. (where 4.212 is the PV annuity factor for 5 years at 6%).

The Advantages of NPV

- It explicitly takes into account the time value of money because it is based on discounted cash flows, recognising that £1 in the future is worth less than £1 today.
- By considering cash flows, NPV is not affected by the company's accounting policies, unlike net profit. For example, net profit is influenced by the company's policies on stock valuation, depreciation and overhead apportionment. Regardless of changes in any of these, the cash flows will remain unchanged.
- NPV takes explicit account of the costs of raising finance via its discounting process. A positive NPV therefore reflects the increase in shareholder wealth that should occur if the project is undertaken.

The Disadvantages of NPV

- In practice it may be difficult to determine the discount rate. This should relate to the cost of finance (or cost of capital, as it is usually known), but calculating the costs of the different elements of finance (e.g. share capital and loans) is difficult.
- The NPV is an absolute figure and it does not allow for the size of the project. For example, in the case of two mutually exclusive projects, NPV would recommend acceptance of a £1 million project with a NPV of £1250 over a £1000 project with a NPV of £500.

Our concern here is very much with the financial bottom line (the net present value), but Lumijarvi (1991) indicates that as long as projects meet the financial criteria, they then have to be sold to senior management based upon their strategic value and use of modern technology. A summary of this article appears at the end of the chapter.

The Impact of the Discount Rate on NPV

Figure 9.1 below shows the NPV for a project with an investment in year 0 followed by net cash inflows in future years. As may be seen, the NPV falls as the discount rate increases. This is because the increasing discount rate results in a decrease in the present value of future cash flows because the discount factor gets smaller as the discount factor increases; the factors in Table 9.3 demonstrate this. When the discount rate is 0, the NPV is simply the net result of subtracting the total cash outflows from the total cash inflows. The figure indicates the importance of using the correct discount rate. If it is too low, NPV will be overstated and possibly the wrong projects will be accepted. If the discount rate is too high, then projects of value to the company will be rejected.

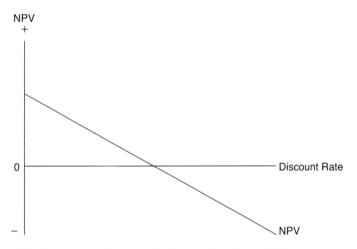

Figure 9.1   The impact of changes in discount rate on NPV

The Internal Rate of Return

The internal rate of return (IRR) is the discount rate that gives a zero NPV. The primary decision rule with IRR is to accept only projects with an IRR greater than the discount rate. If there are mutually exclusive projects each with IRR greater than the discount rate, the rule is to select the project with the highest IRR.

The underlying reason for the primary decision rule is that if the IRR exceeds the discount rate (or cost of capital), the project must be generating a higher return than the discount rate. From a different perspective, the IRR can be regarded as the highest cost of capital that the project could afford to have and still yield benefit to the shareholders.

The IRR can be calculated easily using a computer spreadsheet that will normally include an IRR function. Without a computer spreadsheet, the IRR must be estimated by calculating two NPVs at different discount rates. One of the NPVs should be negative, and this will require discounting at a higher discount rate in order to produce a negative

NPV. Once we have two NPVs, one positive and one negative, we then apply the following formula to estimate the IRR:

$$IRR = DRA + (DRA - DRB)\ \frac{NPVA}{NPVA - NPVB}.$$

Here *DRA* is the first discount rate used to appraise the project, producing a positive NPV; *DRB* is the second discount rate used to appraise the project, producing a negative NPV; *NPVA* is the positive NPV obtained when using *DRA*; and *NPVB* is the negative NPV obtained when using *DRB*.

Let us estimate the IRR for project A. Let *DRA* = 10%, so that *NPVA* = +305, and let *DRB* = 30%, so that *NPVB* = − 60. Then

$$IRR = 10\% + (30\% - 10\%)\frac{305}{305 + 60}$$

$$= 10\% + 16.71\% = 26.71\%.$$

Similarly, the IRR for project B is 38% and for project C is 21%. Calculation of IRR is an estimate and the narrower the gap between *DRA* and *DRB*, the more accurate the estimate. A computer spreadsheet for example will give a value of 25.81% for A. Each project is acceptable as each IRR exceeds the discount rate of 10% used in Table 9.4. If the projects are mutually exclusive, project B should be selected as its IRR is the highest of the three projects.

The Advantages of IRR

- Like NPV, it deals with discounted cash flows and is based upon the time value of money.
- Although the manual calculation of the IRR is more time-consuming than the NPV, the percentage nature of the IRR may make it more acceptable.
- The cost of capital is required for use as the discount rate with NPV but, as has been indicated, its calculation is difficult. Calculation of the IRR does not require a precise cost of capital discount rate and a project's IRR can be compared with an approximation of the cost of capital, avoiding dispute about the precise discount rate to use. The board can decide whether the IRR is sufficiently above the approximate cost of capital for the project to be acceptable.
- The difference between the IRR and the cost of capital indicates the additional return for risk that the project provides.

The Disadvantages of IRR

- If there are negative annual net cash flows later than year 0, this may lead to more than one possible IRR. In this situation IRR must be used with great care.
- If a company has to rank mutually exclusive projects, choosing the project with the highest IRR may result in a suboptimal outcome. (Lumby and Jones, 2003, Chapter 6).

Non-Discounting Methods of Project Appraisal

Payback

Payback is a cash-based technique. The payback period is defined as the number of years required for the annual net cash flows to equal the initial investment in a project. Alternatively, we can look for a cumulative net cash flow of 0. The cumulative net cash flows for projects A, B and C are shown in Table 9.6. By the end of year 2, project A's initial investment is recovered by its net cash flows. In the case of project B, payback occurs between the end of year 2 and the end of year 3. At the end of year 2 we need an additional £100 to payback If we assume that the year 3 cash flows of £600 accrue evenly through the year, then to payback we need 100/600 of year 3 cash flows, which we may assume to take (100/600 × 12 months = 2 months) For project C, payback occurs between the end of year 3 and the end of year 4. The £1600 in year 4 includes £1000 that accrues at the end of the project and £600 that we assume accrues evenly through the year. Therefore, payback in year 4 is at (200/600 × 12 months = 4 months).

Some companies use a 'target payback' approach in which they specify a maximum payback period that projects must meet if they are to be accepted.

The Advantages of Payback

- The underlying concept and the results of applying the technique are very easy to understand.
- It is quick and simple to use.
- It implicitly takes account of uncertainty that characterises the future. The further in the future that a company has to forecast, the more uncertain its forecasts will be. A project with a shorter payback will involve less uncertainty in relation to the forecasting of future cash flows.

Table 9.6   Cumulative NCFs for projects A, B and C (from Table 9.1)

	Project A		Project B		Project C	
Year	Annual NCF	Cumulative NCF	Annual NCF	Cumulative NCF	Annual NCF	Cumulative NCF
0	−1000	−1000	−1000	−1000	−2000	−2000
1	600	−400	500	−500	600	−1400
2	400	0	400	−100	600	−800
3	300		600	+500	600	−200
4	300		700		1600	+1400

Table 9.7 Discounted payback

Year	Cash flow	PV at 10%	Cumulative PV
0	−1000	−1000	−1000
1	600	545	−455
2	400	330	−125
3	300	225	+100
4	300	205	+305

The Disadvantages of Payback

- The payback method ignores the cash flows that occur after the end of the payback period. From our earlier calculations, project A will be selected as it has the shortest payback period, but project B has higher total net cash flows than project A. Project B's total net cash flows amount to £1200 whilst project A's amount to £600. This weakness of payback is in stark contrast to both NPV and IRR that consider *all* cash flows generated by projects.
- It ignores the time value of money. This can be overcome by the use of *discounted payback* in which the cash flows are discounted prior to calculating the payback period.

The discounted payback period for project A is calculated as shown in Table 9.7, giving an estimate of 2 years plus $125/225 \times 12$ months = 6.7 months.

Discounting is particularly useful when cash flows are distant, whereas payback emphasises the early years of the project, so there is an inherent conflict in the technique. Also, discounting assumes that the cash flows occur at the end of the year whereas payback assumes that they flow evenly through the year.

Accounting Rate of Return

The three investment appraisal techniques considered so far, NPV, IRR and payback, are all based on the cash flows generated by the project. Unlike these, the accounting rate of return (ARR) is based on accounting profits.

Accounting profits are based upon a range of concepts, and one effect of these is to convert cash into profits. Examples of accounting concepts at work are as follows:

- At the start of the project, fixed assets are acquired which will result in a cash outflow. However, the cost of such assets is not immediately charged to the profit and loss account of the business. Instead the fixed assets are disclosed on the balance sheet and an annual depreciation charge is made to the profit and loss account over the life of the fixed asset. In the case of land, no depreciation charge is made.
- Payments for raw materials result in a cash outflow for the business, However, the cost of purchases is not charged as an expense to the profit and loss account of the business until the stock is sold. Sales are recognised when the sale is made and not when cash changes hands.

The ARR may be defined as

$$ARR = \frac{\text{Average annual profit from an investment}}{\text{Average investment}} \times 100$$

Where

$$\text{Average investment} = \frac{\text{Initial investment + Scrap value}}{2}$$

The average investment represents the average value of the asset in the accounts of the company. At the commencement of the project, the accounts will include the original cost and at the end of the project the they will include the scrap value. To obtain the average of two figures we add them together and divide by 2.

The decision rule with ARR is to accept a project if the ARR equals or exceeds the company's target ARR. If projects are mutually exclusive, the rule is to select the project with the highest ARR, as long as the ARR equals or exceeds the company's target ARR.

We can use the profit data in Table 9.1 to calculate the average profits and average investment for each project as follows. For project A,

$$\text{Average profits} = \frac{350 + 150 + 50 + 50}{4} = £150,$$

$$\text{Average investment} = \frac{1000 + 0}{2} = £500,$$

$$ARR = \frac{150}{500} \times 100 = 30\%.$$

For project B,

$$\text{Average profits} = \frac{250 + 150 + 350 + 450}{4} = £300,$$

$$\text{Average investment} = \frac{1000 + 0}{2} = £1500,$$

$$ARR = \frac{300}{500} \times 100 = 60\%.$$

For project C,

$$\text{Average profits} = \frac{350 + 350 + 350 + 350}{4} = £350$$

$$\text{Average investment} = \frac{2000 + 1000}{2} = £1,500$$

$$ARR = \frac{350}{1,500} \times 100 = 23\%.$$

In this case, project B will be selected as it has the highest ARR. Both NPV and IRR selected project B.

The Advantages of ARR

- The main advantage is that by using profit figures, projects are appraised by a technique that is closely related to the return on capital employed (or return on investment) by which companies are frequently evaluated.
- It results in a percentage figure that is familiar to business people.

The Disadvantages of ARR

- The main weakness is that the technique, by averaging, ignores the time value of money. Profits in year 4 are treated as having the same value as profits in year 1.
- It makes use of accounting profits rather than cash flows. Accounting profits have been subjected to the application of accounting concepts, whereas cash flows represent power over resources.

The Impact of Taxation on Project Appraisal

In the real world taxation affects project appraisal in several ways. First, companies in the UK are required to pay corporation tax on their profits. So a project that generates profits will incur corporation tax. The amount of taxation must be estimated in the appraisal and then built into the cash flows or profits in the project appraisal.

Secondly, a company pays corporation tax approximately 9 months after the company's accounting year-end. Because of this, it is usual to assume that the taxation is payable in cash one year in arrears.

Thirdly, at the end of the project's life and the disposal of the asset there may be an additional taxation implication. During the project's life a company will claim capital allowances on the assets. These allowances are a legitimate expense in calculating taxable profit and they have the effect of reducing taxable profit and, therefore, the amount of taxation that the company will pay. There are different rates of allowance and they give relief on the difference between the cost and the estimated sales proceeds of the asset on disposal. When the asset is disposed of and the actual sale proceeds are known, the company will calculate whether it has claimed too much or too little in capital allowances. If too much, it will need to make an additional tax payment (termed a balancing charge). If it has claimed too little, it will be entitled to claim further CA (termed a balancing allowance).

Inflation and Project Appraisal

Inflation occurs when there is a general increase in prices; it is measured by an index such as the Retail Price Index (RPI). At the time of writing, inflation is low, between 2% and 3%. Inflation impacts on project appraisal in two ways. First, inflation affects interest rates by increasing rates by the amount of expected inflation. Therefore, higher inflation will mean higher costs of finance and these will have to be incorporated into the discount rate. Secondly, it makes forecasting future cash flows more difficult because they will be affected by inflation. Revenues and costs may well be influenced by inflation in different ways, and it is highly unlikely that inflation will impact on a project precisely in line with changes in the RPI.

There are two main approaches to dealing with inflation in project appraisal.

- *Method 1* uses a real discount rate and projects future cash flows at base year prices with no inflation. A real discount rate is one from which the inflationary effect has been removed. With this approach, inflation is removed from the discount rate and from future cash flows by projecting all cash flows at current prices. In this approach we are using 'real' cash flows and a 'real' interest rate, the term 'real' indicating that inflation has been removed. Inflation is removed from interest rates by the following formula:

$$\frac{1 + \text{Interest rate}}{1 + \text{Inflation}} - 1$$

- *Method 2* uses the current costs of finance and then projects cash flows at expected money prices in future years. This approach starts from the premise that current costs of finance contain an allowance for future inflation. Therefore discounts rates are related to the current costs of capital. This approach allows for forecasts of future costs and revenues to be inflated at different rates.

The following example illustrates these two approaches. A company operates a repairs and maintenance division that is served by a series of diversified local depots. These have experienced difficulty in meeting the demands of the repairs and maintenance division in recent months. A consultant has been approached to investigate the situation and to make recommendations.

The consultant has come up with the following way of effecting improvements. The company is recommended to purchase stores handling equipment. This would require an immediate payment of £220,000 and annual maintenance and operating charges of £40,000 at year 0, subsequently subject to inflation of 5% per year. The equipment is expected to have a four-year life.

The company would like to carry out an appraisal of the option over a four-year period. Its current cost of capital is 16% and the RPI is expected to increase at 5% for the foreseeable future.

First calculate the real discount rate $= \dfrac{1.16 - 1}{1.05} = .105 = 10.5\%$

Then discount at current prices using a rate of 10.5%

Method 2
Forecast future costs including inflationary increases
Discount at the current cost of capital.

Method 1

Yr	NCF	Factor	0.105
	£000s	0.105	PV
0	220	1	220
1	40	0.904977	36.1991
2	40	0.818984	32.75936
3	40	0.741162	29.64648
4	40	0.670735	26.82939
			345.4343

Method 2

Yr	NCF	Factor	0.16
	£000s	0.16	PV
0	220	1	220
1	42	0.862069	36.2069
2	44.1	0.743163	32.77348
3	46.305	0.640658	29.66565
4	48.62025	0.552291	26.85253
			345.4986

As may be seen from the illustration, the two methods produce virtually identical results in terms of the projects net present values. Method 2 has a slightly higher cost by £64, but this difference is due to rounding. Drury and Tayles (1997) found that a high proportion of companies in a UK study failed to deal with inflation correctly. A summary of that article follows at the end of this chapter.

Sensitivity Analysis (or 'what if?' analysis)

Sensitivity analysis represents a non-probabilistic approach to allowing for risk and uncertainty in project appraisal. In consequence, it can be used in situations where information about probabilities is absent. It can also be used in parallel with techniques using probabilities. Sensitivity analysis examines how sensitive the net present value is to changes in key variables, such as increases in capital costs at the commencement of the project, increases and decreases in projected sales volumes, and increases and decreases in variable costs. The methodology of sensitivity analysis is as follows:

1.   Specify a base case or most expected situation. This is the most likely scenario and acts as a core against which the net present values arising from changes in key variables can be compared.
2.   Ask a series of 'what if' questions that explore the effect of changes in the key variables. For example, what if sales fall 5% or 10% below base case or rise 5% or 10% above? The NPV is recalculated for each of these 'what if' questions. For this stage of sensitivity analysis a computer spreadsheet is essential.
3.   Up to this point, one variable has been changed at a time. This next stage involves changing several variables, for example, what if output increases, selling price falls and fixed costs increase?
4.   At this point we evaluate the sensitivity of the project's NPV to changes in the key variables.
5.   Make a decision.

Let us examine an example. Suppose that base-case cash-flow projections (in millions of pounds) are as follows:

Investment (year 0)	800
Annual revenue items	(years 1–10)
Sales	400
Variable costs	200
Fixed costs	40

The cost of capital is 10%.

In Table 9.8, each variable is changed in isolation. In each case the change is 10% above or below the expected outcomes. From this table it is straightforward to see what happens over a range of values of a single variable. For example, as annual revenue changes from £360 million to £400 million and £440 million, net present value goes from – £63 million to £183 million and £429 million, respectively.

Table 9.8   Sensitivity analysis

	Outcomes (£m)			NPVs (£m)		
	Pessimistic	Expected	Optimistic	Pessimistic	Expected	Optimistic
Annual revenues	360	400	440	−63	+183	+429
Annual variable costs	220	200	180	+60	+183	+306
Annual fixed costs	44	40	36	+158	+183	+208

Table 9.9 Two-way analysis of net present value (£ millions)

Annual revenue (£m)	Variable costs 220	£(m) 200	180
360	−186	−63	+60
400	+60	+183	+306
440	+306	+429	+552

To see what happens when we vary two variables, we need to draw up a two-way table. For example, Table 9.9 shows how NPV changes when both annual revenue and variable costs vary.

The Pivot Approach to Sensitivity Analysis

A complementary approach, termed the pivot approach, is to ask by how much a variable must change before the NPV becomes zero. In other words, what level of change can a project sustain and still break even, or what level of change is necessary to turn an acceptable project into an unacceptable project?

The procedure for undertaking this approach is:

1. Find the NPV of the project with the original estimates.
2. For each variable in the NPV calculation (capital cost, revenues, operating costs, discount rate and so on) calculate by how much the variable must change before the NPV becomes zero. This is done independently for each variable.

Table 9.10 illustrates the procedure for capital costs and annual sales for our example. Such a table indicates the variables that the project is most sensitive to. The pivot approach provides more information for the decision maker about an important area of risk in a project. From an operational perspective, it may indicate those variables on which more management time may be worth spending. For example, Table 9.10 shows that the project's NPV is particularly sensitive to annual sales, so that more resources may need to be put into marketing the product, year after year. The table shows that if capital costs increase by 23% over budget this will result in a zero NPV. Recognition of this will highlight to management of the construction phase the importance of completion within budget.

The Value of Sensitivity Analysis

The technique is transparent and readily understood by all. The output of sensitivity analysis may have operational value in allowing managers to resource those variables that are seen to be most critical in terms of their impact on NPV. A range of organisations use the technique; for example, the National Health Service requires it for all project appraisals. We have seen with pivot analysis how it can alert managers to the critical variables in the management of a project. Finally, in the all-pervasive computer environment, it is ideally suited to a spreadsheet package, which takes the cost and drudgery out of the

Table 9.10   The pivot approach

Variable	Expected value (£m)	Expected NPV (£m)	Maximum change in variable to give a zero NPV (£m)	Maximum % change in variable
Capital cost	800	183	+183	+22.875
Sales	400 per year	183	−29.8 per year	−7.45

constant recalculations, and which has facilities to display the information in ways that bring out its significant features; for example, with the use of charts.

On the downside, it increases the amount of information available to the decision maker but does not give a single figure signal as to whether the project is acceptable or not. The basic variant changes one variable at a time, which may limit its usefulness, but we have seen that changes in a number of variables can also be built in.

Non-Financial Appraisal

Desiderata Analysis

The above approaches are purely financial and may need to be supplemented with other techniques in non-profit organisations. One way of dealing with non-financial issues is through the use of desiderata analysis, which was introduced in Chapter 8.

With reference to project appraisal, desiderata analysis has the following methodology:

1. A multi-disciplinary team establishes the desirable features (desiderata) required from a project.
2. The team also assigns weights of importance to the desiderata, with the more desirable outcomes receiving greatest weight.
3. Each option is scored (e.g. from −4 to +4) in terms of meeting the various desiderata.
4. The resultant weighted scores are summed in a table to establish the best option.

An illustration is provided in the following table:

Desiderata	Weights	Option 1 Score	Option 1 Score × weight	Option 2 Score	Option 2 Score × weight
D1	0.4	−2	−0.8	+2	0.8
D2	0.3	+2	0.6	+2	0.6
D3	0.2	+4	0.8	−4	−0.8
D4	0.1	+4	0.4	+2	0.2
Totals	1.0		1.0		0.8

In the table, Option 1 scores a total of 1 and is therefore preferred to Option 2 with a weighted score of 0.8.

The advantages of the desiderata approach are as follows:

- Provided that the staff involved are located in relatively close proximity to each other, it is quick to implement.
- It has low costs, the most significant of which is that of staff time in meeting to determine desiderata and the scoring of options.
- It fosters co-operation as the scoring teams are usually multi-discipliniary, crossing departmental boundaries.
- It produces an auditable trail of the non-financial issues that have been considered in the analysis.

The approach also has some disadvantages:

- The process is, of course, subjective.
- It does provide a recommendation of the 'best' project but this cannot be integrated into the financial analysis. It must be considered by decision makers alongside the results of the financial appraisal.
- Total scores may conceal significant differences between options, so it is important that a full summary of discussions and scoring accompanies the results of the exercise.

There is an opportunity to undertake desiderata analysis in the second case study at the end of this chapter.

Cost–Benefit Analysis

Cost-benefit analysis (CBA) not only looks at the direct costs of an option but also explicitly values indirect costs and social factors. It adds together these costs and benefits and applies discounted cash-flow methods to them.

It was first used in the UK to appraise construction of the M1 motorway and London's Victoria underground line. Later it was used in analysing the costs and benefits of a third London airport. It is used in a day-to-day fashion in appraising schemes for motorway extensions and widening, river crossings, etc.

To provide an illustration, if CBA were used to appraise a proposal for adding an extra lane to a motorway, then it would consider the following costs and benefits:

- The direct costs, which would consist of the costs of the land, the construction costs and the annual maintenance costs resulting from the extra lane.
- The benefits to road users in terms of fuel savings and time savings. These benefits do not have market prices and so ways of valuing them have been created. Fuel savings would occur because traffic might move at a more fuel-efficient rate or because the motorway could carry more cars and reduce total journey time. Time

savings would be estimated based upon the estimated speed of the traffic; they could be valued at different rates depending on whether they are work time or leisure time activities. A new motorway lane will itself generate traffic, and such generated traffic time savings are also input but may be weighted less than existing traffic. These benefits are valued in money terms. They are regarded as benefits of the project as they owe their existence to the project.

- Finally, the costs and benefits would be projected over a lengthy time period and discounted back to the present day.

The advantages of CBA are as follows:

- It estimates the market prices of non-traded costs and benefits and adds these to direct costs to produce a 'bottom line' figure. Desiderata analysis is unable to do this.
- It takes account of the time value of money by discounting to these value flows to obtain an overall NPV for each option.
- CBA attempts to take a global perspective and visualise the whole problem.
- It has developed innovative approaches to the valuation of intangibles such as time savings and the costs of noise pollution.

The disadvantages of CBA are:

- It can take a very long time to complete and it can be very expensive – especially for one-off projects. In this respect it is unlike desiderata analysis. Where the type of analysis can be repeated many times, as with major road schemes, then it becomes a much more manageable and cost-effective technique.
- It is argued that the measurable drives out the immeasurable. Because things such as amenity cannot be valued, they are relegated to footnotes and the focus of attention is located firmly on the value flows and the NPV.

Conclusions

This chapter has shown that:

- The scale of many projects gives them strategic significance.
- In project appraisal the duration of the project is a significant factor, and because of this the idea of the time value of money and discounting is very important.
- There are two discounted cash-flow techniques, net present value and internal rate of return. Both make use of cash flows and of discounting.
- There are two other techniques. Payback is cash-based and emphasises the short-term payback of the project. Accounting rate of return is based upon accounting profits rather than cash flows.
- Taxation impinges on project appraisal because a project will produce profits that will be taxed. The taxes need to be included as cash outflows.

- Inflation is also significant because of the duration of projects, and there are two approaches for dealing with this: the real interest approach and the money interest approach.
- Sensitivity analysis is a valuable tool for dealing with project risk. It does not use probabilities. It may be used contemporaneously with probabilistic approaches.
- Desiderata analysis and cost–benefit analysis represent ways of dealing systematically with non-financial issues.

Summary

There are many examples of projects of a strategic nature. These projects are long-term, extending over several years, and usually involve investments, costs and revenues. After identifying the scope and objectives of the project, the next step is to identify the relevant cash flows for project appraisal. Great care must be taken at this stage to include all relevant cash flows and to exclude those that are not relevant. Following this, the chapter considered different methods of project appraisal and concluded that the best methods were those based upon discounted cash flow – net present value and internal rate of return. Discounted cash flow is considered to be the best technique because it emphasises cash flows rather than profits (which can be manipulated), it considers all cash flows, it allows for the timing of those cash flows and uses the appropriate discount rate. The chapter also considered payback, a very simple cash-based technique that emphasises the short term, and the accounting rate of return that bases its appraisal on accounting profits.

Taxation can have an important influence on the net present value of a project because a company will have to pay corporation tax on its profits and will gain capital allowances on its investment. Because projects may last many years, it is important to take account of inflation, and the chapter discussed two ways of doing so. Finally, the chapter considered the usefulness of sensitivity analysis, a method of looking at a range of outcomes from a project with the objective of better informing the decision maker.

Recommended Further Reading

Drury C. and Tayles M. (1997) 'The misapplication of capital investment appraisal techniques', *Management Decision*, **35(2): 86–93.**
This study is based upon a questionnaire mailed to qualified management accountants in 866 UK manufacturing companies with average annual sales in excess of £10 million. The authors achieved a questionnaire response of 35% (305 usable replies).

The questionnaire responses indicate that payback is the most popular technique in small organisations and discounted cash-flow techniques the most popular in large organisations. The vast majority of organisations used a combination of methods. Small organisations rank payback as the most important technique and large organisations the internal rate of return.

Small firms rate 'intuitive management judgement' highly in project appraisal, whereas this is not the case in large organisations where formal management committees may consider projects for approval. The staff of small firms are more likely to base their individual judgements on knowledge of the business.

A significant percentage of firms use the accounting rate of return, and the authors indicate that the only justification for this is the project's impact on reported profits. Top management may consider these to be significant to the capital markets, whilst the remuneration of top managers may be tied to annual net profit.

The authors stress the importance of the correct treatment of inflation in project appraisal. They indicate that there are two approaches to dealing with inflation: using a real discount rate with cash flows expressed in real terms; and using a money discount rate with cash flows adjusted for future inflation. The latter approach is preferable because expenses and revenues inflate at different rates. The survey discovered that only 53 out of 195 companies (27%) treated inflation correctly in appraisal.

The article also considers the discount rates used by firms. It confirms earlier studies that have found firms to be using excessively high discount rates, thereby leading to underinvestment. A possible explanation for this is that senior managers wish to counteract the tendency to inflate systematically the forecast returns from projects. Additionally, a company is exposed to greater risk than a well-diversified portfolio and the discount factor may reflect this. Finally, it is also suggested that, managers may wrongly use return on investment as a guide to a appropriate discount rate.

The authors consider the appraisal of investments in advanced manufacturing technologies and find no evidence to support claims that for such projects companies set shorter payback periods and/or apply higher discount rates. It is proposed that any underinvestment in such technology may be primarily because of the difficulty of valuing the benefits of such investments.

The authors conclude that managers should take care to ensure that they use appraisal techniques correctly. They recommend that discount rates for appraisal should be established in corporate headquarters. They also conclude that corporate management should provide clear guidelines on how inflation should be allowed for in appraisal.

Lumijarvi, O.P. (1991) 'Selling of capital investments to top management',
***Management Accounting Research*, 2: 171–188.**
This article indicates a weakness with survey techniques based on questionnaire completion relating to the capital appraisal techniques employed by companies. In environments where investment funds are scarce, questionnaires tell us little about the ways in which lower levels of management influence more senior managers to approve their projects. This study is based upon a field study in one organisation of how subordinates attempt to influence senior managers who are decision makers with respect to acceptance or rejection of projects. The company is Scandinavia Corp., one of the largest companies in Finland. It has five divisions and the field study concentrates on three of them: Pulp and Paper, Metal and Packing, and Service. The company appraises projects using internal rate of return and payback.

The results of the study indicate that lower levels of management attempt to 'sell' their investments to senior decision makers in order to obtain approval for their projects. Nine interviewees out of ten said that their investments have to be sold to senior managers such as the heads of divisions. The interviews emphasised that projects were unlikely to be accepted unless the support of the division head was obtained, often well in advance of putting a proposal forward.

The arguments made by managers in their lobbying of senior staff can be categorised as follows:

- Economic arguments: the basic argument is that the project is profitable. Profitability was particularly important if the division's profitability was poor. However, several senior managers indicated that profitability was rarely the most important factor, although it was emphasised that a minimum level of profitability had to be achieved – an internal rate of return of 15%.
- Strategic arguments: within Scandinavia Corp. it is essential that a project fits into an agreed strategy or will permit a planned strategy to be implemented. Strategic arguments have more influence than economic arguments.
- Non-financial reasons, such as employment, may also be used to sell strategies although it is observed that these are rarely used in Scandinavia Corp.
- Production technology arguments such as that the project represents new technology. These arguments were employed frequently and were rated as 'very effective' by the decision maker.

Selling projects took place in formal selling occasions such as (a series of) meetings and also on informal occasions such as trips and phone calls. Where a manager made a personal visit to a decision maker, this could have considerable influence. Once the decision-maker is committed, both the proposer and the decision maker sell and promote the project. The field study finds that submitted proposals are likely to be approved. This is because the proposer will have already sold the idea to the division head, and together they will have sold the idea to other senior executives. Only after the decision makers give their commitment to the project are projects submitted formally for approval.

Case Study: Branchester United

Branchester United is a professional rugby club in the Kingdom of Karibya. The season has recently ended and the club has finished in eighth position in the Kingdom's 20-club Premier Division.

The club was formed into a PLC three years ago when the game first became professional in Karibya. Prior to this the players were semi-professionals and played rugby football on a part-time basis. The last three years have been a period of upheaval, with two of the newly professionalised clubs going into liquidation. Indeed, some commentators consider that the impact of professionalism has been disastrous for the game.

The club's city centre ground has a capacity of only 20,000, which is considered too small for a Premiership club. The ground is easy to access by public transport, although car parking can be difficult on Saturdays when the team are playing at home. The site represents prime building land and is owned by the local authority and leased to the club. The lease has 11 years to run after the end of the current season.

The club has recently been awarded a Heritage grant of £20 million towards the cost of building a new stadium on the outskirts of the city at the Old Grove. One condition of the grant is that the club must leave the current ground at the end of the 2004/2005 season and move to the new ground. Assurances have been received that the new ground could be constructed by the start of the 2005/2006 season (1 July 2005) if a start is made in the next month. The lease agreement with the local authority would then cease at the end of the 2004/2005 season. As soon as the club vacates the current ground, construction of a Heritage Mall will commence. The new stadium would cost £40 million. A sliding roof would be constructed for an extra £10 million.

The new location has several advantages for the club. There would be ample car parking and there would be reserved spaces for the club's directors and key sponsors. The pitch would be surrounded by a running track and the seats would be rolled forward when rugby is being played. Its capacity would be 30,000 for athletics and 40,000 for rugby. The sliding roof would allow rugby to be played in the depths of winter – in the past games have had to be cancelled due to snow and freezing conditions. Finally, the sliding roof would permit pop concerts and other types of entertainment to be put on.

The club has two star players, Andy Mixon and Ryan Donaldson. Leeds Castle has offered £10 million for Mixon and Crystal Glass Corinthians have offered £12 million for Donaldson. The directors have issued a press statement indicating that they propose to sell both players in order to part finance the new stadium, with a further £8 million being borrowed over 20 years at 8%. They are convinced of the benefits of the sliding roof. However, the supporters club is incensed by news of the decision to sell players and a letter from its Chairman is attached as Annex 1 at the end of this case study.

The directors include Charles Proshare, an expert in financial theory. He has advocated in a recent TV interview keeping Donaldson, borrowing £10 million and financing £10 million from reserves. He strongly advises against the issue of shares. An article in the *Karibyan Financial Daily* has claimed that the lack of player sales during 2003/2004 has held back Branchester United's planned stadium development (Annex 2). Proshare dismisses this assertion and has indicated that the company has £8 million cash on short-term deposit. He is supported by the head coach, who has stated that Branchester's coaching policy has provided from its own environment world-class players such as Mixon and Donaldson. He has indicated that he has three very able youngsters with world-class potential currently playing in the reserves. All three will be promoted to the first team squad when Mixon and Donaldson are sold.

The club plays on average 24 home days per year and is entitled to a valuable share of Premiership television proceeds as a Premiership club. Its recent performances and average ticket prices are as follows:

Year	Attendances (000s)	Stadium revenues (£m)	TV revenues (£m)	League position	Net profit before tax (£m)	Dividends per share (p)	Share price (£)	Average ticket price (£)
2000/01	450	4.5	0.56	2	1.2			10
2001/02	450	5.4	1.2	3	1.5	7	3	12
2002/03	419	5.45	1.4	7	7.3	5	2.8	13
2003/04	404	5.25	1.8	8	0.8	4	2	13

The detailed profit and loss statement for the year ended 30 June 2004 is as follows:

	£000	£000
Revenues		
Stadium (attendances plus net concessions)	5250	
TV revenues	1800	
Sponsorship	110	
Sales of players	50	
		7210
Expenses		
Stadium expenses	180	
Stadium rent	50	
Club management and coaching staff	450	
Playing staff (30 players)	2,750	
Advertising	385	
Travel and hotels	170	
Vehicle costs	25	
Interest	2,400	
		6410
Net profit before tax		800
Corporation tax (25%)		200
Net profit after tax		600
Dividends: 10 million ordinary shares at 4 pence per share		400

Transfers to reserves	200

The company's current financial structure is as follows:

	Book value £	Market value £
10 million £1 ordinary shares, fully paid	10,000,000	20,000,000
Share premium account	10,000,000	
Reserves	1,024,000	
Loans (8%)	30,000,000	30,000,000

The company's cost of capital for project appraisal is 20%.

Tenders to build the stadium before the start of the 2005/2006 season have been received from three specialist construction companies; the cheapest of these is Stadium All Stars, which has quoted capital costs as follows:

	£000
Land	5,000
Building	20,000
Fixtures and furnishings	13,000
	38,000
Sliding roof	10,000
	48,000

Branchester RFC will also have to pay planning fees of £2 million; of this, £1.2 million has already been spent. Construction costs and all fees will be fully capitalised.

The company will be able to claim capital allowances at the rate of 4% on a straight-line basis over a 25-year period on the whole of the capital costs (including fees). The company pays corporation tax at the rate of 25%. All tax payments are made one year in arrears. It is estimated that the stadium will be completed on 1 July 2005, the first day of the 2005/06 financial year.

Estimates of revenues and costs relating to the new stadium are contained in Annex 3.

After completion of the building and fitting-out of the stadium there will have to be a fortnight of safety testing so that the stadium will be awarded a Health and Safety Certificate for the start of the 2005/2006 season. The certificate will cost £5,000 and does not attract capital allowances.

A specialist stadium surveyor has just been contacted with reference to the detailed appraisal of the stadium. The surveyor has reported that the proposed stadium should be appraised over a 10-year period, commencing 1 July 2005, in order that it may be compared with the existing stadium. Additionally, the report states that it is usual in stadium appraisals to consider the capital costs, the net revenues of the proposed stadium, and the net revenues of the existing stadium.

1. Using Branchester's cost of capital of 20%, calculate the net present value of the new stadium. State and explain any assumptions that you need to make.
2. Making use of the results of your net present value analysis and the other information (both financial and non-financial), examine whether Branchester United should go ahead and move to the new stadium.

ANNEX 1

BRANCHESTER UNITED RFC SUPPORTERS CLUB (BUSC)

10 May 2004

The Board of Directors

Branchester United RFC

Dear Sir,

I am writing on behalf of the BUSC about the disclosure that Andy Mixon and Ryan Donaldson are to be sold for a total of £20 million. Mixon is probably the best and most dynamic forward we have, and his presence in the team will be essential if we are to avoid relegation next year. Donaldson is a superb attacking full back, first choice in that position for Karibya, and his transfer would cost enormously in attack, defence and goal kicking. Rather than sell the two of them we should be looking to purchase other players to strengthen our squad and progress back up the table to where we were four years ago.

I understand that the sale is to finance the new stadium. This is another thing that concerns the supporters. The existing stadium is well suited for public transport, and many supporters can walk to the ground. What does the club propose to do about these supporters, many of whom have season tickets?

Since the game went professional, prices have increased. The price of a season ticket has increased from £100 to £250 in just three years. Yet the quality of the rugby football has not improved. Please bear in mind that there is lots of other entertainment available on a Saturday afternoon and next season, Leeds Castle, the Premiership champions, will offer a box-office television service on cable and satellite for all their Saturday and midweek home games. The new stadium will have increased capacity – but what is the percentage occupancy of the existing ground, as I noticed lots of empty seats last season?

In conclusion, we request the directors to consider the views of the supporters, the game's true fans.

James McAttee
Chairman

ANNEX 2

FROM THE KARIBYAN FINANCIAL DAILY, 11 MAY 2004

Branchester United yesterday announced reduced estimated post-tax profits because of reduced revenues from player sales. Profits were estimated at £800,000, compared with £7.3 millions last year.

There were no high-profile player sales in the period while the figures for 1998/99 included a significant profit on the sale of Brian Davies to Blackburn Bulldogs. Profits from player sales shrank from £6.34 million to £50,000.

Gate receipts have fallen but media revenues from satellite and cable have increased as more of Branchester's games were broadcast. Next season the picture is likely to be less rosy because of the box office viewing capability to be offered by Leeds Castle.

Branchester United has announced that it is to build a 40,000 seat stadium on a 12.5 acre site at the Old Grove starting in June 2004, with completion in June 2005. It has been offered a Heritage Commission grant of £20 million towards the construction.

Planning permission for the new stadium has been received but the company said it was waiting for an archaeological team to finish work on the proposed site, which is close to an ancient Saxon settlement.

Pre-tax profits per share are estimated at 8 pence, compared with 73 pence last year. Dividends are cut to 4 pence and the share price has fallen by 28% in the past year, closing yesterday at £2.

ANNEX 3

DETAILED ESTIMATES FOR THE NEW STADIUM

Annual running costs

Office staff	£45,000
Security	£45,000
Stadium management	£97,000

Business rates	£15,000
Equipment depreciation	£2,300
Maintenance	£32,000
Electricity	£12,500
Heating	£6,500
Motoring expenses	£8,500
Marketing	£25,000

It will also cost a total of £5,000 each time the sliding roof is closed and then reopened. This is expected to occur on 20 days per year.

Annual gate receipts

Season-ticket holders: 5,500 @ £275
Other paying spectators (19 home Premiership games plus 8[a] home Cup games plus 4 European[b] league games)

Per home match:

Probability	spectators	Ave. ticket price
0.3	25,000	£15.00
0.5	20,000	£15.00
0.2	15,000	£15.00

Notes:
 [a] Assumes that the club will get through to the quarter finals of the competition.
 [b] Assumes that the club will finish in the top four of the Premier Division in 2004/2005.

Other annual receipts

Concerts: 12 × £5,000
Bars and cafeterias concessions
   Sales: Drinks 100,000 × £4.50
          Snacks: 50,000 × £2.60
   Running costs £375,500

Athletics meetings: 10 meetings per year are projected with an average expected audience of 27,500 and an average ticket price of £15.

Case Study: Social Services Agency

The Social Services Agency in Toptown is a branch of the Department of Homeland Affairs. The Agency is currently investigating the possibility of moving from its current office accommodation to larger premises. The number of staff has grown significantly in the last five years from 56 to 103, and the Agency has had to rent two small houses in the near vicinity to provide working space for the extra staff. Many of the additional staff are peripatetic as they are responsible for visiting clients and monitoring projects being undertaken by the local authority on behalf of the Agency.

The current building was acquired several years ago for £560,000, but it is now worth £1.2 million. It is situated in the centre of town near other civic buildings. However, the commercial market is oversupplied in the area and it is not considered a good time to sell the property. The property provides 3500 square feet and, if vacated, would be let for £12 per square foot per year payable annually in advance. The other two houses are both on short three-month tenancies and are let to the Agency for £3600 and £5400 per year, respectively. In total, they provide an additional 900 square feet. The current building has a number of small fixed rooms and lacks flexibility. Both new buildings will offer open plan accommodation and be much more flexible.

There are two options for the new accommodation. One option is to rent 8000 square feet of office space in a new development at Baytown, comprising a large building about 4 miles towards the coast. There are several offices to choose from in the complex and all have plentiful parking, but the location is inconvenient for public transport. The new office would be rented at £9.50 per square foot per year, payable annually in advance. This block is suitable for accommodation immediately and if this option is chosen, the Agency will move to the new accommodation immediately.

The other alternative is to purchase a block in an older part of town, Trafford. The block comprises the ground floor and three upper floors. The ground floor and the top floor are both occupied at present and will continue to be so. The middle two floors are very spacious and offer 9000 square feet of office space. The total rents payable by the tenants amount to £70,000 per year payable annually in advance. The building is expected to cost £900,000, plus a further £650,000 on refurbishment and £110,000 on fees. The refurbishment would take a year, with £900,000 acquisition cost spent at the start of the project and refurbishment and fees payable in one year's time when the building would be occupied. There is an option to incorporate air conditioning which will add £120,000 to the refurbishment costs, and it has been agreed to proceed with this option. The older part of town is well served with public transport and High Street is very busy. Many of the Agency's clients live in this part of town. There is parking for 40 cars incorporated into the area at the rear of the office block. The current tenants will continue to use five of those spaces. The agency would move into the block in one year's time.

Removal costs will amount to £25,000 for either option. Annual building running costs for all buildings included within this appraisal are estimated at £9.04 per square metre per year payable annually in arrears.

It has been estimated that annual car expense payments to staff will be as follows: current, £18,000; Baytown, £27,000; Trafford, £13,500. These may be assumed to be paid annually in arrears.

British Council of Offices has found in recent years that the average gross floor area per person is 8 square metres and this is considered acceptable. Gross floor area includes non-productive space such as corridors, stairwells and meeting rooms.

A meeting of a multi-disciplinary stakeholder group (consisting of three managers and three case officers) identified five qualitative factors for consideration in the appraisal, and weighted them to reflect this:

Factor	Weighting	Reasoning
Public transport service	3	To facilitate access by clients and staff who do not have cars
Adequate car parking	3	Notwithstanding the desire to promote public transport, it is recognised that all peripatetic staff bring a car to work
Efficient working	3	The current office set-up involves the staff being split in three offices and this weakens the service provided. It also leads to a loss in time in travelling between offices
Minimal environmental impact	2	In accordance with central government's objectives to reduce vehicle emissions
A modern office environment	2	To allow ready communication, flexible organisation, air conditioning and internet-ready accommodation

The Agency's scoring methodology is as follows:

Basis	Score
Meets desiderata exactly	4
Meets desiderata well	2
Meets desiderata adequately	0
Satisfies desiderata inadequately	−2
Does not satisfy desiderata at all	−4

Two appraisal guidelines are in force:

- The Agency appraises schemes using a 6% real discount rate.
- The office accommodation scheme is to be appraised over 20 years. The Trafford scheme may be assumed to have a residual value of £1.7million in 20 years' time (in current monetary values).

1. Calculate the net present values of both options.
2. Complete the desiderata table for both options, explaining your reasons for project scoring.
3. Prepare a short briefing note (500 words) for the Agency's chief executive in which you bring together your conclusions about both schemes and make a clear recommendation.

Questions

1. A company is considering the following investment projects. Both would involve purchasing machinery with a life of 5 years.

    - **Project 1** would generate annual cash flows of £150,000; the machinery would cost £350,000 and have a scrap value of £45,000.
    - **Project 2** would generate annual cash flows of £250,000; the machinery would costs £800,000 and have a scrap value of £350,000.

    The company's discount rate is 12%. Assume that the annual cash flows arise on the anniversaries of the initial outlay.

    Calculate the net present value and payback for each project and state which project the company should accept and why.

2. A firm can buy a new printer for £2,000 payable immediately. The new printer would make cash savings for the firm of £2,000 in the first year of operation, £4,000 in the second year and £2,000 in the fifth year.

    The firm makes no savings from the printer in the third and fourth year of its life, and will need to spend £4,000 on it in year 3 because of expensive repairs. The machine is scrapped at the end of 5 years, but there is no scrap value.

    As an alternative to outright purchase, the firm could hire a printer, paying £1000 per annum, in advance, for the 5 years. The firm would still expect to make the same costs and savings as in outright purchase, but the hire company would meet the repair cost of year 3.

    If the going rate of interest is 10%, using net present value, advise the firm as to which of the two methods (buy or hire) should be used to obtain the printer.

3. Trigger PLC is a manufacturer of computer components and a decision is required on a proposal to invest £1,800,000 on a new machine in order to move into a new market for components. The financial details are as follows:

Initial investment:	£1,800,000
Life of project:	10 years
Net cash flows:	
years 1–6	£500,000 per year
years 7–10	£300,000 per year
Residual value	£500,000

The company has a target rate of return of 11% and a payback criterion of 4 years.

    (a) Calculate the payback period.

    (b) Calculate the project's net present value.

    (c) Advise the company on whether it should proceed with the project. Provide reasons for your advice.

4. A company is considering an investment of £1.4 million in a project that has a seven-year life. The company has estimated its discount rate at 12%. Details of the sales and costs arising from this project are as follows:

Sales volume:	250,000 units per annum
Sales price:	£4 per unit

Costs

Direct materials (4 kg at £0.40 per kg)	£1.60 per unit
Direct labour (0.1 hour at £8 per hour)	£0.80 per unit
Overhead	£330,000 per annum

Note that the annual overhead includes £200,000 per year depreciation on the asset. It also includes apportioned fixed overheads of a further £50,000 per year.

    (a) Calculate the net present value of the project. Provide a commentary on the discounting process and on the net present value that you have calculated.

    (b) Carry out a sensitivity anlaysis on five variables of this project, including the life of the project and the discount rate. Identify what you consider to be the most critical variable and advise management what they should do, if anything, before adopting this project.

Table 9A.1   Present value of future cash flows

									Discount rate											
No. of periods	1%	2%	3%	4%	5%	6%	7%	8%	9%	10%	11%	12%	13%	14%	15%	16%	17%	18%	19%	20%
1	0.990	0.980	0.971	0.962	0.952	0.943	0.935	0.926	0.917	0.909	0.901	0.893	0.885	0.877	0.870	0.862	0.855	0.847	0.840	0.833
2	0.980	0.961	0.943	0.925	0.907	0.890	0.873	0.857	0.842	0.826	0.812	0.797	0.783	0.769	0.756	0.743	0.731	0.718	0.706	0.694
3	0.971	0.942	0.915	0.889	0.864	0.840	0.816	0.794	0.772	0.751	0.731	0.712	0.693	0.675	0.658	0.641	0.624	0.609	0.593	0.579
4	0.961	0.924	0.888	0.855	0.823	0.792	0.763	0.735	0.708	0.683	0.659	0.636	0.613	0.592	0.572	0.552	0.534	0.516	0.499	0.482
5	0.951	0.906	0.863	0.822	0.784	0.747	0.713	0.681	0.650	0.621	0.593	0.567	0.543	0.519	0.497	0.476	0.456	0.437	0.419	0.402
6	0.942	0.888	0.837	0.790	0.746	0.705	0.666	0.630	0.596	0.564	0.535	0.507	0.480	0.456	0.432	0.410	0.390	0.370	0.352	0.335
7	0.933	0.871	0.813	0.760	0.711	0.665	0.623	0.583	0.547	0.513	0.482	0.452	0.425	0.400	0.376	0.354	0.333	0.314	0.296	0.279
8	0.923	0.853	0.789	0.731	0.677	0.627	0.582	0.540	0.502	0.467	0.434	0.404	0.376	0.351	0.327	0.305	0.285	0.266	0.249	0.233
9	0.914	0.837	0.766	0.703	0.645	0.592	0.544	0.500	0.460	0.424	0.391	0.361	0.333	0.308	0.284	0.263	0.243	0.225	0.209	0.194
10	0.905	0.820	0.744	0.676	0.614	0.558	0.508	0.463	0.422	0.386	0.352	0.322	0.295	0.270	0.247	0.227	0.208	0.191	0.176	0.162
11	0.896	0.804	0.722	0.650	0.585	0.527	0.475	0.429	0.388	0.350	0.317	0.287	0.261	0.237	0.215	0.195	0.178	0.162	0.148	0.135
12	0.887	0.788	0.701	0.625	0.557	0.497	0.444	0.397	0.356	0.319	0.286	0.257	0.231	0.208	0.187	0.168	0.152	0.137	0.124	0.112
13	0.879	0.773	0.681	0.601	0.530	0.469	0.415	0.368	0.326	0.290	0.258	0.229	0.204	0.182	0.163	0.145	0.130	0.116	0.104	0.093
14	0.870	0.758	0.661	0.577	0.505	0.442	0.388	0.340	0.299	0.263	0.232	0.205	0.181	0.160	0.141	0.125	0.111	0.099	0.088	0.078
15	0.861	0.743	0.642	0.555	0.481	0.417	0.362	0.315	0.275	0.239	0.209	0.183	0.160	0.140	0.123	0.108	0.095	0.084	0.074	0.065
16	0.853	0.728	0.623	0.534	0.458	0.394	0.339	0.292	0.252	0.218	0.188	0.163	0.141	0.123	0.107	0.093	0.081	0.071	0.062	0.054
17	0.844	0.714	0.605	0.513	0.436	0.371	0.317	0.270	0.231	0.198	0.170	0.146	0.125	0.108	0.093	0.080	0.069	0.060	0.052	0.045
18	0.836	0.700	0.587	0.494	0.416	0.350	0.296	0.250	0.212	0.180	0.153	0.130	0.111	0.095	0.081	0.069	0.059	0.051	0.044	0.038
19	0.828	0.686	0.570	0.475	0.396	0.331	0.277	0.232	0.194	0.164	0.138	0.116	0.098	0.083	0.070	0.060	0.051	0.043	0.037	0.031
20	0.820	0.673	0.554	0.456	0.377	0.312	0.258	0.215	0.178	0.149	0.124	0.104	0.087	0.073	0.061	0.051	0.043	0.037	0.031	0.026

Table 9A.2   Present value of annuities

No. of Periods										Discount rate										
	1%	2%	3%	4%	5%	6%	7%	8%	9%	10%	11%	12%	13%	14%	15%	16%	17%	18%	19%	20%
1	0.990	0.980	0.971	0.962	0.952	0.943	0.935	0.926	0.917	0.909	0.901	0.893	0.885	0.877	0.870	0.862	0.855	0.847	0.840	0.833
2	1.970	1.942	1.913	1.886	1.859	1.833	1.808	1.783	1.759	1.736	1.713	1.690	1.668	1.647	1.626	1.605	1.585	1.566	1.547	1.528
3	2.941	2.884	2.829	2.775	2.723	2.673	2.624	2.577	2.531	2.487	2.444	2.402	2.361	2.322	2.283	2.246	2.210	2.174	2.140	2.106
4	3.902	3.808	3.717	3.630	3.546	3.465	3.387	3.312	3.240	3.170	3.102	3.037	2.974	2.914	2.855	2.798	2.743	2.690	2.639	2.589
5	4.853	4.713	4.580	4.452	4.329	4.212	4.100	3.993	3.890	3.791	3.696	3.605	3.517	3.433	3.352	3.274	3.199	3.127	3.058	2.991
6	5.795	5.601	5.417	5.242	5.076	4.917	4.767	4.623	4.486	4.355	4.231	4.111	3.998	3.889	3.784	3.685	3.589	3.498	3.410	3.326
7	6.728	6.472	6.230	6.002	5.786	5.582	5.389	5.206	5.033	4.868	4.712	4.564	4.423	4.288	4.160	4.039	3.922	3.812	3.706	3.605
8	7.652	7.325	7.020	6.733	6.463	6.210	5.971	5.747	5.535	5.335	5.146	4.968	4.799	4.639	4.487	4.344	4.207	4.078	3.954	3.837
9	8.566	8.162	7.786	7.435	7.108	6.802	6.515	6.247	5.995	5.759	5.537	5.328	5.132	4.946	4.772	4.607	4.451	4.303	4.163	4.031
10	9.471	8.983	8.530	8.111	7.722	7.360	7.024	6.710	6.418	6.145	5.889	5.650	5.426	5.216	5.019	4.833	4.659	4.494	4.339	4.192
11	10.37	9.787	9.253	8.760	8.306	7.887	7.499	7.139	6.805	6.495	6.207	5.938	5.687	5.453	5.234	5.029	4.836	4.656	4.486	4.327
12	11.26	10.58	9.954	9.385	8.863	8.384	7.943	7.536	7.161	6.814	6.492	6.194	5.918	5.660	5.421	5.197	4.988	4.793	4.611	4.439
13	12.13	11.35	10.63	9.986	9.394	8.853	8.358	7.904	7.487	7.103	6.750	6.424	6.122	5.842	5.583	5.342	5.118	4.910	4.715	4.533
14	13.00	12.11	11.30	10.56	9.899	9.295	8.745	8.244	7.786	7.367	6.982	6.628	6.302	6.002	5.724	5.468	5.229	5.008	4.802	4.611
15	13.87	12.85	11.94	11.12	10.38	9.712	9.108	8.559	8.061	7.606	7.191	6.811	6.462	6.142	5.847	5.575	5.324	5.092	4.876	4.675
16	14.72	13.58	12.56	11.65	10.84	10.11	9.447	8.851	8.313	7.824	7.379	6.974	6.604	6.265	5.954	5.668	5.405	5.162	4.938	4.730
17	15.56	14.29	13.17	12.17	11.27	10.48	9.763	9.122	8.544	8.022	7.549	7.120	6.729	6.373	6.047	5.749	5.475	5.222	4.990	4.775
18	16.40	14.99	13.75	12.66	11.69	10.83	10.06	9.372	8.756	8.201	7.702	7.250	6.840	6.467	6.128	5.818	5.534	5.273	5.033	4.812
19	17.23	15.68	14.32	13.13	12.09	11.16	10.34	9.604	8.950	8.365	7.839	7.366	6.938	6.550	6.198	5.877	5.584	5.316	5.070	4.843
20	18.05	16.35	14.88	13.59	12.46	11.47	10.59	9.818	9.129	8.514	7.963	7.469	7.025	6.623	6.259	5.929	5.628	5.353	5.101	4.870

Chapter 10
MANAGEMENT ACCOUNTING AND PERFORMANCE MEASUREMENT SYSTEMS

Key Learning Objectives

By the time you have finished studying this chapter, you should be able to:
- explain the need for effective performance measurement in all organisations;
- discuss the influence that the organisation's structure and culture have on its performance measurement systems;
- calculate and interpret commonly used performance measures;
- describe the influence of particular contemporary environments on performance measurement;
- outline the effects of interdivisional transfers on performance measurements;
- describe and apply strategically focused performance measurement techniques.

The Need for Effective Performance Measurement Systems

In earlier chapters we have explored the basic need for accounting control systems and considered and applied some common management accounting techniques. As we saw, management accounting activity is composed of two closely intertwined components, planning and control, each of which can take place at the detailed, short-term level or at the more strategic, longer-term level. One element of management accounting activity that links these two components is that of performance measurement.

Without targets, deadlines and specified levels of acceptable performance, it is unlikely that organisational players will achieve objectives. Thus it is important to consider carefully a number of aspects of performance and performance measurement, such as those in Table 10.1. We will realise (if we take on board the principles of contingency theory) that there is no single way of measuring performance that will suit all organisations' needs

Table 10.1   Issues to consider in performance measurement

- *What* do we want to achieve?
- *When* do we want it to be achieved?
- *Which* performance measures are most closely related to achieving it?
- *What* resources do we wish to commit to achieving it?
- *What* are measuring?

  - The performance of the organisation, or part of it?
  - The performance of an individual, or group of individuals?

- *How* will we measure performance?

  - In terms of time?
  - In terms of cost incurred?
  - In terms of value created (however measured)?
  - In terms of quality?
  - In terms of quantity of inputs and/or outputs?
  - In terms of outcomes?

- For *whom* are we measuring performance?

  - Management?
  - Employees?
  - Owners?
  - Other stakeholders?

- At what level of *detail* do we wish to measure performance?
- *How often* should performance be measured?
- *What effects* on organisational behaviour might performance measurement have?

and circumstances. Thus there is a need to frequently monitor the continuing appropriateness of the performance measurement solution in place.

The area of performance measurement is a huge one with implications for all organisations. Entire texts are devoted to aspects of it, so constraints of space prevent more that a relatively limited coverage of it here. The reader would benefit from reference to more specialised texts for a deeper understanding. An excellent coverage of many aspects of performance measurement is given by Simons (2000), and a robust consideration of the human aspects of performance is presented by Emmanuel *et al.* (1990). Many of the academic accounting journals (such as *Accounting, Organizations and Society*) have devoted much space to this topic.

The Influence of the Organisational Environment on Performance Measurement Systems

We noted in earlier chapters that this area of research activity has been a very active one. The basic maxim of the contingency theory of management accounting could be expressed

Table 10.2   Some contingent factors for consideration

The environment

- Predictability
- Competition
- Number of products
- Market hostility

Organisational structure

- Size
- Interdependence
- Decentralisation
- Resource availability

Technology

- Nature of the production process
- Degree of routine
- Understanding of means–ends relationships
- Task variety

as 'one size does not fit all'. Hence the organisational and environmental settings within which the performance measurement system is to be applied must be considered carefully. Table 10.2 lists some of the key factors to be considered within such a decision (based on Emmanuel *et al.*, 1995).

An excellent model for consideration of the suitability of performance measures for a given environment is given in Simons (2000). Simons' model outlines the importance of the nature of the performance measure (objectivity, completeness, responsiveness) and identifies some dysfunctional effects that may occur.

Public Sector Aspects

The issues within performance measurement exist whatever the organisational setting, but there are, of course, variations of problems and practice across the various sectors. Within the public sector, the cultures that exist (service-focused, rather than profit-focused), the tendency toward bureaucracy, and the inertia that may derive from years of tradition and 'doing things in a certain way' may all mitigate against the successful application of business-based performance techniques and practices. Conversely, one should guard against automatically making the assumption that the public sector is somehow less efficient and/or less professionally managed than the private sector. Every case is different.

Lapsley (1996), in reflecting upon performance measurement in the public sector, identifies environmental factors that may influence the effectiveness of performance measurement systems and considers some of the implications. In particular (see the Recommended Further Reading section at the end of this chapter), he focuses on five aspects of the interface between performance measurement systems and the organisation:

- reasons for increased focus on performance measures in the public sector (political, social and economic);
- problems of transferring 'business' performance measurement approaches to applications within the public sector;
- characteristics of performance measurement problems within the public sector;
- consideration of the optimal 'package' of performance measures within a given setting and the dangers of 'creeping bureaucratisation' and 'spin';
- reflections on the lessons learned to date (in the UK) and possible issues for the future.

People Aspects

An organisation may be defined as the sum of its parts, or as the combined effects of its features (e.g. its structure, its locations, its products or outputs and its people). The people involved in the work of an organisation will have a big effect on how that organisation operates, it effectiveness, it ability to respond to change and its relationships with the outside world. Coad (1999) draws attention to how the individual personal characteristics of management accountants may impact on the performance measurement activities of organisations. He suggests that such individuals may have either an orientation toward learning or toward performance, and that such leanings may impact upon how the performance measurement system is used, or its outputs acted upon or interpreted. He concludes that a *learning orientation* should be promoted and supported by managers as this is more likely to increase openness to new ideas for performance measurement that may increase its usefulness.

Divisionalisation and Decentralisation: Degrees of Responsibility and Power

Organisations may expand and/or grow more complex in a number of ways, for example in terms of:

- geographical expansion – to new regions, either at home or abroad;
- product range – adding new products/services, and/or though increasing the variations available of each product service;
- organisational structure – more complex structures, through specialisation of division by nature or function;
- diversity of customer range.

As organisations expand or become more complex, the practical difficulties of managing the organisation as a coherent whole, maintaining focus on the key organisational objectives, increase. The argument over whether organisations are most effective when managed as individual autonomous units or as large integrated networks continues and there appears to be a cyclical popularity of 'big (or small) is beautiful'.

Decentralisation and Divisionalisation

One of the key decisions to be made within any large organisation is the degree of autonomy to be allowed to individual organisational units. Where organisational units are allowed a high degree of autonomy, the organisation is said to be highly *decentralised*. Note here the difference between decentralisation (relating to the allocation of power/ authority) and *divisionalisation* (relating to the fragmentation of an organisation without any necessary allocation of power). Hence, an organisation may consist of many divisions but none of these division may be able to take any important decisions for themselves – such an organisation would *not* be said to be decentralised.

Table 10.3 identifies some of the performance measurement issues that may arise as an organisation becomes increasingly decentralised. In addition to such issues, there is another major area for attention where there is a degree of trading/service provision between the divisions comprising the organisational whole. Where such interdivisional trading or service provision (or 'intragroup') exists, decisions must be made about the prices, known as *transfer prices*, that the 'selling' division should charge to the 'buying' division. Given that, in many large international organisations, the divisions will be subsidiary companies of a corporate group located in overseas countries and subject to different tax laws, these decisions on interdivisional transfer prices may have taxation, legal and other political and social implications.

Transfer Pricing Considerations

When determining transfer prices, a number of questions need to be asked:

- On what basis should the transfer price be set?
- Who should set the transfer price?
- What are the likely behavioural effects of the transfer prices determined?
- How often should the transfer prices be reviewed?

A number of transfer pricing bases have been suggested and/or applied over the years by organisations. Some of these are illustrated and some of their advantages/disadvantages described in Table 10.4.

Much of the seminal work on transfer pricing considerations was carried out in the 1980s, and the work of Emmanuel and Gee and of Spicer is particularly respected in this

Table 10.3   Issues that may arise as an organisation becomes increasingly decentralised

- How to maintain focus on the organisations' central objectives
- How to maintain adequate communications among divisions and between division and centre
- How to decide on the most appropriate performance measures
- How to avoid over-proliferation of performance measures
- How to ensure that performance measures are used properly, followed up and action taken
- What mix to use of financial and non-financial performance measures
- How to obtain the right mix of long-term and short-term focused performance measures
- How to measure the effectiveness of the performance measures used
- How often to measure performance
- Who should administer the performance measurement system and from where
- How to ensure fairness and consistency of approach across the organisation
- How to minimise the dangers of players' using the performance measurement system to their advantage
- How to counter the effects (in geographically-spread organisations) of cultural differences
- Whether to use the same performance measures across the organisation, or to 'customise' according to local conditions
- How to maintain/increase the level of motivation of the workforce via the performance measurement system
- How to and whether to create and maintain a system of rewards (and/or penalties) related to the performance measurement system
- How to ensure that targets and benchmarks remain appropriate and at the right level

area. Emmanuel and Gee (1982) argue for the use of a market-based transfer pricing approach on the grounds of its being the fairest approach and being verifiable by managers. They construct a model of a 'fair transfer price' based on a two-instalment transfer charge (i.e. a two-part tariff approach) but recognise and discuss a range of shortcomings of their model. Spicer (1988) investigates the various approaches to the transfer pricing issue. He analyses the work of Watson and Baumler, among others, and, using a contingency theory based approach, attempts to place transfer pricing within a wider organisational context and prepares the ground for further empirical research (see also Chapter 8 above).

What appears to be true, as in many other areas of management accounting control, is that there is no single transfer pricing approach that will be optimal under all circumstances. Although some methods are easy to use, they may not yield results that are optimal for the organisation. Other methods may be theoretically sound but may be impractical to use in real life, or the theoretical models on which they are based may be founded on unrealistic assumptions. Other models, based on the existence of markets, may falter where there exist imperfect or sparse markets, or where the data collection and analysis requirements are resource-intensive. All in all, the best method to apply will depend on circumstances and may change over time.

Table 10.4   Some possible transfer pricing bases and some advantages/disadvantages

Transfer pricing basis	Basis of calculation	Advantages	Disadvantages/issues
Cost-based (i.e. 'cost-plus')	The transfer price is set at the cost of producing the intermediate product, or a relatively arbitrary percentage 'mark-up' is added to the cost	• Easy to calculate and administer • Easy to understand	• Does not reflect the economic reality • Difficulty in deciding to which 'cost' (i.e. marginal, variable, full, opportunity) the mark-up should be applied • Arbitrariness of the mark-up • Difficulty in deciding by whom and how the mark-up should be established • May lead to unintended behavioural consequences
Market-based	Transfer prices are set by direct reference to equivalent prices within the external markets	• Transfer prices should be seen to be relevant by users • Easier for proponents to justify the use of the transfer prices as 'based on fact'	• More than one market may exist, or the markets identified may be imperfect • Data collection and analysis may be resource–intensive as markets may be volatile and complex • Differences will exist between external and internal markets and so users may complain that the transfer prices do not reflect the internal organisation realities
Mathematically based	Transfer prices are set via a process of: • identifying the variables and constraints within the decision package • formulating these as a mathematical model • performing mathematical iterations in order to produce a theoretically optimal solution	• Theoretically sound • The process of mathematical formulation helps to clarify the factors within the decision • A clear, prescriptive solution is derived upon which to take action	• Requires refined mathematical and analytical skill • Is dependent upon a full identification of the relevant factors • Difficult for non-technical users to understand • May give a theoretical solution that ignores some aspects and thus leads to unexpected consequences

(Continued)

Table 10.4 Continued

Transfer pricing basis	Basis of calculation	Advantages	Disadvantages/issues
Negotiated	• The transfer price is settled by agreement between the buying and selling division	• Should, by definition, lead to a transfer price that is acceptable to both buying and selling divisions	• May lead to protracted and bitter arguments over what is an acceptable price • The negotiated price, while acceptable to both parties, may not be the best price for the company as a whole • Time-consuming and administratively expensive
Two-part tariff	The transfer pricing mechanism involves two components: • a 'lump sum' amount, paid over after the period end, to cover an appropriate amount of the fixed costs of the supplying division; • a 'per unit' amount to cover the supplying division's variable costs and a profit margin Both components of the pricing mechanism are subject to negotiation and may be adjusted to take account of extra information after the period	• Greater agreement between the divisions involved • Allows divisions to get on with the business of transfer pricing while allowing some negotiation before final settling of prices • Should be seen as fair as specific aspects of cost are identified and covered by the transfer price	• May be time-consuming and costly to administer • The subsequent negotiations may be difficult • May not lead to the most economically sound transfer price for the company as a whole
Dual pricing	A system whereby, because of difficulties within the negotiation process, two separate transfer prices are set: a 'buying price' used for the buying division, and a different 'selling price' for the selling division	• Keeps both divisions happy, assuming that the 'buying' and 'selling' pries are accepted as fair by the respective divisions	• Unlikely to result in the optimal transfer price for the company as a whole • May still require extensive negotiation with each division (or the imposition of a transfer price, with adverse behavioural consequences) • Will require reconciliation exercise at the period end for accounting purposes

Transfer Pricing Example

An organisation has two main divisions, S and B. Division S makes an intermediate product that it could sell in the external market, but also sells this intermediate product to B. Division B buys this intermediate product from S and processes it further, producing a final product that it sells to the external market. Relevant data are as follows:

	£
Division S sells 1000 units per period to Division B	
Division S:	
Variable cost per unit of intermediate product	10
Fixed costs per period	15,000
Market price per unit if intermediate product is sold in the external market	40
Division B:	
Divisional B variable costs per unit processed	5
Fixed costs per period	10,000
Final market price for final product	60

The head office of the company has decided that the divisional managers' remuneration will be based upon the profit performance of their divisions.

Using the data above, let us consider some possible scenarios. In *scenario 1*, the head office decides to set the transfer price for the intermediate product at a level which represents the external intermediate product market price, adjusted for internal conditions, giving a transfer price of £37 per unit (i.e. the external market price of £40 reduced by £3 per unit to reflect savings in advertising, etc.). The divisional results under these conditions are:

Division S:	
	£/unit
Divisional variable costs	10
Selling price = transfer price	<u>37</u>
Contribution per unit	27
No. of units transferred per period	1,000
Total contribution per period	£27,000
Divisional fixed costs	<u>£15,000</u>
Divisional profit	£12,000

Division B:

	£/unit
Divisional variable costs	5
+ Transfer price inwards	37
Total variable cost per unit	42
Selling price (final product)	60
Contribution per unit	18
No. of units transferred per period	1,000
Total contribution per period	£18,000
Divisional fixed costs	£10,000
Divisional profit	£8,000

Total company profits = £12,000 + £8,000 = £20,000

The imposition of the transfer price will result in a number of effects:

- Division S's manager may be demotivated as the transfer price is below that which it can achieve in the market. If Division S has a large potential external market for the intermediate product, then every unit it transfers to Division B loses it a potential £3 contribution. This £3 is effectively transferred to Division B, to the advantage of Division B's manager.
- Division B's manager may feel that, although Division S sells it the intermediate product at £37, Division B could buy externally a perfectly adequate substitute for less than £37. Division B's manager therefore feels that its production costs are unnecessarily high and thus its profit (and its manager's remuneration) depressed.
- The managers of each division are demotivated because they feel that they have no real control over their profits (as, although the transfer price has been based on an economically sound market price, it has been dictated from above, by head office staff).

In *scenario 2*, the head office decides that an arbitrary transfer price £35 per unit should be used. The divisional results under these conditions are:

Division S:

	£/unit
Divisional variable costs	10
Selling price = transfer price	35
Contribution per unit	25
No of units transferred per period	1,000
Total contribution per period	£25,000
Divisional fixed costs	£15,000
Divisional profit	£10,000

Division B:

	£/unit
Divisional variable costs	5
+ Transfer price inwards	35
total variable cost per unit	40
Selling price (final product)	60
Contribution per unit	20
No of units transferred per period	1,000
Total contribution per period	£20,000
Divisional fixed costs	£10,000
Divisional profit	£10,000

∴ Total company profits = £10,000 + £10,000 = £20,000

As under scenario 1, the total company profit remains at £20,000. All that has changed is the allocation of the divisional profits. Under scenario 2, as compared with scenario 1, Division S ends up with £2,000 profit less and Division B is allocated an extra £2,000 profit.

Evidently, this reallocation of profits will be seen as more unfair (given its arbitrariness) than scenario 1. Division S's manager will feel particularly aggrieved as her/his profit has been decreased at a stroke by an arbitrary decision by head office.

Under *scenario 3*, the managers of divisions S and B have negotiated a transfer pricing agreement between themselves. The agreement is that each unit transferred will be charged to Division B at Division S's variable cost plus a mark-up of 80%. Additionally a lump-sum transfer of 80% of Division S's actual fixed costs will be made at the end of the period. The variable cost-plus charge will be revisited and renegotiated retroactively at the end of each period to take account of unexpected circumstances. The divisional results under these conditions are:

Division S:

		£/unit
Divisional variable costs		10
Selling price = transfer price [= £10 + 80%]		18
Contribution per unit		8
No. of units transferred per period		1,000
Total contribution per period		£8,000
Divisional fixed costs	£15,000	
Less fixed cost transfer to Division B	£12,000	
		£(3,000)
Divisional profit		£5,000

Division B:

	£/unit
Divisional variable costs	5
+ Transfer price inwards	18

Total variable cost per unit		23
Selling price (final product)		60
Contribution per unit		37
No. of units transferred per period		1,000
Total contribution per period		£37,000
Divisional fixed costs	£10,000	
Plus lump sum transfer inwards	£12,000	
		£(22,000)
Divisional profit		£15,000

∴ Total company profits = £5,000 + £15,000 = £20,000

Here, again, we see the same overall company profits of £20,000 but now Division S has only £5,000 of these.

This reallocation of profits between divisions may have a number of effects depending upon a number of factors:

- the extent to which the negotiation was undertaken without the interference of head office;
- the extent to which the pricing structure represents, overall, the external market;
- the basis on which the managers' remuneration is related to the absolute size of the divisional profits earned.

All of the transfer pricing approaches taken within these scenarios have a degree of artificiality and bias. Additionally, the assumption has been made that the total production of Division S will be taken up (and must be taken up) by Division B. In reality, the degree of authority that the divisional managers have to decide whether to transfer internally or to buy/sell externally will bring into play a range of opportunity costs to be taken into account.

We have seen that interference by head office in the transfer price setting will be seen by divisional managers as removing some of their independence and as reducing their ability to influence their remuneration. One possible solution might be to remove the link between performance, as measured by divisional profits, and remuneration. Maybe an increased focus on overall, more strategic and qualitative objectives, rather than on short-term profitability might enhance organisational coherence.

Practical Realities and Theoretical Ideals

Any of the transfer pricing approaches outlined in Table 10.4 may be found in practical situations. Additionally, there are some further practical considerations that affect all of the approaches:

- Where the selling of the intermediate product, or service, has implications for taxation, cross-border regulations, political or social aspects, then the transfer prices should be set in such a way as to comply with the rules in place in the external environment.
- There is always a balancing act to be achieved when setting a transfer price:
  - The economically optimal (ideal theoretical) transfer price is unlikely to be that achieved through practical means.
  - Theoretical perfection may lead to the transfer mechanism's being difficult to understand for many organisational players.

    ○ There is a payoff between accuracy and administrative cost.

    ○ Inappropriate transfer prices (or transfer prices that are seen to be inappropriate) are likely to lead to dysfunctional actions by those affected.

Accounting Measures of Performance and Financial Ratio Analysis

A large range of individuals and organisations might be interested in the performance of an organisation. Table 10.5 suggests some of the most significant interested parties. These

Table 10.5 Some of the parties interested in performance information

Type of organisation	Interested parties
Small/medium company	Shareholders Management Employees Suppliers Customers
Large listed company or multinational/global group	As small/medium companies *plus* Government agencies Central government Analysts Credit rating agencies International organisations
Central government organisation	Managers Voters (the public) Politicians Employees Central government of other countries/states International organisations
Local government organisation	Managers Employees Central government Other local government organisations Local taxpayers Service users Providers of services to local government
Charity	Managers Donors and benefactors Employees Beneficiaries and representative bodies Regulators Central government

would in most cases be interested in both financial performance measures (e.g. profit margins, stock turnover rates, return on capital) and non-financial performance measures (e.g. productivity, market share, staff turnover). Each user will, of course, have his/her own areas of interest and so you might wish to give some thought to the types of measures that each would apply.

So what are the actual performance measures that organisations might use?

Exhibit 10.2 illustrates some of the 'standard' *financial* performance measures that might be used.

<table>
<tr><td>EXHIBIT
10.2</td><td colspan="4">Illustration of the Use of Financial Performance Measures</td></tr>
</table>

Holby plc has obtained the following data from its management accounting system, relating to the previous period:

Profit and loss account data

	£000	£000	£000
Sales			1,000
Cost of sales:			
Opening raw materials stocks	50		
Purchases	100		
Closing raw materials stocks	(70)		
Materials cost of production		80	
Direct labour	100		
Production overheads	250		
	350		
Opening work in progress (WIP) stock	80		
Closing WIP stock	(100)		
Cost of goods produced	(20)	410	
Opening stock of finished goods	120		
Closing stock of finished goods	(90)		
	30		
Cost of sales			440
Gross profit			560
Administration overhead			(250)
Selling and distribution overhead			(180)
Net profit			130

Balance sheet data:

	£000	£000	£000
Fixed assets			1,000

Current assets:		
Stocks (as above)	260	
Trade debtors	200	
Cash and bank	100	
		560
Current liabilities:		
Creditors		50
Net current assets		510
Total assets less current liabilities		1,510
Long-term loan		500
Net worth		1,010

When addressing the matter of financial performance measures, we need to ask who wants the information. The *shareholders* of the company will primarily want to know how their investment in the company is performing. Such information is not available directly from the type of management accounting data given above. To answer the shareholders' questions we would need to have data on the company's share price, its price–earnings ratio, earning per share, and so on. Such analysis is possible only where the company has a market price for its shares. This 'higher level' analysis is covered in texts on financial management. We can, however, address the question of the company's performance indirectly by analysing its apparent performance based on its accounting data from its internal management accounting system.

A number of measures are available concerning return on investment, depending upon how we define 'return' and how we define the investment base. 'Return', for instance, might be defined as gross profit, net profit, or sales income. 'Investment' might be defined as total assets, current assets, net assets etc.

The most probable 'overall' measure of return on investment, given the above data, would be

$$\frac{\text{Net profit}}{\text{Net worth}} = \frac{130}{660} = 19.7\%.$$

We could then ask what caused the return on investment to be 19.7%.

One approach here is to apply what is sometimes called the 'pyramid' or 'hierarchy' of ratios:

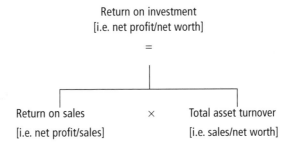

Return on investment
[i.e. net profit/net worth]

=

Return on sales   ×   Total asset turnover
[i.e. net profit/sales]   [i.e. sales/net worth]

So, for this example, the calculations are:

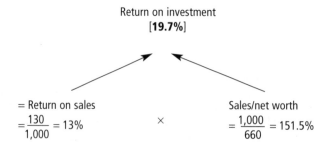

Return on investment
[19.7%]

= Return on sales
$= \dfrac{130}{1,000} = 13\%$

×

Sales/net worth
$= \dfrac{1,000}{660} = 151.5\%$

We could now ask further questions such as: What caused the 'return on sales' to be 13%? What caused the 'sales/net worth' to be 151.5%? 'How do these performance figures compare with other time periods' performance and comparable companies' results? The last two questions are very useful and important in practice, although in many cases the necessary comparative data may not be available. Let us concentrate on the first two questions.

We begin with the return on sales. The 'return' is composed of two elements – sales and cost of sales. Focusing on the cost aspects as a proportion of sales income, a number of subsidiary ratios can be calculated:

$$\frac{\text{Material cost of sales}}{\text{Sales}} = \frac{80}{1000} \times 100 = 8\%,$$

$$\frac{\text{Production overhead}}{\text{Sales}} = \frac{250}{1000} \times 100 = 25\%,$$

$$\frac{\text{Gross profit}}{\text{Sales}} = \frac{560}{1000} \times 100 = 56\%,$$

$$\frac{\text{Administration overhead}}{\text{Sales}} = \frac{250}{1000} \times 100 = 25\%,$$

$$\frac{\text{Selling and distribution overhead}}{\text{Sales}} = \frac{180}{1000} \times 100 = 18\%.$$

Note that all of these ratios are only of use in a comparative sense. The figures calculated have no intrinsic information value but, to become useful, must be compared with similarly calculated figures for previous periods or other divisions, subsidiaries, and so on.

Concentrating on the make-up of the costs, a number of further ratios may be calculated, for example:

$$\frac{\text{Materials cost}}{\text{Total production cost}} = \frac{80}{410} \times 100 = 20\%$$

A number of similar ratios could be calculated concentrating on other cost aspects such as labour and overhead costs. Note that some of these costs will be the periodic costs (e.g. the materials cost of the goods produced in the period), whereas the total costs figure will be adjusted for the changes in work in progress stocks. Thus, for accuracy, care would need to be taken that costs are compared on a like-with-like basis.

Using a similar approach, the overall 'total asset turnover' ratio can be analysed into a number of subsidiary indicators:

$$\frac{\text{Sales (the 'fixed asset utilisation ratio')}}{\text{Fixed assets}} = \frac{1000}{1000} \times 100 = 100\%,$$

$$\frac{\text{Sales}}{\text{Stocks}} = \frac{1000}{260} \times 100 = 3.85 \text{ time per year, or } 365/3.85 = \text{a turnover of 96 days.}$$

Stock 'turnover rates' could be calculated for the different aspects of stocks:

Raw materials stock turnover $=$

$$\frac{\text{Raw materials stock (average)}}{\text{Raw materials purchases}} = \frac{60}{100} \times 365 = 219 \text{ days,}$$

$$\frac{\text{WIP stock (average)}}{\text{Cost of production}} = \frac{90}{410} \times 365 = 80 \text{ days,}$$

$$\frac{\text{Finished goods stocks (average)}}{\text{Cost of sales}} = \frac{105}{440} \times 365 = 87 \text{ days.}$$

Of course, with all the ratios above, we are comparing static, balance sheet figures, at a specific date, with profit and loss based figures that cover a period of time. Thus, the figures being compared are not on a strictly comparable basis and so the resultant ratios must be used with care. Also, naturally, various ideas will exist about the 'best' ways to calculate such performance indicators.

The figures calculated seem, however, to indicate that the company is taking a long time to pass its stocks through the system. All such stock is effectively 'money tied up' within the company and efforts to speed up the process of converting stocks into saleable goods and, eventually, cash must be beneficial.

One of the important aspects of a business that can be the 'make or break' of its success is the way in which it manages working capital and financing. For example, it will need to monitor cash flows to and from its debtors and creditors. Two *credit management indicators* are the following:

$$\text{'Debtors' turnover'} = \frac{\text{Average debtors}}{\text{Credit sales}} = \frac{200}{1000} \times 365 = 73 \text{ days,}$$

$$\text{'Creditors' turnover'} = \frac{\text{Average creditors}}{\text{Credit purchases}} = \frac{50}{100} \times 365 = 183 \text{ days.}$$

Holby is taking around 2 months to collect from its debtors. Any improvements possible here will be rewarded by an earlier reinvestment of the cash received, thus giving further opportunities for making profits. (Note that, due to lack of data we have had to use year-end debtors and to assume that all sales were on credit.) Furthermore, Holby is taking 6 months to pay its creditors. This is, of course, a very poor state of affairs and, if the data are reliable, Holby is likely to be experiencing great problems with its supplier relationships. It could be, however, that the 'snapshot' figures used are untypical.

Two important *Working capital indicators* are:

$$\text{'Working capital ratio'} = \frac{\text{Current assets}}{\text{Current liabilities}} = \frac{560}{50} = 11.2 \text{ times}$$

$$\text{'Acid test'} = \frac{\text{Current assets} - \text{Stock}}{\text{Current liabilities}} = \frac{560 - 260}{50} = 6 \text{ times}$$

For safety reasons, we would hope that the level of current assets would cover the level of current liabilities (i.e. a ratio of 1). What is 'normal', however, depends on the industry sector's practices and economic conditions, therefore contextualisation is necessary. The 'acid test' attempts to be a more testing indicator by removing the 'cover' provided by stocks, a relatively illiquid asset. Finally, in this category, we have the

'Cash operating cycle' = Total debtors' days + Total stock days − Total creditors' days

$$= 73 + 219 + 80 + 87 - 183 = 276 \text{ days}$$

The company is taking around 276 days to convert its initial investments in stocks into cash!

The main *financing ratio* in use is the gearing ratio which may be calculated as:

$$\frac{\text{Fixed interest debt}}{\text{Shareholders' funds}} = \frac{500}{1010} \times 100 = 50\%.$$

A number of other versions of the calculation of this indicator will be found in other texts.

As we have noted above, the analysis must be used carefully and comparisons made to contextualise the data. Although the indicators calculated will have to be used carefully, they do at least provide a basis for further investigation and clarification. In the context of specific organisations, other quantitative indicators may additionally prove useful. They also provide data that may be useful in 'benchmarking' the organisation's performance against other similar organisations.

Non-Financial Aspects of Performance Measurement

All of the analysis above is *quantitative* in nature. But organisations are much more complex than the numerical data that may be utilised to describe them.

There has been an increasing tendency in recent years to turn attention towards the non-quantitative, *qualitative* side of performance measurement. There are various facets to this:

- the aspects of productivity, absenteeism, staff turnover, morale, public image, customer satisfaction, environmental responsibility, etc. Many of these aspects are, of course, people-focused in nature. Few, if any, of these areas are quantified easily in financial terms.
- the issue of separating the performance of *people* from the performance of departments, divisions, etc. A good manager, who makes a great effort and acts strategically, may have her/his true performance 'masked' by being situated within a division that performs poorly overall, when assessed according to the 'usual' financial performance indicators. It is thus important to attempt to isolate the actual performance of that manager and to reward it. Such an approach will be likely to involve the use of non-financial indicators.
- the issue of *input measures* as compared with *output measures*. The efforts of individuals form inputs into the organisational production processes. Most performance measures, however, tend to focus on outputs. There is thus the risk that the efforts that an individual makes will be hidden behind the multitude of complex events that take place in converting inputs into organisational outputs.
- the issue of *outputs* versus *outcomes*. In much of the literature discussing performance measurement in the public sector – (see, for instance, Lapsley (1996) – attention is

paid to the differences between outputs (the immediate products of an organisation, e.g. products made or services sold) and the outcomes of the organisation's activities (i.e. the longer-term effects, such as local levels of health as the result of a hospital's strategies). It is thus important that sufficient attention is paid to all aspects of performance and to recognise individuals' contributions to the organisation's success, both immediate and eventual.

Performance Measurement and Contemporary Organisational Environments

A wide range of organisational types exists. We looked earlier, in Exhibit 10.2, at typical financially based performance indicators that might be applied within a manufacturing organisation. What about service and public sector organisations?

The public sector operates in a rather different way from manufacturing organisations. Although a small number of public sector organisations act as semi-commercial organisations (e.g. nationalised industries), most public sector organisations have the provision of services as their prime objective, with cost and quality criteria acting as constraints. Naturally, then, performance measures used in such settings should focus upon these organisations' objectives and constraints.

Lapsley (1996) considered the 'state of play' of performance measurement in the UK public sector (see the recommended further reading section at the end of this chapter). Lapsley focused on five main areas:

- The rationale of performance measurement in the public sector – i.e. what was the driving force for performance measurement?
- Performance measurement in action – here Lapsley looked at some of the issues that arose when trying to apply business-based performance measures within a public sector setting and identified some suitable models, including the 'three Es' (see below).
- Performance measurement as a management process – including the use of 'checklists' and the problems of performance measurement systems' stifling innovation.
- Performance measurement in specific (nationalised) industries.
- Performance measurement in the future.

In his analysis, Lapsley draws attention to the problems of over-bureaucratisation, stifling of creativity, establishing valid and appropriate performance measures as well as considering others' ideas on what constitute 'ideal' models for performance measurement in this setting. Many of the issues that Lapsley discusses, however, are not peculiar to the public sector. The problems of performance measurement, although contingent upon organisational setting, technology and culture, are relatively consistent across organisational types.

One of the useful ideas that emerged from early developments in public sector performance management was a relatively simple one, which said that performance consisted of three main components:

- *Economy* – in simple terms, obtaining resources at the lowest possible price (obviously when pursuing this goal, the constraints of quality and timeliness will need to be considered).
- *Efficiency* – in simple terms, undertaking processes in ways that make the best use of available resources. Efficiency is thus a matter of maximising the outputs from the available inputs. Here, also, the constraints of required quality, timeliness, etc. must be taken into account.
- *Effectiveness* – in simple terms, the degree to which the organisation's objectives are achieved.

The 'three Es' are hierarchical in that efficiency will not be achieved without economy, and effectiveness will not be achieved without efficiency. However, being economical and efficient will not necessarily result in effectiveness. Why not?

As mentioned above, effectiveness is the degree to which the organisation's objectives are achieved. How we define effectiveness therefore depends upon how we define our objectives – broadly or narrowly, short-term or long-term, financial or non-financial, quantitatively or non-quantitatively.

How might a hospital apply the 'three Es'?

- *Economy* – an example might be that supplies (of pharmaceuticals, laundry services, staff costs, etc.) would be obtained at the lowest cost commensurate with required quality levels. Obviously, falling below the required quality could be disastrous within any of these criteria, and this failing would have a direct impact upon the hospital's overall effectiveness.
- *Efficiency* – the hospital will want to make best use of its resources. It will therefore make efforts to ensure that surgical procedures are carried out on time and quickly, to reduce the time that patients wait in hospital beds until their operations are carried out, to reduce the amount of time that patients spend in recovery wards before being discharged. Again, however, any overenthusiasm in these respects will lead to poorer health care and an increase in re-referrals, with consequent effects on overall effectiveness.
- *Effectiveness* – a big question for a hospital is 'how should effectiveness be defined. Simple measures such as 'number of operations carried out' or 'percentage reduction in waiting lists' are readily distorted by creative accounting and may not be directly linked to longer-term objectives such as improving the general level of health of the community served by the hospital. There is in this context, the need to distinguish between *outputs* (e.g. number of operations performed) and *outcomes* (improvements in health levels). One approach to this issue was found within UK health authorities that made, in the 1990s, an attempt to follow two linked objectives:

'adding years to life' (i.e. making people live longer via preventative and corrective medicine) and 'adding life to years' (i.e. improving the quality of people's lives via improving their general health and well-being). What was not done quite so successfully, however, was identifying appropriate performance measures that linked to these composite objectives.

Strategic Aspects of Performance Measurement – Taking a Broader View and Avoiding Short-Termism

Much has been written in recent years on the shortcomings of financially based and short-term focused performance measurement systems. Such systems, it is argued, increase the risks of taking a short-sighted view of the objectives and strategy of the organisation and thus increase the risk of a divergence between the actions of organisational players and those actions that are more likely to increase the overall longer-term effectiveness of the organisation.

Additionally, the organisational environment has changed markedly in recent years, and will continue to change, owing to changes in areas such as technology, communications and globalisation.

Kaplan (1983) – see the recommended further reading section at the end of this chapter – drew attention to the non-financial aspects of performance control, particularly the issues of *quality* and *stock levels*. He argues that the contemporary short production runs, flexibility, reductions in stock levels, technical innovation, supplier and customer relations, and efficiency must all be taken into account by the performance measurement system. He criticises the 'automatic' use of discounted cashflow narrowly (taking a narrow view of financial effects) without consideration of the broader issues involved in an investment decision which are, of course, more difficult to measure. He suggests that financial 'experts' have a tendency toward myopia and that reward systems should be tied to achieving strategic, rather than only financial goals – though this has the problem that shareholders tend to think in financial terms.

Otley (2001) argues that, by the mid-1980s, management accounting had become largely outdated and risked obsolescence. He indicates the importance of the strategic management accounting ideas of authors such as Johnson and Kaplan (1987) with their more forward-looking and market-focused emphasis, including the balanced scorecard (BSC). He also discusses the merits of the economic value analysis (EVA) technique, designed to increase 'shareholder value', and argues that such techniques as the BSC and EVA are most likely to be effective when used together. He identifies the need to recognise the increased application of strategic management accounting within the public sector (see Chapters 7 and 8 for more on Otley's work).

Cooper *et al.* (2002) note the popularity of shareholder value analysis (SVA) amongst blue chip companies (see also Chapter 3). They argue that SVA focuses on value drivers but that SVA's potential benefits are not always realised in practice, as companies fail to put their faith in the use of the measure. Research by Cooper *et al.* established that a number of shareholder value based techniques, including EVA and SVA, were in use, although shareholder value was not always treated as the most critical issue. Interestingly, the use of SVA and similar techniques did not seem to have improved the profit performance of its users, although the researchers suggest that this may be the result of the relative infancy of such applications.

In Chapter 5 we discussed techniques such as activity-based cost management (ABCM), benchmarking, value chain analysis, the balanced scorecard, business process re-engineering and economic value analysis. It is not intended here to undertake further in-depth analysis of some of these strategic management accounting approaches.

Conclusions

This chapter has shown that:

- effective performance measurement is required in all organisations;
- an organisation's structure, culture and environment will have a direct effect on which performance measurement systems will prove most effective;
- performance measurement and transfer pricing are closely interrelated – the objectives of transfer pricing may have a distorting effect on performance measures;
- a range of strategically focused performance measurement approaches have been developed and promoted in recent years – these should be analysed carefully for their applicability in any given situation.

Summary

In this chapter we have considered some of the fundamental aspects of performance measurement in modern organisations. We have seen that the process of performance measurement requires careful consideration of a range of behavioural, organisational, environmental and strategic factors. As with all techniques that are dependent for their success upon a range of contingent factors, there is no 'right answer'. Thus, performance measurement is a process of learning and being flexible to change. This need for flexibility and learning has been a common theme throughout this book and it is particularly pertinent to the area of performance measurement. We have also given some attention to the more strategic approaches to performance measurement. As these new approaches are relatively untested, and because new approaches appear continuously in the accounting press, this is an area upon which you should keep a regular watch. Nevertheless, there is often a degree of 'the emperor's new clothes' about these new developments and there is always uncertainty as to which of such techniques will stand the test of time. You should therefore maintain a critical stance when considering such developments.

Recommended Further Reading

Lapsley, I. (1996) 'Reflections on performance measurement in the public sector', in L. Lapsley and F. Mitchell, *Accounting and Performance Measurement: Issues in the Private and Public Sectors.* London: Paul Chapman Publishing, pp. 109–128.

Lapsley addresses five main areas:

1. *Rationale of performance measurement in the public sector:*
    Lapsley asks why accountants and managers should focus on performance measures. He identifies forces such as fiscal pressures, perceived inefficiency, lack of clear 'commercial' objectives and the 'dependency culture'. He also expresses the opinion that Thatcherite views on the need for devolved management and accountability may have led to the proliferation of performance measurement activity in the public sector since the early 1980s.

2. *Performance measurement in action:*
    Lapsley explains the relevance of the public sector focus on the 'three Es' (effectiveness, efficiency and economy) as a market surrogate toward value-for-money in the public sector. He draws attention to the problems of complexity and definition that may occur in attempting to implement such performance measurement models. He comments on the questionable validity of transferring private sector models to the public sector, pointing to factors such as the problems of variation in practice (accounting 'noise') and the various possible models/frameworks, e.g. 'three Es', FEE and Mayston that may be put forward as 'optimal'.

3. *Performance measurement as a management process:*
    Lapsley gives examples of checklists, such as Likierman's '20 lessons', when considering the effectiveness and/or relevance of public sector performance measurement systems. He points to the problems of clarity, consistency, contingency, measurability, controllability and reductionism that may occur, and to the stifling of innovation, ambiguity, displacement, omission and conflict that may result from the enforcement of such systems.

4. *Performance measurement in specific (nationalised) industries:*
    Lapsley considers issues such as:

    *   which mix of key performance indicators is optimal,
    *   the tendency to concentrate on inputs,
    *   the danger/natural tendency towards budget 'padding',
    *   the problem of 'general' objectives – tenuous links to key performance indicators,
    *   the problem of over-bureaucracy, data overload, 'death by 1000 initiatives',
    *   the effects of patients, citizens, and customer charters in massaging of information and compartmentalization, and
    *   the tendency for concentration on measures of efficiency rather than effectiveness and equity.

5. *Performance measurement in the future:*

   Lapsley comments that, in the future, we will probably see 'more of the same', but many issues need to be resolved. (Note that the current UK administration, the Labour Party, has slowed the 'privatisation' process a little.)

Coad, A.F. (1999) 'Some survey evidence on the learning and performance orientations of management accountants', *Management Accounting Research*, 10: 109–135.

Coad suggests that management accountants are not the proactive business consultants (skilled in design/implementation of systems, involved in business decision processes and innovation) that the literature suggests they should be. Maybe this is because they have a *performance* rather than a *learning* goal orientation:

- A *performance goal* orientation is a concern with achieving positive evaluation from others – this leads them to fear poor outcomes and thus they tend to avoid challenges. They may suffer from anxiety, defensiveness etc when difficulties are encountered.
- A *learning goal* orientation is a concern with increasing their *real* competence – they are interested in work, curious, and not too bothered by mistakes.

He also suggests that this (suboptimal, undesirable) goal orientation may be due to management accountants' perception of their leaders' behaviour. These conclusions were based upon a postal questionnaire based survey, which is in the process of being supported by a case study based investigation.

Coad comments, based on the literature, that goal orientation may be contingent upon environmental conditions and personal attitudes to or interpretations (social constructions) of events.

Coad proposes that management accountants who are *involved* are less likely to have a performance goal orientation, and those management accountants who see themselves as *independent* are more likely to have a performance goal orientation. He argues that many of the 'new' ideas relating to management accounting (ABCM, theory of constraints, value chain analysis, balanced scorecard, kaizen, etc.) have not been taken up by management accountants. He argues that this failure to embrace change may partially be explained by the goal orientation of management accountants. (i.e. predominantly a *performance* goal orientation).

He argues that it is *leaders* who should, by example, inculcate a *learning* goal orientation in management accountants and managers. Leaders, he argues, should be more *transformational* and less *transactional*, thereby stimulating innovation and questioning of assumptions via *inspirational* motivation. He comments that, in recruiting and retaining management accountants, attention needs to be given to which type of goal orientation is required for the work area intended. He indicates that leaders may exhibit both transactional and transformational leadership, depending upon circumstances.

He also argues that there are important implications for the *training* of management accountants. Existing training emphasis technical and *domain-specific skills*, with a scarcity of broader, *intellectually creative aspects*. Both sides, he exhorts, need to be developed.

Emmanuel, C.R. and Gee, K.P. (1982), 'Transfer pricing: a fair and neutral procedure', *Accounting and Business Research*, Autumn: 273–278.
Emmanuel and Gee argue for the use of a market-based transfer pricing approach on the grounds of its being the fairest approach and being verifiable by managers. They recognise, however, that fairness/neutrality might be compromised as:

- internal markets may be (are most likely to be?) imperfect;
- transfer prices tend to be agreed for time period, whereas external market prices are changing constantly;
- if the selling division is working below capacity, problems (or deadlock) might be encountered relating to what represents a *reasonable* transfer price between the external price and the in-house costs.

They construct a model of a 'fair transfer price' based on a two-instalment transfer charge which would consist of a charge based upon the selling division's variable cost per unit, and a period cost (charged *ex post*, at the period's end) which is based on the quantity transferred and which takes account of errors in the discount (below market price) allowed in the transfer price because of erroneous assumptions made (about quantities, etc.) at the year's commencement. Emmanuel and Gee argue that such a model does not require accurate market price inspection in advance (as the period cost is calculated *ex post*), and avoids the need for negotiation (as all errors are put right *ex post*) – although the 'discount' still needs to be negotiated in advance. Under such a regime, they explain, the selling division, if it has spare capacity, will resist setting a transfer price below market price – this should be allowed for in the model's period cost calculation that includes a 'lost contribution' charge.

They identify some shortcomings of their model:

- The period (including the various adjustments) may be distorted by significant differences (e.g. in size) between internal and external markets.
- The price which the buying division's manager would charge to external and internal markets would differ because of the different respective risk premia, and this might lead to distortion of the transfer price.
- How should the true production capacity of the selling division be defined? This would cause obvious problems for the calculation of the period cost.
- The model may lead to inefficient marketing by the final division if transfer prices are high and the final product seems to make a loss (although it might generate some contribution).
- Distortion will be caused by the different cash-flow implications of internal and external markets.
- The buying division may require more than one source of the intermediate product, for safety's sake – hence distortion of the transfer price.

Kaplan, R.S (1983) 'Measuring manufacturing performance – a new challenge for MA research', *Accounting Review,* **LVIII: 686–705.**

Kaplan draws attention to the non-financial aspects of performance control, particularly emphasising the issues of *quality* and *stock levels.* He argues that management accounting techniques (in the 1980s) were based on mass production rather than the more flexible, diverse methods used in many industries today – for example, the USA learning from Japanese production practices and philosophies. Short production runs, flexibility, and reducing stock levels must all, he argues, be taken into account by the management accountant in future, as must measures indicating technical innovation, supplier and customer relations, and efficiency.

Kaplan refers to the inadequacy of economic order quantity models (see below) for capturing the true costs of excessive stocks and refers to the ideas inherent in just-in-time. He focuses on 'missing measurement', for example with regard to:

- quality – zero defects (as in just-in-time, total quality management, etc.);
- stock (inventory) – degree to which uncertainty can be reduced (and therefore the need for stock);
- productivity (i.e. *not* costs).

Kaplan says that management accountants must focus on the new product technologies, (e.g. CAD/CAM, flexible manufacturing systems, robotics, etc.) and that the focus of performance measurement differs over a product's life cycle (e.g. the need for flexibility in the early stages of a product's life). He criticises the 'automatic' use of discounted cash-flow narrowly (taking a narrow view of financial effects) without consideration of the broader issues involved in an investment decision which are, of course, more difficult to measure. He suggests that financial 'experts' have a tendency toward myopia.

Kaplan also suggests that reward systems should be tied to achieving strategic, rather than only financial goals – though this has the problem that shareholders tend to think in financial terms.

He goes on to suggest a range of research objectives based on his above observations, for example:

- new management accounting procedures designed to replace the old standard costing approach;
- new management accounting procedures to deal with shorter production runs, increased flexibility and the greater percentage of fixed costs found in modern production environments;
- new measures of productivity (probably non-financial);
- new measures related to achieving higher quality;
- new measures designed to promote optimal stockholding;
- improved capital budgeting procedures to incorporate wider effects, uncertainty, the costs of reducing uncertainty, etc.;
- the need for management accountants to gain a good understanding of the evolving production environment.

Gould, S. (2002) 'Rough guide', *Financial Management*, April: 30–31.

Gould notes the growing popularity of the EBITDA (earnings before interest, taxation, depreciation and amortisation) but cautions against using it carelessly, drawing attention to some of its flaws.

The increasing use of EBITDA is partially due to use by investors and analysts as the result of an increasing 'cash is king' attitude amongst such parties. Increasingly, EBITDA is being included within the published annual report of companies (around 16% at the time of Gould's article, including such large companies as Cable and Wireless, BT, Vodafone, BT, and Reuters).

Gould notes that EBITDA has the tendency to flatter performance and may therefore be used for this end. He points to the particular popularity of the measure within start-up and telecoms companies disguising the fact that such companies may in their early years be making no profit. He argues that the use of EBITDA may have given an early warning of the problems at Enron, since its reported profit figures disguised the fact that they were not backed up by any cash generation.

Conversely, Gould identifies that EBITDA is not a direct measure of cash generation (and thus not a direct indicator of a company's ability to service its debt). Additionally, the fact that EBITDA is an unofficial measure of performance allows it to be calculated in a number of ways, to the particular firm's advantage. Gould gives examples of such variations in calculation.

Keef, S. and Roush, M. (2002) 'Does MVA measure up?', *Financial Management*, January: 20–21.

In discussing the use of the market value-added (MVA) approach, Keef and Roush suggest that a main reason for its use is that it focuses upon the maximisation of shareholders' welfare. He notes that MVA's acceptance as a performance measurement technique is evidenced by Fortune magazine's having reported the rankings of companies, based on their MVA performance, since the early 1990s.

Keef and Roush refer to a seminal definition of MVA given by Stewart (1991) as 'the difference between a company's fair market value, as reflected primarily in its stock price, and the economic book value of capital employed.' Keef and Roush define economic book value, in this context, as 'the best estimate of the monies shareholders have invested in the company. It consists of the sum of the monies subscribed for new shares, together with retained earnings, which are profits that could have been paid out as dividends, but have been reinvested for shareholders'.

Keef and Roush suggest that part of MVA's popularity may be due to its apparent ability to convert accounting numbers into measures of *economic* value, that is, to be a measure of 'true' economic performance.

Keef and Roush criticise MVA in several respects:

- MVA is a 'hybrid' performance measure in that it is partly *ex post* and partly *ex ante*, and thus may give unclear signals regarding what it is actually measuring.

- MVA is essentially the present value of future EVA. They argue that there is no systematic link between the cost of an investment and the NPV that it creates (small investments can create large NPVs and vice versa). They argue that the value created by an investment is no more or less important than its cost. It is the net effect that is important. Secondly, they criticise MVA for incorporating economic book value which they argue includes past sunk cost aspects.
- The evidence suggests that MVA is of limited value in predicting the financial future of a firm, Keef and Roush arguing that strategic decisions, rather than the assets employed, by a firm are more important in determining share prices.
- MVA is distorted by the size of the company, therefore a size-adjusted MVA calculation would be more appropriate.
- The MVA of the firm represents the MVA of the shareholders who bought their shares when the company was set up. What, ask Keef and Roush, is the MVA of shareholders who have acquired their shares since then? They answer that there will be almost as many MVAs as there are shareholders, each shareholder having a different MVA.

They conclude that, rather than attempting to maximise MVA, an imperfect measure, one should concentrate on the matter that really interests shareholders: maximising the orthodox risk-adjusted abnormal return.

Azofra, V., Prieto, B. and Santidrian, A. (2003) 'The usefulness of a performance measurement system in the daily life of an organisation: a note on a case study', *British Accounting Review*, 35: 367–384.

This paper takes a case study approach to the use of performance indicators by a Spanish subsidiary of a North American multinational. The plant had turnover of $87 million and employed 340 people. Its sphere of operations was car production for such companies as Volkswagen, General Motors and Renault. Managers saw the plant as operating in a 'war economy' (p. 370) where error led to loss of profits and potential impact on the level of employment. Initial stimulus for change came from a major customer.

The indicators were designed in the Spanish plant and were the result of negotiation and consensus in the plant. The primary objective of such changes was to motivate behaviour. The paper points out the substantial competitive pressures that companies are under and that these have led to substantial modifications of productive processes. Such approaches include TQM and JIT, which seek rationalisation of the production cycle as well as continuous improvements in quality, time and cost. It is also seen as important to recognise that such practices cannot be introduced in an isolated and unconnected way but must also be accompanied by innovations in other areas of the organisation. Such changes are seen as including a need to develop both qualitative and quantitative measures, as the use of financial indicators alone to assess performance is seen as inadequate. The system in the paper is known as Performance Indictors System for Continuous Improvement (PISCI) and is divided into five areas – Finance, Materials, Human Resources, Production, and Quality.

The principal characteristics of the system introduced were:

- A combination of financial and non-financial indicators (164) which are revised annually.
- Workers are seen as owners of at least one indicator and have to answer for both its evolution and the actions needed to correct deviation.
- Each indicator has a comprehensive definition including name, area to which it is linked, code, unit of measurement, how calculated and key individual accountable.
- Data exchange between areas through computerised systems to improve information flow and to detect potential manipulation.

The paper concludes with the view that the inclusion of non-financial performance indicators is a valuable means of disaggregating strategy and communicating to workers the objectives of the company. Despite the large number of indicators, there seems no confusion or tension and they are seen as a valuable tool to mark responsibilities and involve workers, thus increasing the potential motivation of the workforce. Head office strategic control is limited to 12 indicators as internal management at plant level influences internal behaviour through both monetary (bonus incentives) and non-monetary rewards (gifts and congratulatory letters).

Case Study: Callas plc

Callas plc is a large company that manufactures and sells a wide range of goods to the clothing and personal accessory markets. It has a range of retail outlets across the UK and has recently expanded its retailing and manufacturing activities into mainland Europe. Callas plc's current product range is aimed primarily at the under-20, high street fashion market. Its products have been losing their appeal to this sector in recent years and a new marketing team has recently been appointed in an attempt to revitalise sales. The new team has spent a significant amount of time and money on a new televised promotion/marketing campaign although, it argues, it is too early yet to see the results of the campaign.

Callas plc's main administrative, accounting/finance and marketing activities are dealt with by its head office in London. A certain amount of authority for local advertising, manufacturing management, product distribution and human resource management (HRM) matters is, however, given to regional headquarters based in Cardiff (Wales), Glasgow (Scotland), Lille (France) and Borlange (Sweden). Callas plc's head office management insist that, wherever possible, administrative, financial, reporting and HRM procedures are standardised across all regions.

Managers in the retail outlets are paid bonuses based upon their outlets' quarterly operating profits and, additionally, a regional managers' profit-sharing scheme is in place which is related to the company's after-tax profits for the past year. Retail operative staff and other administrative staff are not entitled to participate in the bonus scheme, although they are able to earn overtime pay. Additionally they may receive awards for good performance, following an annual individual performance appraisal carried out by their direct supervisors. The profit margins in Callas plc's line of business are not great and this is the justification given by the company for its paying relatively low amounts to its retailing and administrative staff.

A management control system was put into place by Callas plc's central management accounting staff in 1990. The control system is based on an annual budget, calculated at headquarters level, for which regional and outlet managers have responsibility. Monthly management accounting control reports are produced by Callas plc's headquarters which indicate actual and budgeted results for the past month. Managers are required to explain the differences (variances) between actual and budgeted figures to Callas plc's management team, within one week following the month's end. Comparisons are made between the performances of the various outlets and regions of the company, the results of these comparisons being made available to all company personnel via the Callas intranet. An award is made, each quarter, to the manager of the region that has performed best, although the basis of comparison has changed from time to time. The budgeted figures for the month are calculated from the actual budget upon a time-based, pro-rata basis. A pro-forma for the monthly performance report forwarded to outlets is shown below:

Monthly Performance Report – Pro Forma   *Date produced:................*
Region:............................
Outlet: ....
Outlet Manager: ....

You are required to explain all variances to Headquarters Management Accounting Division by one week following the date of production of this report.

Product Line	Fashion Clothing			Personal Accessories		
	Actual	*Budget*	*Variance*	*Actual*	*Budget*	*Variance*
	£	£	£	£	£	£
Sales						
Cost of Sales:						
Bought-in materials:						
Consumables:						
Direct Labour:						
Supervision:						
Factory overheads:						
Non-factory overheads:						
Net stock adjustment:						
GROSS PROFIT						
Marketing and distribution:						
Product development:						
NET PROFIT						
Net profit margin %						
Sales per person						
Sales per m²						

Managers at both regional and outlet level have complained about the validity of the budgets and variance calculations sent to them by headquarters, but Callas's accountants have responded that, each year, budgets are updated for known trends, inflation, and so on. Additionally, the head office management accountants select outlets, on a cyclical basis, for cost-cutting exercises, in an effort to optimise cost efficiency.

The company announced earlier this year that its strategy is moving towards customer satisfaction as a key issue and that managers at all levels need to ensure that customer satisfaction and product/service quality show a clear improvement year-on-year. The head office accountants made an attempt in 1997 to put into place a set of non-financial performance indicators. This was fiercely resisted by managers at the regional and outlet level who complained that they did not understand what these measures were for and that the mode of calculation was unclear and subjective. A new initiative has now been put in place, by the managing director, who has forwarded a memorandum to all managers instructing them to implement a new set of non-financial measures within the next month. Additionally he has instructed all managers to inform him as to how they could implement the principles of the 'balanced scorecard' within their divisions. The four balanced scorecard perspectives, which the managers are to consider within their divisions, have been identified as follows (based on Kaplan and Norton, 1996: 9):

Perspective	Meaning
Financial	'To succeed financially, how should we appear to our shareholders?'
Customer	'To achieve our vision, how should we appear to our customers?'
Internal business process	'To satisfy our shareholders and customers, what business processes must we excel at?'
Learning and growth	'To achieve our vision, how will we sustain our ability to change and improve?'

Callas's top management has recently made moves into marketing the business via the Internet, with the intention of an eventual full e-commerce capability.

Additionally, it has been undergoing negotiations with a UK government organisation regarding the supply of large amounts of uniforms for use by government employees. If obtained, this large contract would form a significant part of Callas's UK business and, if successful, this type of business would increasingly be sought in Callas's other geographical locations. Such new business would, however, stretch Callas's UK production and distribution capacities to the limit. It would therefore need to consider other means of servicing the business, such as outsourcing. All government contracts would need to be gained by tendering for contracts against competitors, an unfamiliar aspect of business for Callas.

Management at Callas's headquarters has found it increasingly difficult to make decisions about the company's product and customer mix. Despite the company having made and sold more in recent years, its profitability has declined. The management team feel that the company's new customer-focused strategy will have a positive effect but are unsure of how to gauge the effectiveness of its efforts in the short to medium term.

Regional managers have been complaining recently that they are under constant pressure from their production staff who argue that the cost targets within which they are required to operate are impossibly tight. The regional managers have stressed that a complete review of the cost targets should be undertaken in order to establish which products are worth manufacturing. Callas's financial director has recently become aware of the concept of target costing and has instructed the head office management accounting team to investigate the potential of this approach.

Based upon the above information:

(i)   Discuss the possible behavioural, motivational and ethical issues that might arise out of Callas plc's use of its management accounting control systems.

(ii) Given the company's new strategic focus upon customer satisfaction, analyse the type of information which managers at regional and outlet levels might require in order to monitor their performance and to control operations. Give examples of specific performance indicators that might be usefully applied, within each of the balanced scorecard perspectives, and discuss the advantages/disadvantages of such indicators.

(iii) Critically analyse the potential implications for Callas plc's management accounting systems of the possible changes in the nature of the company's business.

(iv) Outline the possible value of applying a target costing approach within Callas plc.

Information related to Callas Plc – Period since May 2003

Several developments regarding Callas Plc have taken place since May 2003.

Firstly, sales in the personal accessories aspect of the business have decreased, although profits seem to have been relatively unaffected (as far as can be ascertained from the accounting system). In the fashion clothing side of the business, the opposite effect seems to have occurred, i.e. sales have increased but profitability seems to have decreased.

At the manufacturing level, the monthly performance reports have indicated a continuing trend of increasingly adverse cost variances, but production managers have been unable to ascertain the reasons underlying this. This has led to an escalating amount of pressure upon production managers from the head office staff. A member of the head office management accounting staff has suggested that a system of activity based cost management (ABCM) might assist in the resolution of this issue.

Callas Plc has been successful in obtaining its first government contract for the supply of uniforms and has already tendered for a further four major government contracts, two of which are in the UK, one in Sweden and one in France. Having obtained the first contract and now preparing for success in the other tenders, the company is reviewing its operations to maximise the chances that the new contracts will be profitable. The production managers within the manufacturing plants have warned that, if all tenders are successful (and this seems likely), the company's production capacity will be exceeded greatly. The head office management team has been considering, therefore, strategies to overcome this problem. Their favoured option, at present, is to outsource at least 50% of the government contracts and to cut costs, wherever possible, by launching a further efficiency drive aimed at the manufacturing plants. The government sector business is very price competitive and it has been suggested, by an external consultant, that the introduction of *target costing* systems is now an urgent requirement.

The e-commerce side of the business has taken off and is growing quickly. Initially, head office staff manned the Internet-based business, but the head office has now passed this responsibility to the retail outlets, on the basis that the outlets are more skilled in selling. The Callas plc website's popularity and competitive strategy was based upon promising delivery times that were faster than those of competitors. While this has been maintained to date, increasing pressure has been mounting upon the company's warehousing and distribution capabilities and some custom has been lost.

Retailing staff turnover has increased markedly during the past few months and the head office management team suspects that this may be caused partly by the relatively low pay levels. Outlet managers, however, feel that a more likely cause is decreased job satisfaction.

Little progress has yet been made on the implementation of Balanced Scorecard (BSC) approaches. Operational managers have argued that they are too busy, under conditions of increased pressure of work, to devote time to a new system that is seen to be inadequately defined, and arbitrary. They have also demanded that, should a performance system based on the BSC be introduced, they would expect to be rewarded adequately. Relationships between the head office, regional offices and outlets have worsened recently, probably due to the increased pressures felt by most staff. An air of conflict between the management accountants and other managers is noticeable and the Financial Director is pondering how matters can be improved.

Based upon the additional information provided post May 2003:

(1) Analyse Callas plc's recent history and discuss the extent to which it demonstrates the use of effective feedback systems.

(2) Discuss the extent to which the application of systems of activity-based cost management (ABCM) and Target Costing might be able to assist in dealing with Callas plc's problems.

(3) Given Callas' plc's plans for the future, and the problems which it is experiencing currently, analyse how improvements to its management accounting information system (MAIS) might assist in the management of the company. Give examples of specific information that the improved MAIS might produce.

Case Study: Fantasy Planet University

Fantasy Planet University is a former polytechnic which became a new university in 1992. One of its major departments is the Business School, which comprises 90 academic staff and 20 administrators. The School is led by a head of school and split into five divisions – Strategy, Enterprise, Accounting and Finance, Human Resource

Management and Professional Courses; the latter teaches the courses provided by the School. Research is carried out in the School but has to be covered by the teaching and consultancy income the School earns, as the research assessment exercise found the quality of research did not reach a sufficient standard to attract government funding.

The budget for the School is approximately £9 million in 2003/04. There are over 5000 full-time equivalent students who are taught on undergraduate, postgraduate and professional courses. In 2003/04, 45% of the income for the School is payable into the centre to support non-teaching departments such as the library, computing and the directorate of the University. Approximately two-thirds of the sum payable to the centre is used to fund support departments such as Finance, while the remaining third is used to provide a Strategic Adjustment Fund and capital projects. The Strategic Adjustment Fund is used to help fund schools where student income is insufficient to meet the schools' costs. Such funding is only provided for a maximum of three years to allow the School to develop plans to turn itself around. After that date the School must be self-financing through whatever means. This includes potentially closure and certainly staff redundancies to bring cost and income into balance.

Up until 2000/01 the Business School was a 'cash cow' for the University but there has now been a downturn in demand for business courses since that date. Due to a feared shortfall in funding across the University in 2000/01, targets for the School were increased by the University's central directorate. In 1999/2000 actual income was £8 million, but the target for 2000/01 was set at £10 million based on increased student numbers. Actual income was £9.5 million. Target income was again increased in 2001/02 to £10.5 million. Actual income was again below target at £9.6 million. The deduction in 1999/2000 for support costs was 40% of target income, but this was increased in 2001/02 to 45%. The target income was reduced in 2002/03 to £9.5 million but actual income fell to £9 million. In 2003/04 target income remained at £9.5 million and in April 2004 it was anticipated that a small surplus would be made in 2003/04. Prior to 2002/03 income was paid by the funding body to the University for teaching purposes on the basis of enrolments. From 2002/03 income is only paid if students complete the assessments set. This means that no funding is available for students who fail to submit any assessment and drop out. The funding body has also reduced the amount payable to try to ensure the University makes efficiency gains. The centre still takes 45% of target income as the contribution to central costs.

The bulk of the costs of the School are staff costs. Supplies and services costs (photocopying, transport, etc.) have been as high as 20% of the expenditure budget. Limited monitoring information is provided during the course of the year and the School has developed its own internal monitoring systems. This has resulted in supplies and service costs being reduced to 12% of the expenditure budget by 2003/04. Additional staff were recruited (5) in 2001/02 and there is a need to find increased pension costs and national insurance taxes. Staff levels have remained consistent since 2001/02.

The Business School also undertakes consultancy activity. This is commercial work charged at commercial rates and is outside the government grant. The University system is that 20% of the income from consultancy is paid to the University's consultancy company for undertaking the relevant administration associated with the activity, 20% is payable to the Business School, and the balance is payable to the staff member who undertakes the activity. The Business School also employs outside consultants to undertake these activities. The payment system is the same as for internal staff. At the end of the year the Business School's share of the income is transferred to the School from the consultancy company but there is no knowing what this transfer is until the end of the year, although again the University provides a target for the School to achieve.

It is now half way through 2004/04 and the Business School has a cumulative deficit of £2.5 million and has approached the centre for support from the Strategic Adjustment Fund. The University's directorate is currently considering this request.

Finally, the Business School is also to reorganise into four new departments which will act as profit centres in the next academic year.

(i)   Identify the main features of the budgetary system outlined above.

(ii)   Comment on any advantages and disadvantages that may exist in respect of the features you have identified.

(iii)   What would you advise the Business School to do about the situation?

(iv)   What would you advise the University's directorate to do and why?

(v)   How would you reconcile your advice to the School and the directorate where it differs?

(vi)   What issues would you need to consider in establishing the new profit centres?

Case Study: Sioca PLC

Sioca PLC started life as a regional electricity generating company in Ampland, a European country. Such regional companies were nationalised by the Ampland government in 1945 in order to safeguard the reliability of service provision. There was, however, concern that the nationalised electricity service was being operated inefficiently and that costs to the consumer had spiralled upwards. There was a governmental decision in 1990 to reprivatise such service providers in order to motivate them to produce better value for money through the mechanisms of customer choice and competition between providers.

Sioca PLC has been the licensed provider of electricity in the South East Ampland area since 1991 and, during the intervening period, it has responded to relaxations in government regulations such that it now supplies water and gas services to the same geographical area. The nature of Sioca PLC's business activities has thus evolved significantly since the early 1990s. While Sioca PLC still provides electricity to its consumers, it does so via a network of smaller, privately owned generating companies. These companies are entirely separate from Sioca PLC and are dealt with by Sioca PLC on an 'arm's length' basis. In order to supply its customers, Sioca PLC uses the electricity cable network owned by K-Bel PLC, for which it pays a two-part fee which comprises a fixed annual charge and a variable charge based on usage.

Sioca PLC supplies water and domestic gas to its consumers by similar mechanisms. Sioca PLC effectively acts as a licensed 'wholesaler' whereby separate water and gas companies sell their output to Sioca PLC which then sells it to the end-users. In doing so, Sioca PLC must pay the owners of the water and gas supply networks for the use of their distribution networks.

Competition exists within Sioca PLC's operating environment in that, while it is essentially an electricity company which also trades in water and gas, other companies exist which operate in the same markets within the local area. Hydra PLC, the company originally licensed to supply water in the South East Ampland area, now offers electricity and gas supplies, amongst other products, in competition with Sioca PLC.

In addition to the competitive activity which exists for the supply of power and water, several of Sioca PLC's competitors have now widened their product portfolios to include the financial services area, offering personal loans, mortgages, insurance, and so on. While Sioca PLC has not moved into these activities as yet, it is giving serious consideration to including such operations in the near future.

The increasing level, and increasingly diverse range, of competition has had many side effects within Sioca PLC. The advent of competition led to the need for intense marketing activities in order to maintain Sioca PLC's market share. Legislation has made it easy for consumers to change suppliers whenever they decide. There has been a need to attempt to differentiate products and to convince consumers of the quality of the services provided. Pressure to maintain the reliability of the services provided has also increased. Continuous downward pressure on prices to consumers has resulted from two sources: competitors' tactics and government watchdogs' moves to limit excessive profiteering and large price rises.

The cost pressure on Sioca PLC has led to a need for rationalisation, and the company has recently completed the first stage of its 're-engineering' project, which has resulted in the redundancy or forced retirement of approximately 300 staff. Many of the redundancies, however, were carried out on a last-in, first-out basis, with the result that a large proportion of the remaining staff have worked within the industry for quite some time and originate from the period when the company's main line of business was the generating of electricity. Significant staff retraining has been necessary and Sioca PLC has been enlisting the help of several local educational institutions to run training courses on an *ad hoc* basis as skills shortfalls have become evident. Such training courses have proven to be very expensive and Sioca PLC's board is not yet convinced of their effectiveness.

There has been a considerable amount of movement of senior staff between Sioca PLC and its competitors as the market for capable senior managers has heated up.

Sioca PLC's profits have fallen considerably, year-on-year, during the past five years although it has managed to maintain its dividend yield to date. Its share price has fallen gradually over the same period. It is estimated that, if current trends were to continue, Sioca PLC would have difficulty in stabilising profitability. Given the need for sustained investment in technology in its business environment, the directors of Sioca PLC are becoming concerned about the company's ability to obtain financial backing in future years. Additionally, the government is maintaining a programme of monitoring the quality of services to customers with which Sioca PLC will need to comply. The board has not yet been able to obtain a clear answer from its management team as to whether a service quality shortfall exists in this respect.

Since privatisation, Sioca PLC has developed a large range of sophisticated and complex tariff systems for the purposes of charging its customers in the domestic and commercial sectors. Sioca PLC has developed a far wider choice of tariffs than its competitors in an effort to become more attractive to consumers. Sioca PLC also offers a 24-hour telephone helpline service to all its customers and the majority of its workforce have been equipped with pagers or mobile phones in order to ensure their 'around the clock' availability. Last year, Sioca PLC's board decided to make a one off payment to employees to reward them for their increased commitment to the company.

All managers within Sioca PLC have been given delegated budgets, and managers are expected to control the costs within these budgets strictly. Middle managers receive an annual bonus based on the total savings made during the control year, while senior managers receive bonuses in the form of Sioca PLC ordinary shares. The senior managers' bonuses are calculated in relation to Sioca PLC's after-tax profit levels for the previous year.

Sioca PLC has recently experienced some trouble in dealing with customer complaints because of higher than previous levels of absenteeism and sick leave. It has also suffered some poor publicity recently related to its responses to customer queries and complaints. Complaints from customers have covered a range of matters including slow responses to call-outs, failure to complete repairs satisfactorily first time, unprofessional or abrupt telephone manner of helpline staff as well as matters such as frequent power cuts or surges, water shortages and gas pressure falls.

Sioca PLC's managing director, Joules Van Den Graaf, has spearheaded a number of investigations in recent months in an effort to sort out some of the company's problems. In investigating the problem of the poor publicity mentioned above, he was informed by the company's senior managers that the appearance of adverse articles in the local press was the first that these managers had known about the customer complaints problem.

They were, they argued, too busy managing the physical provision of electricity, gas and water services to be able to allocate time to such problems.

The company's middle managers complained that they had more than enough work with which to fill their time, given the complex nature of their day-to-day tasks and the need to control their budgets. Several such managers commented that much of their time was spent poring over their weekly budget reports, arguing with Sioca PLC's accountants about the amount of overheads with which they had been charged and looking for ways to reduce their overhead costs. Most middle managers seemed to have little idea about how the overhead costing system really worked. There was a common attitude amongst middle managers that there was little to be gained from questioning the validity or reliability of the costing system as the Sioca PLC accountants (the 'budget police' as they were called by these managers) made it very clear that a clear understanding of the company's complex costing system required an accountant's mind. Many of these managers seemed to have reached the point whereby they had given up attempting to discuss such matters.

In the course of his investigations, managers at all levels within Sioca PLC had complained to Mr Van Den Graaf that they had insufficient information to manage effectively. This Mr Van Den Graaf found puzzling. He had been made aware of the comprehensive budget reports received by managers each week. Indeed, it had taken him more than two hours to make sense of one such report, although he had put this down to his lack of experience of the detailed complexities to which the report had related. Van Den Graaf had queried why this weekly report contained so many estimated figures. The accountant responsible for producing the report had replied that the fault lay with the manager of the cost centre to which the report related. There was a general problem, the accountant explained, that managers did not seem to be able to understand or take an interest in the company's accounting systems. Many of these systems were well proven, he argued, having been established in the company's early days and having been expanded and further sophisticated as time had passed. Although many detailed forms were sent out to managers every month, so that they could enter the details required to allow the calculation of accurate apportionments and so on, managers seemed to have little commitment to the system. This lack of commitment had, the accountant explained, been the main reason why no attempt had been made to computerise the data entry process.

In an attempt to air these problem, and possibly move towards alleviating some of them, Mr Van Den Graaf had called several joint meetings of accountants and managers. On each occasion it had been difficult to stick to the agenda, as the meetings tended to degenerate into unproductive slanging matches. Neither the management nor accounting parties seemed to be able or willing to see the other's viewpoint. Managers complained that accountants used the costing systems to 'confuse and demoralise the managers and to increase the power of accountants', while accountants argued that such systems were 'in existence to protect the investors, not to support the managers' ailing departments'.

Mr Van Den Graaf had done his best to discharge the atmosphere at the meetings but was left feeling that he needed to generate some powerful new ideas in order to move the company forward and to give it the potential to succeed.

1. Analyse the implications of recent changes in Sioca PLC's operating environment which are likely to affect the effectiveness of its management accounting information systems (MAIS).
2. Identify the principal MAIS components which Sioca PLC would require in order to achieve its immediate and longer-term control and decision-making objectives.
3. Discuss the behavioural, motivational and ethical aspects of Sioca PLC's activities, and of the MAIS which you have specified in your answer to question 2.

Additional Information for the Period from February 2003 to August 2003.
The board of Sioca PLC made a decision in March 2002 to move into the financial services markets in order to compete effectively. Among its initial developments in the financial services markets were:

- the provision of personal loans to private individuals.
- home buildings and contents insurance.
- consumer goods repairs insurance (on such goods such as personal computer systems, 'white goods' etc).

Additionally, the company has commenced acting as a management consultancy organisation although, in this respect, it acts as a middle-man whereby it sub-contracts educational organisations and small firms of accountants and other professionals to carry out consultancy and training activities for it, under the Sioca Consultancy name. Apart from initiating the contracts with, and paying fees to, the sub-contracting bodies, Sioca PLC has little direct involvement in these activities.

Similarly, Sioca PLC's new activities in the loan finance and insurance markets are, in reality, largely delegated to banks and insurance companies already operating within these fields. The fees paid to the banks and insurance companies consist of a fixed management fee, fixed in advance and based on estimated business volume, plus a variable commission based on amounts of loan/insurance raised.

Staff morale problems have intensified within Sioca PLC over the past 6 months. The company has been taken to court by several employees on the grounds of its allegedly having placed employees under excessive stress. Many of its longest serving employees have sought early retirement recently and a considerable number of intelligent but inexperienced young staff have been recruited to replace those staff who have left.

To a large extent, the majority of Sioca PLC's staff are involved in administrative, marketing and public relations activities and the already heavily criticised weekly budget reports are seen, by most staff, to have become even less useful than before. A number of managers have created their own unofficial management accounting systems and therefore tend to ignore the official system. Indeed, several managers have argued strongly that they should no longer be charged with the costs of the official system and this has resulted in a higher charge being levied upon the remaining system users, halfway through the budgeting year. The remaining system users have been criticised heavily for their failure to control overhead costs.

The training of the new young managers has concentrated on the use of the existing reporting systems although some of these managers have commented that they need to be involved in the design of a new management information system The accounting department has argued that the new managers lack sufficient experience to enable them to make a meaningful input and that thus the management information system should remain the province of the accounting department for the time being.

Given the wide range of Sioca PLC's activities, an Assistant Director position has been created to head up each of the company's main activities, e.g. electricity services, water services, insurance services etc., and each of these activities is to be treated as an investment centre (even though all major investments must be authorised by Head Office). Each assistant director is responsible for the return-on-capital of his/her activity and for developing new markets and products. Several of the new assistant directors have already complained that the existing budgeting system does not help in the latter respects.

The accounting department has warned that the degree of uncertainty experienced in many of the company's newer markets will lead to less frequent reports being available, if reporting accuracy is to be maintained.

A bonus system for both assistant directors and key staff within their activities has been introduced whereby bonuses are based upon the overall turnover generated by the activities. This seems to have had some positive effects in increasing turnover.

At a recent meeting of the board of Sioca PLC, concern was expressed that, despite Sioca PLC's having expanded its range of activities greatly, its profitability had continued to decrease.

In relation to the additional information provided subsequent to January 2003:

1. Critically analyse the events which have occurred *within* Sioca PLC since January 2003 and the management accounting information systems related problems that have resulted.
2. Discuss the extent to which Sioca PLC's new products and markets might affect the nature of the management accounting information it will require in future.
3. Write a brief report to Sioca PLC's managing director which provides an action plan designed to overcome the problems which exist, or may exist in future.

Be specific about what needs to be done and who will be involved.

Questions

1. Discuss the extent to which 'strategic management accounting' represents a new dimension of management accounting.

2. Critically examine the interrelationships between motivation and performance appraisal and discuss the implications of such interrelationships for management control systems.

3. Examine the extent to which it is possible for a multinational organisation to specify an optimal transfer pricing system.

4. For a university library that provides services to other university departments:

   (i) explain, and evaluate the suitability of, the transfer pricing mechanisms that might be used to charge library services to other departments;

   (ii) outline the effects that the resultant library charges might have on the levels of innovation and creativity within the client departments.

5. As the management accountant of an international distribution company, you have been asked to make a brief presentation to the company's senior management on the nature and coverage of strategic management accounting (SMA). Prepare some notes on the content of the proposed presentation which should:

   (i) discuss the coverage of SMA;

   (ii) analyse the claimed advantages of SMA;

   (iii) discuss the possible problems of implementing SMA within the company.

6. Assess the relevance to today's management accountant of the economics-based analysis of the transfer pricing problem. Assess critically the alternative practical approaches to the establishment of transfer prices.

7. Discuss the extent to which activity-based cost management and business process re-engineering fall within the domain of management accountants. What do you consider to be the main limitations of these approaches?

8. It has been suggested that the nature of management accounting is changing such that management accounting may cease to exist as a separate discipline in future years. Give, and justify, your opinion on whether management accounting is doomed to extinction.

9. Examine the management accounting related difficulties encountered within an internationally divisionalised organisation.

10. 'Strategic management accounting is merely *good* management accounting'. Critically assess this statement.

11. Emmanuel and Gee (1982) discuss the strengths and weaknesses of a two-part, fairer approach to setting transfer prices. Discuss the validity of such a transfer pricing approach for the recharging of the computer services department of a health authority to other departments within that authority. Your discussion should include an evaluation of the suitability of other transfer pricing approaches that might be used in this context.

12. (i) Discuss the extent to which practical methods of setting intracompany transfer prices represent a compromise.

    (ii) Critically analyse the extent to which transfer pricing is relevant within a public sector organisation of your choice.

13. Outline and discuss the economic, practical and ethical aspects of multinational transfer pricing.

14. Wilson (1995) proposes that 'The emergence of strategic management accounting ... is a recent phenomenon and there is, as yet, no unified view of what it is or how it might develop'. Discuss.

BIBLIOGRAPHY AND RECOMMENDED FURTHER READING

Amigoni, F. (1978) 'Planning management control systems', *Journal of Business Finance and Accounting*, 5(3): 279–92.

Argyris, C. (1953) 'Human problems with budgets', *Harvard Business Review*, 31(1): 97–110.

Ashton, D., Hopper, T. and Scapens, R. (1995) *Issues in Management Accounting* (2nd edition). Hemel Hempstead: Prentice Hall.

Azofra, V., Prieto, B. and Santidrian, A. (2003) 'The usefulness of a performance measurement system in the daily life of an organisation: a note on a case study', *British Accounting Review*, 35: 367–84.

Bannock, G. and Manser, W. (1999) *International Dictionary of Finance*. London: Penguin Books.

Baring Asset Management (1997) *Lamont's Glossary*, (8th edition). London: Advanced Media Group.

Bhimani, A. and Piggott, D. (1992) 'Implementing ABC: a case study of organisational and behavioural consequences', *Management Accounting Research*, 3: 119–32.

Brealey, R.A. and Myers, S.C. (2002) *Principles of Corporate Finance*, 7th edn. New York: McGraw-Hill.

Briers, M. and Hirst, M. (1990) 'The role of budgetary information in performance evaluation', *Accounting, Organisations and Society*, 15(4): 373–98.

Bromwich, M. and Bhimani, A. (1989) *Management Accounting: Evolution not Revolution*. London: CIMA.

Burns, J. (2000) 'The dynamics of accounting change – Interplay between new practices, routines, institutions, power and politics', *Accounting, Auditing and Accountability*, 13(5): 566–96.

Chandler, A.D. (1962) *Strategy and Structure: Chapters in the History of the Industrial Enterprise*. Cambridge, MA: MIT Press.

Chwastiak, M. (1999) 'Deconstructing the principal–agent model: a view from the bottom', *Critical Perspectives on Accounting*, 10: 425–41.

Coad, A.F. (1999) 'Some survey evidence on the learning and performance orientations of management accountants', *Management Accounting Research*, 10: 109–35.

Collin, P.H., Collin, F. and Collin, S.M.H. (2001) *Dictionary of Business*. Peter Collin Publishing.

Collins (2000) *Collins English Dictionary*. Retrieved from xreferplus, http://www.xreferplus.com/entry/2669715.

Coombs, H.M. and Evans, A. (2000) 'Managing central support services through service level agreements', *Government Accountants Journal*, 49(1): 54–9.

Coombs, H.M. and Jenkins, D.E. (2002) *Public Sector Financial Management* (3rd edition). London: Thomson Learning.

Coombs, H.M., Hobbs, D. and Jenkins, D.E. (2000) 'Management accounting for the new millennium and beyond', in S. Saunders and N. Smalley (eds), *Simulation and Gaming Research Yearbook*, Vol. 8. London: Kogan Page.

Cooper, R. (1990) 'Cost classification in unit-based and activity-based manufacturing cost systems', *Journal of Cost Management*, Fall: 4–14.

Cooper, R. and Kaplan, R.S. (1987) 'Measure costs right: make the right decisions', *Harvard Business Review*, September/October: pp. 96–103.

Cooper, S., Davies, M. and Davis, T. (2002) 'Value judgement', *Financial Management*, February: 31.

Drucker, P.F. (1994) *Managing the Future*. New York: Penguin.

Drury, C. (2004) *Management and Cost Accounting* (5th edition). London: Thomson.

Drury, C. and Tayles, M. (1997) 'The misapplication of capital investment appraisal techniques', *Management Decision*, 35(2): 86–93.

Drury, C. and Tayles, M. (2000) Cost system design and profitability analysis in UK companies. Chartered Institute of Management Accountants.

Eccles, R.R. (1985) 'Control and fairness in transfer pricing', *Harvard Business Review*, November – December, 149–61.

Emmanuel, C.R. and Gee, K.P. (1982) 'Transfer pricing: a fair and neutral procedure', *Accounting and Business Research*, Autumn: 273–8.

Emmanuel, C., Otley, D. and Merchant, K. (1990) *Accounting for Management Control* (2nd edition). London: International Thomson.

Ezzamel, M., Morris, J. and Smith, J.A. (2004) Accounting for New Organisational Forms. Research Update, 8–9 September, CIMA.

Foucault, M. (1977) *Discipline and Punish: The Birth of the Prison*. London: Allen Lane.

Garcke, E. and Fells, J.M. (1887) *Factory Accounts, Their Principles and Practice*. London: Crosby, Lockwood & Co.

Garrison, R.H. and Noreen, E.W. (2000) *Managerial Accounting* (9th edition). Boston: Irwin/McGraw-Hill.

Gietzmann, M. (1995) 'Introduction to agency theory in management accounting', in D. Ashton, T. Hopper and R. Scapens, *Issues in Management Accounting* (2nd edition). Hemel Hempstead: Prentice Hall, pp. 259–72.

Goldratt, E.M. (1990a) *The Haystack Syndrome: Sifting Information out of the Data Ocean*. Croton-on-Hudson, NY: North River Press.

Goldratt, E.M. (1990b) *What Is This Thing Called Theory of Constraints and How Should It Be Implemented?* Croton-on-Hudson, NY: North River Press.

Goldratt, E.M. and Cox, J. (1984) *The Goal: A Process of Ongoing Improvement*. Croton-on-Hudson, NY: North River Press.

Gould, S. (2002) 'Rough guide', *Financial Management*, April: 30–1.

H.M. Government (1994) *Better Accounting for Taxpayers' Money: The Government's Proposals*, Cm 2626. London, HMSO.

Hofstede, G.H. (1968) *The Game of Budget Control*. London: Tavistock.

Hopwood, A.G. (1972) 'An empirical study of the role of accounting data in performance evaulation', *Journal of Accounting Research*, 10: 156–82.

Hopper, T. and Armstrong, P. (1991) 'Cost accounting, controlling labour and the rise of conglomerates', *Accounting, Organizations and Society*, 16(5/6): 405–38.

Hopper, T., Tsamenyi, M., Uddin, S. and Wickramasinghe, D. (2003) 'The state they're in', *Financial Management*, June: 14–19.

Hopwood, A. (1974) *Accounting and Human Behaviour*. Englewood Cliffs, N.J.: Prentice Hall.

Hussey, R. (1999) *Oxford Dictionary of Accounting*. Oxford: Oxford University Press.

Innes, J. and Mitchell, F. (1995) 'A survey of activity-based costing in the UK's largest companies', *Management Accounting Research*, June: 137–54.

Johnson, H.T. and Kaplan, R.S. (1987) *Relevance Lost: The Rise and Fall of Management Accounting*. Cambridge, MA: Harvard Business School Press.

Kaplan, R.S. (1982) *Advanced Management Accounting*. Prentice Hall.

Kaplan, R.S. (1983) 'Measuring manufacturing performance – a new challenge for MA research', *Accounting Review*, LVIII: 686–705.

Kaplan, R.S. (1994) 'Flexible budgeting in an activity-based costing framework', *Accounting Horizons*, June: 104–9.

Kaplan, R.S. and Norton, D.P. (1996) *The Balanced Scorecard: Translating Strategy into Action*. Boston: Harvard Business School Press.

Keef, S. and Roush, M. (2002) 'Does MVA measure up?', *Financial Management*, January: 20–1.

Kennis, J. (1979) 'Effects of budgetary goal characteristics on managerial aspects of performance', *Accounting Review*, 4: 707–21.

Lapsley, I. (1996) 'Reflections on performance measurement in the public sector', in L. Lapsley and F. Mitchell, *Accounting and Performance Measurement: Issues in the Private and Public Sectors*. London: Paul Chapman, 109–28.

Locke, E.A. (1968) 'Towards a theory of risk motivation and incentives', *Organisational Behaviour and Human Performance*, 3: 157–89.

Loft, A. (1995) 'The history of management accounting', in D. Ashton, T. Hopper and R. Scapens (eds), *Issues in Management Accounting* (2nd edition). Hemel Hempstead: Prentice Hall.

Lumby, S. and Jones, C. (2003) *Corporate Finance Theory and Practice* (7th edition). London: Thomson.

Lumijarvi, O.P. (1991) 'Selling of capital investments to top management', *Management Accounting Research*, 2: 171–88.

Lyne, S. (1995) 'Accounting measures, motivation and performance appraisal', in D. Ashton, T. Hopper and R. Scapens (eds), *Issues in Management Accounting* (2nd edition). Hemel Hempstead: Prentice Hall, pp. 237–58.

Mak, Y.T. and Roush, M.L. (1994) 'Flexible budgeting and variance analysis in an activity-based costing environment', *Accounting Horizons*, June: 93–104.

March, J.G. (1976) 'The technology of foolishness', in J.G. March and J.P. Olsen (eds), *Ambiguity and Choice in Organizations*. Bergen: Universitetsforlaget.

Merchant, K.A. (1998) 'Management control-related ethical issues and analyses', in *Modern Management Control Systems*, Hemel-Hempstead: Prentice Hall, pp. 697–712.

Mintzberg, H. (1975) *Impediments to the Use of Management Information*. New York: National Association of Accountants.

Otley, D.T. (2001) 'Extending the boundaries of management accounting research: developing systems for performance management', *British Accounting Review*, 33(3): 243–61.

Otley, D.T. (1980) 'The contingency theory of management accounting: achievement and prognosis', *Accounting, Organisations and Society*, 5(4): 413–28.

Otley, D.T. and Berry, A.J. (1980) Control, organisations and accounting, *Accounting, Organisations and Society*, 5(2): 231–44.

Otley, D.T. (1978) 'Budget use and managerial performance', *Journal of Accounting Research*, 16: 122–49.

Ouchi, W.G. (1979) 'A conceptual framework for the design of organisational control mechanisms', *Management Science*, 25(9): 833–48.

Pass, C., Lowes, B. and Pendleton, A. (1995) *Collins Dictionary of Business*. London: Peter Collin Publishing.

Pass, C., Lowes, B. and Davies, L. (2000) *Collins Dictionary of Economics*. London: Peter Collin Publishing.

Penguin (2000) *The Penguin English Dictionary*. London: Penguin.

Porter, M.E. (1985) *Competitive Advantage: Creating and Sustaining Superior Performance.* New York: Free Press.

Preston, A. (1995) 'Budgeting, creativity and culture', in D. Ashton, T. Hopper and R. Scapens (eds), *Issues in Management Accounting* (2nd edition). Hemel Hempstead: Prentice Hall, pp. 273–98.

Proctor, R. (2002) *Managerial Accounting for Business Decisions.* Harlow: Pearson Education.

Robson, K. and Cooper, D. (1989) 'Power and management control', in W.F. Chua, E.A. Lowe and A.G. Puxty (eds), *Critical Perspectives in Management Control.* MacMillan, pp. 79–114.

Roget (1995) *Roget's II: The New Thesaurus* (3rd edition). Boston: Houghton Mifflin. Retrieved from xreferplus, http://www.xreferplus.com/entry/746368.

Ronen, J. and Livingstone, J.L. (1975) 'An expectancy theory approach to the motivational impact of budgets', *Accountancy Review*, 50: 671–85.

Roslender, R. (1995) 'Critical management accounting', in D. Ashton, T. Hopper and R. Scapens (eds), *Issues in Management Accounting* (2nd edition). Hemel Hempstead: Prentice Hall, pp. 65–86.

Samuels, J.M., Wilkes, F.M. and Brayshaw, R.E. (1999) *Financial Management and Decision Making.* London: International Thomson Business Press.

Shim, J.K. and Siegel J.G. (1995) *Dictionary of Economics.* New York: Wiley. Retrieved from xreferplus, http://www.xreferplus.com/entry/2764220.

Simon, H.A. (1953) 'Theories and decision making in economics and behavioural science', *American Economic Review*, XLIX: 253–83.

Simons, R. (2000) *Performance Measurement and Control Systems for Implementing Strategy.* New Jersey: Prentice Hall.

Spicer, B.H. (1988) 'Towards an organisation theory of the transfer pricing process', *Accounting, Organizations and Society*, 13(3): 303–22.

Stedry, R.C. (1960) *Budget Control and Cost Behaviour.* Hemel Hempstead: Prentice Hall.

Stewart, G. (1991) *The Quest for Value.* New York: Harper Business.

Swieringa, R.J. and Waterhouse J.H. (1982) 'Organizational views of transfer pricing', *Accounting Organizations and Society*, 7(2): 149–65.

Upchurch, A. (1998) *Management Accounting Principles and Practice.* London: Financial Times/Prentice Hall.

Walker, M. and Choudhury, N. (1987) 'Agency theory and management accounting', in J.A. Arnold, R. Scapens and D. Cooper (eds), *Management Accounting: Expanding the Horizons.* London: Chartered Institute of Management Accountants, pp. 61–112.

Watson, D.J. and Baumler, J.V. (1975) 'Transfer pricing: a behavioural context', *Accounting Review*, July: 466–74.

Wilson, R.M.S. and Wai, F.C. (1993) *Managerial Accounting: Method and Meaning* (2nd edition). Singapore: Chapman & Hall.

Zimmerman, J.L. (1979) 'The costs and benefits of cost allocations', *Accounting Review*, July: 504–21.

INDEX

Note: page numbers followed by *t* refer to tables

Performance Measurement and Management

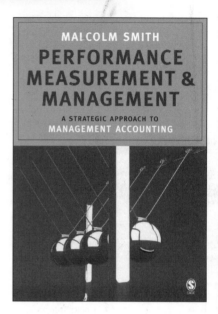

A Strategic Approach to Management Accounting

Malcolm Smith *University of South Australia*

Management accountancy has a dynamic role to play in the competitive strategy of modern global businesses. This book sets out key strategic principles and then assesses how management accountancy can affect and direct these strategies. Engaging case studies reveal how theories and concepts translate into real business practice. Throughout, the book emphasizes:

- how accounting initiatives can trigger assessment and improvement of performance management

- the importance of managerial decision making to good business practice

- how today's management accountancy measures against current research

Written for advanced undergraduate, postgraduate and MBA students taking courses on management accounting and performance measurement and management, the book will be also of interest to management and business consultants, professional accountants and accounting academics.

Table of Contents:

Introduction / Emerging Issues / Performance Measurement and Analysis / Strategy Alternatives / Product and Customer Profitability / Know Your Process / Know Your People / Management Information Systems / Financial Modelling

March 2005 • 312 pages
Cloth (1-4129-0763-2)
Paper (1-4129-0764-0)